ARCTIC OCEAN

SIBERIA

RUSSIA

FINLAND

Sea of
Okhotsk

BERING SEA

TURKEY

Sea

TRANSPORTATION

PERSIA

CHINA

TRADING

WATERWAYS THE
ONLY HIGHWAYS

EMPIRE
of JAPAN

TOWING CHINESE BOATS

PACIFIC
OCEAN

EXPLORING

ARABIA

INDIA

CRUISING

TREASURE

Philippine
Islands

RICA

Sumatra

Borneo

New GUINEA

SAMOAN
ISLANDS

INDIAN
OCEAN

MADAGASCAR

FIJI
ISLANDS

PROSPECTING

AUSTRALIA

SYDNEY

MELBOURNE

NEW ZEALAND

TASMANIA

NEWSPAPER MEN MEET
H.R.H. PRINCE OF WALES

Chris-Craft

Ye Mappe of
Chris-Craft Activities
throughout the World

© 1930 CHRIS SMITH AND SONS BOAT COMPANY

THE LEGEND OF CHRIS-CRAFT

THE
LEGEND
OF

Chris-Craft®

BY

JEFFREY L. RODENGEN, Ph.D.

PUBLISHED BY WRITE STUFF SYNDICATE, INC.

WRITE STUFF SYNDICATE

Write Stuff Syndicate, Inc.

1108 Citrus Isle
Ft. Lauderdale, Florida 33315

(305) GO BOOKS/462-6657

Library of Congress Catalog Card Number; 88-50102

ISBN 0-945903-02-2

This book was composed by Friedrich Hofer, The Type Studio, Inc., Ft. Lauderdale, Florida. Color separations, color printing, jacket and endpapers were accomplished by Graphic Dynamics, Inc., Pompano Beach, Florida. Binding was by Nicholstone Book Bindery, Inc., Nashville, Tennessee. Transcription: Grace Silvis; Preef Rooder: Betsy Holt.

Art Director: Karine N. Rodengen

Yoda: Alfred "Ted" Straw

Completely produced in the United States of America

10 9 8 7 6 5 4 3 2 1

TABLE OF CONTENTS

ACKNOWLEDGEMENTS

The author wishes to thank the many people who have assisted in the research, photographic acquisition and identification, interviews, travel, transcription, layout, consultation, inspiration and encouragement, without whose assistance this work would not have been possible.

The Antique and Classic Boat Society, Bud and Pat Aikens, The City of Algonac, Michigan, George Abrams, John Almquist, Tom Avers, Anna Beach, Abram and Denise Berens, Danny Berenberg, Kathryn B. "Katie" Braig, Pete and Carol Beauregard, Frank Bronson, Bill Buckley, F. Lee Bailey, Peter A. Bailey, Greg Bohn, Frank and Marcia Bronson, Scott and Kathy Campbell, Jim Chominski, Tim Clarke, Don Cuthbertson, Tom Cuthbertson, Chris-Craft Industries, Inc., Joe and Dee Caimi, Myron L. "Mike" and Cynthia Carlson, Nancy Donaldson, Pat Doyle, Ed and Kate Drouillard, James Duke, Michael M. Dixon, Peggy Cox, Marian Dawson, Harry H. Coll, Jeanne Craig, The Dolphin Book Club, John Eidt, Errand Express, Larry Folker, Kelly Foster, Abbot and Barbie Geer, Judd Gilbert, Joseph A. Gutierrez, Jr., Vic Hanna, Gunnar Hansen, Tom Heath, Lee Holland, Lawrence Holly, Bud Holowicz, Historical Society of Michigan, Gen. Alexander Haig, Sharon M. Gwin, Barry Greene, Graphic Dynamics, Inc., Mike Hobren, Mike Horowitz, Louanne Jeffries, Geraldine Johnson, Mel Johnson, Patrick Kelley, John Kovach, Jean Lerche, Carl J. Lisee, Richard and Paullette Louzon, Ken MacStephen, Mike Mason, Thomas W. and Peg Maher, Joe and Jenny Morrison, The Mariners' Museum, Jim Mertaugh, Jack Mertaugh, Mint State, Gary Merrill, William McKeand, Anthony S. Mollica, Mike Mason, Samuel L. Martin, Ed McMahon, Dan Modas, Angela Moses, Craig R. Muir, Tracey A. Muhlfeld, Winslow C. and Helen Morrow, Jack Naber, Mel Mathias, Bill Munro, Murray Chris-Craft Cruisers, Inc., Murray Chris-Craft Sportboats, Inc., Murray Chris-Craft Aqua-Homes, Inc., Murray Chris-Craft Yachts, Inc., Murray Chris-Craft Cruisers-West, Inc., Murray Boat Administrative Services, Inc., Robert F. MacNeill, Nordstrom/Cox Marketing, National Marine Manufacturers Association, Stacy O'Hare, Mary Olmscheid, Mark Paulhus, Judy M. Peterson, Robert Pocock, Herb Pocklington, Don Pruett, Patsy Recor, Tom Reeves, Riley Richardson, Marvin A. Rodengen, Roy and Gloria Royal, Shattuck School, Donna Schaal, Bob Schubert, Julie Shumpert, John L. Simons, Christopher James Smith, George Smith, Harsen Smith, Emerson Shaffer, John Stevens, Emily Stuart, Bob Speltz, Luke R. Stephen son, Robert W. Smith, Walter K. Schumacher, Henry "Hank" Tinnerman, TIME, Inc., Donald Thornburg, The Type Studio, Donna Tellefson, Roger Tyzzer, Charlotte Valentine, Dana and Darlene Wagenhals, Dennis Wegley, Sharon Wible, Witkop Office Machines, Garfield A. Wood, Jr.

A very special thanks to: Arthur N. and Janie Armstrong, Jr.; Maynard Bray, *Wooden Boat*; Brian Callaghan; *Lakeland Boating*; Joel Coigney; Peggy Cox, Murray Chris-Craft; Thomas Crew, The Mariners' Museum; Marian Dawson; Betty and Keith Droulard; Ron and Sarah Danneels; Bruce J. Donaldson, Murray Chris-Craft; Frederique and Jean Dorgambide, D.P. Marine; Abbot Geer, *Abbot Geer Public Relations*; Richard E. "Dick" Genth, Donzi Marine; Jim Gilbert, *The Yacht*; Ken Gidney, *Graphic Dynamics, Inc.*, Mary M. Glass; Pete and Jean Henkel; Jim Holcomb, Graphic Dynamics, Inc.; Jack and Deona Holmes, *Southern Star*; Betsy Holt; Andy Hough, Southeastern Printing Co.; C. Gordon Houser, Donzi Marine; Irwin Jacobs, Genmar Corporation; Peter A. Janssen, *Motor Boating & Sailing*; Sharon Khan, Graphic Dynamics, Inc.; Fred and Carol Kiekhaefer, Kiekhaefer Aeromarine, Inc.; Ray and Geraldine LaParl; G. Dale Murray, Murray Industries, Inc.; Cornelius N. "Connie" Ray, Ray Industries, Inc.; Elizabeth Reed, Murray Chris-Craft; Jack Reichert, Brunswick Corporation; James M. Rodengen; Karine N. Rodengen; Dan A. Rothwell, *Rusty Rudder*; Joel A. Schleicher, Murray Industries, Inc.; Doug Schryver, *Boating*; Rick Shank, CCS Clearwater; Grace and Ed Silvis; Ralph Simonsen, Arandell-Schmidt Corp.; Christopher James Smith; George Smith; Harsen Smith; George Stern, Graphic Dynamics, Inc.; Charles D. "Charley" Strang, Outboard Marine Corporation; Alfred "Ted" Straw; Roy Taylor, Graphic Dynamics, Inc.; Marian Thompson, Southeastern Printing Co.; Norm Wangard, *Classic Boating*; Wilson Wright, *Brass Bell*; William D. Wilkinson, The Mariners' Museum; Jim Wynne, Wynne Marine; and especially for the total patience, dedication, perseverance and photography of my beloved Karine.

Acknowledgement is gratefully made to the following authors and publishers for permission to quote and reprint from their work:

Algonac Courier; Business Week; Courier Journal/Independent Press; Chronicle of the 20th Century, Chronicle Publications, Inc.; *Detroit News;* Kevin M. Desmond; Michael M. Dixon, *The Flats Golden Era; Florida Journal; Florida Trend; Forbes; The Gray Goose News;* Joseph Gribbins; Historical Society of Michigan, *Speed Boat Kings; History of the Great Lakes,* J.H. Beers & Co.; *Iacocca – An Autobiography,* Bantam Doubleday Publishing; *Journal of the Industrial Designers Society of America;* Peter A. Janssen, *Motor Boating & Sailing;* The Mariners' Museum, Newport News, Virginia; Robert McNeil; *Miami Herald; Motor Boating & Sailing; Motor Boating; Nautical Quarterly;* National Marine Manufacturers Association Hall of Fame; *New York Herald-Dispatch; New York Times; News Tribune;* Nordstrom/ Cox Marketing; *North American Decoys; Racing with Cornelius Shields and the Masters,* Prentice Hall; *Port Huron Daily Herald; Port Huron Daily Times; Power Boating; Powerboat; Rudder; Sports Illustrated; Southern Star; The Star and the Laurel,* Beverly Rae Kimes; *St. Ignace News; TIME,* The Weekly Newsmagazine; *Websters New Universal Unabridged Dictionary,* Simon & Schuster, Inc.; Garfield A. Wood, Jr.; *Yachting.*

FOREWORD

Well over a million people have commanded a Chris-Craft. Since volume production began in 1922, nearly 250,000 boats have left Chris-Craft factories and in some ways forever changed the lives of their owners. If you accept the formula that most boats change owners at least four to five times, a million owners is well within reason. These owners have families, these families have friends. If each of those families gave just 20 lucky outsiders a ride in their Chris-Craft, you have well over a hundred million people who have experienced a ride in a Chris-Craft. It's a safe bet you're one of us.

This is a book about that experience. The origins of Chris-Craft stretch back to the beginning of America's Civil War, with the birth of its founder, Christopher Columbus Smith. Since the beginnings of the Age of Industrialization, few ventures have left such an indelible mark. The name Chris-Craft is one of only a handful of trademarks universally recognized throughout the world, and in fact, some dictionaries have the word Chris-Craft as a synonym for pleasure craft.[1]

There is a mystique, an elusive magic about the name and the products which have borne the signature in script. If the voyages of Chris-Crafts were placed one after the other, they would have made a round-trip to the moon by 1927, and made it to Mars before 1960.[2]

The Legend Of Chris-Craft is not meant to be an encyclopedia of Chris-Craft boats, nor an accounting of the screws, planks, frames and stringers that have been united throughout the years, nor even a documentary of each model and variation, for there were thousands. Even the most fervent technical connoisseurs of Chris-Craft will find fascination, however, in the depth and surprising biographical exploration of the Smith family, truly America's First Family of boating, along with a generous selection of Chris-Craft's most notable boating achievements and products.

There has been an assumption, through the years, that by and large the facts about Chris-Craft have been unearthed, and that each stone along history's path had been duly turned over. Not so. In fact, a great many facts which have been printed about the Smiths and the evolution of Chris-Craft have been

VII

honest mistakes. As early as the late nineteenth century, errors crept into print, and generations of innocent, well-meaning writers promulgated and added slowly to the chaotic and checkered historical record, until even the obituary of Christopher Columbus Smith was riddled with seemingly incontrovertible error.[3]

The author has traveled a distance equal to a circumnavigation of the world in a small research vehicle, complete with telephone, computer and copying machine to explore the subject. In the reading of over 300,000 pages of documents, articles, ads, brochures, releases and publications, the elusive facts slowly emerged. A comparison of over 25,000 photos and illustrations cleared up a sea of conflicting captions. And finally, the interviews of production line workers from the '20's to the '80's, and of members of the Smith family, helped to explore the many personal and passionate dimensions of the Chris-Craft boat building legacy.

The research has uncovered surprising new facts, and much data never before accessible to marine historians. To this end, a great debt is owed the Mariners' Museum in Newport News, Virginia, the recipients of the Chris-Craft archives, generously donated in May of 1987 by Chris-Craft Industries, Inc. The scope, access and condition of these archives represents unquestionably the finest historical record within the marine industry, and is discussed in *Appendix A.*

Some confusion exists about the various Chris-Craft organizations. Chris-Craft Industries, Inc., the donator of the Chris-Craft archives, is a publicly traded organization which has evolved in name, since its purchase of Chris-Craft Corporation from the Smith family in March of 1960, from National Automotive Fibers, Inc., to NAFI, to Chris-Craft Industries, Inc. in 1962. For the nineteen years until December 1981, the manufacture of Chris-Craft boats was among the various activities of Chris-Craft Industries, which also included automotive fibers, energy, chemical and broadcasting interests. Though the Chris-Craft boat production companies were acquired in 1981 by Murray Industries, Inc., the name Chris-Craft was retained by Chris-Craft Industries, as both a registered trademark and corporate allonym. The name Chris-Craft is licensed to the Murray Companies[4] by Chris-Craft Industries, and by this modern and circuitous route, graces the line of boats which has been in continous production longer than any other pleasure boat manufacturer, and is today the largest independent pleasure craft builder in the world.

The Legend Of Chris-Craft examines much unexplored ground, to offer the reader a well-rounded perspective, touching on areas as diverse as the day Christopher Columbus Smith narrowly escaped murder, to the nearly miraculous rescue of the young corporation by an unwitting and unwilling savior. From The Girls of Chris-Craft, The Chris-Craft Railroad, The Kit Boats, to Boats You Never Saw, an attempt was made to present new and fresh material.

In so many ways, Chris-Craft established the runabout and the cruiser as "expressions of the American Dream incarnate."[5] This rich heritage and colorful history has provided American boating enthusiasts with a "distinguished succession of innovative product and industry milestones."[6]

Most of all, Chris-Craft has provided generations of families with the irreplaceable excitement and memories that only waterborne recreation can supply.

For the Mothers:
Gerry, Moony and Frederique.

Photo courtesy Christopher James Smith.

Interior of one of the early Smith duckboats, from the hand-tinted original.

CHAPTER I

Origins

"In the new world lies a cluster of inland seas, matchless in extent, about which has been growing for three centuries a new civilization, surpassing in splendor and in might the sea-girt empires of the past. Upon these Great Lakes are fleets that excite the wonder of the world."

J. H. Beers, *History of the Great Lakes*[1]

NINE YEARS BEFORE HIS death, in a rare gesture of historical preservation, Christopher Columbus Smith presented to each of his eighteen grandchildren a little homemade book, detailing as he knew it, the history of the Smith family. Though Chris never knew his grandparents, on either his father's or mother's side, he believed that his grandfather was of Holland-Dutch descent, and that his grandmother's maiden name was Graves.[2]

His father, James G. Smith, was born in Camilues, Onondaga County, New York on July 28, 1823. According to Chris, there weren't any schools in this area of New York when his father was growing up, so "consequently he grew up without book knowledge."[3] He did have superior skills, however, including traits that would serve his son Chris well, and come to characterize the Smith generations to follow. He was an "ingenious mechanic", as Chris explained, and had the ability to make "most anything he chose with iron or wood."[4] He tackled among the most demanding and exacting metal engineering and woodworking challenges, such as making many firearms from scratch, and, as Chris put it "quite a number of violins." Among the more revealing discoveries concerning Chris' father's projects is that they were all fashioned with hand tools and by hand alone. He was also an accomplished blacksmith, not an uncommon aptitude among farming families of the day.

Chris' mother was Harriet D. Hazard, born in Burns, Allegheny County, New York on February 5, 1833. "My mother was a medium sized woman with a light skin and a very wonderful head of coal black hair," Chris recalled. "I can remember seeing her stand up with her hair hanging down her back and it touched the floor." James and Harriet were married in Oregon, Ogle County, Illinois by a Reverend Woolley.

Christopher Columbus Smith was born in Cottrellville Township, St. Clair County, Michigan on May 20, 1861, an area sometimes referred to as *back of the marsh*.[5] His parents moved to Algonac, Michigan in 1868, when Chris was about seven years old. He began school in Algonac, in a building known as "The Old Red House", and there completed the eighth grade. Chris was one of six children, including Henry the oldest; Elsie, sometimes known as Elma;

Mary, Lucinda who died very young, and Nellie, who was the only child younger than Chris.[6]

Algonac is located some forty miles northeast of Detroit, Michigan, along the western shores of the St. Clair River, flowing southward from Lake Huron into Lake St. Clair, thence through the narrows of the Detroit River on into Lake Erie. It is an anomaly of geography, and only one of a few locations in America, that by looking south it is the Canadian shore observed.

The river flows south past Algonac at a brisk and tireless five knots, through all seasons, though it freezes over with sufficient thickness to drive teams of horses, or now, automobiles and snowmobiles across its surface to Walpole Island on the Canadian side, or to Russel and Harsens Island, among the many islands of the river delta. This St. Clair River delta region, known popularly as the St. Clair Flats, is a large expanse of channels, islands, marshes and reed-laced shallows that was a fishing and hunting paradise during the late nineteenth and early twentieth centuries. Deer, moose, beaver, muskrat, and otter once abounded throughout the region, along with pickerel, bass, northern pike, perch,

Photo courtesy Marian Dawson.

From an 1870's tintype, the only known image of Henry Smith the backwoodsman, with his younger brother Christopher Columbus Smith.

catfish and lake trout. It was throughout this spectacular natural oasis of prolific wildlife and cool, swift waters that young Chris Smith would learn, grow and mature.

Chris had an older brother to help him learn the ways of hunting and fishing on the Flats, and it was Henry, or Hank as he was sometimes called, who was to have the greatest influence on Chris during these formative years. Henry, eleven years Chris' senior and already a successful market duck hunter, was to pass along his skills in marksmanship, wildlife marketing, decoy preparation and boat handling to an eager and resourceful younger brother. It is impossible to confirm the well-circulated story that, at age 11, Chris would whittle or hew his first small boat from a log in 1872, having selected an appropriately bent log on Walpole Island to assist in shaping the bow. The obscure episode has never, however, been denied by surviving generations.

Chris was destined to become a market duck hunter alongside Henry. It was a hard, yet satisfying means of survival, supplying game birds for the voracious appetites of fast-growing Detroit. Chris abandoned school at between 14 and 15 years of age, and began to hunt duck in earnest with Henry.[7] For the Smith brothers, successful market hunting required a great deal of ingenuity, stamina and preparation.

Chris and Henry built two duck hunting shacks at Baltimore Bay, on the mainland side of the North Channel of the St. Clair River, and alternately selected one or the other depending on the location of rafting ducks.

To understand how the Smiths first became interested in boat building, it's important to recognize the original applications required of the Smith boats. The usual method employed by them as hunters is somewhat different than modern techniques. They used a large rectangular sinkbox structure which contained a small boat in the middle. "A coaming at the top of the box kept out some of the sea; a large canvas skirt with wood floats around it also helped in breaking up the waves. Iron decoys, weighing from 30 to 40 pounds each, were used to weigh down the sink box so that most of the structure was below water level."[8] It's really not a romantic notion to consider that probably the first boat the Smiths constructed was a sinkbox, a boat designed to sink.

The Smith brothers developed several preferred systems for hunting, which nearly guaranteed good results with each outing. In one version, they would let out somewhere around 200 wooden decoys on a single string, lie back in the middle of the sinkbox and wait for flocks to land among or near this raft of deception. On a mutual signal, they would sit up and shoot the first couple of rounds into the raft of swimming ducks, and then start shooting the flock on the rise. Chris was highly regarded as a marksman, and it has been said that he could get off six shots during a single rise. More than this, he was

selective. "He had the knack of picking out the large white-breasted birds which brought the highest prices from the servant-buyers for the wealthy families and clubs, although these ducks were actually not as good to eat as the brown, first-year birds. Canvasbacks and Redheads were in greatest demand, with Scaup (Bluebill) next. Mallards were not popular and as for Black Ducks — they couldn't be sold at any price so the Smiths ate them."[9]

"Picking up a big rig of decoys after hunting was quite a job, especially when ice was forming on all 200 birds and strings. They came home many a time completely soaked from head to foot after lying in the sink box with the waves throwing a spray of icy water inside, and from picking up the decoys afterwards."[10]

Another technique which they employed certainly won't draw praise from today's average sportsman, but it must be remembered that the Smiths didn't hunt for sport. It was a living, and

a respected profession that they and their family relied upon for income and sustenance. According to Christopher James Smith, grandson and namesake of Christopher Columbus Smith, at one point Chris mounted a rather large "cannon" on the front of his duck boat. "It was just like an overgrown shotgun is what it was. Mounted solid right on the bow of the duck boat."[11] They would set their decoys, and when conditions were favorable, lie back in the duck boat, drifting towards a raft of ducks, and, "... they'd blow this cannon off and then they jumped up and tried to shoot the cripples."[12]

Phenomenal results ensued. To support his growing family, Chris needed to bag somewhere between seven hundred and eight hundred ducks a week. He regularly met and exceeded his needs. "Chris' record bag was 387 Scaup shot in one afternoon. Mallards were shot in quantity at Dickerson's Island. Chris could punt [push with a pole against the bottom] his small layout boat into the rushes and lie there and shoot these big birds anytime. He seldom shot teal because they were so small that there was no market for them."[13]

The ducks were iced down in barrels, or hung out for a long and tenderizing cure before taken to Detroit for sale or possible shipment to Cleveland and points east.

There was no such thing as a duck hunting season to the Smiths, except of course that they were more plentiful during the late fall and early winter months. The winters were spent in trapping and hunting the plentiful fox, muskrat and otter in the region, and selling the hides.[14]

Most market hunters of the Lake Erie and St. Clair and Detroit Rivers region would deploy anywhere from 150 to 200 decoys in a single location rig. Their duck boats were generally small, so it was important that their decoys were designed to be both light and compact. Since Midwest hunters didn't leave their decoys in the water overnight, or for months the way the Eastern market hunters would, the Smith decoys were handled a lot, and had to be made to last.[15]

Chris learned to make decoys most likely from just about every member of his family. His brother Henry must have made them for his own market hunting before Chris was out of grade school. Some evidence suggests that both of the boys learned decoy making from their parents, however, which is quite feasible considering their father's unusual craft abilities. An insightful description of Chris' early decoy carving techniques and designs was provided by an authority on decoys appearing in a 1970 issue of *American Decoys:*

> During all of these years Chris had been turning out decoys for his own use as well as for sale. His method required few tools. First a wooden stake was driven into the ground and a large screw set in the top with the sharp end up. Wood was sawed to lengths and then shaped to a pattern by a nearby wood shop that owned a band saw. The resulting blanks were screwed down onto the post and held fast for the draw shave work. After the body had been carved the bottom of the decoy was sawed off so that the body could be hollowed out with a special hand bit known as a Dutch bit.
>
> The decoy heads were carved, separately, by hand and fitted very carefully to the bodies. Chris' head styles range from medium high to hunkered-down resting positions. Usually the heads look straight forward, but occasionally they turn sideways. His low-head models are especially well designed to create the feeling of a resting bird.
>
> A characteristic of Chris' work with decoys having upright head positions is that the lower part of the neck is carved as a part of the body with the joint perhaps an inch or two above body level. While there are other Michigan and Canadian makers of flat, hollow decoys who also used this method, most of the earlier carvers (and probably all of the modern ones) have the base of the neck set flush with the body.[16]

One source close to Chris during the 1920's said that Chris explained to him how his mother taught him the art of making duck heads. "He said she had an old pair of scissors, and sharpened them up. He said she could cut a duck head out while you were just standing there looking at her."[17] He went on to explain that Chris continued to make decoys well into the 1920's, and was observed making decoys one day outside the Chris Smith & Sons Boat Co. One of the men would cut the rough shape of the bodies and heads out on a band saw in the lumber mill for Chris, resulting in about a six-inch by eight-inch block of soft pine. Chris would mount the body plug on a post, and then begin pulling chunks off with a draw knife that looked something like the curved blade of a linoleum knife. "He'd take that point and he could cut out a [big] chunk with that." When he attached the heads to the bodies, he'd line them up for painting, applying one color after the next, so that when he started down the line again the first color was already absorbed by the soft pine. "Anybody that hunted knew a Chris Smith decoy, and boy, they were after them."[18]

Chris could turn out about five bodies an hour when he got going, and five heads the next, so including painting he could produce five completed decoys every three hours. The Smith decoys have become collectors items, and are becoming in greater demand with the passage of time. Today, a Chris Smith original can bring from several hundred to five hundred dollars.

Hundreds were burned as firewood before alarmed family members rescued them from garages and sheds throughout Michigan.

It was during this market hunting era, somewhere around 1874, that the Smith brothers would together construct their first boat. It was for their own use, most likely, and its construction was more of a financial necessity than anything else. The hardship duties required of the market hunter's boat, combined with the fast flowing currents of the St. Clair River, dictated a rugged yet clean design that could be rowed for miles with facility.

Oak-ribbed, lapstrake clinker-built style hulls were built, no doubt one for each brother, so that by splitting up they could increase their hunting productivity. The boats weren't so much of an unusual design as they were well-built, pleasing to the eye and thought of as very practical.[19]

The Smiths had gained a solid reputation as hunters and fishermen, and during this period they began to guide small parties of affluent Detroit businessmen through the convoluted waterways of the Flats in search of fish, game and waterfowl.[20] Their reputation spread rapidly, not only because of the superb hunting and fishing, but also as a result of the Smith brothers' relaxed, affable and humorous leadership. It wasn't long before their patrons noticed the workmanship and utility of the Smith boats, and talked the brothers into building one for them.[21] In 1881, when Chris was 20, he and Henry "built a duck boat along different lines than the then prevailing style for shooting boats that they sold to a hunter for what they considered a high price. Other hunters liked the boat and it wasn't long until the Smith boys were kept very busy supplying the demand."[22]

In the early spring of 1884, Chris made a promise to his bride-to-be, Miss Anna Rattray of Harsens Island, that he would settle down and open a commercial boat house and livery. Chris had been rowing across the St. Clair River for quite some time as their relationship blossomed. Anna, the daughter of a hardy and pioneering family,[23] was also an excellent oarswoman, and could negotiate the swift St. Clair with strong dexterity and confidence.

Chris, 23 and Anna, 20 were married on April 13, 1884. They boarded the steamship *Mary* for the one-hour cruise upstream to Port Huron, which is where the official County offices were located, with brief stops at Marine City and St. Clair enroute. When the newlyweds returned to Algonac, they boarded another boat and headed right for the Flats. Perhaps to persuade his new bride that he was serious about getting ahead in life, he immediately put her to work on their honeymoon "picking ducks" and preparing barrels for brother Hank to take to a hotel in Detroit. "She loved to tell that story," a granddaughter would reveal, "That's the way they earned a lot of their cash money, shoot ducks down in the St. Clair Flats, put them in barrels and took them to Detroit by boat."[24]

Testimony of Chris' promise kept, is a reference in a 1905 *Algonac Courier* wherein it states, "Practically the only manufacturing plant in town belongs to Chris Smith. Everybody knows Chris. He has been in the boat building business in the same spot *for over 25 years* and has built some of the fastest motor boats afloat."[25] His modest shop and boat house was located in the 1200 block of Riverside Avenue.

Photo courtesy Marian Dawson.

Christopher Columbus Smith (standing) near the year of his marriage, along with best friend Bernard Townsend after whom he would name his second son, Bernard Townsend Smith. From the original tintype, approx. 1884.

More evidence suggests that Chris indeed went right to work. In the same year, 1884, Chris would already have a small boat livery business operating, and would rent a boat to a young O. J. Mulford, who, as an adult, would organize the Gray Motor Company.

> I remember when I was a kid of fourteen or fifteen. I went up to Algonac and rented an old two-master sailboat, known to fisherman as a pound boat, from Chris Smith. I still get a thrill when I recall that ride. It was the first time I had ever met Chris Smith. Docking, Chris came over to me, shaking his head: "Son, you were edging yourself into trouble out there. I spotted you coming down, wing and wing, beating that tug. Thought you were going to blow the stick out of my boat. Don't do that again."[26]

Settling down also meant an increased awareness of the community, and Chris would invest greatly of his time and energy into community service over the next twenty-five years. Chris became Postmaster of the Village of Algonac by at least the year 1899, a position he would hold for at least 12 years.[27] When the Algonac Post Office was raised from a fourth class to a third class office in 1903, it must have been cause for celebration at the Smith household, for the new designation carried with it a salary of $1,000 per year and the assistance of a postal clerk. Chris would also become a member of the school board, be elected president of the Algonac Chamber of Commerce in 1900, while still Postmaster, *and* while developing his growing boat business. To say that he had his hands full would be a gross understatement. Chris almost lost the whole works the week of May 27, 1904, when, "A spark from a chimney came near burning C.C. Smith & Co.'s boat house." Fortunately for Chris, "Had it not been for the discovery by neighbors, the whole boat house might have been burned. Mr. Smith soon had a hose playing on the blaze which was extinguished before much damage was done."[28] It's a good thing, too, for the Post Office was located in the same building next door, and he would have lost everything. Chris was an indefatigable worker, a reputation that would spread to his growing family in the years to come.[29]

From the date of his marriage in 1884, and over the course of the next fifteen years of market hunting and field guide activities, Chris and Hank expanded their reputation by building a number of simple duck boats, canoes, rowboats, sailboats and ultimately launches for both a local and Detroit marketplace. The rental of their rowboats and sailboats brought in a modest income, the rowboats bringing in probably about fifty cents a day according to one competitor's flier of the day.[30]

The launches of the late 1880's and early 1890's were powered either by steam or naphtha engines, and would accommodate up to 30 people depending on the design. A few surviving photographs of the launches built by Chris and Henry Smith show narrow beamed vessels of between 25 and 40 feet, looking almost like enormous canoes, with large coamings to keep splashing water from the passengers. It is debatable whether any of the Smith launches were steam powered, but more than likely were powered by naphtha engines.[31]

Steam engines were generally in use in larger vessels of the day, as a steam plant's sheer size and weight limited the possible applications. Though today memories of the steam engines in small launches conjure up romantic visions of well-dressed ladies and dapper gentlemen, the truth is that they were far from ideal. As Edward T. Birdsall wrote in *Rudder* in 1896, "One who

Smith Boat House, Algonac. Mich.

Photo courtesy Marian Dawson.

The enterprise that fulfilled a marriage promise. The Smith Boat House on the St. Clair River at Algonac in the late nineteenth century. In front, the large, powered launches were a popular specialty of Smith construction.

has never been off for a day's pleasure in a small steam launch cannot imagine the amount of misery that one of these crafts is capable of creating. The trip is usually extended beyond the capacity of the supply of fuel, with the result that the boat arrives home minus seats, lockers and floorboards."[32] The complex mechanisms were in need of vigilant attention and constant adjustment, while the hot fire and dirty work of feeding coal into the furnaces often relegated them to service as public launches and water taxis rather than private transportation. Moreover, many passengers were leery of the hot, oily-smelling contraptions, and fearing, though of rare occurrence, the possibility of a steam boiler explosion.

The naphtha engine was a step in the right direction, however it still left a great deal to be desired. Instead of water, naphtha was vaporized in the boiler. One advantage over the steam engines it replaced was that "provision was made to condense the naphtha vapor after it had

passed through the engine, it could be used over and over again."[33] To some passengers, the thought of sitting next to a boiler of boiling naphtha must have made them yearn for the good old days of steam, as even the smell of the occasionally released naphtha was most peculiar and unpleasant. But naphtha engines became quite widespread, and, "up until the time the internal combustion engine was developed, small naphtha launches flourished. Shipments were being made to all parts of the world, and to all the prominent watering places of this country, both inland and along the coast."[34]

The busy waterways of the St. Clair River and delta, along with its close proximity to metropolitan Detroit, would suggest that very soon after naphtha engines became available, the Smiths would be sure to have early exposure, and be among the first to investigate this new technology. By 1894, Chris and Hank had saved enough money from their work as sportsman guides, market hunters, log salvagers and duck boat builders to buy one of the new naphtha engines for themselves. They carefully bolted their prize to one of their rowboats and fired the boiler. According to family oral histories, this combination was the genesis for further explorations into powered boating, and is generally considered a benchmark achievement for powered sport craft. At least one grandchild remembers Chris saying the boat performed well enough that rides were sold to daring customers.[35] Naphtha engines, like their steam ancestors, were generally of low power, so most estimates of this combination would have these devil-may-care thrill seekers zooming across the St. Clair River at somewhere around 4 or 5 miles an hour.[36]

The speed wasn't so important as the implications of the Smiths' accomplishment. They had powered a small pleasure boat designed for personal use, and though it may have been cumbersome, crude, cramped and slow, it stirred their imaginations and they were seemingly smitten and spoiled. The oar and the sail would seem quite archaic, once they had begun to turn heads with the Great Lakes' first runabout.

Photo courtesy Marian Dawson.

Christopher Columbus Smith on his docks with one of the early Sintz gasoline engines. It never ran well until Charles Sintz showed up with a gadget he called a "carburetor".

Two years of toying with their new contraption, and no doubt two years of frustrating modifications in an attempt to squeeze minute improvements in performance, were overshadowed by a dramatic watershed event. Isaac Colby, a long time resident of Algonac, and the man who would present the Village of Algonac with the Soldier's Monument to commemorate the Algonac men who had fallen in battle during the Civil War, bought one of the first small, internal combustion engines to run on gasoline.[37] The engine, a two horsepower Sintz, was just about the first small gasoline engine to be offered to the public.[38] The trouble was, Isaac Colby couldn't get it to run, which isn't really too surprising considering the fact that this early engine didn't have a carburetor. He gave up, much to the amusement of the many sidewalk engineers of Algonac, and found an eager buyer in Chris and Henry Smith.[39]

The early Sintz engine was a one-cylinder, two-cycle, two-port type with a touch spark ignition, which, with refinements to come in following years, would run quite well. The problem that Colby and Smith would encounter, centered around the air-gas mixture. These crude gasoline engines used several means for metering and mixing fuel and air, for carburetors were mostly unavailable for the smaller engines. One method entailed the use of a vaporizer, which consisted "of a number of vertical sheets of blotting paper or similar material dipping in gasoline, and so arranged that the air drawn into the cylinder was forced to travel over and around these sheets. This device was simple, but did not allow much speed variation by throttling."[40] The other method simply entailed dribbling gasoline directly into the intake valve, as Henry Ford did during the earliest testing of his gasoline engine.[41] It would be two more years before the ultimate solution would arrive. As Jay Smith recalled in a 1959 *TIME* interview, "It never ran well," Jay, then 74 explained, "until Charles Sintz showed up from Grand Rapids two years later with a gadget he called a carburetor."[42]

Chris and Henry managed to overcome this obstinate and cantankerous obstacle, and installed the little engine into another of his row boats. Thirty years later, Chris would describe this, possibly the first gasoline engine on the Great Lakes.[43] "Well maybe you've heard them thrash grain," he reminisced, "the motor would go bang, then it would turn over a couple of revolutions, and then bang, that's the way that little

Photo courtesy Marian Dawson.

Beautiful workmanship is apparent in this, the only surviving image showing the interior of the Smith Boat House, taken in 1896. Some of the timber used in these launches may have been salvaged by Chris Smith from the St. Clair River.

motor went."[44] Chris also said part of his growing family was on the dock when he first made the little engine run. His oldest son, Jay W., would have been eleven, and Bernard would have been seven. But it was Chris, now thirty-four years old, who got down on his hands and knees, cranking the little Sintz over and over and over, coaxing and fiddling, until the first muffled explosion broke the long silence in front of the Smith boat house. Turning a slender three-quarter-inch shaft and two-bladed propeller,[45] the little engine was a remarkable enrichment to the Smith product,[46] and, "under favorable conditions, he was able to get seven miles an hour in this, the first speed boat."[47] It marked the beginning of a new direction for the Smiths, and the final link in a chain of events which was destined to change American boating forever.

CHAPTER II

Speed Merchants

BY THE TURN of the century, Chris and Hank had firmly established themselves as not only the leading hunting and fishing guides in the region, but had secured a solid reputation as first-class boat builders.[1] Among the earliest published accounts of their activities occurred in an 1899 edition of the *Algonac Courier*. The article also conveys the great affability and fellowship which was characteristic of the brothers, contributing to their early business success as much as their boat building and sporting prowess. Identifying "C. C. & H. M. Smith" as "the Oldest Boat Builders in Algonac."[2] The little-known article details the full measure of their activities in the waning days of the nineteenth century:

They are practical men who thoroughly understand their work and take great pride in turning out a first class article. They not only build boats, but keep them to rent or sell, in other words they carry on a first class "boat livery" using oars, sail or gasoline for propulsion.

They are noted sportsmen with gun or rod, and are called upon by businessmen who wish to take a few days outing to act as guides. They know the rivers and lakes thoroughly, the hiding places of the water fowl, and the haunts of the finny tribe. Chris and Hank are well known to most of the sportsmen of Michigan and Ohio, and their jovial earnest hard working proclivities make them favorites and their quaint way of telling stories and cracking jokes make them most enjoyable companions. Proud? Well, no. They are not ashamed of honest toil, nor too weary to earn an honest dollar.

They are favorites with both ladies and gentlemen, and in the summer season enjoy a very large trade. A boat with the Smith Bros. mark means style, stability, swiftness and safety. C. C. Smith has held many offices which attest the esteem and confidence in which he is held by his fellow citizens. He is now P. M. [Postmaster] and a member of the School Board. H. M. [Henry] would not take an office if it was handed to him on a golden platter and the platter included in the gift. Both good-fellows, good business and good family men. They deserve the success they have attained.[3]

Early differences appear between the brothers. Chris is more inclined to social and civic activities while brother Henry, though gregarious and equally good-natured, is the more independent. Another source quotes Henry, being the more backwoodsman of the two, as boasting that he "never changed his winter underwear in the summer."[4] It is during this period of quickening business activities and boat speeds that Chris assumed full responsibility for the fledgling boat company, while Henry would continue to earn an income as a market hunter, professional field guide, and expand his hobby as a naturalist and amateur ornithologist.[5] Chris continued to hunt and fish, but the small enterprise will change its name for the first of eleven times. From simply *Smith Bros. Boat Builders,* Chris continued alone as *C.C. Smith, Boat Builder.*[6] Within a few short years, Chris would change the name of the company to *Chris Smith & Co., Boat Builders and Boat Livery.*[7] He gradually expanded his activities to include the construction, sale and rental of canoes, sailboats, launches, his traditional duck boats, along with his new gasoline runabouts. He inaugurated ferry services from Algonac to the popular Camp Algonac [situated on Russel Island], and to Grande Pointe and Tashmoo Park recreational areas which had become increasingly in vogue with Detroit and Cleveland vacationers. He also established *Chris Smith's Injun Ferry*[8], to deliver passengers and goods between the Canadian Indian reservation on Walpole Island and Algonac. At each phase of Smith's professional career, it was always a wide assortment of modest business interests that, when added together, represented genuine security for his growing family.

But Chris had become a man with a mission. Over the next few years, he generated hull and gasoline engine combinations that combined increased speed with greater detail, style and comfort, and his sales began to manifest the wisdom of his choices.

It was somewhere within this time period that Chris began to smoke cigars. You could generally tell Chris was in the vicinity just by the omnipresent blue haze and odor of stale tobacco. Chris was picky about his cigars. He bought only the cheapest and crudest that money could buy. "He used to call them *El Ropos,*" a granddaughter remembers, "and boy they were. He used to buy them by the boxes of hundreds so that he wouldn't run out. He'd buy three boxes at a time, and he was *never without one.* And the house *reeked* of it. He'd sit in his

Typical of the Chris Smith displacement hull designs was this milk boat used to deliver fresh milk and dairy products to Algonac area residents. Notice how far aft the spray line begins, and how high the bow is raised, a design handicap which Smith would soon conquer.

Chris Smith was afraid that a competitor might steal the plans for his boats, so he always developed his hull lines from models he would whittle himself, as opposed to full scale blueprints. In this rare photo, Chris is shown seated with an unidentified acquaintance while working on a model for a new runabout.

Photo courtesy Marian Dawson.

big chair and smoke his big fat cigars and say 'Good tobacco would kill me.' They weren't very good quality. He smoked all the time, and he loved to tease my grandmother. She took it in stride, he never got a rise out of her."[9]

Chris worked season after season to increase the speed of his runabouts, usually by small improvements in horsepower and propeller design. His hull designs had shown very little improvement since the emergence of his first duck boat. The deep draft of Smith's design was virtually identical to the steam and naphtha launches of the area, well suited for the leisurely five to eight m.p.h. speed their slow-turning power plants could supply. When Chris began to increase the speeds of his boats, the sterns would pull down hard in the water, dragging tons of water and limiting his speed. By 1905, he had managed to move one of his runabouts at somewhere around sixteen miles an hour, quite a respectable speed for the time. It also made Chris the fastest man on the Flats, a dis-

tinction that he had now cherished for over nine years. Smith wanted to move faster, though, and like the Sintz engine, once again it was a member of the Algonac community that helped to supply the solution.

In the summer of 1905, J.W. Gilbert, prominent member of Algonac's growing community, bought a boat hull in New York from William Scripps, the famous newspaper publisher and magnate. Gilbert also bought among the first four-cylinder gasoline engines to be built by a young Joseph Van Blerck of Detroit. The Ecce was an immediate success, and at 21.5 miles per hour, beat Smith's fastest combination by over five miles an hour.[10]

Chris dispatched his top men, including Ace Jackson and Fokert Endelman, to the Gilbert boatwell, armed with clipboards, rulers, pencils and pads. They measured every inch of the Ecce, from rail to rail and from stem to stern. This became a turning point for Chris, because for the first time he began to realize that subtle differences in hull design would make the difference between fast and *fastest.*

Chris received a commission to build an adaptation of this new design, a slim displacement runabout, as opposed to a hydroplane, from Algonac sportsman and businessman Neil McMillan. McMillan entered the boat in the annual races in Detroit, and "figured well."[11] It is uncertain whether the *Dart,* as McMillan's new boat was aptly christened, had a four-cylinder Van Blerck like the *Ecce,* or whether it contained a heavier Pope-Toledo power plant.[12] If it was the Pope-Toledo, it was an engine called *The Man Killer,* acquired at some time by Smith, and so-named because it had been responsible for the deaths of six men when used in a racing car.[13] Whichever, the *Dart* was to restore the speed record to Smith at between 23 and 26 miles per hour.[14]

It would also be in 1905 that Chris would hire a man who was destined to have the most influence on his sprawling career. Joseph Napoleon Lisee was a short, plump gentleman of French descent with a pinched face sporting wire-rimmed glasses that made his hawkish eyes look even bigger. At 34 years of age, "Nap," as everyone knew him, was already a master wood turner living in nearby Marine City, just nine miles upstream from Algonac. "Nap" started work in the Sicken Lumber Mill in Marine City when he was only twelve years old, and by the time he was sixteen, he was considered one of the finest wood craftsmen in the trade. "I don't think there was a finer wood turner in the country," his son Jack remembered. "He never used gauges or other measuring tools. He did his work by hand, his eye was sure and accurate. Why I believe he could spot a 1/8-inch variance in a joint at 150 feet away. He knew wood and he knew boats. Some people say that it is impossible to build a boat without a model. Dad never used a model, he constructed the hulls from plans drawn full scale on the floor of the plant."[15]

Chris, on the other hand, always developed his hull lines from models. "Smith does not work from blueprints," William A. Moffett wrote; "He builds the hull from a model he has fashioned. The only blue print employed is for the contour of the hull. He does this because blue prints may be obtained by a competitor. He believes a rival cannot do much with a model."[16]

"Most of the timber used," Moffett continued, "outside of the mahogany planking in the hulls, is cut and seasoned under Smith's supervision. He goes to Walpole Island or some other wooded tract and picks out the particular tree he desires, [and] has it cut, the lumber sawed and seasoned."[17]

The success of the *Dart* and the fortuitous acquisition of the skills of Nap Lisse, were events that by 1908 had launched Smith on a long voyage of innovation, acceleration and perseverance that would grow to challenge the entire science of boat building. The race for speed was on.

Photo courtesy Carl Lisee.

Joseph Napoleon "Nap" Lisee showing the fine touch which gave him the reputation as the finest wood turner in the country. It was said he could spot a ⅛-inch variance in a joint from 150-feet away. "Nap" was to design many of Chris-Smiths racing hulls, and eventually the Miss America and Miss Detroit series which would set new world records.

CHAPTER III

Murder Over Hull Timbers

FIVE YEARS BEFORE Chris Smith would show his first boat at the New York Boat Show, he narrowly escaped violent murder. Though he was spared by scant inches, one of Algonac's most respected and beloved citizens would be slaughtered over Smith's refusal to abandon twenty dollars worth of logs for his boats.[1]

Smith was the archetypical entrepreneur. Always searching for the profitable opportunity no matter how small or entangled, it was often his intricate network of secondary pursuits that added up to financial security for his family. The Hall Lumber Company, just upstream from Algonac on the Canadian side of the St. Clair River at Sarnia, provided one such opportunity. The lumber company would assemble great rafts of cedar and oak timber for drift shipment to Detroit down the river under steam tug escort. Occasionally, in the course of these log flows, a few logs would be shed from the raft and beach along the shoreline. Smith struck a deal with the lumber company, that he would retrieve any strays and pay them twenty-five cents a log.[2] These were pretty good sized logs, in some cases thirty feet long and two to three feet in

diameter, though most were smaller. They were "saw logs,"[3] suitable for milling into lumber, frames, stringers or planking, and represented a real bargain for Smith.

As soon as Chris secured this evidently exclusive arrangement with the lumber company, more logs seemed to drift away from the pack. Chris, it seems, was a friend of the tug captain whose job it was to escort the raft past Algonac to Detroit.[4] The gunplay and tragedy which ensued, however, bore no connection to Chris' secret, inside connection. That is, unless of course his bountiful river harvests helped to sow the seeds of a deadly jealousy.

It was a chilly January morning in 1905 when Chris realized some of his usual cast-offs were missing. He also had a pretty good idea where to look. It was only last year that Chris had experienced trouble from the Sauer brothers, William and Norman, who lived about six miles downstream from Algonac.[5] Chris drove a team of horses to the lower end of the middle channel, and there found nearly a hundred of his logs stacked in piles. Confronting the Sauers proved useless, and Chris decided his best course would be to return with a writ of replevin.[6]

By 7:00 the next morning, Chris had set out with veteran constable Elisha B. Moore of Algonac with documents in hand. Confident of his success, Chris also brought three teams of horses pulling three bob sleighs, and seven men as teamsters and timber handlers. All were unarmed. Two years later, one of these men, Leigh Merrill, would marry Chris' daughter Laura and become his son-in-law.[7]

By eight o'clock, the party of men had driven their teams the six miles to the Sauer home below Algonac. While the teams proceeded past the house to begin loading the first sleigh,

Smith and Constable Moore attempted to serve their papers on the brothers.

The older brother at 38, William Sauer, Jr., was over six feet tall, well built and described as "a fine specimen of manhood."[8] This morning, Wednesday, the 18th of January, he was wearing a soft black shirt, corduroy cap, a dirty brown vest, "slouchy looking" coat, grey trousers,[9] long rubber boots, and in his hands was a time-worn Winchester double barrel shotgun. His younger brother Norman, 21, also wearing high top rubber boots, casually rested a rifle on his shoulder.

The Sauers were living on "unsurveyed

were quickly loading the second. William Sauer, leveling his shotgun at the horses of the second team, told the teamster in charge, "if they valued their teams not to load any more of the logs."[13] William, taking aim at the startled teamster, told his brother Norman, who had produced a large butcher knife, to cut the tugs of the horses.

Smith now knew that events had gotten out of control, and that lives had become imperiled over what amounted to twenty dollars in drift logs. He instructed Constable Moore to have the men abandon the logs for the time being. Moore approached the older Sauer with his right hand raised. As he got to within twenty feet, Sauer swung the muzzle to cover Smith and Moore. "For God sakes don't shoot," Moore said. "If you come another step I will shoot you in your tracks," Sauer swore. With Smith and Constable Moore standing shoulder to shoulder, and before Moore could react, Sauer pulled the trigger. Moore, clutching his breast, covering a jagged hole the size of an apple, groaned, fell to his knees and rolled over in the snow, dead in an instant. Sauer immediately trained the gun at Christopher Columbus Smith and proclaimed, "You're next."[14]

Smith, now 44 years of age and never known for athletic prowess, must have realized that his only means for survival lay in flight. And fly he did, according to witnesses,[15] in a flurry of snow, no doubt dodging the expected blast through the woods until out of range of that second deadly chamber.

William Sauer, training the still-smoking murder weapon on the frozen and unarmed teamsters, told them to unload the logs from their sleighs and take Moore away.[16]

By 10:30 the first reports of savage murder had reached Algonac, and the news flashed from house to house with such great commotion and speed that within the hour every home in the village had been alerted, and "the streets thronged with people and guns and revolvers were in prominent display everywhere."[17] "Hundreds crowded together on the different corners and discussed the affair." Smith and the other witnesses of the shocking murder corroborated their accounts to authorities.[18] "Excitement was at a fever heat and the more lawless among the crowd called for ropes and a lynching."

A posse led by the Sheriff, Turnkey, and a large contingent of frenzied and slavering Algonac citizens set out through swamp, marsh and frozen fields in desperate pursuit. "The trip through the swamp was completed with much

land,"[10] a euphemism for squatters on the Flats bordering the Village of Algonac. It might help to explain the argument over the logs, as one who would claim land by popular sovereignty might even more readily profess title to the unescorted drift logs of the St. Clair River.

On review of the writ of replevin, Smith and Constable Moore were told by the obdurate younger brother Norman, that "This is not any good; it is not made out properly,"[11] and made remarks to the effect that they "wouldn't bulldoze the people of the Flats."[12] By this time, one of the three bobs was loaded, and the men

difficulty," according to eye witnesses, "the upper layer of the ice broke through in places and the horses were submerged in slush and water knee deep."[19]

The posse discovered the Sauers at 4:30 in Gus Hahn's hotel at the Flats, and arrested them without incident. Back in Algonac, however, an angry mob of 600 men and boys, presumably including Smith, waited in ambush for the posse and prisoners. When news spread that the victorious posse approached, "suspicious looking ropes were tucked into the sleighs, and there is but little doubt that had the murderer been found...lynching would have followed."[20] "The saloons were well patronized, and many men were led to recklessness by drink."

Fortunately for the Sauers, the Sheriff was alerted of the danger, and circled Algonac with his prisoners and sleighs, boarding the Rapid Car[21] for Port Huron with his deadly cargo before the lynching mob realized the deception.

The officers among the posse would report

that, "Sauer has always been on good terms with Moore, and they never before had trouble. Against Smith, however, he has a grudge, and as long as the trouble had to come he was sorry that it had not been Smith, instead of Moore."[22]

Sauer was sentenced to 15 years in Jackson prison following his conviction on manslaughter charges. Judge Law, presiding over the case, said, "It was the most outrageous case of manslaughter I have ever heard of," and further, "Human blood is too precious to be spilt over a sawlog."

And so Christopher Columbus Smith narrowly escaped an untimely death at the hands of a murderer. His legacy would have ended as the obscure, boat-building craftsman who assembled a few rowboats and launches in somewhere called Algonac, Michigan. The world could never have imagined how fast and how famous his creations were to become, and the legend of Chris-Craft would have abruptly ended on that cold January morning of 1905.

CHAPTER IV

The Smith-Ryan Boat Co.

THE CATALYST which Chris Smith needed to propel his work and reputation from the drowsy Village of Algonac to the world of power boat racing arrived one spring day in 1910. It came in the blithe form of Johnny J. "Baldy" Ryan, a light-hearted, debonair and charismatic gambler and financier. Ryan was a wealthy and well-known Cincinnati and St. Louis area sportsman, so when he bought a summer home on Harsens Island, across the St. Clair River from Algonac, he would naturally come to know Chris Smith.

To say that these two men were an odd pair is an egregious understatement. Smith, the conservative, unassuming, humble country craftsman and Ryan, the rakish and spectacular diamond-studded big city gambler. It wouldn't take long for Ryan to observe Neil McMillan's *Dart* flashing by on the St. Clair River overtaking everything in sight. He went to Chris Smith and ordered a boat to beat the *Dart*.[1]

It was Ryan's unwavering goal to be the fastest. Chris designed and built a similar but slightly improved boat for Ryan that would make 31 miles per hour. The *Reliance I*, a 28-foot displacement boat, surpassed the *Dart's* best speed by a com-

fortable margin, and made Ryan the fastest man on the Flats. His appetite whetted for higher speeds, Ryan commissioned Smith to build a second boat, the *Reliance II*, again a 28-foot displacement boat with a 100-horsepower engine, most likely supplied from Joseph Van Blerck in Detroit. The *Reliance II* would hit 33 miles per hour, a speed approaching the fastest competition boats of the day. Ryan was understandably impressed with Smith, and approached him with an offer of partnership.

Smith was already shipping his gasoline-powered runabouts throughout the country, and had carefully built a reputation for durability, style and speed. Chris was still largely isolated within the Michigan and Ohio territories, however, and the promise of national exposure, along with a generous cash offering, was the incentive which Baldy Ryan represented to Smith. It would be the first of only four times in which external or investment capital would be received by the Smiths, and not from the direct production and sale of boats.[2]

Algonac, with a permanent population of only 1800, had been home to the Smith boat house

The *Reliance I* was built by Chris Smith for Johnny J. "Baldy" Ryan so that he could beat the fastest boat on the "Flats". At 31 miles per hour, it was approaching the fastest speeds known for displacement hulls. Aboard in this rare 1910 photo are Bernard Smith with "Baldy" Ryan at the wheel.

Photo courtesy Pete and Jean Henkel.

for over a quarter century,[3] and the C. C. Smith Boat Co. represented nearly the full measure of Algonac manufacturing industry. The demand for the Smith product had turned the small boat house into a flourishing enterprise, with sometimes as many as fifty men working long hours during the spring and summer months, turning out a motorboat about every five weeks.[4] The Smith boat house was also well-known throughout the lakes as a reliable refuge for repairs, modifications and overhauls. Smith accepted the lure of J. J. Ryan, and streamlined his operations for speed.

The Smith-Ryan Boat Company was formed in the latter part of 1910 with a two-fold ambition. The new venture would develop an unprecedented line of fast, economical runabouts for a wider market, and display new models at the major boat shows of Chicago and New York. The more dramatic initiative would be the construction of a series of strictly race craft that would compete in the nation's preeminent motorboat races in an attempt to showcase and prove the superiority of Smith design and craftsmanship. This combination of sophisticated production, marketing and competition could only be ac-

complished with the financial panache of Baldy Ryan, and would establish precedents in merchandising strategy to be imitated by generations of boat builders to follow.

The Smith-Ryan Boat Co. runabouts were designed in two basic models, a 25-foot and 33-foot model. Drawing only 22 inches of draft, the boats were found to be extremely practical and were even adopted by the St. Clair River Game Warden who abandoned their clumsy, expensive cruiser.[5] It should be remembered that 1910 was a period of shifting sentiment concerning the gasoline-powered runabout. The prevailing opinion that these seemingly complicated, dirty and unreliable motor boats could offer their owners only headaches and embarassment was slowly being eroded by the efforts of Chris Smith and his sons.

The only brochure of the Smith-Ryan Boat Co. pointed out that "A Smith-Ryan Runabout will convert your 'motor-boat night-mares' into endless dreams of pleasure. Engine trouble is forever ended, for we have replaced the uncertain 'go-if-I-please' two-cycle popper (the 'Ogre' of all motorboat enthusiasts) by a steady, *4-cylinder, 4-cycle Engine* — sure as the flight of time.

And by building the only scientific, minimum-friction hull, we've eliminated the constant heavy pull and drag which relegates so many good engines to the scrap heap." The alluring brochure also stated that "Smith-Ryan Runabouts are handsomely finished in Oak or Mahogany. They're built big and roomy — for solid comfort. The upholstery is luxuriously cushioned. *They're boats to be proud of.*"

Of this there can be little doubt, for Chris had consistently maintained a reputation for premium and highly-regarded boats, and developed a large following of eager buyers. Among the more revealing developments about the Smith-Ryan partnership is that Chris was able to offer his new 25-foot runabout, complete with engine and upholstery, for only $475 F.O.B. Algonac. Boats of a similar class, unable to approach Smith's 26 miles per hour for a standard model, could cost anywhere from $900 to $1,200 on the East coast. The 33-foot Smith-Ryan runabouts were designed and built along almost identical lines as the 25-foot models. As the brochure re-

veals, "In class and construction it is exactly like the 25-footer. It's simply roomier — built for the man who wants super-comfort."[6]

Closer to Ryan's heart, though, was the development and competitive exhibition of faster and faster race craft, for he was certain that Smith could build the fastest boats on earth. Chris Smith was keeping abreast of new racing hull designs through his readership of popular periodicals like *Rudder* and *Motor Boating*, and was well aware of international hull design developments which had led to significant speed improvements over the past several years. Among the more successful configurations was the *hydroplane*. Smith and Ryan had decided that the next Ryan boat, *Reliance III*, would be a new and *improved* style of hydroplane.

Jay Smith recalled late in life that Chris observed the water bugs that would scoot so effortlessly over the water. "Some day," he told Jay, "somebody is going to build a boat like those bugs — one that will go on top of the water instead of through it."[7] Chris knew that the Amer-

The Smith-Ryan Boat Company was formed in 1910 to produce runabouts for the boating public and racing craft to prove the superiority of Smith designs. Notice the post office to the left, where Chris Smith also hung his hat as postmaster of Algonac.

Photo courtesy Pete and Jean Henkel.

ican, W.H. Fauber, residing in Paris, had successfully patented the hydroplane concept.[8] In his analysis of the hydroplane patent, Chris realized that the Fauber claim was for a hull which had multiple steps from bow to stern which progressively raised the boat as boat speed increased. "That's fine," Chris is quoted as saying, "I'll build a *single-step* hydroplane."[9]

The concept behind the single-step hydroplane is remarkably simple. At a precise location between the bow and the stern of the boat, a step is placed, the hull being slightly lower in the water forward of the step. At low speed, the boat is supported by the entire length of the boat, across the step. As speed increases, the bow raises up and more and more of the hull surface is supported by the area behind the step until no portion of the front surface is supported by the water. At high speeds, less than a third of the length of the hull is touching the water, also admitting great volumes of air beneath, so the drag and resistance of the hull with the water is significantly reduced, allowing the boat to go much faster. Even a crude single-step hydroplane hull would be at least fifteen percent faster than a similar boat with an ordinary displacement hull, pushing *through* the water rather than skimming *on top.*[10]

Chris, without formal education of any variety, was able to design what was probably America's first single-step hydroplane by keen boat-building instincts alone. He would move the step an inch or a fraction of an inch in a continuous stream of trial and error modifications until the desired result was achieved. A few years later, when Chris attended the National Motor Boat Show in New York, a technical discussion ensued. According to J. Lee Barrett in *Speed Boat Kings*, when the experts began exploring "friction, wetted surfaces, air resistance and model testing in the government tank at Washington, Smith admitted openly that he knew nothing of these things; that he was just an ordinary speedboat builder who got his ideas for speed under actual tests out on the St. Clair River."

"Well, what about displacement. How do you figure displacement?" they asked him.

"Displacement?" he said, surprised. "I don't care about displacement. All I need is enough water to cool the engines, that's all."[11]

Only 26-feet long and powered by a smaller and lighter, 75-horsepower Van Blerck engine, the *Reliance III* carried a jubilant Ryan to 34.7 miles per hour, making her one of the fastest boats in America. The success of the first single-step hydroplane was a great turning point for the young Smith-Ryan partnership. Ryan had Chris design another boat, *Baby Reliance IV,* using the considerable knowledge gained on the first experimental single-step configuration. The new ship, 25 feet 11 inches long, with a 4-foot 6-inch beam, was also equipped with the 75-horsepower 6-cylinder Van Blerck engine.

The *Baby Reliance IV* was ready in early September of 1911 in time for shipment to Buffalo, New York, where Ryan, along with Jay Smith, entered her in The Motor Boat Club of Buffalo races on the Niagara River. Three days of races were scheduled for the 14th, 15th and 16th of September, and the best American boats arrived from all quarters for the competition. On hand was *Dixie IV,* the boat that had won the British International Trophy, the *Harmsworth,* in 1910. It was the *Reliance IV,* however, that caught the appreciative eye of a journalist before the first race, and he was able to jot down an excellent, and the only existing description of the boat for his readers.

I passed on to another boat, the 26-footer, *Reliance IV,* designed and built by C.C. Smith of Algonac, Mich., an insignificant looking craft compared to the big *Dixie,* but one that excited a great deal of admiration by her speed and the manner in which she planed. *Reliance* is a single-step hydroplane with a round, canoe-shaped forebody, very different from the knuckle-bowed kind. Air is admitted to the step through two wide, flat S-shaped metal slots, fitted with a sort of damper with which to regulate the amount of air taken in. They said that her hull weighed only 400 pounds. She carried her racing number, 10, thumb tacked on each side of her stem, making a white square against the black painted side. A little aft of amidships there is a step in her sheer line about 3 inches deep, the after deck being lower. Inside her hull was bare, showing the frames bent "on the flat" about ¾" by ⅝", spaced 4 inches, as nearly as I could judge, with a wide, flat arch or hog frame fitted inside the frames to stiffen her in the way of the big six-cylinder 80 h.p. Van Blerck motor fitted with single exhaust pipe slanting aft and out over the starboard side. The shaft goes through a stuffing box on the inside of her step, a jog of apparently 6 inches at the keel molding in flush at the bilges. She carries her gasoline in a red, cylindrical tank with cone-shaped ends, chocked up fore-and-aft on her deck aft of the helmsman. A deep V-shaped strut steadies the propeller shaft just forward of her three-bladed propeller. She has twin rudders.[12]

Reliance III demonstrating the abilities of the first single-step hydroplane hull, was able to reach 37 miles per hour. Aboard in this rare photo are Johnny J. "Baldy" Ryan at the wheel (his bald head was always covered), and Jay W. Smith (highest).

The first day of racing was dedicated to the 32-foot class, the winner claiming the coveted *Evening News Tribune Edward H. Butler Trophy* valued at over $500. Three boats challenged for the cup *Reliance IV, La Truda,* a 32-foot multiple-step hydroplane with a 100-h.p. Sterling engine, and *Niagara II,* a 32-footer with a 60-h.p. Herschel-Spillman engine. The *Niagara II,* by contrast, was the only displacement-type hull in the race, and, "the difference in the running of this narrow hull with her bow down cutting a sheet of spray clear from the forefoot aft, looked queer when compared with the way the hydros lifted out forward."[13]

The race course was designed with two 2½ mile legs, requiring six laps to complete 30 miles. Ryan and the *Reliance IV* executed a near-perfect flying start at the gun. "*Reliance,* half out of the water forward, bouncing and splashing, with Mr. Ryan standing up and crouched over her steering wheel, like a jockey urging his boat on, jumped to the leading position."[14] Ryan won almost effortlessly, and at the end of the race, "*Niagara* was on her 25-mile lap, when down the

river against the black, smoky background the two white spiderlike legs of spray from *Reliance* could be seen. She was hitting it up at the finish, as the fountains of spray showed, and was given a gun and wild salute of whistles as she dashed across the line a winner."[15] In fact, Ryan and *Reliance* passed over the line at the same moment as *Niagara,* lapping the slower boat by exactly five miles.

The following day, Ryan and *Reliance IV* were admitted to race in the largest class, against the giant 32-footer *Dixie IV,* which had only two weeks earlier been proclaimed fastest in the world by winning the *Harmsworth* at Long Island with a course average speed of 34.66 miles per hour. Though the *Dixie* far outstripped the *Reliance* in terms of sheer horsepower, the speed and capability of the smaller boat caused a great stir along the banks of the Niagara.

"At the crack of the gun, *Reliance* was off in the lead...It was *Dixie's* first appearance here, and it was a revelation to the spectators the way that big racer slid through the fleet into the lead. A start like that is hard indeed to describe; so much happened in so few seconds, and there was such a cloud of spray and smoke that one couldn't tell exactly what was happening behind it. But we could see that big *Dixie* hull forge to the front, and close behind her, like a terrier chasing a horse, went *Reliance*, wide open, running with her bow away up in the air. *Reliance* caused a flutter of excitement by getting in *Dixie's* wake. She took a sheer across her wake, another sheer back across it again, half drowned in spray, and finally straightened course. When *Dixie* swashed past, a can of oil upset on *Reliance's* floor, and [Ryan] slipped and slid on this, and once fell down on his knees; by kicking off his slippery, rubber-soled shoes and standing in his stocking feet, he managed to keep his footing."[16]

At another point in the race, *Reliance* ran "dangerously close along the line of spectator boats, for a sudden sheer would mean certain disaster, but she runs true, there being two metal fore and aft fins under her aft, which prevent skidding."[17] It is testimony to the stability of the Smith design, for on the following day, *Dixie*, attempting a similar course, lost control, making a "fatal dash into the crowded bank, causing the probable death of one person and seriously injuring two others."[18] Ironically, *Reliance* had been barred from the race because of her diminutive size in comparison to the field of 40-footers that had arrived for the third day of competition.

Two weeks later in St. Louis, at the first annual regatta of the Carondelet Motor Boat Club, Ryan, Jay Smith and the *Reliance IV* scorched to a dramatic victory, and in the process completely upset the American motorboat racing establishment. A prominent marine publication put Ryan's victory into perspective. "It is reported that a distinct shock, followed by a series of waves coming apparently from the west, was felt about 4:30, September 30, at a large number of prominent power boating centers. The origin of this shock was at St. Louis. It was caused by *Reliance IV.*"[19]

That the race provided the most equitable test of the Smith design is undeniable. Another competitor, the *Kitty Hawk*, was almost an exact copy of the *Reliance*. Both boats were single-step hydroplanes. Both were 25-foot 11-inches in length, 4-foot 6-inches in beam, and both were equipped with a 6-cylinder 75-h.p. Van Blerck engine. In the twenty mile race at St. Louis, *Reliance* beat the *Kitty Hawk* by over three miles, thrashing her best speed by over seven miles an hour.[20] Earlier in the year, *Kitty Hawk* had beaten the *Reliance* at the races in Detroit, and Ryan was out for vengeance.

In a calm wind and flat course, five 26-foot boats jockeyed for position at the starting gun. The start was said to be picturesque:

"A better start has not been seen in the west this year; no boat could be said to have had the advantage. In a screen of smoke the whole five dashed for the north turn. At Detroit, *Kitty Hawk* had beaten *Reliance* decisively. Now the tables are turned. This race might be entitled "Ryan's Revenge, or What Happened in the Smoke," for when the leading boat emerged from obscurity on the down stretch, eager glasses identified the long black hull of *Reliance* in the lead. When the afternoon was over and the news spread that *Reliance* had covered 20 miles in 31:33...or at a little over 37 ½ miles an hour, smashing all 26-foot class records beyond recognition, there was an awed silence."[21]

Actually, Baldy Ryan and Jay W. Smith had demolished the old record by over four miles an hour. In all of American motorboat racing, only two boats had been witnessed going faster, *Dixie IV*, while winning the international title, and *Disturber*, whose 2,500-horsepower had only gone 3 miles per hour faster than the 75-horsepower *Reliance*. Through the test of competition, the Smith-Ryan Boat Co. had proven their products and workmanship to be the best and most innovative in the country.

As dramatic evidence of the success of their marketing strategy, at the New York Boat Show of 1910 The Smith-Ryan Boat Co. would display a newly-designed, 29-foot single-step hydroplane, the *Queen Reliance*. To call attention to the unusually high speed of the *Queen*, they advertised her for sale at $100 per mile of speed. At an advertised 35 miles per hour it drew considerable positive publicity and securely established the Smith-Ryan hydroplane as among the fastest in the business.[22]

One of the first contacts which Baldy Ryan would make following the formation of the partnership proved to be the most successful. In the early days of the American motion picture industry, few companies could rival Vitagraph Pictures, both in sheer volume of production or in scale of overseas distribution. By 1911, J. Stuart Blackton was internationally renowned as the owner of Vitagraph, and equally esteemed as the Commodore of the Atlantic Yacht Club. Blackton owned a palatial estate and motion picture studio at Oyster Bay, Long Island, and could claim President Theodore Roosevelt, fresh from the Oval Office, as his next door neighbor. In 1911, Blackton was attending a New York motor-boat show and was interested in buying a fast boat. "Ryan told me about a fellow in Algonac, Michigan who was the best designer and builder in the business," he would tell a *Detroit News* reporter later. "Ryan — I think they called him 'Baldy Jack', said Smith could build a boat that would beat *anything afloat*. I learned later that Ryan had money in the Smith boat business. But Chris was all Ryan said he was. I came out here and Chris told me he would build me a boat that would do 40 miles an hour — or I wouldn't have to pay for it."[23]

Blackton was well aware that the fastest boat in the world was *Dixie IV*, the boat owned by E. J. Shroeder and F. K. Burnham that had won the British International Trophy — the *Harmsworth* — the previous year with an average speed of 34.66 miles an hour.[24] Blackton had every right to be skeptical, for it was also an era of speedboat braggadocio, when wild and unrestrained claims of faster speeds and abilities flew from Europe to America. As J. Lee Barrett suggested in *Speed Boat Kings*, "Boat builders were promising speeds as high as sixty miles an hour. Alexander Graham Bell, inventor of the telephone, had just returned from Europe with the story that he had traveled in a new kind of boat — a hydroplane with an air-propeller built by Enrico Forlanini, of Milan, Italy, at forty-five miles an hour. Another man, Comte De Lambert, was building "hydroplanes" on the Seine River, France, that he said traveled almost fifty miles an hour. These, of course, are not official records, timed by a governing body of race experts as the world records are today. Some Americans said that these boats must have been timed with an alarm clock. Americans then were

Photo courtesy Marian Dawson.

The 250-horsepower Van Blerck engine is clearly seen in this portrait of *Baby Reliance I*. The man without a bowler in the boat is Johnny J. "Baldy" Ryan. Holding the rope is Jay W. Smith, and behind his neck can be seen the head of Chris Smith.

Baby Reliance I designed for Vitagraph Pictures owner J. Stuart Blackton. Ryan had promised Blackton that the boat would do 40 miles an hour or he wouldn't have to pay for it. Aboard the 20-foot Smith hydroplane in 1912 are Jay W. Smith at the wheel and Johnny J. "Baldy Ryan".

secure, even haughty, about speedboats and world records."[25]

Chris was convinced he could produce the boat Ryan had promised Blackton in New York. In fact, he told Ryan that someday he would build a boat that would travel a mile a minute.[26] Smith went right to work, knowing that he would have to break new ground in hull and engine design to meet his commitment to Blackton.

As Chris and his sons began work on Blackton's single-step hydroplane, his chief mechanic, Jack Beebe, was addressing the engine side of the Blackton challenge. The gasoline engines of

the day were going through rapid improvements in reliability and performance, but weight was still a major problem. Smith and Ryan researched the new engine-builders, and settled on a new design by Joseph Van Blerck in nearby Detroit. The 250-horsepower cast iron engine was too heavy for the graceful little twenty-foot hull of the *Baby Reliance I*, so Beebe attacked the problem quite creatively. He bored holes through the connecting rods, which not only reduced the overall weight of the engine, but also increased performance. He cut away large sections out of the heavy cast iron crankcase, filling back in with lighter metals, like brass. It is said that with this piece-by-piece weight-reducing system, Smith and Beebe developed "the lightest marine engine for its power in America."[27] The significant improvements that were consistently made to the leading gasoline engines by Smith and his crew led to the decision in late 1911 to change the name of the partnership from the Smith-Ryan Boat Co., to the *Smith-Ryan Boat & Engine Company.*[28]

The Blackton gamble was lowered into the St. Clair River for preliminary speed trials. Should the boat not perform as Smith and Ryan had pledged to Blackton, the losses could be spectacular, possibly even fatal in terms of money, honor and reputation. What seemed to be a major problem developed early in the trials. The boat was having great difficulty getting up on plane, or *on the step.* It seems that a powerful vacuum had developed in the pocket formed by the single step. Chris, with characteristic pluck, drilled a hole in the vertical surface of the step, breaking the vacuum. It worked, and the boat rose up on plane without a struggle. Now, would it be fast enough for Blackton?

Baldy Ryan and Jay Smith took the *Baby Reliance I* to New York for Blackton's inspection. Blackton took the boat for a trial spin out on Oyster Bay. He sped out about four miles, then unexpectedly turned around and headed back to his boat well. Jay, alarmed and perhaps suspecting the worst, asked Blackton if "he wasn't going to give it a further try before bringing it in."[29] "No, no," he shot back, "This boat has got *something.* I'm afraid something will happen to her." As he was gliding into his boat well, he made his decision clear, "Get out of here, fellows. This boat is mine." When Jay Smith and Baldy Ryan went into the house, Blackton presented Ryan with a check for $8,500.[30] They were in the racing business.

A week later Blackton entered the *Baby Reliance I* into an exhibition race on Long Island Sound at Gravesend Bay. Fog shrouded the waters on the Bay when Jay Smith, riding as mechanician, and Blackton maneuvered into position for the start. Blackton remembered the *Baby Reliance I* "skimmed out into the lead so fast it wasn't long before I couldn't see the boats behind me. We decided to open it up. I don't know how fast we were going but it was a lot more than 40 miles an hour."[31] Then, catastrophe. At somewhere near top speed, the *Baby Reliance I* struck a log, crushed in the hull, and promptly sank. Jay Smith and Stuart Blackton both tread

water and swam around in the fog for quite some time until they were fortunately picked up by a passing Coney Island ferry. Though the $8,500 boat went down in sixty feet, Blackton was reportedly more upset about losing his $2,000 watch during the accident. "We were picked up without knowing just how fast the boat was, but I knew Chris could build fast boats so I had him build another."[32]

Actually, Blackton's enthusiasm was so great that he commissioned Smith and Ryan to build two boats almost immediately following the destruction of *Baby Reliance I* at Long Island. The *Baby Reliance II* at 20-feet, and *Baby Reliance III* at 26-feet were both built along the same lines as the first, but with minor modifications.[33] The *Baby Reliance II* contained a new 250-horsepower engine designed by Charles Criqui of the Sterling Engine Company at Buffalo, New York. 1912 was destined to be a year of spectacular, though mixed success for Blackton and his Smith-Ryan hydroplanes.

The Blackton boats were finished in time for the Fourth of July races held annually at Davenport, Iowa to determine the Mississippi Valley Championships. Baldy Ryan and Jay Smith entered the tiny 20-foot *Baby Reliance II* in its own 20-foot class, but also in the 26-foot class, the 32-foot class, and the unheard of rodomontade of entering her in the 40-foot class, the ultimate class in powerboat racing. In an unthinkable display of superiority, Smith and Ryan won *every race,* and captured the Championships in *all four classes.* American racing was stunned. The news startled the New York racing establishment like a cannon shot. "They almost ruined powerboat racing in America," one source later reported; "It was unheard of for a 20-foot boat to win over the 40-foot class."[34] As if they hadn't proved their point with *Baby Reliance II,* they casually rolled out *Baby Reliance III* following the races, and, over an officially measured mile set a new American, and probable world record, at a sizzling 53.7 miles an hour. It was officially the first time that any boat had traveled faster than 50 miles an hour, much less nearly 54. In one glorious, delirious weekend, the Smith boats were proclaimed the fastest in America, and probably the world.

In fact, it was the international title that Blackton now contemplated. The most coveted prize in all motorboat racing was the British International Trophy, The *Harmsworth,* which was to be challenged at Huntington Bay, Long Island in a few short months. The race is the ultimate test of design and skill, with scant limitations on power or configuration for the entrants. The British had shipped their two finest boats to Long Island for the 1912 contest. The *Maple Leaf IV* built for E. Mackay Edgar and driven by the famous English aviator T.O.M. Sopwith, was a massive 39-foot 11-inch Fauber-Saunders five-step hydroplane powered by *two* 600-horsepower 12-cylinder Austin engines. Twelve hundred English horsepower against 250 for the Smith-Ryan *Baby Reliance II*. Britain's other entry was the *Mona,* owned by the Marquis of Anglesey. To round out the competition, the other American entry was Count Casimir Mankowski of Lake George, New York, with *Ankle Deep.*

The course for the *Harmsworth* was a thirty-mile triangle, with one leg protruding well out of Huntington Bay, past the headlands, and into the open sea. At this north end of the course, the seas built up conspicuously, and much conversation centered on the ability of the tiny *Baby Reliance II* to weather the heavy swells and towering waves of the open ocean.[35] The Blackton boat, detractors charged, was a fast, light skiff designed by Chris Smith for sheltered bays, rivers and lakes.

It was Bernard Smith, now just 23 years old, along with Wallace Pugh, Commodore and renowned driver of the famous *Disturber* series of race boats from Tonawanda, New York, who would pilot for Blackton in defense of the trophy. The *Harmsworth* is decided in three heats, and it was in the first heat that an international audience would first bear witness to the capabilities of the Smith-Ryan product. The *Baby Reliance II* sped around the course, setting a new course record at 42.679 miles per hour, and winning the first heat far ahead of the pack. On the smooth straightaways, Bernard calculated that he and Pugh were accelerating to over 50 miles an hour, faster than the capabilities of even the mammoth *Maple Leaf IV.* Problems were encountered in the open sea on the northern legs of the course, however, and the tiny boat pitched and lurched wildly, so that Bernard Smith at times only caught the wheel at the last second before rolling the boat over in the troughs and crests of the exposed seas.[36] By contrast, the much heavier *Maple Leaf IV* plowed through the rolling ocean quite comfortably, and with her enormous power was able to negotiate the course within a scant sixty seconds of the *Baby Reliance II* over the thirty mile circuit.

During the first heat, the Sterling engine aboard the *Baby Reliance II* was drenched by the salt water and spray of the seaward leg, and while leading the *Maple Leaf IV* by over a mile

Baby Reliance II was the first boat to travel 50 miles per hour. With Bernard Smith aboard, the Chris Smith hydroplane barely missed winning the 1912 British International Trophy, the *Harmsworth,* when the magnetos got wet from spray. With a 250-horsepower Sterling engine aboard the 20-foot Smith hydroplane, the following year J. Stuart Blackton beat the 40-foot, 2,500 h.p. *Disturber* in Chicago.

Courtesy of the Mariners' Museum, Newport News, Virginia.

The *John J. Ryan* was an all-weather displacement launch designed and built by Chris Smith for partner Johnny J. "Baldy" Ryan. Notice the large navigation lamps on the cabin roof, for being seen at night among the heavy Great Lakes freighter traffic of the St. Clair River area.

Photo courtesy Marian Dawson.

in the second heat, the soaked magneto shorted out and a paralyzed silence swept over the Blackton boat. The *Maple Leaf IV* completed the race and the following heat to return the *Harmsworth* to England, where it would remain for the next eight years. The Americans were devastated.

Baldy Ryan, incensed with the unfortunate malfunction, boarded Sir Mackay Edgar's yacht, owner of the victorious *Maple Leaf IV,* brandishing a check for $20,000. In a rash act of crowing vanity which characterized the career of J.J. "Baldy" Ryan, he challenged the British baronet[37] to a match race between the two boats the following spring on the River Thames in London. "I'll bet this check against yours," Ryan gambled, "that my *Baby Reliance* (meaning Blackton's) can beat the *Maple Leaf.*"[38] The race would never be held. Years of horse betting, living beyond his means and the fantastic cost of his own fleet of race boats had taken its toll on Ryan's fortune, and he would be broke within six months.[39] On September 27, 1913, Johnny J. "Baldy" Ryan and Chris Smith would dissolve their partnership.[40] The world would endorse the ingenuity of the Christopher Columbus Smith design, however, which was to change virtually all efforts at high speed competition which would follow.

Blackton was invited the following year, 1913, to Chicago by Mayor Bill Thompson to compete in a regatta that Blackton would recall later as the most satisfying of his career.[41] Among the competition was Commodore Pugh's notorious *Disturber IV,* powered by a pair of twelve-cylinder Dusenberg engines, which was scheduled to

challenge the English in the 1914 *Harmsworth* competition. "The *Disturber* had 2,500 horsepower, and was 40-feet long," the Commodore recalled. "My *Baby Reliance II* was only 20 feet long and, at that time, had a 250-horse Sterling motor in her. I had entered in every class, had won several trophies and hadn't worried until the big race against the *Disturber.* With the start of the race, I got out in front and expected every minute she would sweep by me. But she didn't, and it wasn't long before I realized she wasn't functioning 100 per cent that day, so I slowed down and made a race of it, winning easily."[42] The *Disturber* would never challenge for the *Harmsworth* trophy because of the outbreak of hostilities in Europe signaling the start of the first World War. The 40-foot behemoth would later record 61.503 miles per hour in 1915.

The next autumn, Blackton captured the highest prize in American powerboat racing, the 1914 Gold Cup, campaigning *Baby Speed Demon II,* the renamed *Baby Reliance III* built by Chris Smith. It was to be Blackton's crowning achievement, and though Smith would build *Baby Reliance IV,* and ultimately *Baby Reliance V,* the Gold Cup would be the zenith of Blackton's racing career.

Without Johnny J. "Baldy" Ryan, and now known as simply the *C. C. Smith Boat & Engine Company,* Chris was counting on continuing his exemplary relationship with the Commodore. But Blackton's fortune was beginning to erode as a result of the broadening war in Europe. Vitagraph Pictures' largest market, it seems, was Germany. And Chris Smith's largest market was Blackton.

Chris-Smith was stripped down to his last seven cents in a poker game
before he had the dream that would change his life.

CHAPTER V

Vision of Victory

IT WAS PERHAPS the lowest point in Chris Smith's career. Ryan had squandered and dissipated his fortune, trifling away over a million 1912 dollars at the track, on a swelling stable of racing boats and impulsive private wagers. One who knew Ryan wrote, "Ryan was glinted with the flame of daring adventure. He did things. He came to Algonac with a million dollars. Then, after two swift, exciting years of speedboat building with Chris Smith, he was penniless. The man would wager thousands on the turn of a card or the chances of a horse to hit the wire first. He'd walk up the slumbering streets of Algonac rolling diamonds in his short, fat hands, looking for excitement — some place to spend his money."[1]

The loss of Ryan alone was a setback, but in combination with the loss of Blackton it was devastating. Following Blackton's 1914 Gold Cup victory aboard *Baby Speed Demon*, actually *Baby Reliance III,* Smith was hopeful of convincing Blackton to commission another contender, perhaps even a challenger for the *Harmsworth.* Smith went to see Blackton at Oyster Bay, but it was too late. Blackton would maintain the boats that he campaigned, and could not be persuaded to contract for more.

After a depressing few days in New York, Smith, now 53 years old, was unceremoniously skinned down to his last seven cents in a poker game.[2] He then purportedly received a telegram from Detroit, "tipped the messenger boy the seven cents and went to bed."[3] Perhaps it was the agony and despair of his situation, but alone and penniless, that night Chris Smith had a dream that would change his life. As Smith later described to J. Lee Barrett in *Speed Boat Kings,* "He saw a beautiful speedboat being displayed on Cadillac Square, Detroit, beside the Pontchartrain Hotel and hundreds of beautiful flower girls were throwing basketsful of dollar bills into the boat. The money had been given by the people of Detroit. In his dream Smith even began to lay out plans for the boat. 'That's the idea,' Smith told himself the next morning. 'Build a speedboat for Detroit and raise the money by popular subscription'."[4]

Since one of his boats had already won the Gold Cup, Chris was confident he could build a boat for Detroit and convey the Cup, a tradi-

Hamilton Smith, here about age eleven in 1914, looks right at home behind the wheel of one of father Chris Smith's big displacement runabouts.

Photo courtesy Marian Dawson.

tional East coast privilege, to his home state of Michigan. He had to borrow a hundred dollars to return to Detroit. There, on March 30, 1915, at the Pontchartrain Hotel, he organized a meeting with a wealthy collection of the most influential civic and industrial leaders of Detroit. According to J. Lee Barrett who would be appointed secretary of the organization formed that day, the *Miss Detroit Powerboat Association,* "Among those present were Hugh Chalmers, head of the Chalmers Motor Company; William E. Metzger, one of the original organizers of the E. M. F. Automobile Corporation; William E. Scripps, publisher; Horace E. Dodge, Sr., head of Dodge Brothers; Otto Barthel, Detroit attorney; Paul H. Deming, Dr. Crevier, C. Harold Wills, of the Wills St. Clair Company; Frank Boydell, John J. Barlum, Arthur Waterfall, Chas. T. Bush, Havelock Northmore, [and] Dr. James W. Inches."

It is amazing that, although these assembled gentlemen represented tremendous, almost fabulous wealth, they were unable to raise enough money in all of Detroit to pay Chris Smith for the design and production of the boat they authorized that day, *Miss Detroit.* Smith, ever the optimist, and believing his dream boat would somehow be paid for, went ahead and built her anyway.

Miss Detroit was another single-step hydroplane, built mostly along the lines of the Blackton boats, and was powered by a 250-horsepower Sterling engine designed by Charles Criqui. During performance trials on the St. Clair River,

Chris invited William E. "Billy" Metzger, a founding member of the *Miss Detroit Powerboat Association,* and elected pilot, to take the boat for a spin. As Metzger was climbing into the boat, Chris said, "Be careful, Billy. This is the fastest boat I've ever built." When Metzger had completed his turn at the wheel, he said to Chris, "For the first time, Chris, the West will win the Gold Cup."[5]

The 1915 Gold Cup Trophy Race was held in New York, starting on Saturday, August 14, at Port Washington, Manhasset Bay. Chief among the competition would be Blackton's two entries in defense of the Trophy, the *Baby Speed Demon II* (Baby Reliance IV), and *Baby Reliance V.* Blackton wasn't the only threat, however, for scheduled to race in the crowded field was a broad collection of motor boating luminaries which included Charles F. Chesebrough's *Tiddledey Wink,* which he claimed had sped over 80 miles an hour; Count Mankowski's *Ankle Deep Too; Tech, Jr.,* owned by T. Coleman du Pont; *Hawkeye; Little Joker; Peter Pan VII,* owned by J. P. Bicknell, representing the Royal Canadian Yacht Club of Toronto, *P.D.Q. VI,* owned by Mrs. Henry Devereaux Whiton and A. Graham Miles; and finally *Presto,* owned by Carl Fisher, upon whose Indianapolis Motor Speedway, the first Indianapolis 500 Race was run four years previously.

Two weeks before the first heat, *Ankle Deep Too* would hit a rock and sink, *Peter Pan VII* would rip off one of the metal plates protecting

The *Miss Detroit* series of Chris Smith-designed racing hydroplanes were to become the fastest boats on earth. Here, Jay W. Smith is shown in classic repose, aboard *Miss Detroit II* mechanician to the 250-horsepower Sterling engine

her forward step, the *P.D.Q. VI* would blow out a cylinder, blasting away part of her crankcase, and the *Hawkeye* would be disabled by severe backfiring. In fact, out of the twelve contenders for the Cup, only *Miss Detroit* would be able to race in each of the three heats without mechanical problems. The 1915 races represented perhaps the poorest showing in the history of the prestigious Gold Cup, and was generally thought of as an embarrassment to the sport in general.

Surrounded by a sea of frantic mechanics and boat owners, it isn't too surprising that confusion reigned at the dock of the *Miss Detroit* as well. It seems that within five minutes of the starting gun for the first heat, the driver, Billy Metzger was nowhere to be found. In an act of desperation, and at the last possible moment, A. A. Schantz who was chairman of the *Miss Detroit* committee, asked if anyone from Detroit was in the crowd that knew how to drive a boat. The humorous incident was described by J. Lee

Barrett, secretary of the *Miss Detroit Powerboat Association* as follows:

A freckled face kid from Algonac, Michigan, stepped up.
"What's your name?" Schantz asked.
"John Milot."
"Can you drive a boat?"
Milot said he could.
"All right," said Schantz. "Get in there and drive."
Milot jumped into the cockpit beside Jack Beebe, the mechanic. He had no goggles, gloves, knee-pads — nothing. Before the heat was over Jack Beebe was driving the boat, taking care of the engines, and trying to hold Milot in the boat. The constant pounding in the rough sea had almost jarred Milot into insensibility.

But they won the race. At first Milot didn't know the course. *Baby Reliance V,* Blackton driving, was first over the line at the gun; *Little Joker* was second; Blackton's *Baby Speed Demon II,* with Robert Edgren driving, was third; *Miss Detroit I* was fourth.

Courtesy Mariners' Museum, Newport News, Virginia

Milot followed Blackton around the course for two laps — to get acquainted with the position of the buoys. At the start of the second lap *Baby Reliance V* was leading but the *Miss Detroit I* had pulled up into second place. Milot stayed in second place for another lap. Then Beebe began pulling out the throttles. They passed Blackton and were leading at the beginning of the third lap. They stayed in the lead and won the heat, averaging 48.5 miles an hour.

As the *Miss Detroit I* swept across the finish line the gun on the judges' stand blasted the finish signal. But Milot and Beebe, strangely enough, kept going for two more laps while boat whistles blew and the crowds yelled to them to stop their boat. When they came near the judges' stand finally, engines throttled, someone yelled, "Why didn't you stop? You won the race long ago."

Beebe yelled back, "We forgot to count the laps."[6]

Miss Detroit I went on to victory in the next two heats, one each on successive days, to be the first boat west of New York to win the Gold Cup. Detroit rejoiced, a major sporting trophy had drawn attention to the fast-growing city. There could be no doubt of the abilities of Chris Smith and his sons now. Even so, the *Miss Detroit Powerboat Association* still owed Smith $1,800 for the championship boat, and wasn't about to risk ordering a new boat for the 1916 Gold Cup competition.

This was a matter of some concern to Chris, for now he had six children, Jay, 31; Laura, 29; Bernard, 27; Owen, 21; Catherine, 16, and Hamilton, 13. One other son, John, had died from what was believed to be meningitis as a young boy. Without exception, all of the Smiths were contributing to the family enterprise in one fashion or another. It is this unified family strength that was to pull them through the tough times, both in 1916 and in the years ahead. It was almost unheard of to hear the Smiths argue, they were a quiet, dignified family that seldom went out of their way to promote their own individuality. Even Jay's son, Harsen, only eight years old, was already learning his way around the Smith boat house. Among the first jobs that the young Smiths would learn was to sort through the sweepings at the end of the day, sorting out the various sizes of brass screws. The boat company was a wonderland for the young children. Another grandchild remembered the wonderful innocence of being part of a family business.

We were allowed to go down there and play, you know what I mean. We spent a lot of time running up and down the canals and getting the men to cut us out a pointed boat out of a piece of scrap lumber, putting a nail in front of it, taking a string and pull it along the canal. Your first job down there was to sort screws. When they dropped screws they didn't bother to bend over and pick them up. It was all saw dust and everything under the boat, and the fellows that swept up at night [would] sweep those all into a dust pan and empty them into a pail. You got the job of sifting the saw dust out of the screws with a screen, shaking it out, and then you sorted screws, and you salvaged the good ones. Once in a while to this day, when I go out to the marina, I find myself picking up a box of stuff, junk, and I'll start sorting it. And then I start to laugh and I think it sure stuck with you, that job of sorting screws was very valuable.[7]

Fortunately, Smith received an order to build a challenger for a group of Minneapolis sportsmen. The twenty-foot single-step hydroplane was powered by a 250-horsepower Sterling engine. The *Miss Minneapolis*, with seasoned race veterans Jay and Bernard Smith aboard, won all three heats at the 1916 Gold Cup Races on the Detroit River, and returned to Minneapolis with the Cup. In the bargain, with the Smiths piloting, *Miss Minneapolis* became the first boat in history to officially travel over a mile a minute, clocked at 61.083 miles per hour on the Detroit River following the competition for the Gold Cup.

The bankrupt *Miss Detroit*, which naturally competed in defense of the Cup, was left a "broken, battered hulk after the race, fit only for junk."[8] The *Miss Detroit Powerboat Association* decided to wind up its affairs by offering *Miss Detroit I* for sale to the highest bidder. Secretary Barrett described the ensuing negotiations, which were to have a profound influence on the future of Smith and his family.

So one day I made a plea at the noon-day meeting of the Detroit Exchange Club for some loyal Detroiter to buy the boat. It so happened that the one man in all the world who was interested in a "used" speedboat was in that room when I spoke. He stood up — a slim, dark-haired, modest fellow about thirty-five years old. I had never seen the man before.

"How much do you want for that boat?" he called out from the back of the dining room.

Silence swept the room. The man didn't look to me like he could buy an $1,800 boat. I leaned over to Judge Sherman Callender sitting at my side, said, "Shall I tell him the price?"

"Sure," the judge said. "Take a chance."

I straightened up and told the stranger the price.

"I've got $1,000," he said. "I'll give you a six-months note for the balance."

I whispered to the judge; "Is his note good for $800?" The judge replied, "His word is good for a million." The boat was sold — to Gar Wood.[9]

Chris Smith's boats had won the Gold Cup for three straight years, and he must have imagined a bright and independent future for his company. Little did Chris know, however, that the events unfolding in Detroit would remove control of the C.C. Smith Boat & Engine Co. from Chris and his sons for the next six years.

GARFIELD ARTHUR WOOD

1880-1971

Illustration courtesy of the National Marine Manufacturers Hall of Fame,
National Marine Manufacturers Association, NMMA,
sponsored by the Attwood Corporation.

CHAPTER VI

Racing Dynasty

GARFIELD ARTHUR WOOD, named after two American presidents, was born on December 4, 1880 in Mapleton, Indiana. By his thirteenth birthday he was operating a launch out of Duluth, Minnesota on Lake Superior, and soon after developed an acute affinity for speed. "My first 'speed' craft was a 16' boat with a three-horsepower engine," he once reflected. "With it I succeeded in getting 8 m.p.h. running up and down the harbor at Duluth near my home, merely by squirting raw gasoline into the bell of the motor with an oil can."[1]

By 1911, when Chris Smith and Baldy Ryan set a scorching new 37½ m.p.h. record for 26-footers with *Baby Reliance IV,* Gar Wood quite accidentally began his career in racing. Gar was employed as a traveling lightning rod salesman for a midwest territory, and so employed wound up watching preparations for the annual Fourth of July Motor Boat Races in Dubuque, Iowa. He was looking at the boats from the dock when he observed *Leading Lady* experiencing motor problems. Gar, already quite familiar with gasoline engines, suggested to the owner, Mr. W. P. Cleveland from Kansas, that faulty ignition was the source. While Gar was out in the boat with Cleveland helping him get the engine firing properly, the race began. Wood, dressed in his "Sunday best", helped Cleveland win the race that day, and discovered himself hopelessly addicted to the rush of the checkered flag.[2]

Gar was exceptionally creative, having designed and built his own boats, and had an eye for technical improvement in all he surveyed. In 1913, he watched a coal truck driver laboring over the discharge of two tons of coal in St. Paul, Minnesota. It was a filthy, sweaty and inefficient operation, and one which was repeated thousands of times every day in a world powered and heated almost entirely by coal. Gar began to wonder if there might be a better way.

"Mrs. Wood and I had just $200 between us at the time," he later explained. "'I've got a new idea,' I told her one day, 'a mechanical device for dumping trucks. Shall I put the money in it?' She was a good sport and said to go ahead — that $200 wouldn't make or break us."[3] Using only about $100 of their savings, Wood developed the first hydraulic lift for truck bodies, secured a proper patent, and formed the Wood Hydraulic Hoist and Body Company. It was an overwhelming

"They are the captains of my fate," Gar Wood (left) once exclaimed. Here pictured with Jay W. Smith, mechanician, they hold "Teddy" and "Bruin" the mascots, which were strapped to the engines to bring luck to Wood's racing efforts.

Courtesy Mariners' Museum, Newport News, Virginia

success, and Wood made a sizable fortune from his new device.

Freed from financial constraints, in 1914 he built another boat, *Little Leading Lady.* His wife Murlen had bought a little teddy bear, which Gar promptly pressed into service as mascot and good luck charm for his boat. When Mrs. Wood bought another little bear, Gar enlisted him for duty as well. "Teddy" and "Bruin", lashed to the engines, were to be Gar's constant racing companions, Gar even once describing them as *"The captains of my fate."*[4]

By the time 1915 rolled around, Gar Wood was ready to "get into motor boat racing with a vengeance."[5] Immediately after purchasing the battered hull of the *Miss Detroit I* from the now disbanded *Miss Detroit Power Boat Association,* Gar set off for Algonac to speak with Chris Smith. Gar was very impressed with Chris' boat building operation, and also with the considerable mechanical abilities of his sons Jay and Bernard Smith. Gar commissioned the design and construction of a boat capable of winning the Gold Cup back from the Minneapolis sportsmen, and bring it home to Detroit once again. He was so confident of the Smiths' abilities, that in a shrewd move destined to limit the possibility of racing against other Smith designed and built speedboats, he negotiated and secured a controlling interest in the C. C. Smith Boat & Engine Co. Jay, although he would remain very closely

aligned with his father's business and Wood's racing program, accepted a generous position as a technical superintendent in Gar's hoist factory. It would be the start of the most successful motor boat racing dynasty in history.

The new 20-foot boat, *Miss Detroit II,* contained the 250-horsepower Sterling engine which had driven *Miss Detroit I* to victory in the 1915 Gold Cup. With Jay Smith riding as mechanician, Gar Wood won the 1917 Gold Cup in Minneapolis from the Smith-built defenders, *Miss Minneapolis. Miss Detroit II* also set a new American Power Boat Association speed record following the race heats, at a scalding 61.724 miles per hour. The Cup was returned to Detroit, and Chris Smith could now claim four straight Gold Cups to his credit.

The motor boat racing fraternity of the East coast was seething. *Their* beloved Cup was still stubbornly in the hands of midwesterners after two grievous years, and they intended to pull out all the stops to retrieve it. The president of the American Powerboat Association, Albert L. Judson of New York, had *Whip-po 'Will, Jr.* constructed to take on the Smith boats. Though he snobbishly announced to the racing community "I'm going to bring the Gold Cup Trophy back East. That's where it belongs — in the East", he actually had his 27-foot boat built in Detroit, by Martin and Jack Beebe, previously Smith's ace engine mechanics, and equipped her with a 400-

horsepower Van Blerck engine, also from Detroit. When Judson and Beebe claimed an *unofficial* one mile record of 69.39 miles per hour, Gar Wood was impressed, but naturally suspicious.[6] He understood the potential threat of a serious Eastern effort, and worked on a solution to increase his advantage.

The greatest obstacle to significant speed increase in boats was the power plant. The heavy, relatively slow-turning marine engines then in production also required a suitably beefy hull structure to support them. Aircraft engines, on the other hand, had a much more impressive horsepower-to-weight ratio, and steady progress had been made at government expense due to the continuing demands of WWI, which the United States had joined in the spring of 1917.

Down in Miami, Glen Curtiss of the Curtiss Engine Company had demonstrated an aircraft engine in his *Miss Miami*, which, by using an air propeller, had been clocked at 55-miles per hour. As part of Britain's war effort, Curtiss was contracted to build a high power, lightweight V-12 engine. He built several of the engines, which were all refused by the British government.

Through mutual friends, Wood was able to secure one of the prototypes, and scrambled throughout the winter of 1917 in the Smith boat house to modify it for marine use. They managed to increase revolutions from 1,650 to 2,000, while at the same time trimmed over seventy pounds of fat from the engine, now weighing-in at a slender 1,250 pounds and 400 horsepower, compared to 1,650 pounds and 250 horsepower

Courtesy Mariners' Museum, Newport News, Virginia

Miss Detroit II being prepared for a race. The 250-horsepower Sterling engine was taken from the *Miss Detroit I.* Pictured in the forward hatch is Jay W. Smith, with Gar Wood standing in the engine compartment. Jay W. Smith was considered by many to be the best racing mechanician in the world.

Gar Wood and Jay W. Smith win the 1917 American Power Boat Association Gold Cup in Minneapolis aboard *Miss Detroit II.* They had to beat the Smith-built defender, *Miss Minneapolis.*

Courtesy Mariners' Museum, Newport News, Virginia

for the Sterling aboard *Miss Detroit II.*[7] This special power plant would require a special hull, and plans were laid out for the new *Miss Detroit III.*

The new boat was considered a masterpiece of engineering and strength. The Smiths used seven different woods in her construction, and particular attention was given to her single-step planing angle, so that no part of the hull back to her step would be in the water at high speeds. The combination of the experimental engine turning a twenty-five pound, twenty-inch manganese bronze propeller accelerated Wood and Jay Smith to 56 miles per hour during preliminary trials on the St. Clair River. Though certainly not a blistering speed, after all, *Miss Detroit II* had gone nearly 62 miles an hour to beat the *Miss Minneapolis* record, but more importantly, they were the first in America to successfully modify an aircraft engine for marine use.

The 1918 Gold Cup Races were held on the Detroit River, and Gar Wood, taking the Eastern challenge quite seriously, entered both boats in defense. *Miss Detroit II* with the Sterling engine, would be piloted by his brother George Wood along with Bernard Smith, while the *Miss Detroit III*, powered with the new *Curtiss-Smith* engine, would be commanded by Gar Wood and Jay Smith. To round out almost a two-family race, driving *Miss Minneapolis* would be Gar Wood's other brothers, Winfield and Louis. Driving the Eastern threat *Whip-po 'Wil, Jr.* for A. L. Judson would be George Reis.

Though Gar Wood and Jay Smith won the first two heats against the stiff competition, Gold Cup rules made it mandatory for *Miss Detroit III* to take at least third place in the third and final heat to win on points. The defense of the Cup had taken its toll on both men and machines, as Bernard Smith and George Wood, driving *Miss Detroit II,* had demolished an engine in each of the first two heats, and a third was being overhauled for the final day of racing. In *Miss Detroit III,* both Gar Wood and Jay Smith had sustained burns, "when the flames of the Curtiss engine shot out of the exhaust stacks in front of them as they were roaring down the backstretch of the course. [Mrs. Wood] nursed their burns, bandaged Smith's fingers... ."[8] During the second heat when the crankshaft broke on the *Miss De-*

Courtesy Mariners' Museum, Newport News, Virginia

Seven different woods were used in the construction of *Miss Detroit III*, here seen at the docks prior to winning the 1918 Gold Cup Races in Detroit. It was powered by the new Curtiss-Smith 400-horsepower V-12, the first successful marine conversion of an aircraft engine.

troit II, a fire broke out. "George Wood was just getting ready to leap into the river when Bernard Smith held him down, calmly picked up the fire extinguisher and put out the flames."[9] It wouldn't be the last time that Bernard Smith would show great courage and quick thinking in the series of races. Again, J. Lee Barrett describes the incident in *Speed Boat Kings.*

The second heat was run just as Wood had planned. The SECOND *[Miss Detroit II]* went across the line first; the *Whip-po 'Wil* following. On the second lap the SECOND and the *Whip-po 'Wil* came into the west turn bow to bow, with only two feet of water between them. George Wood was frightened, desperate. His hands tight on the wheel of the SECOND, he didn't know what to do. How could two boats get into that sharp turn at full throttle without an accident?

He didn't have time to think it all out. Bernard Smith, with one hand holding out the throttle and the other steadying the wheel for George, put the boat around on her heels and guided it to the inside track. It was a swift piece of snap judgment and uncanny mastery. The SECOND went into the straightaway in the lead. But in a moment a connecting rod snapped and tore through the cylinder head. The boat gave a tremendous shudder, died. It was towed off the course.

Meanwhile, the *Whip-po 'Wil* had taken fire near the Belle Isle Bridge. Johnson and Kneeshaw [mechanicians] worked furiously putting out the flames. The boat shot ahead again and went on to finish the heat in first place.

Miss Minneapolis finished second; Gar Wood finished third. The Gold Cup Trophy was safe for another year.[10]

Gar Wood had unquestionably proved his point about the performance and reliability of aircraft engines in high performance boats. As word spread of his success and methods, other competitors began experimenting as well. Wood entered into partnership with Carl Fisher, builder of the Indianapolis Motor Speedway, and purchased over 1,000 surplus aircraft engines from the U.S. Government. Jay Smith, who had demonstrated superior engineering abilities, was chosen to lead the technical development for the project. The venture was quite successful, and shortly there was a clamor for the Smith — Wood conversions for high performance craft.

Smith and Wood repeated their performances by winning the 1919 Gold Cup Races in Detroit the following year with *Miss Detroit IV,* a virtual twin of *Miss Detroit III,* again powered by the 400-horsepower Smith-Curtiss engine.

Gar Wood, according to those around him, was becoming quite bored with winning the Gold Cup year after year, with little difficulty.[11] He had now won with Smith boats in 1916, 1917, 1918, and 1919, which for Chris Smith made a total of six straight years holding the national crown. Sometime after his victory at the 1918 Gold Cup, Gar began to look into the rules and history of the British International Trophy, the *Harmsworth.*

Since J. Stuart Blackton's mechanical difficulties in the 1912 *Harmsworth,* the coveted symbol of world supremacy in motor boat racing had remained in England. Only one other race, 1913, had taken place before Europe was ensnarled in the paroxysms of World War I. With the signing of the Treaty of Versailles in 1919, Gar Wood wanted to be the first to challenge England for the Cup of Cups, the owner of which could claim to be the fastest and the best in the world.

Among the rules in the deed of gift for the *Harmsworth* Trophy was the stipulation that challenging boats must be constructed, powered and piloted by strictly national resources. Hulls, engines and drivers had to be all American. Gar Wood had been using Honduras mahogany for his boats, and Honduras was a British protectorate. He had also been using Bosch carburetors and magnetos from Germany. He switched, for the first time, to Philippine mahogany, perfectly within the rules as the Philippine Islands had long been under United States protection. Accordingly, Chris and his sons began construction of two new boats, both primarily of Philippine mahogany. Wood then canvassed America's leading carburetor and magneto companies to secure their best efforts for his challenge.

The first boat, *Miss Detroit V* was to be the larger and stronger of the pair, designed to weather the often-belligerent seas of the English Solent, the semi-protected waters near the Isle of Wight, which are almost perpetually exasperating. Wood and the Smiths remembered well the near swamping that the lightweight *Baby Reliance II* endured during Blackton's unsuccessful assault on the *Harmsworth* in 1912. *Miss Detroit V* was built of sturdy, double-planked Philippine mahogany, 38-feet in length and nearly 8-feet abeam. It was the largest race boat that the Smiths had ever built, and it was only two feet short of the *Harmsworth* limitation of 40-feet.

Courtesy Mariners' Museum, Newport News, Virginia

The bow rudder is easily seen aboard *Miss Detroit III*, as she easily wins the 1918 Gold Cup with Gar Wood driving and Jay W.

Smith, mechanician. In many respects today's race craft can't match the turning ability of the Smith-Wood boats.

She is a Chris Smith design pure and simple. She has all the earmarks of the Smith 20-footers — just enlarged, one step in the underbody, a bow rudder, broad bow and wide stern, a sharp chine and all the other details so common in the 20-footers. Her power consists of two twelve-cylinder Liberty motors driving twin screws. The motors are set way aft in the boat and follow the usual practice of leading to a reduction gear forward. These gears drive the propeller shafts at about one and one-third engine speed. The engineers [mechanicians] sit aft of the motors while the boat is steered from a small cockpit forward of the motors. There is no engine control from the forward cockpit.

In workmanship and finish the whole outfit is about the finest ever turned out by a builder of racing boats. The installation of the motors appears perfect and there is an abundance of room both outside and between the motors for the mechanicians.

In her actual running *Miss Detroit V* does not fall short of her other excellent characteristics. The self-starters get her motors under way at the first turn, and when the gears are thrown in, there is no hesitation about planing. The big hull seems to get up on top of the water at once and starts off more like a locomotive at express train speed than a race boat. While no official speed trials have been held or speeds given out, yet it is certain that on the short stretches which *Miss Detroit* ran on the day she was launched her speed did not fall much short of seventy miles an hour.[12]

The other boat, *Miss America I*, was built purely for the slim chance that the English Solent would be calm on the day of the race, and a lighter boat would be able to make the highest speeds. At only 28 feet, she is the same length as Blackton's *Baby Reliance III* in which Jay Smith set a new speed record in 1912. Blackton had equipped her with a 150-horsepower Sterling engine, while the new *Miss America I* would have two Liberty aircraft engines of 500 horsepower *each*. It should be noted that Chris Smith used American cedar for the Blackton boat, while the much heavier and less resilient Philippine mahogany would make the *Miss America I* capable of supporting the more powerful engines. Although most racing historians, and even writers of the day, considered the *Miss America I*, the first twin-screw raceboat in the country, the fact is that the *Miss Detroit V* was running in the water almost a month before *Miss America I* came out of the Smith boat house, which would give *Miss Detroit V* the honor.

Wood's strategy turned out to be inspired. August 10th, 1920, on the day of the first *Harmsworth* heat, the English sea was as smooth as glass. "Harry G. Hawker, one of England's famous war aces and pilot of the defending *Maple Leaf VI*, told Wood the morning of the race, 'Listen, old fellow,' he said, 'I've lived on this strip of water all my life and never, NEVER have I seen it as calm as it is today.' Wood chuckled and said, 'Well, you see, sir, I brought my Teddy Bears with me.' Harry Hawker thought it another strange attempt of Yankee humor."[13]

The Liberty aircraft engines which Gar Wood and the Smiths used for both challengers were developed by Colonel J. G. Vincent and were used extensively by the American Army Air Corps during the War. Col. Vincent, by this time vice president of engineering for the Packard Motor Car Company of Detroit, had overseen over one half million dollars of research and development for the Liberty, and was willing to assist Wood and Smith with their critical marine application. The brawny 12-cylinder engines were designed to develop 500 horsepower at 2,500 revolutions per minute. Wood was able to secure an entire boxcar of spare Liberty parts, some of which had been rejected by United States government inspectors. Chris Smith always enjoyed among the most enviable mechanical reliability records within the sport, but now in combination with all the considerable financial resources and extreme competitiveness of Gar Wood, the team would leave absolutely nothing to chance.

Unfortunately, things began to go wrong almost from the beginning for the other American challenger, *Whip-po 'Will, Jr.* First, illness prevented her owner, Commodore Albert L. Judson from attending the races in England. Then, the daring but cantankerous combination of two 16-cylinder, 450-horsepower Bugatti engines harnessed together driving a single prop, required almost constant attention. The 27-foot hull, smallest in the races, is the same which was defeated by *Miss Detroit III* in the 1918 Gold Cup races with the 400 h.p., 12-cylinder Van Berck power plant, and was timed in trials then at 63.498 miles per hour. It is interesting to note, that the *pair* of 450-horsepower Bugatti engines aboard for the *Harmsworth* races weigh less than the single 400-horsepower Van Blerck which they replaced.

Disaster struck the Judson entry three days before the race. In practice trials, a backfire ignited the engines in flames so quickly that two of three crew members had to abandon ship almost immediately. After the fire had burned itself to the waterline, the *Whip-po 'Will, Jr.* slipped beneath the blackened surface of the English Solent, never to be seen again. Watching the catastrophe was the hapless Lloyds of London insurance agent who had just insured the ship for 15,000 pounds, for the miniscule premium of only three hundred dollars. It would be the last time that Lloyds would ever insure high speed competition boats.

The English had three boats prepared to defend the Cup. *Sunbeam-Despujols*, an exact duplicate of a French boat which had performed impressively at the Monaco races the previous season, was powered by four 12-cylinder, 450-horsepower aviation engines, for a whopping total of 1,800 horsepower. The greatest threat, however, was posed by *Maple Leaf V*, and *Maple Leaf VI*, both prepared by the holder of the Cup, the same Sir E. Mackay Edgar which Baldy Ryan had challenged to a $20,000 match race following Blackton's defeat with *Baby Reliance II* in the 1912 *Harmsworth* contest. Sir Edgar would claim over 66 miles per hour for *Maple Leaf V* in one-mile speed trails, and tauntingly suggested that the new 39-foot *Maple Leaf VI*, powered by a pair of 550-horsepower Rolls-Royce Condor engines was even *faster*.

The first heat of the race was filled with tension and excitement, as the field of competitors prepared to do battle. Aboard *Miss America I* was Gar Wood, with Jay Smith and Phil Wood as mechanicians. Piloting the *Miss Detroit V* was George Wood along with Bernard Smith and Clarence Mericle as mechanics.

The Cannon on the Judges' barge boomed the five-minute signal. Wood and his mechanics stepped into the cockpit. Smith touched the

Chris Smith found a comfortable seat to watch his *Miss Detroit IV* win the 1919 Gold Cup Races in Detroit. His unbeatable hulls and engines had won the nation's most coveted racing trophy six years in a row.

After winning the *Harmsworth* trophy, *Miss America I* set a new international speed record of 76.655 miles per hour on the Detroit River with Gar Wood driving, seen here along with "Doc" Sanborn and Jay W. Smith.

starting button, warmed the engines, jerked the throttle down. The *Miss America I* rose on her step, leveled off and charged ahead.

Wood, handling the wheel, streaked up the mainland side of the course, going west. His boat planed perfectly; the bright Philippine mahogany gleaming like fire beneath the English sun; the white spray spreading like wings poised for the dive. He cut a wide arc beyond the extreme westerly buoys and headed back, pointing the bow of his boat straight for the towers of Queen Victoria's palace rising above the tree tops. He had previously chosen to run down along that line marked by the palace towers.

He could see the last disc hanging above the judges' stand but his watch told him the time was crowding. He signaled Jay Smith for more throttle. The two Liberties in his boat answered with 1,000 horsepower.

Wood was fearful that he would not be able to hear the starting gun over the roar of his two Liberties. But when he put his Miss America across the line the blast of the six-inch cannon on a battleship above his head almost pitched him out of the boat.

Wood...was having a good deal of trouble. It was only his fast turning at the buoys that kept him up there near the lead. He could turn much faster than any of the English boats because of his bow rudder. Before the race, when the English engineers examined the American boats, they ridiculed the bow rudder on Wood's boats. "You can't turn a boat with a rudder way up there," they said.

But now, with Wood's spark plugs fouling, his bow rudder was keeping him in the race. The English would sweep far wide of the buoys and before they could get their boats back on the

Miss Chicago, the boat built by Chris Smith for Sheldo Clark. Clark would claim that *Miss Chicago* held the world record for single-engine speedboats for sixteen years. Th boat may have been among the reasons for the growin disenchantment between Chris Smith and Gar Woo

stretch again, Wood was taking the turns with all his power, trimming the buoys. [The following year the English put a bow rudder on their boat]. On the fourth lap Wood took the lead with his Miss America I.

After Wood had gone over the finish line he headed his boat back toward the judges' stand. For the first time he noticed that the faces of his mechanics and the American flag at the stern of his boat were as black as coal. When they neared the judges' stand Sir Mackay Edgar, owner of the *Maple Leafs*, yelled out, "What kind of fuel are you burning in that boat?"

Wood answered, "We're using soft coal today. But watch out for tomorrow — we're going to use gasoline."[14]

Indeed, it was superiority of the Wood-Smith and Nap Lisee designed hulls that made the dramatic difference. Even though both *Miss Detroit* and *Miss America I* experienced severe carburetion problems during the first heat, it was the obvious conclusion of all onlookers that the British boats were poorly designed. One leading publication reported "Evidently the widely different atmospheric conditions had entirely upset carburetion and there had not been time to get this right. The fact that the boats could win, and win easily, under such conditions, is most wonderful testimony to the genius dis-

played by the designers and builders of the hulls."

Ironically, the same Lloyds of London agent that had insured *Whip-po 'Wil, Jr.* had insured the American hulls, and insisted on a sheet metal shroud to protect the engines from salt water spray. The closely fitting cowling choked off the air supply for Wood's deep breathing Curtiss engines, and "His engines were smoking and in his wake was an immense black ring around the entire rim of the course."[15]

Admiration was unbounded at the way the two American boats skimmed over the water without any fuss, without any pounding, and with the minimum disturbance of water. But the greatest surprise of all was the way the two United States boats went around the buoys. While the best of the Britishers threw up a rudder wave twenty feet high, the American craft slipped round with no trace of a wave, and even had they been no faster than their rivals on the straightway, they could have won by reason of this feature only.

In contrast with these, the Saunders-built *Maple Leaf VI* advanced with a long series of bounds which were often described as "rocking horse motion," "kangaroo leaps" and "speeding hound." The sea in Osborne Bay was calm with a fresh breeze; had the water been at all rough,

Courtesy Mariners' Museum, Newport News, Virginia.

it is likely that this boat would have broken its back before that race had been run. The pounding appeared to be in irregular intervals of thirty to fifty seconds, when the whole forward portion of the boat came out of the water and pounded down most violently, throwing up a spray on each side fifty or sixty feet high.[16]

After minor adjustments to both boats, including removing the Lloyds recommended engine shrouds, Gar Wood's boats were running perfectly. During the second heat, they completely outclassed the English defenders, and for the most part put on an exhibition race between *Miss America I* and *Miss Detroit V.* Her best speed over the course was over 65 miles an hour, actually the fastest on earth. The team of Wood and Smith had won the championship of the world, and returned the *Harmsworth* Trophy to American shores.[17]

Almost exactly a month later, in defense of the Gold Cup at Detroit, *Miss America I* shattered every Gold Cup and international speed record with a blistering 76.677 miles per hour. Gar Wood was the idol of speedboating, and America was the toast of the seas.

In 1921, Gar Wood accepted the expected challenge from Sir Mackay Edgar from England to compete for the *Harmsworth,* and preparations began in earnest in the C.C. Smith Boat & Engine Co. in Algonac. *Miss America II* was slowly taking shape, a bold adventure of 32-feet housing *four* Smith-Liberty engines for a total of 2,000 horsepower. Occasional disagreements would arise between Smith and Wood over hull refinements, and may have sown the seeds of future discontent between the two independent thinkers. "Wood instructed his men to reduce the wetted surface on the new boat," J. Lee Barrett wrote in *Speed Boat Kings.* "We're getting too much water friction. Reduce the beam below the water line." Chris Smith was opposed to the idea, and advised Wood that the, "beam should be the same below the water line as it is above."[18] Wood, not surprisingly, prevailed. When *Miss America II* was tested on the St. Clair River it wouldn't plane. It had to be returned to the boat house, the forward step broadened to Smith's original specifications, and during subsequent trials planed well. This small incident is mentioned only as a premonitory of disaffection which would arise between the two men in the coming months and years, and at its peak would lead eventually to the renewed independence of the C.C. Smith Boat & Engine Co.

Another early indication of the growing independence of the Smiths was their ability to build *a rival entry* to compete against Wood in the 1921 *Harmsworth* competition. Sheldon Clark, the Commodore of the Chicago Yacht Club, conspired with Gar Wood's brother Phil to finance a threat to Gar's possession of the trophy. Clark's Chicago syndicate commissioned Chris Smith to construct *Miss Chicago,* a lightweight 22-foot bolt of lightning powered by a single Smith-Liberty engine. The boat was so successful that Clark would claim that *Miss Chicago* held the world's record for *single-engine* speedboats for 16 years. It seemed that none of the boats designed and built by the Smiths were ever destined to be average or ordinary.

A series of setbacks befell the English challenger, *Maple Leaf VII,* long before the starting gun echoed across the Detroit River on September 5th. First, the exotically constructed hull slipped its loading tongs on arrival and fell two feet to the dock, jarring its four Sunbeam engines out of line. The hull was constructed with a patented lamination of two-ply mahogany held together with oiled and sewn aircraft silk in diamond-shaped sections.[19] When Wood first saw the *Maple Leaf VII,* "...a smile escaped him. The English had put on a bow rudder."[20]

Even though the *Maple Leaf VII* was pitching and porpoising hopelessly during trials, the English crew continued preparations for the race. Wood passed along some good advice to Colonel A.W. Tait, pilot of the *Maple Leaf VII.*

> When Tait came into the boatwell after one of his trial runs, Wood went up to him. "Your boat is out of line, Colonel. Your men have got to straighten that hull. She won't take the power."
> The English crew was under-manned and they did what they could on the hull. But the engines were their greatest concern. "If we get these engines working the way they should," Tait said, "you'll see something."
> Wood didn't believe this. He always believed that hull construction, balance, alignment, lifting surfaces, these things were as important as the engines. "You can pile a lot of horsepower in a boat," he's often said, "but if the hull isn't balanced, what good is your power?"[21]

Then, with only a day remaining before the big race, Tait burned out a bearing aboard *Maple Leaf VII.* They didn't have a spare, and the *Harmsworth* rules specifically require that only English parts and English personnel were to be used on the English entry. Wood magnanimously waived the rules, fashioned a bearing for the British, delayed the start of the race for two days, and then assigned his own crew to assist the challenger.

The race itself was quite anticlimactic. On the second lap, *Maple Leaf VII* tore a large hole in her hull just forward of the step and began to sink. Even as she was being towed off the race-course she caught on fire. Any British hopes for retrieving the lost trophy were extinguished along with the flames.

But Gar Wood could not claim the Cup unless he defeated his brother George and Bernard Smith, not to mention the single engine *Miss Chicago.*

...Wood and Jay Smith in the *Miss America II* drove a wild, mad, daring race against the *Miss America I*, driven by George Wood and Bernard Smith. Taking the first east turn on the second lap the *Miss America I* was in the lead, ahead of Gar Wood. Wood and Jay Smith were roaring up the back stretch. They began to push their boat in an effort to catch *Miss America I*. George Wood, driving the *First*, kept hugging the buoys, on the inside track. Bernard Smith kept the throttles out. They weren't going to let Gar Wood beat them if they could help it.

But just beyond the far east turn...Gar Wood cut his boat dangerously across the bow of the *Miss America I*. His propellers threw a sheet of boiling spray into the cockpit. George Wood and Bernard Smith were blinded, for a moment. The spray hit them like bullets at that speed. Bernard Smith threw down the throttles to keep his boat from hitting the *Miss America II*, which had now gone into the lead. Just as the boat checked, George Wood had to swing the wheel fast to keep from hitting the second easterly buoy.

"George was ahead of me," [Gar] Wood said later. "I had to take him as soon as I could. That's racing. If I cut dangerously across his bow — well, that's racing too. I wanted the lead and I got it. That's what counts."[22]

Clark's *Miss Chicago* developed engine difficulties, and wasn't competitive during the event. Gar Wood had successfully defended the *Harmsworth* Cup, and America loved him for it. During official one-mile trials following the race, *Miss America II* captured a new international speed record at 80.567 miles per hour. Boats built by the Smiths had been the first boats to do 50, 60, 70 and 80 miles per hour. It was also destined to be the last time that the Smiths would team up with Gar Wood in defense of the *Harmsworth* Trophy.

It is against this backdrop of massive publicity that the C. C. Smith Boat & Engine Co. began

a series of advertisements in the major marine publications to promote their new *Smith Marine "Twin Six,"* the world's champion motor. Actually, the *"Twin Six"* was the successful Curtiss-Smith aircraft engine conversion used aboard the triumphant *Harmsworth* challengers, *Miss America I*, and *Miss Detroit V*. In their advertisement of October 1920, they proclaimed in part:

Records speak for themselves. *Miss America*, winner of the *Harmsworth* trophy and Gold Cup, is a SMITH-BUILT boat, powered with SMITH MARINE "TWIN-SIX" engines which easily won over all American and European contenders powered with the best European and U.S. made engines. To defeat these products of skilled foreign mechanics it required the highest efficiency, extreme power for weight and reliability. This record speaks for itself.

SMITH MARINE "TWIN-SIX" engines in combination with SMITH-BUILT hulls have proven their supremacy over all competitors. They have stood the test.

Boats equipped with SMITH MARINE "TWIN-SIX" engines are: *Miss America, Miss Detroit V, Miss Toronto II, Miss Detroit II, Miss Detroit III,* hydroplanes; *Unique, Tallyho, Gar, Jr., Gar, Jr. II, Commander,* express cruisers; *Sure Cure, Miss Nassau, Heldena II, Pam, Emma K, Miss Los Angeles II,* runabouts. These are the fastest boats in the world.

These engines are the lowest priced power plants per horse-power in the world.

Write for catalogues and descriptive matter on SMITH MARINE "TWIN-SIX" engines, SMITH-BUILT Express Cruisers, runabouts, and speedboats to the

C. C. Smith Boat & Engine Co.
Builders of Speed Boat Champions
For Ten Straight Years

In fact, during almost their entire association with Gar Wood, the Smiths were building an assortment of enviable runabouts and express cruisers for a well-heeled clientele. Naturally, since a majority interest in the C.C. Smith Boat & Engine Co. was held by Mr. Wood, *his* racing projects and other hull-building assignments would receive first priority. But where time permitted, the Smiths were still building a solid reputation among discerning pleasure craft buyers throughout the country. Among the Smiths' accomplishments during this landmark year, was their successful display at the 1921 Motor Boat, Ship & Engine Show, held at the Grand Central Palace, New York City, December 10-18, 1920.

Two of the Gar Wood specialty commissions built during this period are quite remarkable,

Gar, Jr., and *Gar, Jr. II.* The term *express cruiser,* as applied in 1920, generally extended to a class of seemingly overgrown speedboat hulls with traditional cruiser-style conveniences for travelers. The *Gar, Jr.'s* were 50-foot express cruisers built to demonstrate the superior speed and dependability that the new aircraft engine conversions could offer to cruiser owners. Equipped with two Smith-Liberty engines developing 900 horsepower, she was able to capture the express cruiser record for her class at 48.7 miles per hour in 1921. Designed along the lines of the Nap Lisee mono hulls, the *Gar, Jr. II,* "was fully equipped for long comfortable open water travel and had sleeping quarters for eight persons."[23]

Gar, Jr. II had a long and astonishing career, and, "set more distance speed records, marks that stood up for a longer period of time than any other boat ever has. In fact, each of these records held for more than forty years and the record runs from Miami and New York to Detroit *still stands,* [over] sixty-five years to this date."[24] One of the most publicized records was accomplished with *Motor Boating* editor Charles F. Chapman aboard as navigator, when *Gar, Jr. II* raced the east coast's fastest train from Miami to New York, beating the locomotive by 21 minutes. As described in an ad for the Valspar varnish that covered the boat, "Nothing daunted by rough weather and a two day fog which forced her 25 miles off shore, the determined little craft, with her daring owner at the helm, forged ahead through the open sea and put the 1,260 miles behind her in 47 hours and 23 minutes running time — 21 minutes less than the train time of the famous "Havana Special.""[25] Even though *Gar, Jr. II* was not designed as a race boat, "... sometimes the large windshields and part of the upper cabin top would be removed for strictly racing events.[26] The famous boat explored more than 20,000 miles of territory including the "Florida Straits from Palm Beach to Cuba, all over the Great Lakes including Superior, Michigan, Huron and the Georgian Bay, and throughout the entire Bahamas."[27]

Though *Gar, Jr. II* was the *last boat* built for Gar Wood by the Smiths, it became the prototype for a series of boats still unmatched in perfor-

Charles F. Chapman was navigator aboard *Gar, Jr. II* as Gar Wood beat the east coast's fastest train from Miami to New York. Chapman is remembered as the long-time editor of *Motor Boating* magazine, and as the author of *Chapman's Piloting, Seamanship and Small Boat Handling,* the "bible" of seafaring rules and techniques.

Illustration courtesy of the National Marine Manufacturers Hall of Fame, National Marine Manufacturers Association, NMMA, sponsored by the Attwood Corporation.

CHARLES FREDERIC CHAPMAN
1881-1976

Courtesy Mariners' Museum, Newport News, Virginia

The only known photo in existence of a runabout produced by the C.C. Smith Boat & Engine Co. The photo is dated 1919, and shows the unique design of a roomy single cockpit runabout of approximately 28-feet.

mance today. Gar Wood advertised a 50-foot boat with a guaranteed 50 miles an hour speed for $50,000. As Gar Wood, Jr. explains, "The speed guarantee, which was always reached, is amazing when one considers modern day boats of similar size and accommodations and power cannot reach thirty miles an hour and sometimes struggle to reach twenty-five."[28]

It was, though, the end of a dramatic era for the talented and now seasoned band of Smiths. Chris had led the industry in technical innovations and racing accomplishments for over a decade. Jay had gained a reputation as the best mechanician in America, and was considered an authority on marine propulsion. Bernard was a world champion mechanician whose cool and level head had saved more than one race. Both Owen, 27, and young Hamilton, now seventeen, had proved a valuable addition to the growing Smith boat building talent pool. Catherine, now 20, was already tackling the family bookkeeping, paperwork and business correspondence. In all, the Smiths represented a well-balanced, disciplined and unusually hard-working family, well suited to the unique challenge of history they were to face together.

Once again, they were to become *independent* boat builders.

The Smiths had gained a reputation for superb quality and craftsmanship from their very first designs.
This scene from the early twenties depicts the skill of driving the thousands of
Philippine mahogany bungs to seal the holes left by bronze fastening screws.

CHAPTER VII

Chris Smith & Sons Boat Co.

IT WAS MORE A combination of factors rather than a single event which caused the dissolution of the Wood-Smith partnership. Chris was anxious to begin volume manufacture for a wider market, while the demands of the Wood racing program could at times be formidable. Also, a sort of intra-company rivalry slowly evolved, as Chris would take on contracts to build boats which would ultimately, as *Miss Chicago* did, compete against the majority shareholder, Gar Wood. It was primarily this purely business decision that led to the establishment in February of 1922 of the independent Chris Smith & Sons Boat Co. Other events, in later years, would lead to decades of bitter estrangement between the two celebrated marine authorities.

Following Gar Wood's easy victory in the 1921 Gold Cup races aboard *Miss America II*, the American Power Boat Association met to map out new rules which would diminish the possibility of a complete Wood domination of the event in perpetuity. "Besides," J. Lee Barrett wrote, "they wanted the Trophy returned to New York."[1] Two critical changes completely eliminated Wood's possibility of competing with his existing

record-holding hulls. First, they ruled out hydroplanes entirely; competing boats must be the much slower displacement style hulls. Secondly, they limited engines to just 625 cubic inches of piston displacement. Their rationale was that the unlimited nature of Gar Wood's assault on the water was too expensive, and that only a very few could afford to mount an adequate challenge. "The officials also claimed that hydroplanes could never be made practical for the public," Barrett recorded, "and with the coming of hydroplanes there had been a serious lack of development in displacement boats. A displacement boat rides *through* the water. There is a strong suction at the stern that keeps it balanced, safe. With hydroplanes this is not possible. Hydroplanes are racing boats only, built for speed. They ride *on top* of the water, eliminate the suction and drag at the stern, [and therefore] are faster."[2]

Wood was incensed. To him it seemed, "...like they were trying to take the Gold Cup Trophy from him by making *rules* instead of *boats.*" Wood knew there was no way to challenge the politics of the governing body. "I'm being robbed," he retorted.[3] It must have been good news for Smith, however, for the opening up of the Gold Cup to displacement runabouts with modest engines would mean a landslide business in affordable boats for many more competitors. It would be this considerable business opportunity that motivated Chris Smith to negotiate the repurchase of Wood's majority interest in the C. C. Smith Boat & Engine Co. Chris and the Smith family would be in control of the now world renowned Smith boat house again.

Among their first income was the production of bailers, a sort of small wooden bucket well-suited for getting rain water or seepage out of the bottom of a boat. Two dozen were sold to the Hacker Boat Company for $3 apiece within a week of opening up shop, and hundreds would be sold each month until they stopped production in 1927.[6] Thirty men were listed on the

Photo courtesy Betty Droulard

Chris Smith seems quite proud of his growing crew in front of the C.C. Smith Boat & Engine Company in about 1921. Chris and his sons were about to be independent boat-builders once again.

By-laws of the new *Chris Smith & Sons Boat Company* were drawn up on February 15th, 1922. Four of the Smiths, Chris, now 61 years old; Jay W., 37; Bernard, 33; and Owen, 27, each received one-fourth of the capital stock, for a total of $8,000 initial investment. Their very first entry in the general ledger was already one of expansion. They listed the first payment on 20 acres of land, $300 down, "$2,700 to be paid on delivery of land contract, balance of $7,000 to be paid $1,000 or more annually."[4] They then began to construct a 50-foot by 150-foot building on the land in order to expand production.[5] The land, at what is called Point du Chene, is located at the western edge of Algonac, and would become their base of operations for the next nearly 40 years.

payroll, including seventeen-year company veteran Napoleon Lisee, whose starting salary was $48 a week, which was double that of a new man, 27-year-old A. W. "Bill" MacKerer, who started in March. The four oldest Smiths would receive $4,000 a year, payable when the company could afford it.

Orders flowed in at a steady pace during the year, so that by December 31, 1922 they would show 24 boats shipped, all of them from April to September, for an average of about a boat a week. In addition to these powered boats, the industrious crew produced no less than 22 *Chris Smith Rowboats* during the summer, knocking out a couple a week for a sale price of $621.37, selling 11, stocking 11, which represented a full fourth of their annual revenue. Based on checks issued during the year, it appears that the company's vast majority of board stock was oak, and to a much smaller extent, mahogany. A generous portion of their business during 1922 was still with Gar Wood. Among the most interesting discovery in the records recently made available, reveal that Chris Smith & Sons Boat Co. actually made quite a few of the Gar Wood *Baby Gar* runabouts during this period. The records show several 28-footers with Liberty engines shipped to Gar Wood, repair work on *Miss America, Miss Detroit*, and other Wood boats, as well as the *Baby Gars* which they built for Gar Wood at about $1,700 apiece, complete. Total sales for 1922 would be $53,825.[7]

Wood's premonition of being "robbed" of the Gold Cup proved to be prophetic. For the 1922 Gold Cup regatta on the Detroit River, Chris Smith and his sons had built *Baby Gar, Jr.*, conforming to the new rules. Chris also built *Miss Packard* for old friend Col. Jesse G. Vincent, developer of the Liberty engine, and now chief of engineering for the Packard Motor Car Company in Detroit. In fact, because of the tightened rules for the Cup, Chris Smith was able to watch no less than nineteen *Chriscraft*, the name coined by his son Hamilton, start the race. The catchy name, appearing as a single, non-hyphenated word, first appeared on the general ledger on August 31, 1922, a few days before the Gold Cup races.

The unthinkable happened. *Miss Packard* beat Gar Wood. The Gold Cup was gone. "It was the first race Gar Wood had lost in years. That Chris Smith should betray him by building a quicker boat for Colonel Vincent was hard to believe. ...Although he raced *Curtiss Baby Gar* in 1923, and *Baby America* in 1924, Wood was never able to regain his hold on the APBA's Gold Cup."[8] But it was only the first Smith-generated embarrassment that would occur within a year.

When the Gold Cup rules were altered, Gar Wood retaliated by forming the *Yachtsmen's Association of America*, an organization which would sponsor an annual 150-mile speed and endurance race with a $25,000 purse. Though Wood's large boats were still ineligible under the guidelines, it was a much more demanding challenge than the Gold Cup under the new rules. During the inaugural *150 Mile International Sweepstakes Race* on September 3, 1923, an incident occurred which shook any remaining foundation of the Smith-Wood relationship.

Gar Wood prepared two boats for the event,

Teddy, and *Bruin,* named after his two teddy bear mascots. The Bruin, made with light 5/16-inch veneer plywood planking, was destined to be unsuitable for the purpose, and never completed a full lap of the race. *Teddy,* however, was built with solid 5/8-inch planking, and would be piloted by George Wood with mechanic Orlin Johnson.

Chris Smith built three boats for Col. Vincent. *Miss Packard, Packard Chriscraft II*, and *Packard Chriscraft III*, all powered by 12-cylinder Packard engines.

An eyewitness to the race described the strange contest.

> Col. Vincent, piloting the *Packard Chriscraft II,* led the way for thirty-two laps (almost 100 miles). Not one of the 400,000 spectators on the Detroit River could deny that it was a remarkable performance. For almost 100 miles it set the pace and stayed there. But suddenly a tiny pin came out of the governor on the distributor head. It put six cylinders out of order. The other six kept the boat going. But George Wood and Orlin Johnson passed them in the *Teddy.* Vincent finished the race with only half his engine power. And he finished second. His other boat. *[Packard Chriscraft III]* finished third. Gar Wood's *Teddy* finished first.[9]

But just after Wood's *Teddy* had taken the lead, a judge noticed that she had lost her engine hatches during the race. One of Wood's crew went out and brought the hatches to the dock. It was pointed out to Gar Wood, observing the race from the judges' stand, that the rules of the race were specific about a boat finishing the race with all her equipment in order to be eligible for the prize money. "That boat can't go on without her hatches, Gar," the judge said, "We've got to flag her in."[10] When the judge ordered the flagman to wave the boat in, Wood protested, was overruled, and then took the flag himself to the dock to wave his men into the pits. They wouldn't come in. Orlin Johnson said later, "I wasn't going to stop that boat. I saw Mr. Wood waving the flag. Of course I did. But Mr. Wood isn't one of the judges and the judges are running the race, aren't they?"[11] After another thirty miles, *Teddy,* now two miles ahead of Col. Vincent in the disabled and limping *Packard Chriscraft II,* streaked over to the dock, picked up the hatch covers and sped back out on the racecourse. They came in first place, beating *Packard Chriscraft II* by only two lengths, while *Packard Chriscraft III* came in third.

Wood was celebrating his victory on the dock. As the secretary of the Yachtman's Association of America later recalled,

> Then the fireworks started. Someone walked up to Wood and said, "Did you know Vincent is going to protest the race?"
>
> Wood stiffened. "He is? What for?" he asked. "The hatches."
>
> Wood went up to Chris Smith, who was just then coming down the dock toward him with his daughter, Catherine. "Did you hear, Chris, that Vincent is going to protest?"
>
> Chris didn't hesitate. "If he doesn't, he should,"....Chris was serious. He and his sons had built Vincent's boats.
>
> Suddenly, Wood caught sight of Vincent climbing out of his boat at the end of the dock. He called to him. "Is that right, Colonel — you going to protest?"
>
> "It's in the rules," Vincent called back.[12]

Tension reigned during the post-regatta meeting at the Detroit Yacht Club. The *New York Times* of Sept. 5, 1923 said, "The protest climaxed a feud in motorboat building that for a year had as its principals Gar Wood and Chris Smith, Algonac boat builder. Wood and Smith had broken relations following Wood's defeat in the Gold Cup race of 1922. Yesterday, Colonel Vincent, for whom Smith now is building boats, was drawn into the vortex of animosity by his protest."

"So strong has been the feeling between Smith and Wood that before the Gold Cup Regatta started, the town of Algonac, the home of both, was divided into two factions, the one favoring Wood and the other Chris Smith. Yesterday the Detroit Yacht Club membership fell in with the feeling and views of the townspeople of Algonac. Half the membership is now pro-Wood and the other pro-Smith and Vincent. Colonel Vincent had nothing to say tonight, declaring he would abide by the committee's ruling."[13]

The potential explosion of personalities over *Teddy's* hatches was on everyone's mind. Gar Wood, certainly the most powerful man in the world of motor boat racing, addressed the gathering of drivers, boat owners, boat builders and judges. He left absolutely no doubt as to his own feelings on the matter. After he introduced his brother George and Orlin Johnson, crew of the *Teddy*, he admonished the crowd. "These men," he said, "have raced the finest and fastest boats in history. In spite of what they had against them they turned out the winning boat. No one can take that from them — *no one*."[14] The race committee let the results stand. Wood's *Teddy* was the winner, the Smith-Vincent boats could claim only second and third. The following day, the entire race committee resigned. The *New York Times* would say, "The cause of the wholesale resignation of the committee was that it had permitted Commodore Wood to dominate its decision in disallowing the protest of colonel Vincent...."[15]

The controversial decision was the last straw in cementing decades of disaffection and alienation between Chris Smith and Gar Wood, and one of the reasons which led to fierce competition between the two boat builders, both with an eye towards building in quantity for a national marketplace. Chris Smith would turn nearly all of his attention now to producing pleasure craft of celebrated distinction, and carry forward with a name that would transfix the novelty of boating for the few, into a revolution of pleasure for a worldwide following.

This runabout was among the first to be built by the Chris Smith & Sons Boat Co. in 1922. Notice the wicker seats still used in the aft cockpit of this approximately 26-foot double cockpit runabout.

Jay W. Smith, at age 42 in 1927, was appointed President and General Manager of Chris Smith & Sons Boat Co., a position he would hold for the next thirty-one years before his retirement in 1958. His far-sighted leadership and superior mechanical skills set the course for a boat and engine empire that became the largest on earth.

CHAPTER VIII

The Twenties

FROM THE DAY of their restructure in 1922, the Chris Smith & Sons Boat Co. began to expand at an exponential rate. Though the widening feud between Gar Wood and Chris Smith would result in a raid on Smith's personnel that would claim designer Nap Lisee and a number of other top men, sales and deliveries continued to climb.

The decade of the 20's would emerge as the most important in the entire history of the company, as sales would surge past the three million dollar mark by the end of 1929. The volume of boats produced each year during this same period would grow from 24 in 1922 to 946 in 1929. Virtually each year produced a doubling of both sales and deliveries. A chart of this era of fabulous growth reveals the meteoric climb.

By 1923 the dependability and utility of a well-designed runabout was becoming quite fash-

YEAR	SHIPMENT	SALES
1922	24	53,825
1923	33	67,642
1924	48	165,485
1925	111	431,737
1926	134	523,391
1927	447	1,339,109
1928	830	2,037,218
1929	946	3,254,932[1]

ionable, and all over America bashful buyers were starting to compare features, engines and prices. One of the new terms being discussed was *standardized runabout*. Certainly, a number of companies had been building the same model of runabout year after year, but essentially they were still crafted as unique creations, each one built to order and each one slightly different than the last. There was really no benefit to develop mass production techniques, because the market wasn't actually quite ready to absorb a large quantity of boats. Chris Smith & Sons Boat Co. was also still building by *contract number;* that is to say each boat had its own separate specifications, and a team of men tackled it until it was done, and then they moved *en masse* to the next contract number. The general ledger of the company illustrates the technique quite vividly, for Catherine Smith, Chris' youngest daughter, 23

By 1924, Bernard Smith became responsible for product development, quality control and testing. He is seen here supervising the cradling of another Chris-Craft runabout for shipment.

years old in 1923, would enter into the books each hour that each worker spent on a particular contract number. In fact, the Smiths were very careful and scrutinizing as a whole, and practiced rigid cost control measures in order to keep the costs of their product to an acceptable level, while insuring a respectable profit for their labor. So conscious were they of the direct contribution of labor to a particular boat, that the principals, Chris, Jay, Bernard and Owen, though they worked day and night at their jobs, were always characterized as *unproductive*

labor in the books, as if they had nothing to do with the product itself.

In 1923, a boat was built which would be declared, in 1975, over half a century later, as the "oldest living Chris-Craft." *Miss Belle Isle,* a 26-foot double-cockpit, 10-passenger runabout, was acquired by Chris-Craft following a nationwide search. The boat, in superb condition, was part of the extensive archives donated to the Mariner's Museum in Newport News, Virginia in the spring of 1987. The boat originally retailed for $2,950, and, like the majority of the Smith runabouts during the early 20's, it was powered by the 90-h.p. Curtiss OX-5 aircraft engine marinized primarily by Jay Smith and his engine technicians, and which they sometimes referred to as the Smith-Curtiss V-8.

By 1924 a significant change was underway at Chris Smith & Sons Boat Co. They had been selling every boat they could build, and construction was going on at a feverish pace. They could not keep up with the demand during the spring and summer months, although great pressure was put upon their craftsmen to increase production. Though the company managed to squeeze out 48 boats during the season, it was frustrating, knowing that the market was willing to absorb a much higher volume. The first sincere efforts at standardizing the Chris Smith product was undertaken. The majority of ship-

ments during this year were 26 and 27-foot runabouts, powered by the Smith-Curtiss engines, and capable of 35 miles per hour. The engines were highly regarded, as they were complete with electric starter, generator and reverse gear, popular accessories that weren't universally available in 1924.

By May of 1924, the company was making almost complete use of the Chris-Craft name, and for the first time displaying the words in *script*, and including the dash between the words becoming so well known to boatmen. The name, however, really only applied to a single model and was not universally used. To herald the introduction of this *standardized runabout*, they ran a full-page ad in *Motor Boating* that month, describing in detail their flagship, the 26-foot runabout.

Courtesy Mariners' Museum, Newport News, Virginia

By 1927, Christopher Columbus Smith had established his "office" in the boiler room by Chris Smith & Sons Boat Co., where he decided the fate of scrap wood and could smoke his cigars in peace.

A Smith-Built Standardized Runabout
at a Remarkably Low Price

To realize that Chris-Craft is a remarkable boat at a remarkable price about all you have to know is that it is designed and built by the same men as Miss America, Packard Chris Crafts (I, II, and III) and scores of other famous boats which have figured in the foremost events of motor boat racing history —

that it is powered by a 100 H.P. Smith-Curtiss 8 cylinder V-type engine, fully guaranteed by this company and equipped with electric starter, generator, reverse gear, etc., —

that it is 26' over all length by 6'8" beam and 24" draft, with seats for ten. Mahogany planking and decking, double planked bottom, removable upholstery, polished deck hardware, manganese bronze strut, rudder and propeller. Completely equipped with everything needed for high class runabout.

The speed of 32 to 35 miles an hour is not merely the designer's estimate but it means real miles over a measured course as we have already built and delivered many boats of the same design and with the same motor.

Chris-Craft is dry, comfortable to ride in, very seaworthy and thoroughly reliable. Our guarantee covers both the boat and engine.

Prompt Deliveries on Early Orders as we are now finishing Chris-Crafts at the rate of three a week. Write today for detailed specifications.

Chris Smith & Sons Boat Co.
Algonac, Michigan[2]

The majority of their powered shipments during 1924 would be the 26-foot models, at $3,200 a copy, with an option of either a single or double cockpit forward of the engine. During Detroit's Annual Motor Boat Regatta, proof of the tremendous popularity of the new runabouts was a special "Chriscraft Race, the most spectacular of the Detroit Regatta."[3] "That the Chriscraft is a real as well as a popular boat," an announcement claimed, "is proven by the fact that over 50 have been built and sold during the past year. About 20 competed in the Detroit races."[4]

1925 would prove to be among the most remarkable years in the company history. Critical changes were undertaken that would transform the small company from regional celebrity to eventually near national resource. A.W. "Bill" or "Mac" or "the Boss" MacKerer was by now fully in control of the manufacturing process, serving as factory superintendent and production manager. Jay, Bernard and Owen had each assumed specialized duties and responsibilities which would shape the company's future. Bernard was

slowly emerging in a role of product development, testing and quality control, while Owen, now sales manager, was increasingly absorbed with sales and distribution. Jay, just turning 40, as vice-president and general manager, had near total control over Chris Smith & Sons Boat Co., with Chris, 64, though still president, working more and more in a strictly advisory capacity and as nationally respected figurehead of the organization.

Production began early the spring of that year at the rate of a boat and a half a day on their newly introduced 22-foot runabout model. For production to increase substantially, new methods would have to be instituted. Under the leadership of Bill MacKerer and Jay Smith, an "in-line" or "straight-line" manufacturing process was being fine tuned. Though already in common use in other industries, particularly the automobile industry in nearby Detroit, it represented a radical change in a boat-building industry dominated by autonomous craftsman builders. Rather than large teams of craftsmen working on an individual contract, lines of production were established so that men with individual specialties would contribute to the product at a regulated point in the process. Standard keels, frames, stringers, rails and decking components were cut using precise templates in the wood milling operation, so that each boat being produced would be as identical to the next as possible. Slight modifications in design of the templates would modify each successive boat produced.

Early in the critical transition from contract number production to in-line production, it was still largely the increased pressure applied to the skilled workers that contributed to the expanded volume. A 17-year-old Tom Cuthbertson was working in the plant at the time and remembers how increased production was often accomplished.

We were building a 22-foot boat, and the production boat was almost unheard of in those days. I recall Jay Smith asking [Bill] MacKerer whether they could get two boats a day out of the setup we had which was doing a boat and a half a day at full capacity. Before the summer was over, we were getting four boats a day.

It wasn't so much the organization as it was, to me, more of a push. You take your key man who had experience and put a bunch of kids, farmers, whatever you could get a hold of, and put them with him and tell them how much work you expect out of them and they'd try it and eventually they got that production out.[5]

The Smiths were the first boat-builders to employ in-line production of standardized boats in the world. By May, 1926 these workers were able to complete a new runabout nearly every other working day. Notice the young men at far right using the new electric screwdrivers to set bronze screws into the double planked bottom.

Tom remembers his starting salary vividly. "I didn't ask them what they were going to pay me. Algonac was a summer resort town, and board and room was high for those days. My first week of board and room was fifteen dollars, and my first week's pay of thirty-five cents an hour was about sixteen dollars, so I had a whole dollar left."[6] Wages ranged from a base of $16 a week for unskilled labor and office girls, to $28 to $30 a week for highly skilled and master craftsmen.

By contrast, Smith family salaries in 1925 ranged from Catherine and Hamilton at $26 a week; Owen and Chris at $7,500 a year; Bernard at $10,000 a year; and Jay Smith at $15,000 a year. It is interesting to note that most of the family members collected the majority of their yearly salaries at the end of December, rather than at regular intervals throughout the work year, another indication of the careful money management philosophy shared by the Smiths.[7]

Another crucial change occurred early in 1926, that of slowly moving from a factory direct distribution scheme, to that of establishing dealers and franchises which would in turn buy boats direct from the company. The concept was working well, again in the automobile industry, but was largely untested in the boat-building business. Up until late in 1925, advertisements for Chris Smith & Sons would proclaim the advantages of dealing direct with the factory, with justifications such as, "One great advantage in buying a Chris-Craft is the fact that you deal direct with the builders. There is no confusion as to responsibility for service."[8] Service wasn't

Courtesy Mariners' Museum, Newport News, Virginia

The very first Chris-Craft franchise was awarded to Eugene J. Mertaugh of E.J. Mertaugh Boat Works in Hessel, Michigan on February 18, 1926. Mertaugh used to drive even small runabouts across enormous Lake Huron from Algonac to Hessel. The business still flourishes, managed by his sons Jim and Jack.

really the issue, however, because the products were so well built that they offered among the most extensive guarantees in the industry. "The entire craft is fully guaranteed against repair and replacement due to construction, for *one year* from date of purchase. The Chris-Craft are so nearly 100 percent trouble-proof that this guarantee has cost us an average of only $6 a boat."[9]

The very first franchise was awarded to Eugene J. Mertaugh, owner of E. J. Mertaugh Boat Works in Hessel, Michigan, on February 18, 1926.[10] Mertaugh "held exclusive rights to the territory north of Bay City, including Canada."[11] Paved highways didn't exist to bring the boats up to his yard in northern Michigan, so Mertaugh would make the long and often dangerous passage across Lake Huron to get them to Hessel. "Stories of Mertaugh's daring include an event in which he knocked a bear out of his boat four times before he made it to the dock. After pulling the bear to shore by a noose, he weighed it, with some help... 175 pounds."[12]

That year, Chris Smith & Sons Boat Co. offered 11 models of boats in four basic lengths. Two variations of a 22-foot runabout; a 24-foot runabout; four versions of the venerable 26-foot runabout including sedan and hydroplane versions; a 30-foot runabout, and a 30-foot commuter. Dealers could expect discounts ranging from 15% on a 22-foot runabout listing for $1,995 to 25% off on the 30-foot commuter listing for $9,750.

Nonetheless, by far the most popular of the offerings was the 26-foot double cockpit 9-passenger runabout, powered by the new 6-cylinder Kermath marine engine. The 960-pound engine would develop 150-horsepower at 1800 r.p.m., which would guarantee the Chris-Craft owner better than 35 miles per hour. It is interesting to remember that sixteen years ago, in 1910, it was a truly radical proposition for the Smiths to offer the *Queen Reliance* for "$100 per mile of speed", but now the 38 to 40 mile per hour Chris-Craft was offered at $3,500, F.O.B. Algonac.[13] "For those who are satisfied with less speed", another ad stated, "we offer optional equipment of the 100-horsepower Kermath at 30 to 32 miles per hour. Price complete with Kermath "100"— $3,200.[14]

You could also buy the runabout with the aging Smith-Curtiss 8-cylinder OX-5 at a $600 discount for $2,900. It is significant that Chris Smith & Sons Boat Co. were the first boat builders to announce a considerable price *reduction* in their stock production boats. It was so unusual that they had to explain their reasoning carefully.

A Greatly Increased Production Permits this Astounding Price Reduction. The Famous Chris-Craft with the Smith Curtiss Motor is Now $2900

Why can Chris-Craft sell for $600 less? The one answer is quantity distribution. Quick to recognize the desired qualities of workmanship and sound construction, coupled with ample speed and power, many men bought Chris-Craft for $3,500. Unhurried, but steady, consistent production has done the rest.

This greatly increased production with the added economies of quantity buying and a constantly reduced sales expense makes possible this astounding price reduction.[15]

In fact, by 1926, while building only 134 boats, the Chris Smith & Sons Boat Company would claim, quite correctly, that they were the *Largest Builders Of Fast Runabouts.*[16] During the National Motor Boat Show in New York, the week of January 22-30, 1926, "Twenty-eight bona fide orders [with deposits] were placed for Chris-Craft, making this all mahogany boat the outstanding "buy" in the field of fine runabouts."[17]

During the four years of *standardized* construction, the Smiths were building production facilities at an impressive rate to keep up with the burgeoning demand for their Chris-Craft runabouts. The first article dealing with the Smiths' newly-devised techniques of *produc-*

By 1929, Chris-Craft were delivered to thirty countries around the world, and a full fifteen percent of sales were for export. Chris-Craft commanded a large exhibit at the *Salon Nautique* marine exhibition in Paris on December 15, 1929, through European distributor Arthur Bray.

1—General Office.
2—Service and Repair Dept.
3—Hardware Construction.
4—Machine Shop.
5—Storage—22 Foot Runabouts.
6—Stockroom, Runabout Manufacture.
7—Stockroom Service Parts.
8—Service Boat Wells.
9—Storage—24 Foot Runabouts.
10—Boat Wells Storage No. 1
11—Upholstering Dept.
12—Air Suction Blower.
13—Boat Wells Storage No. 2.
14—28 and 30 Foot Assembly Plant.
15—Boat Wells (Test and Driveaway)
16—28 Foot Hull Storage.
17—Mill Room and Wood Working Plant.
18—22 Foot Assembly Plant.
19—Boat Wells Storage No. 3
20—Power Plant.
21—Chris-Craft Marine Motor Plant.
22—22 Foot Hull Storage.
23—24 and 26 Foot Assembly Plant.
24—24 and 26 Foot Hull Storage.
25—Garage.
26—Shipping Dept.
27—Mahogany Storage.
28—Cruiser Millroom and Woodworking Plant.
29—Cruiser Assembly Plant.
30—Cruiser Power Plant.
31—Cruiser Launching Docks.
32—Channels to St. Clair River f Water Testing

Courtesy Mariners' Museum, Newport News, Virginia

By 1927 Chris Smith & Sons Boat Co. had 114,517 square feet of floor space under cover. These facilities were the equivalent of 2.86 covered acres spread out amongst 26 sheds, warehouses, manufacturing buildings and offices. Hard work had earned the Smiths the distinction of being the *World's Largest Builders of All Mahogany Motor Boats.*

tion boat building appeared in May 1926, and offers a considerable insight into their early *in-line* or *straight-line* production strategies.

The Chris Smith organization is one of the best examples of a boat factory that has established a reputation for inaugurating production methods never before attempted in the boating field. This naturally came about only because they found a very ready market for their product, the Chris-Craft runabout, which enabled them to take advantage of the many features which come with quantity production.

The most recent addition to the Smith plant is a large, well lighted, airy building of 150 x 275 feet which houses the Chris-Craft from the time the keel is laid until the boat leaves the drying rooms, a complete unit ready to run.

After a keel has been laid down; the sawed shapes are clamped to the keel and the side planking is in place, the boat is automatically lifted up and moved into the next position where the engine stringers are bolted into place and the chines are bolted to the sawed shapes. It is then turned over, again bottom up, and the first layer of planking is laid on diagonally, — the heavily oil-soaked mahogany used in the first layer is first varnished and then canvassed. The next process is the laying on of the fore and aft planking which is screw fastened to the sawed shapes. The ribs are then fastened into the bottom and screwed to the double planking of the bottom from the inside. The sides are then bunged and plugged with mahogany plugs to cover up the screw heads and from this junction the hull is moved along the production line where the sides and bottom are planed, scraped and sanded, after which a heavy coat of green bottom paint is applied. The sides are now ready for the mahogany filler which is applied and rubbed, then the inside is given a heavy coat of hot oil below the water line and two coats of Valspar over the entire inside with a top coat of battleship gray paint.

In line with the unusual methods which are employed in the Smith plant, which are original in the extreme and highly efficient, we find the boats, after arriving at the previously mentioned spot, being moved down into slips or platforms where gangs of workmen furnished with all their needs rapidly prepare the boat with engine room and fore peak flooring and the next operation is to strike or mark the shear and trim it; whereupon another crew then come on the boat, installing the deck carlins, hatch headers and cockpit trimmers, followed by the fastening on of the covering boards, and the laying of the deck; next fastenings are bunged, decks are planed, scraped and sanded and a painting crew take charge of the boat and a mahogany filler is applied to the decks.

The next wave of production includes the joinery operations, which really complete the runabout, making it ready for the finishing room. In this process, the skilled joiners install the combing, engine room, hatch frames and hatches; then comes the flooring of the forward and after cockpits, accompanied by the installation of the engine room bulkheads. The seat frames are now ready to be set up, together with the side cockpit paneling.

The cowl and instrument board are now installed at this point and the wind shield mountings are put in place. The runabout is ready to be checked and inspected for the scratches and blemishes which might have occurred during these operations. These are carefully removed before the final mahogany filling is applied and the boat is ready to enter the finishing room. This room is artificially heated and absolutely dust proof. Four coats of varnish are applied in succession to both the hull and the finished mahogany wood work and trim.

The upholstery is made in a separate building where it is put on the boat together with engine snaps and all the nickel deck hardware and fender streaks. The boat is now ready for the final operation which is the motor installation.

A crew of expert mechanics now install the motor, fastening it rapidly into place. The gasoline tanks are connected up, the shaft is lined up and the steering gear, instrument board, and engine controls are put into place.

The boat is now ready for launching and testing under the general supervision of Bernard Smith and a staff of skilled testers. Everything is checked, including alignment, rudder controls, engine revolutions and the boat is run over a measured course to see that it comes up to the guaranteed speeds and an O.K. is then attached to it, or it is brought back for adjustments or corrections.[18]

Though not generally known, Chris Smith and his sons also built custom runabouts and even cruisers for a small number of clients during these years. Contained within a recently discovered personal notebook of W. A. "Bill" MacKerer, Plant Superintendent, were prices for custom designs ranging from a 30-foot double cockpit runabout, less engine, for $5,750, to cruisers in lengths from 28 feet to 55 feet, priced without engines respectively from $3,000 to $24,000.

Though the Chris Smith & Sons Boat Co. by 1927 had 114,517 square feet of floor space under cover, an equivalent of 2.86 acres spread out amongst 26 sheds, warehouses, plants and office buildings, they were still largely isolated from the Village of Algonac.[19] On April 4, 1927, Chris Smith appeared before the village council asking that the village extend the water main from where it ended short of his facilities, and "if, at the present time, the village funds were insufficient to warrant such extension, that he would loan the village $4,000 for a period of two years at 5% interest." Chris, now 66, certainly hadn't lost his touch. The council approved his request, borrowing the money from Chris. Not only did Chris get the village treated water he needed urgently for his sprawling plant, but he also made 5% on his money, more than he could make in many banks of the day. On a roll, later in the month Chris asked that the city guarantee fire protection for his complex, which they agreed to "so far as possible at all times."[20]

A strategic addition of great importance was made to the Smith marketing efforts in 1927, the recruitment of John E. "Jack" Clifford as general sales manager. Clifford was sales manager of the C.H. Wills & Company in Marysville, Michigan, makers of the unique Wills Saint Claire automobile. Everything about the Wills Saint Claire was first class; they even built the chassis out of molybdenum steel. The four models of passenger cars were so overly engineered that its price was nearly double their

John E. "Jack" Clifford is credited with establishing a new national and vibrant image for Chris Smith & Sons Boat Co. from the moment he arrived in 1927. He was very successful in converting automobile agencies and showrooms into successful Chris-Craft dealerships. He is seen here with his daughter (right) and neighborhood friend.

competitors'. "They built their car too well to make money", recalls a lady whose sister became Clifford's secretary.[21]

Clifford, though, was up to the task. When he was called upon to liquidate the over-priced cars at dealerships, he attacked the problem with a passion. "Jack Clifford made the transition from cars to boats easily since he was a born salesman, a real 'straw hats in February', 'air conditioners to Eskimos' type salesman", another remembered. "Jack's talent was much appreciated by car and boat dealers alike. Jack hadn't really thought about his next job as he traveled around the country 'cleaning house' for Wills dealers in late 1926. When the last cars had been liquidated, Chris-Craft was waiting."[22]

Among Clifford's first priorities was to organize and expand a nationwide system for distribution and sales, a goal which he accomplished with great speed and aplomb. Very early in 1927, a New York office, across from Pennsylvania Station at 393 Seventh Avenue, was stocked with boats and staffed with an eager sales staff managed by the capable Arthur J. Utz.[23]

Not long after Clifford's arrival, ads became more artistic and professional, taking on a more national scope. Florida markets were targeted in January as the company geared up for year-round production. Before 1927, no shipments had been made from January through March, and most line employees would dread the prospect of a long layoff which stretched from the end of September until April 1st, as only the most skilled and productive employees were retained, building show boats throughout the winter months for display at the National Motor Boat Show. But Clifford's strategy paid off. The company shipped seven boats in both January and February, and eighteen in March. The ability to remain open for 12 months out of the year was a signficiant accomplishment, and allowed them to solicit advance orders from Clifford's new dealers and distributors well in advance of delivery schedules. Dealers were required to display at least one Chris-Craft, and sell a minimum quantity during the year depending upon their territory. Dealerships were eagerly acquired, and quickly disseminated to virtually every major center of commerce in America.

1927 also started off with a bang because of the introduction of the 22-foot *Cadet* runabout,

destined to rival the 26-foot Kermath or Scripps-powered Chris-Craft in sales popularity. The eight-passenger Cadet was an almost exact duplicate of the 26-foot runabout, simply shorter with a slightly narrower beam, and carrying the smaller, 800-pound, 70-horsepower Kermath power plant, which would push the little boat to 25 miles per hour. "The Cadet will not supplant the 26-foot model," an ad explained, "it will simply fulfill the need for a smaller boat where less speed is required."[24] The smaller price tag, $2,250, attracted a lot of new customers. The maturation of motorboat marketing meant increased competition from many builders, including old partner Gar Wood. When Gar Wood opened a national office in New York a few months after Smith, an article in *Motor Boating* entitled *Modern Merchandising of Motor Boats* summed up the trend of the industry.

What the stock boat industry has long needed but lacked has arrived. The amount of business which has been lost can hardly be even estimated but with the change in selling plans recently put into effect in New York...merchandising of stock boats [has been] put on the business basis which it deserves.

Not more than a few years ago, the sale of motor craft was in the proportion of 90 percent to the yachtsmen who had previously owned boats to 10 percent going to those who had not. Today this ratio is exactly reversed. Over 90 percent of the sales are made to persons without any boating experience. The causes for this change are several. It can be partly attributed to the improvement in the stock runabouts of 1926 and 1927, partly to the great trend toward yachting on the part of the general public but it is principally due to the fact that the manufacturers of this popular type of craft have at last decided to make it easy for the public to buy boats as is done in other fields.

With 90 percent of the sales going to those inexperienced in boats and engines, many requirements must be met which were not in the picture, so to speak, a few years ago. Seeing what you are to buy, and service are the two most important factors. A demonstration of the particular boat or engine is the least important of the many considerations. Both of the first two mentioned problems can be easily solved by the establishmment of National sales rooms. The demonstration factor is so unimportant that it can be disregarded altogether. Boats and engines have been so perfected within the past year or two that there is no question as to whether they will perform satisfactorily. The person who buys on demonstration alone no longer exists and the firm which sells only by this method is fast shifting into the background.[25]

Chris-Craft, as the 26-foot runabouts were known, took Florida by storm between 1927 and 1928, and became possessions of great social consequence. "In fact the interest and curiosity for this new form of fast water travel has grown so rapidly," one magazine reported, "that many men and women, too, for that matter have lately become owners of runabouts. The Chris-Craft Cadet, a 22-foot duplicate of the already famous 26-foot Chris-Craft is now vying in popularity with its bigger brother. Both boats have proven exceptionally popular during the winter at the fashionable watering places on both the East and West coast of Florida."

"The strange thing about this," the writer continued, "is the fact that as a rule whenever you see one of these forty mile boats dashing by you will invariably find it loaded with passengers enjoying the sea breezes and the sunshine. Those fortunate enough to own a Chris-Craft runabout never seem to lack for friends to take a spin along the shore or out to sea."[26]

Among those most interested in the burgeoning sales of small motor boats was Walter P. Chrysler of the Chrysler Corporation in Detroit. Evidence suggests that Chrysler developed the new Chrysler Imperial marine engine specifically for the Chris Smith & Sons Boat Co. products, knowing that if the Smiths would standardize on their engine, he would hardly need any other clients within the marine field. As one periodical of the time commented, "[the engine] is the product of the combined genius of Walter P. Chrysler and the Chris Smith & Sons Boat Company."[27] With a slim weight of only 835 pounds, and packing over a hundred horsepower, the new Imperial was perfectly suited for the 22-foot Cadet, and promised 32 to 35 miles per hour, as opposed to 25 miles per hour for the 70-horsepower, 800-pound Kermath. For a penalty of only 35 pounds and $100, Cadet buyers could now get a substantial improvement in performance. Beyond performance, however, the successful application of the Imperial in the Cadet made available to owners the nationwide service of Chrysler, and an army of Chrysler factory trained mechanics. "Designers are congratulating the Chris Smith & Sons Company on having been the first to adopt the new engine and avail themselves of the wider mar-

ket afforded by the Chrysler prestige and widespread organization."[28] The engine would prove so universally popular, that within two months of its introduction, Chrysler would claim sales of over $500,000 worth of boats powered by the new power plant.

By May, 1927, the month that Charles Lindbergh made his record-making solo flight across the Atlantic in *The Spirit of St. Louis*, production of the Cadet had reached three boats a day, and a rising backlog of orders forced Jay Smith and Bill MacKerer to further automate the assembly process.

> Not long ago it took a good man the best part of the day to turn out one keel; now the stick of wood for the keel passes through a machine and the finished keel comes out in a very few moments, rabbetted, cut to length, shaped and planed in one operation. The same is true of the other major parts of the boat construction, ribs, frames, engine bed, floors, planking, transom, interior trim, bulkhead parts, seats, deck beams, and deck planking, in fact everything is machine made and finished. A keel set up has the frames and ribs in place and is ready for the planking within hardly more than an hour. The double planking is put on in short order by a gang of men who do no other work in the boat's construction. The lumber, screws, hardware, fittings, etc., are delivered to the men in the construction gangs in the proper amounts for each job, completely cut to size, and finished so that there will be no delay.[29]

The Smiths became vitally concerned with the vertical integration of nearly every component for their boats, now that volumes would warrant almost any component manufacture. By 1927, Chris had developed a scheme whereby he took over about half of Warner's Brass Foundry in Algonac for casting Chris-Craft metal components. Cap Warner allowed Chris to pay for labor directly, even though the business was never owned by Chris Smith & Sons Boat Co. At one point, as many as twenty men were casting propellers, rudders, stepping [stuffing] boxes, and brass structural strapping. Three furnaces were kept white hot in the foundry, and one bleak afternoon human error caused one of them to explode, hurling steel, molten brass and bricks through the air as easily as sawdust. "It was raining," a victim of the blast recalls, "the guy who was supposed to close the vents missed one, and it stayed open about an inch. Water poured down into the hot furnace and it blew."[30] A fourteen-year-old worker was flung through the air by the explosion, and when he regained

Courtesy Mariners' Museum, Newport News, Virginia

The roaring twenties were a time for daring adventures, like this 26-foot Chris-Craft in a race with a new type of amphibian aircraft. Because of the volume of fast runabouts built in the 1920's by the Smiths, it is estimated that more bootleg and illegal booze was run across U.S. borders in Chris-Crafts than all other makes combined.

consciousness, discovered his eyes were burned, and that several pounds of molten brass had attached itself to his bare back. He lay in a pool of linseed oil for weeks until he was separated from the residue in birth of a Chris-Craft rudder.[31] The tenacious Luke Stephenson recovered, and Chris hired him at the main plant to fire the boilers there, with a handsome increase in pay for his trouble of five cents an hour.

From January 1st to August 3rd of 1927 the Smiths bought 338,101 feet of Philippine mahogany at a total cost of $50,595.60. This represents an average price of less than 15¢ per foot. Clearly, volume purchasing affected dramatic savings for the company. The bottom line on the mahogany doesn't show the whole picture, however, for in the tradition of old Chris Smith himself, the Smiths were getting a lot of their wood *free.*

There was an art to ordering hardwoods like mahogany and teak, as the Smiths soon figured out. For a shipment of teak to arrive at Algonac all the way from India, or a shipment of mahogany to arrive all the way from the Philippine Islands, it would have to be handled at least six times, sometimes more, moving from land to ship, ship to rail, boxcar to boxcar, etc. until it was trucked from nearby Marine City on Smith trucks to the company mill rooms.[32] The clever ploy worked like this. The Smiths would order more of the one-inch-thick teak wood for trim than they really needed. When the teak arrived, more often than not it would be ⅛ of an inch under the requirement near the ends of the board. They could cut off the end pieces up to the point where the board measured the full one inch thick, only paying for the new length of board. The perfectly good end pieces, sometimes up to four feet long, would be milled down to ¾ inch and made perfectly good finished steps, trim and cabinetry. Free.

The case with mahogany was even more extreme. An agreement with the supplier stipulated that wood that didn't match Smith specifications *exactly,* they would pay for the next smaller size. For example, most of the Chris-Craft mahogany ordered was 4½ inches thick by two feet wide by 16 feet long. If it measured an eighth of an inch under in thickness, they only paid for 3 inches. "We got two extra boards on every piece," a man who worked in the mill remembers; "People don't realize how much free wood that came through."[33] By 1927, Chris Smith & Sons Boat Co. would be the *World's Largest Builders of All Mahogany Runabouts,*[34] and by 1928 they would claim, "Contracts placed to cover this year's program call for one million feet of this costly wood. This is a larger contract than will be placed by any other manufacturer, even the largest furniture maker. This lumber, when it is received at the Chris-Craft factory, is carefully air seasoned, the various hull parts are then laid out by means of templates or patterns, great care taken that the grain and color are well matched for each and every boat. Needless to say, the cutting is done so as to avoid all possible waste. Even pieces that are too small for anything else are used to make the small mahogany plugs which are driven with special glue into the countersunk holes of the screws."[35] Even then, scraps too riddled with bung holes to extract another single plug were taken to the boiler room to produce heat for the buildings. Nothing was wasted.

Once, a boxcar arrived with a nightmarish cargo aboard. The men wouldn't go near the box-

Opposite: In 1927, Chris Smith & Sons Boat Co. were contracting one million feet of mahogany a year, more of this exotic wood than ev the largest furniture makers in the world. This scene, taken in New Yc during the 1920's, shows a busy lumber yard much like those that su plied the Algonac runabout production lines.

car; the stench was overbearing. "I said, 'That's a human being'", an eyewitness recalls; "They stink more than an elephant."[36] Wearing masks, authorities opened the boxcar to find two decomposing corpses. They had evidently hopped the car for a free ride when the door became locked. Not wishing to waste even this *horrendously-smelling* wood, it was stacked far away from the plant, with two-inch ventilation spacer boards between the planks, and within three months in the fresh air of Algonac, it was unceremoniously milled and converted into Cadets and Chris-Craft runabouts.[37]

At least one request was made for an *all teak* Chris-Craft. In a memo to sales manager Clifford, Bill MacKerer explained that the additional material cost would be $308.75, additional labor would be $200, the teak hull would weigh 1,134 pounds more than the mahogany hull, and speed would be reduced from 40 to 35 miles per hour.[38]

By this time, much of Chris Smith's time was spent in the boiler room of the complex, where he could relax and smoke his cigars in peace. Among the favorite stories told about Chris during his years of maintaining his "office" there, is that of the coal passer furiously finishing stoking the boiler before the five o'clock whistle signaled the end of his shift. As he bolted for the door, Chris allegedly stopped him. "Wait just a minute," Chris is reported saying, "where do you think you're going? Brush yourself off young man, that coal dust belongs to me!"[39]

One of Chris' responsibilities was the fate of scrap wood. Wood that was scarred in some way, unsuitable for boat construction, and too good for the boiler, was sold to eager employees at miniscule prices. For example, quite often wood arrived with chunks of lead buried within, a result of the numerous battles which had been fought through the years in the Philippine mahogany forests. Throughout Algonac, many

Courtesy Mariner's Museum, Newport News, Virginia

Photos by Karine N. Rodengen

The Algonac, Michigan home of Jay W. Smith is rich with beautifully joined and finished Philippine mahogany accents, including a massive fireplace which was built at the nearby Chris Smith & Sons Boat Co. factory. As Jay W. advanced in years, this Agatha Christie style stairway chair elevator assisted him in ascending the solid mahogany staircase.

Evidence suggests that Walter P. Chrysler developed the Chr[ysler] Imperial engine specifically for Chris Smith & Sons Boat Co.'s new [25] foot *Cadet*. Here, the new Imperials are installed into *Cadets* as a le[ad]ing specialist applies the final touches.

homes of the day sported beautiful mahogany cabinetry, gloriously varnished mahogany tables, many joined, bunged and finished just like the boats themselves. It is probably safe to say that, per capita, more Algonac furniture was made from exotic imported hardwoods than in any other community in the world.

One of the most beautiful homes in Algonac was that of president Jay Smith and his family. Facing the St. Clair River, the three-story Victorian house was the northernmost along Algonac's main thoroughfare, and commanded an unobstructed panorama from the Canadian shores at Walpole Island to the Flats. Interior accents include a formidable solid mahogany staircase, and solid mahogany door frames, sills and doors.[40]

By late summer of 1927, two months before Al Jolson would star in the first "talkie", *The Jazz Singer*, Owen Smith opened up the company's second 'Direct Factory Branch' at Detroit, Michigan.[41] By fall, the company would announce that Chris-Craft had taken "...first place in the standardized runabout events of

every important motor boating regatta so far this year... ."[42] Their seven unbroken string of victories included the Miami Beach Regatta, Thousand Islands Regatta, Boston Regatta, Algonac Regatta, Gold Cup Regatta, Toledo Regatta, and the first stock boat trophy of England, the Atlantic Gold Challenge Trophy. By year's end, the list would swell to include regattas at Newport, Lake George, Westport, Greenwich, Lake Hopatcong, Baltimore, Washington, Burlington, and Barcelona, Spain. Chris-Craft were the undisputed stock runabout champions, both in performance and popularity.[43]

The high-speed runabout was also proving to be a useful business tool, from commuting executives, to getting the news on the streets of New York City on time. As the *New York Times* reported, "Photographs of the Vienna riots and the damage done by the earthquake in Palestine, which arrived last night on the liner *Olympic*, were rushed from Quarantine in record time to permit their being published in the first edition of the *New York Times* today. Aboard a Chris-Craft speedboat, they were brought from the

Courtesy Mariners' Museum, Newport News, Virginia

Left: Each piston was carefully weighed on a balance beam against the exact required weight. Any excess weight was filed off the skirt of the piston before released for assembly into a Chris Smith & Sons Boat Co. engine. This scale can now be seen at the Mariners' Museum in Newport News, VA.

Courtesy Mariners' Museum, Newport News, Virginia

Courtesy Mariners' Museum, Newport News, Virginia

Jay W. Smith (center), within the new marine engine assembly building, where the new 200-horsepower, eight-cylinder 90-degree V-8 engines (shown) were assembled. Also introduced in 1928 was a 150-horsepower six-cylinder motor.

Olympic at Quarantine to the boat landing at the foot of West Forty-Second Street in twenty minutes and reached the Times Annex on West Forty-Third Street fifteen minutes later."[44]

And then in November, 1927, a string of important announcements issued from Algonac. First, Jay Smith, 42, had been appointed president and general manager of Chris Smith & Sons Boat Co., Bernard had been promoted to vice-president and treasurer, while Chris, now 66, was elevated to the lofty, though comfortably effortless, position of Chairman of the Board. In the same announcement, we find that, "Factory facilities have been increased to care for a tremendous production of mahogany runabouts for 1928. 54,000 square feet have been added to the 114,517 square feet under roof providing a total of 168,517 square feet devoted to the manufacture of Chris-Craft runabouts."[45]

Of greater significance was the announcement that a new Marine Engine Division had been formed, and that two marine engines had passed exhaustive testing and were now in production. One of the engines, a 200-horsepower eight-cylinder V-type 90-degree motor, and the other a 150-horsepower six-cylinder motor, would both be unveiled and showcased at the National Motor Boat Show at New York in early 1928. As one writer would extol, "This announcement is a striking innovation — a wonderful testimonial to the progressive attitude of these boat builders. Nothing comparable to it has ever been attempted in the boating field in magnitude or initiative. This practice of building the completed unit has for years been justified in automotive circles. Almost every successful car manufacturer builds the motor for the complete automobile which he produces. The Chris Smith organization is evidently prompted by the same economic and sound principles of manufacture."[46]

At the New York Boat Show of 1928, the Smiths would reveal an unprecedented eleven models of boats, and for the first time, demonstrate a wide range of fresh approaches to both standard and regional requirements. The breadth and superiority of the new Smith line left at least one reporter reduced to *the ecstatic babblings of a child.*[47] Here's a rare opportunity to go along on a personally guided tour of the exhibit, as each new model is revealed by the president, Jay Smith.

The full significance of this announcement cannot be grasped by those accustomed to think of the boat builder as a skillful mechanic

Courtesy Mariners' Museum, Newport News, Virginia

The marine engine program at Chris Smith & Sons would become among the most successful motor manufacturing operations in America, owing to the simple, hard-working designs and vast quantities which would ultimately be required to supply the national demand for runabouts and cruisers.

who turns out a boat or two at a time, and not as a manufacturer of completed merchandise.

Can this program be more than just a dream? Dawn and cold reality awaken us rudely to find that even the program is past tense. The boats are here — glistening in their new and lustrious coats of Valspar — with an endless string of others following off the production line as fast as fine machinery and human ingenuity will permit.

"This one is under $2,000." "Why man alive it can't be done." But Jay Smith smiling, nods his head, "Yes! a 30 mile, nine passenger Chris-Craft all mahogany runabout!" But then we remember that some one predicted that boating would become a universal pastime for old and young America and we try to conceal our astonishment.

"Here's a Chris-Craft Cadet powered with a 100 horsepower Chrysler marine motor. We have improved the lines and put an additional 20 horsepower in the engine cockpit. "This boat," and our genial guide points to another sleek looking hull, "is the new 24-foot 35 mile runabout." Before we have a chance to open up we are informed that the new Chrysler 120 is the power unit.

Then we come to the famous 26 foot Chris-Craft. Four distinct models are represented in this size. There is the 40 mile boat powered with the Kermath valve-in-head 150 horsepower motor — the same boat with a rakish looking sedan top that slides back permitting easy boarding or disembarkation. It strikes us peculiar that no one has thought of this splendid expedient before. The price on this model is $4,600 with every possible luxury associated with a closed car incorporated in it. The next boat is a duplicate in appearance of the standard 26 foot Chris-Craft, but when the hatches are lifted we see the glistening V of the new 90 degree eight cylinder 200 horsepower Chris-Craft motor promising unlimited get away and speed. A sedan runabout with the same power plant is next encountered, but Jay Smith is already looking at the model beyond. "This is our 26 foot sport Hydroplane runabout." We discover that it has a speed rating of 55 miles per hour with the 200 h.p. Chris-Craft motor. And any one, we predict, with an ounce of red blood in their veins will never be satisfied until they can call it their very own. This Chris-Craft model is certainly a veritable knock-out in appearance, with the lines of a graceful greyhound and a business like step that puts it on top of the water and keeps it there.

Photo by Karine N. Rodengen

A high degree of craftsmanship is apparent in the cockpit of this 1927 22-foot runabout, *Miss Blue Water.* Soon to be known as *Cadet,* these quick runabouts would take Florida by storm in late 1927 and 1928. It would be for this boat that Walter P. Chrylser would develop the new Chrylser *Imperial* engine.

It almost seems that anything from this point will only get a casual glance — but we see two boats resting on cradles in the corner. They are much larger and we learn with some chagrin that our eye has lost its cunning to gauge sizes. Only 30 feet — but 30 feet of Custom runabout that leaves you breathless until your attention is drawn to the companion of this aristocrat. A commuter with a speed of 38 miles per hour and a luxuriousness of upholstering, lockers, toilet, and fitments that reduces any poise we might have retained to the ecstatic babblings of a child. Even the price doesn't deter us from sitting in the driver's seat — testing the softness of the cushions, examining the ice box and cleverly concealed lockers — but why ruin the anticipation of a perfectly wonderful tour of inspection that you must promise yourself at the first opportunity.[48]

Well on the way to their second million in sales, the Smiths broadened their target market even further, proclaiming that, "Anyone Who Can Drive a Car Can Drive a Chris-Craft."[49] It would be the beginning of an assault upon the sympathies of generations of *families,* a careful erosion of all possible objections to buying a runabout. The Smiths were the first to refine this powerful technique, and with an advertising budget of over a quarter million dollars, they were the only company in the business that could effectively inaugurate this highly effective seduction of the American family.

> OF COURSE anyone can drive a Chris-Craft who can drive an automobile. In fact, many women and children who drive Chris-Craft have never driven a motor car...
>
> A Chris-Craft can be stopped as quickly as a motor car equipped with four-wheel brakes. It reverses, turns or backs with ease. It can be driven moderately or made to vie with the wind in speed...
>
> Think, then, what a Chris-Craft would mean to your family — access to the waterways of the world — thrills, luxury, convenience, comfort. Permanently it costs little if any more than the six-mile stodgy tubs — the thousands of putt-putters about the shores — yet, it glides over the waves with velvety smoothness, carries two or three families in utmost comfort.[50]

Having softened up the average American's emotional defenses, the Smiths unleashed a bold economic initiative which was to have a far-reaching effect on the entire pleasure craft industry. *Credit.*

"This is one of the most important announcements we have ever made," the ad trumpeted;

Courtesy Mariners' Museum, Newport News, Virginia

The 1928 30-foot *Custom Commuter* was the first hint of things to come from the Chris-Smith & Sons Boat Co. It was the first enclosed Smith design that wasn't converted from a runabout hull. At $9,750 equipped with a new 200-horsepower Chris Smith & Sons engine, it was the first equipped with a toilet, roll-down windows, and a hinged entry-way hatch for easy access.

"Effective immediately, all Chris-Craft motor boats are made available to the retail purchaser on a unique 12-month deferred payment plan sponsored by the well-known Commercial Credit Company, with offices in all leading cities throughout the world. Now you can buy your Chris-Craft and pay for it out of income. Just think...a year to pay for it and a whole lifetime to enjoy it."[51]

Business was booming, and for portions of the summer of 1928, Chris Smith & Sons Boat Co. factories were "...working day and night, but even with our capactiy as the world's largest builders of all-mahogany runabouts, we are unable to accumulate stocks for future delivery."[52]

With a stable of designs ranging from $1,995 for the 22-foot runabout with the newly introduced 86-horsepower Chrysler engine, to $9,750 for the opulent 30-foot Custom Commuter with the 200-horsepower Chris-Craft engine, the first full menu of standardized motor boat selections was available. Before 1928, the only enclosures available on the standard models were adaptations of the 26-foot Chris-Craft for yacht tenders, or the folding "One Man Top" offered as an accessory for the 26-footer. For the first time, you could get out of the elements with a Chris-Craft. The only difference between the two 26-foot sedans with texti-leather tops and water-tight hatches was the power, $4,600 for the 38-mile-per-hour, 150-horsepower Kermath version, and $5,350 for the 43-mile-per-hour, 200-horsepower Chris-Craft equipped model. The 30-foot Custom Commuter would be America's first hint of things to come from the Smiths, for equipped with a toilet, curtains on roll-down windows and a hinged entryway hatch, a novel attention to group entertainment was indelibly etched into the design lines of America's most prolific boat builders.[53]

In November, the other shoe fell. It would be their first production *cruiser*. "From Chris-Craft proving grounds comes a sensational, new enclosed Chris-Craft," the announcement began, "combining all the speed and easy controllability of a runabout with the seaworthiness and luxury of the finest ocean-going yacht. Lines that are long, low and streamline...a spacious, luxuriously appointed cabin...eating, sleeping and lounging accommodations for the entire family. A boat that will move your pleasure horizon back hundreds, yes, thousands of miles!"[54] Before the first boat could be built, fourteen advance orders were taken by customers totally confident of the Smiths ability to deliver what they promised. Two passengers on the maiden test voyage of the boat each bought one before anyone could even tell them the price.[55] Its introduction left the marketplace thunderstruck, for the stylish and swift 38-foot, 30-mile-an-hour cruiser was introduced for only $15,000. "Nowhere in boating history or experience is there a parallel to this new cruiser," the premiere advertisement suggested, "either in design or performance. Long, low, racy, nimble, easily maneuvered; its gleaming mahogany encases the coziest, smartest cabin and cockpits ever built into a craft. Eating, sleeping and lounging quarters are superb."[56]

In 1928, their year of greatest *technical* achievement, the Smiths introduced their first marine engines, their first sedans, a production hydroplane, a commuter, and now a cruiser. They built three hundred thirty-one 22-foot runabouts, two hundred ninety-six 24-foot runabouts, one hundred thirty-four 26-foot runabouts, forty-four 26-foot sedans, four 28-foot runabouts, two 28-foot sedans, ten 30-foot commuters, two 38-foot cruisers, and still had time to build two experimental prototypes for future designs.[57]

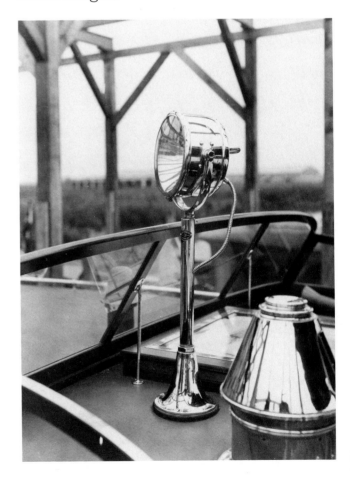

Courtesy Mariners' Museum, Newport News, Virginia

Above and opposite: The revolutionary Model 276, 38-foot *Commuting Cruiser* was Chris Smith & Sons *first cruiser*, and boasted 30 miles per hour. The open forward cockpit, luxuriously furnished cabin, bridge and rear cockpit accommodated 20, with sleeping quarters for four, including galley and private lavatory. It was introduced in November of 1928, and here displayed for the first time at the January, 1929 National Motor Boat Show in New York. Completely found, and featuring the new Chris Smith & Sons 250-horsepower V-8 engine, this first cruiser retailed for $15,000. A beautiful example of this boat can be seen on display at the Mariners' Museum in Newport News, VA.

Photo by Karine N. Rodengen

It was for the 26-foot runabouts that the name *Chris-Craft* was coined by Hamilton Smith. In 1928, one hundred thirty-four 26-foot runabouts like the *Phantom*, shown here, were built in Algonac, Michigan. This one, equipped with the popular 150-horsepower Kermath engine, was guaranteed to make 38 miles per hour.

As 1928 drew to a close, the Smiths would reveal a remarkable statistic. More Chris-Craft had been purchased during the last two years than all other makes *combined*.[58]

For the Smiths, 1929 would solidify their formal entry into the cruiser and yacht marketplace, for of the 18 models offered, fully *half* would be enclosed Chris-Craft ranging from the 24-foot, 10-passenger sedan at $3,300, to the 38-foot 26-passenger V-Bottom Commuting Cruiser at $15,000. Each of these all-weather boats would be powered by the firmly established Chris-Craft engines, some models employing the new 225-horsepower version of the 90 degree V-8 announced in late 1927.

Also new for '29 would be the intermediate, 24-foot 10-passenger runabout, accommodating two more passengers than the 22-foot models. All the runabouts were available with the one-man tops, and *every* boat in the fleet, for the first time, would carry the designation *Chris-Craft*.[59]

A long and prestigious list of Chris-Craft owners would be published this year, and advertising would focus on both the upper and middle class markets respectively. "Bank presidents and brokers whose names are news everywhere," the 1929 brochure explained, "heads of great institutions and high officials have found their Chris-Craft most useful and enjoyable. It gives them complete relaxation and change and clears away nervous fatigue."[60] It seems the best known names in the world preferred Chris-Crafts, from Harvey Firestone taking Thomas Edison for a spin, to Vincent Astor, Charlie Chaplin, Walter P. Chrysler, F. V. DuPont, Wm. A. Fisher, K. Lee Guiness, W. A. Lambert, Eli Lilly, Wm. F. Pelham, H. A. Quakenbush, H. S. Reynolds, His Grace the Duke of Sutherland, Philip K. Wrigley, among a small army of dignitaries, socialites and titans of both industry and commerce.

Capturing the attention of the average family man, the Smiths would extol the virtues of ownership as a reward for the entire household. "Every family is entitled to at least know the delight of Chris-Craft riding," one approach argued, "— its usefulness — its joy-bringing and health-building properties. Let the tired business man lengthen his life and give happiness to the whole family by providing them with the multitude of clean thrills and joys available only through Chris-Craft ownership.... Chris-Crafting is recreation in itself. It recreates those who use it both in body and mind."[61] And, targeting the family with *awkward* aged children even more directly, "Son and daughter were no longer rebellious at the dullness of home — Chris-Craft offered them so many safe thrills — so much clean amusement — such a delightful and distinguished means of entertaining friends — such a flexible form of speedy transportation to swimming raft — the distant dance — the hotel across the bay."[62]

And to quicken the jealous heart of society, "Years ago, society discovered in Chris-Crafting an opening to many exclusive methods of entertainment and diversion...Fortunate were those with a Chris-Craft at their hand...society took Chris-Crafting unto itself — made it a part of social life. Wherever society gathers at seashore or lake, river or ocean, you will find Chris-Craft. The list of Chris-Craft owners comprises many famous names — many who can buy any craft they choose — an ocean liner as easily as a canoe.

The Social Register — Who's Who — the Directory of Directors — all are well represented by Chris-Craft enthusiasts. In Buenos Aires — at Port Said — on the Riviera and on the Nile, Chris-Craft is as much at home as in New York — or exclusive inland lake. Hardly a port exists the whole world round where social and business leaders have failed to make Chris-Craft a part of their equipage. Purchasers in thirty different countries have recently received new Chris-Craft."[63]

Actually, a full fifteen percent of Chris-Craft sales would be made outside of the United States in 1929, and Chris-Craft were enthusiastically received at the major boating shows of Europe, particularly at the newly established Salon Nautique in Paris. Overseas representation by Arthur Bray of London included the majority of continental Europe. Viscounts, Dukes and royalty clamored for their own Chris-Craft.

Of the elegant 30-foot custom Commuter the Smiths would proudly say, "In the first year of its introduction many men of great prominence sought to buy this remarkable new craft; a few who placed late orders were disappointed in not being able to secure one. The demand exceeded our expectations because so many had been waiting for just such a craft. A busy year has now put us in position to supply a larger number of these weather-closed, twelve-passenger, drawing room commuters...Here is, in truth, a

traveling home, where one may comfortably pass the time between office and home. Seclusion, reading, writing or games, luncheon or business meeting are available to every owner of a Chris-Craft Custom Commuter."[64] The Custom Commuter was now provided with the quicker 225-horsepower Chris-Craft engine, whisking business travelers to work at 40 miles per hour.

The Queen of the fleet, though, was the new 38-foot 30-mile Commuting Cruiser, and arguably the Smiths' crowning achievement for the decade. It truly was a marvelous machine, far exceeding the modest competition for a speedy well-appointed mahogany cruiser. Within Bill MacKerer's notebooks was a detailed analysis of every commuting type cruiser on the market, some seventy-three models ranging from custom to production, from 33-feet to 100-feet, and representing the very best cruisers the world had to offer. Within their engine rooms thundered power from sixty-five to twelve hundred horsepower, and *not one boat listed* in the Commuting Cruiser size could come close to the performance of the new Smith flagship.

It was the first Chris-Craft to have berths, galley, wash basin, table, boarding ladder and bilge pumps, but also mattresses, bedding, table linen, china, glassware, silverware, and galley with stove. When you took delivery of your Chris-Craft Commuting Cruiser, all you needed to do

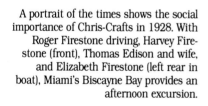

A portrait of the times shows the social importance of Chris-Crafts in 1928. With Roger Firestone driving, Harvey Firestone (front), Thomas Edison and wife, and Elizabeth Firestone (left rear in boat), Miami's Biscayne Bay provides an afternoon excursion.

Courtesy Mariners' Museum, Newport News, Virginia

CHRIS-CRAFT
ALL-MAHOGANY MOTOR BOATS

1929 Condensed Specifications and List Prices
F. O. B. ALGONAC, MICHIGAN

WORLD'S LARGEST BUILDERS OF ALL-MAHOGANY MOTOR BOATS

Model   **Length**

1. Chris-Craft 22' all-mahogany Runabout, 8 passenger, speed up to 30 M. P. H. 82 H. P. Marine Motor_____ $2235.00

2. Chris-Craft 22' all-mahogany Runabout, 8 passenger, speed up to 35 M. P. H. 106 H. P. Marine Motor_____ 2495.00

3. Chris-Craft 24' all-mahogany Runabout, 10 passenger, speed up to 33 M. P. H. 106 H. P. Marine Motor_____ 2750.00

4. Chris-Craft 26' all-mahogany Runabout, 11 passenger, speed up to 30 M. P. H. 106 H. P. Marine Motor_____ 2975.00

5. Chris-Craft 26' all-mahogany Runabout, 11 passenger, speed up to 42 M. P. H. 200 H. P. Marine Motor_____ 4000.00

6. Chris-Craft 26' all-mahogany DeLuxe Cabin Sedan, 11 passenger, speed up to 40 M. P. H. 200 H. P. Marine Motor_____ 4850.00

7. Chris-Craft 26' all-mahogany Runabout, 11 passenger, speed up to 45 M. P. H. 225 H. P. Chris-Craft Marine Motor_____ 4300.00

8. Chris-Craft 26' all-mahogany DeLuxe Cabin Sedan, 11 passenger, speed up to 43 M. P. H. 225 H. P. Chris-Craft Marine Motor_____ 5150.00

9. Chris-Craft 26' Sedan, 11 passenger, speed up to 43 M. P. H. 225 H. P. Chris-Craft Marine Motor_____ 4850.00

10. Chris-Craft 30' all-mahogany Custom Runabout, 12 passenger, speed up to 40 M. P. H. 225 H. P. Chris-Craft Marine Motor_____ 7000.00

11. Chris-Craft 30' all-mahogany Custom Commuter, 12 passenger, speed up to 38 M. P. H. 225 H. P. Chris-Craft Marine Motor_____ 9750.00

12. Chris-Craft 24' Sedan, 10 passenger, speed up to 32 M. P. H. 106 H. P. Marine Motor_____ 3300.00

13. Chris-Craft 26' Sedan, 11 passenger, speed up to 40 M. P. H. 200 H. P. Marine Motor_____ 4550.00

14. Chris-Craft 28' all-mahogany Custom Runabout, 11 passenger, speed up to 42 M. P. H. 225 H. P. Chris-Craft Marine Motor_____ 4975.00

15. Chris-Craft 28' all-mahogany DeLuxe Cabin Sedan, 11 passenger, speed up to 40 M. P. H. 225 H. P. Chris-Craft Marine Motor_____ 5850.00

16. Chris-Craft 38' all-mahogany V-Bottom Commuting Cruiser, 26 passenger, speed up to 30 M. P. H. 225 H. P. Chris-Craft Marine Motor_____ 15000.00

17. Chris-Craft 28' all mahogany Custom Runabout, 11 passenger, speed up to 40 M. P. H. 200 H. P. Marine Motor_____ 4675.00

18. Chris-Craft 28' all-mahogany DeLuxe Cabin Sedan, 11 passenger, speed up to 38 M. P. H. 200 H. P. Marine Motor_____ 5550.00

THERE IS ONLY ONE *CHRIS-CRAFT*

Courtesy Mariners' Museum, Newport News, Virginia

The 1929 catalog showed a remarkable diversity of craft from Chris Smith & Sons Boat Co., including the new 30-foot *Custom Commuter* which was the forerunner of the first cabin cruiser, the new 38-foot *Commuting Cruiser* which was announced too late to make the catalog.

was fill up the 138-gallon gas tank, stock your favorite food and you were on your way; everything else was provided for immediate cruising enjoyment. At 12,000 pounds, you could own her for $1.25 a pound, less than the cost of ground beef sixty years later.

It was the vision of Jay Smith that gave birth to the first Chris-Craft engines, and the superior design and performance of the 200 and 225-horsepower V-8's was testimony to his keen mechanical judgment and perseverance. In a portion of the 1929 brochure dedicated to the marine engines, praise is heaped upon the creator of the division.

> The final development came in 1927. The new motor finally answered the designer's vision — a vision far beyond any layman's expectation. That it speeds a 38-foot cruiser along at 30 miles an hour, day after day, is only a hint at its power and performance.
>
> Those who have had a full year's use of the new motor feel that, in spite of the outstanding success in building the Chris-Craft organization, the largest of its kind in the world, the real Jay W. Smith is best expressed in this superb mechanism.[65]

The decade of innovation, standardization, expansion and diversification had firmly established Chris-Craft as the dominant producer of boats in the world, and had popularized the Smith legacy through millions of words in articles and advertisements. "The eyes of the boating world are on Chris-Craft," the last brochure of the 20's honestly maintained. Indeed, in the coming years, the mettle of the Smiths, along with the national marine industry, would be tested to the limit.

On October 24, 1929, a wave of panic rolled over a sea of dazed brokers, investors and bankers on Wall Street, as the stock market plummeted to an unprecedented and spectacular loss. Within an hour during the frantic day, blue chip certificates of companies like General Electric, Johns-Manville and Montgomery Ward tumbled, in some cases losing 25% of their value. The tickers couldn't keep up with the rush of selling orders, and by the time the gavel mercifully fell at three o'clock, the tape was running an unbelievable *four hours behind* transactions. Rumors, later confirmed, of speculator suicides fueled the frenzy of portfolio dumping, and late in the day stocks were nearly given away.

Black Thursday would consume the livelihoods, dreams and dignity of millions of American workers and families, with a voracious and cancerous attrition in the months and years to follow.

Popular among taxi and thrill-ride operators were the 28 and 30-foot Chris-Craft runabouts, models 114, 117 and 120. They could carry up to twelve passengers in three cockpits, and with speeds up to 42 miles per hour, would in many cases be the fastest speed passengers would experience in life.

CHAPTER IX

Taxis & Tenders

OVER THE YEARS, Chris-Craft boats have been pressed into a wide variety of special service, from fireboat to tugboat, rescue craft to landing craft, and from taxis to tenders. During the 1920's and '30's, many people experienced their first speedboat or *thrill* ride in a Chris-Craft, particularly the popular 26-foot *Chris-Craft* runabout, and later, the 22-foot Chris-Craft *Cadet.* Variations on this popular hull were used as urban water taxis and also as specially-prepared tenders to many of the most fabulous yachts of the era.

Chris Smith & Sons Boat Co. began to take the yacht tender business quite seriously by 1927, and even promoted these models apart from other runabouts.

Yacht builders and yacht designers have accorded Chris-Craft tenders warm praise and an enthusiastic reception. They have expressed complete satisfaction with the Chris-Craft modified in design to meet the needs of the yacht owner. These mahogany tenders are ultra smart, handsome in appearance and very special. Two sizes — the large 26-foot yacht tender and the smaller 22-foot model are built.

The 22-foot Tender powered with Kermath 70 H.P., has a speed of 25 m.p.h. Price $5,500.

The 26-foot Tender powered with Kermath 100 H.P. or 150 H.P., having speeds of 30 to 40 miles per hour. Price $7,000 and $7,500.

Either size will accommodate 9 passengers — the choice depending largely on the size yacht to be equipped. These tenders are safe and comfortable and a fast means of travel is assured the owner and his guests aboard ship.[1]

On December 14th, 1927, a 26-foot Special Yacht Tender was completed for Samuel Untermeyer's new yacht *Nirodha.* Though the fast-flowing St. Clair River was free of ice, in order for Bernard Smith to test the tender, a channel had to be cut through four inches of ice in the canal leading to the Smiths' production buildings. "Chris Smith & Sons Boat Co. are so sincere in the testing of their boats that a mere matter of extremely cold weather [eighteen degrees below zero] and 4 inches of ice could not stop them from thoroughly testing these boats before they are shipped to their customers."[2]

The *Owner's Special Tender* aboard the 294-foot motor yacht *Savarona* owned by Mrs. Richard Cadwalader, Jr., of Philadelphia, was typical of the prestigious applications for Chris-Craft Special Tenders.

Luxury, smartness, speed and dependability of high order are all happily combined in the 26-foot, 40-mile-an-hour Chris-Craft which has

been selected as the owner's boat on the *SAVARONA*.

Whether riding smartly in the davits or speeding to or from shore, this tender will ever reflect the good judgment of those who selected it.

The sheltered cabin over the after cockpit seats seven passengers in comfort and the driver's seat provides seating space for an additional three. The hull is constructed of mahogany — staunch, sturdy, smooth. The deck and upper-works are made of teak, adding a delightful note of contrasting color.

Courtesy Mariners' Museum, Newport News, Virginia

President Franklin D. Roosevelt seemed to be posing beneath a Chris-Craft tender while he was a guest aboard Vincent Astor's yacht *Nourmahal* in 1935. Perhaps the President wasn't aware that a fully equipped 26-foot tender weighed over 4,000 pounds.

Lifting rings, fore and aft, permit easy raising and lowering in the davits.

Although basically the same in design as standard Chris-Craft Runabouts (any one of which may be readily converted for such service) Chris-Craft yacht tenders embody certain features which make them eminently suited to their purpose.[3]

A 1939 *Motor Boating* magazine headline proclaimed *"Round The World in a Dinghy"*. Actually, the *dinghy* was a special, 41-foot Chris-Craft Yacht Tender.

Misleading, perhaps, but in this case, the dinghy is a 41-foot Chris-Craft and sleeps eight persons. She proudly rides the davits of *Fantome*, a 257-foot four-masted schooner, owned by the Honorable A.F. Guinness, brewer of the famous "stout".

Fantome is painted and decorated like a British man-o'-war of one hundred and fifty years ago. It is one of the world's largest privately owned pleasure yachts. After crossing the Atlantic, exploring the East Indies and Panama Canal, *Fantome* picked up her luxurious dinghy at Seattle, Washington. She will eventually circumnavigate the globe before returning to England.[4]

Courtesy Mariners' Museum, Newport News, Virginia

Also of service to President Franklin D. Roosevelt was this 26-foot Chris-Craft runabout pressed into service to pick up the mail pouch from a Navy amphibian aircraft to be delivered to the President aboard Vincent Astor's yacht *Nourmahal* in 1935.

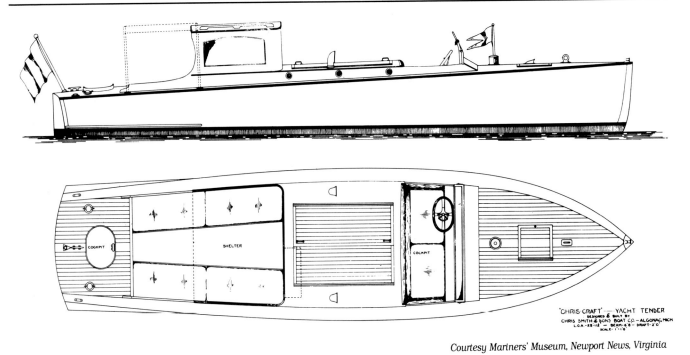

Courtesy Mariners' Museum, Newport News, Virginia

The 26-foot Chris-Craft *Yacht Tender* was a specially-equipped 26-foot runabout. A speaking tube enabled the privileged passenger within the enclosure to communicate with the driver who remained exposed to the elements. Aft of the mahogany cabin was an additional canvas shelter which could be extended when transporting a large party.

Cornelius Vanderbilt used his 26-foot Chris-Craft tender for reaching his 225-foot yacht *Winchester*, here pictured in 1927.

Courtesy Mariners' Museum, Newport News, Virginia

W.A. "Bill" MacKerer broke out a list of extra material required to turn a 26-foot *Chris-Craft* runabout into a 26-foot *Yacht Tender*.

QTY.	SPECIFICATIONS	COST
4	Deck Sockets for Navy Top	$ 7.68
20'	3/4" Tubing	8.97
22	Rings & Wingbolts	3.87
1	Set Canvass Covers Complete	32.00
1	Pc. Convass 60" x 72" — 8-oz — For Shelter Deck	.82
4	Cleats — 7"	3.52
2	Vents	1.76
10'	1" Speaking Tube	.40
4	1" Speaking Tube Ells	.38
2	1" Speaking Tube Flex. Terminals	6.00
	Polished Brass Rod for Handrails	7.50
4	Hinges - 1 1/2" x 2 1/2"	.86
2	Casement Adjusters	2.80
2	Cigar Lighters	4.42
1	Aft Hoisting Yoke	6.75
	Pike Pole Holders	.50
	Binding for Sides Aft Cockpit	.75
	Extra Shafting 2'-10"	6.00
	Extra Exhaust Pipe 3'-0"	1.50
2	Extra Exhaust Pipe Couplings	2.12
2	Dome Lights	3.20
	113.21 Board Feet Mahogany @ .20/Bd. Ft.	22.65
	48 Board Feet Spruce @ .05/Bd. Ft.	2.40
	TOTAL	$124.85[5]

The additional components brought the weight of the 26-foot Special Yacht Tender to 4,040 lbs.[6]

Among the many yachts of distinction during the '20's and '30's which carried either Chris-Craft auxiliaries or Special Yacht Tenders, were:

Courtesy Mariners' Museum, Newport News, Virginia

Edsel Ford was in Palm Beach, Florida in 1931 aboard his 125-foot yacht *Onika*. A 26-foot Chris-Craft tender hanging in the davits was a common sight aboard the greatest yachts of the era.

Alfred P. Sloan, New York	*Rene*	William Randolph Hearst	*Oneida*
Frederick J. Fisher, Detroit	*Nakhoda*	E. W. Grove, Jr., St. Louis	*Margrove III*
Walter O. Briggs, Detroit	*Cambriona*	T. O. M. Sopwith, London	*Vita*
Vincent Astor, New York City	*Nourmahal*	Edsel Ford, Detroit	*Onika*
R. C. Durant, California	*Vidor*	Jack Withers, London	
Robert Law, New York City	*Robador*	W. B. Armstrong, New York City	*Miramar*
David Whitney, Detroit	*Sumar*	K. Lee Guinness, London	*Migrant*
Harrison Williams, New York City	*Warrior*	J. D. Hurd, New York City	*Natalon*
George F. Baker, New York City	*Viking*	Robert Law, New York City	*Robador*
Mrs. Robert Cadwalader, Philadelphia	*Savarona*	B. E. Pollak, New York City	*Tropic*
Joseph P. Grace, New York City	*Jessie Fay*	Geo. W. Pennington, Maryland	
A. W. Atkinson, Philadelphia	*Lycellma III*	Colin Cooper, London	*Karen*
E. W. Grove, Jr., St. Louis	*Margrove III*	His Grace the Duke of Sutherland, Eng.	*Sans Peur*
Mrs. Charles N. Strotz, Norfolk, VA	*Miss Strozzi*	Lt. Cmr. Mantague Grahame White	*Alacrity*
H. E. Manville, Jr., New York City	*Hi-Esmaro*	Monsieur R. Monsegur, Paris, France	
Frank V. Dupont, Delaware		Sir Herbert Samuelson, London	*Endymion*[7]

Alfred P. Sloan, Jr. used a 26-foot Chris-Craft Yacht Tender as equipment aboard his million dollar yacht, *Rene.*

Courtesy Mariner's Museum, Newport News, Virginia

Courtesy Mariner's Museum, Newport News, Virginia

J.P. Morgan is here seen boarding his yacht *Corsair* from his 26-foot Chris-Craft tender in New York.

Courtesy Mariners' Museum, Newport News, Virginia

In the 1930's water taxi services blossomed around the country. Here, from the Chicago Navy Pier, guests eagerly line the docks to tour Lake Michigan or return to the Edgewater Beach Hotel. Note the extra stepping pads along the side decks to help passenger footing and protect the boats.

Chris-Smith & Sons Boat Co. were enthusiastic promoters of the *water taxi* business. Chris-Craft water taxis ranged anywhere from a boy taking a boatload of sightseers around a resort lake in a 22-foot *Cadet*, to a regularly scheduled, professional excursion company taking up to 32 or more passengers aboard a specially-designed Chris-Craft taxi on a tour of a national attraction like the Boulder Dam. By 1930, Chris-Craft had developed a promotional booklet to persuade small businessmen to start up their own water taxi business.

Hundreds of beaches, amusement parks, and summer resorts are calling to operators of water taxi service. There's big money to be made with speed boats for hire. All the world is getting out on the water. Spend 25c. for the new 40-page book, "Water Transit Service." It tells you how to set up and operate your own water taxi service.[8]

Many *Thrill Ride* operators, offering fast, 40-mile per hour action for a squirming, delighted clientele, chose Chris-Crafts because of their rugged durability, built-in safety features and strong, dependable engines. Often, though, it was hard to distinguish between an enthusiastic taxi ride or a thrill ride; the effect could be equally stimulating.

Above: Many Americans' first speed boat ride was a thrill ride aboard a 26-foot Chris-Craft runabout. For fifty cents, it was possible to experience the fastest ride of the times, except perhaps for the quickest passenger trains. Souvenir tickets, like the one shown, were pressed between the pages of thousands of vacation scrap books in the late 1920's and 1930's.

Left: Typical of the taxi applications for Chris-Craft was this speed boat taxi service across Casco Bay near Portland, Maine.

Opposite below: The 48-foot taxi *Florence K* was b in 1934 to accommodate up to sixty passengers in open forward cockpit, central enclosed cabin and o aft seating areas. The enclosed flying bridge wa relatively new development for Chris-Craft, and helm station was the very model of depression simplic

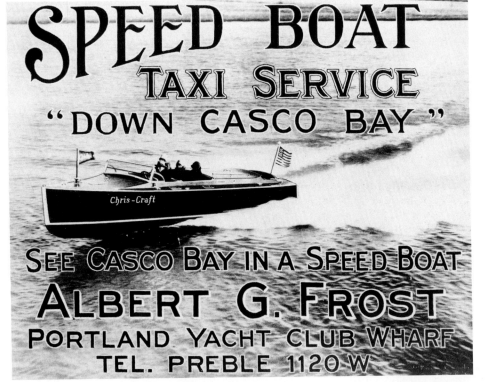

Right: Sixteen passengers sat in the open forward cockpit of this 1930 36-foot V-bottom taxi, while another sixteen could be seated across the exposed stern and aft section. Powered with either the Chrylser Imperial 106-horsepower or Chris-Craft 250-horsepower engine, the practi cal taxi could make 33 miles per hour.

*Courtesy Mariners' Museum,
Newport News, Virginia*

Left: This 31-foot Chris-Craft taxi known as *Strollerette*, could seat thirty-six passengers under cover. The austere 1934 taxi *Syracuse* is shown.

Courtesy Mariners' Museum, Newport News, Virginia

No matter the adversity, the indomitable spirit of Chris-Craft and the American people
would shine through the clouds of the Great Depression.

CHAPTER X

The Thirties

We, in our rush toward God knows what, acquire, or spend our earthly span trying to acquire wealth, culture, fame, luxury, scientific efficiency — and more wealth. We surround ourselves with telephones, tickers, jazz orchestras, subways, bootleg gin, dress clothes, taxicabs, motor parkways, science, glittering hotels, psychoanalysis, alarm clocks, forty thousand brands of phony religion, squawking movie palaces, nickel-in-the-slot divorce. We call it civilization. But we know darn well there's something wrong with it.

Charles F. Chapman[1]

THE HORROR OF the nation's depression was slow to reach Algonac. As business began to increase during early 1930, it may have led the Smiths to assume that their burgeoning enterprise was somehow insulated from the downward spiraling economy. By April 1st, it was clear to Jay Smith that sales had started climbing faster and earlier in the season than in previous years, signaling a stable if not dramatic growth in revenues.

On April seventh, Robert Heller, a salesman for the New York investment banking firm of Childs, Jeffries & Co., Inc., left Jay Smith's office with an option to buy a full third of the family business for $1,125,000.[2] Frankly, the Smiths didn't *need* the money. They had managed to build a surplus of over $640,000, accumulating nearly half a million dollars over the past two years alone. Business was good, profits were continually given over to expansion, and a dividend had not yet been paid the four principals to date. It was, rather, the lure of substantial, fast and effortless profit from taking the family business public through a stock offering that motivated their decision. It was a strange and fateful decision.

Strange because the Smiths, though good-natured and enjoyable company, were a very closed group, almost a knot when it came to family matters. Jay and Bernard were somehow distant from outsiders, "hard to get to know" was the comment of the casual acquaintance, while "very private, almost reclusive" were portraits drawn by those with years of association. They felt awkward and gangly on social occasions, would shy from direct publicity, had a small, exceedingly tight circle of friends, and never,

Courtesy Mariners' Museum, Newport News, Virginia

Chris Smith turns the first shovel of earth for the new office building at Algonac, Michigan, September, 1931. Left to right: Harsen Smith, Jay W. Smith, Chris and Bernard Smith.

never discussed the financial details of the family enterprise with anyone having less than a lifetime commitment to the cause. Whether genetic or environmentally nurtured, this demure and self-effacing reserve became strongly rooted in the third generation personality of Harsen Smith, son of Jay.

One of Harsen's boyhood friends remembers the self-imposed isolation that would permeate even enthusiastic social activity. "We all used to like to ice boat together in the winter," his old friend explained; "We had some nice boats. A bunch of us would come in from ice boating to one of the restaurants, and Harsen would sit at a different table all alone."[3] Another childhood companion recalled Harsen's more adventurous side. "His folks [Jay & Mabel] had a Willis automobile, and one day when they went away Harsen got in the car, turned the key on and pushed ahead right into a barrel of glass fruit jars. He went the wrong way."[4] It seems that was about the extent of the mischief in the conservative and serious-minded Harsen. As *Time* would report in 1959:

> The eldest of Jay's three children, Harsen was born in 1908, grew up among a cluster of relatives and the sights and smells of the Algonac shop. By the time he was nine, he was hanging around the launching slips so much that father

Jay, a firm, nonsmoking teetotaler, ordered him to learn to swim before showing up again in the factory. "This really upset me," says Harsen, "so I practiced for two straight weeks, then told my father I could swim. He threw me off the dock and I made it back."

Harsen left Algonac long enough to attend the University of Michigan and play Big Ten football, returned after three years to work in the shop. One day a flutter of 40 sorority girls showed up in Algonac for a boat ride. Harsen took them out and, says he, "picked the best of the 40." He and May Doherty of Detroit were married in 1929.[5]

By 1930, Harsen, then twenty-two, assumed the ubiquitous duties of Assistant to the President, and was carefully being groomed to someday succeed his father as president of the business.

When Jay Smith negotiated the option to sell a third of the company to the Wall Street investment firm, he had carefully penciled in a clause in one of the earlier drafts which provided for a $250,000 deposit, which, in case of the bankers backing out of the deal, would be retained by the Smiths. Both sides had a list of tasks to accomplish for the transaction to be completed. Chris Smith & Sons Boat Co. was required to form a new corporation, *Chris-Craft Corporation*, give up a seat on the Board of Directors, supply certain financial documents and quarterly audits of the company until November 1st, 1930, at which time Chris-Craft would deliver stock to the bankers and pick up a check for over $1.1 million. The bankers were required to place $250,000 in a Detroit bank to be held in escrow, handle a public offering not later than January 1, 1931, return 50% of any price over $20 per share they would get for the stock, become the bank of preference for any future company financing, and more or less coordinate all events leading to the listing of the Chris-Craft Corporation on the New York Stock Exchange.

On May 5th, five days following the execution of final contracts, the quarter million dollar deposit was placed in the National Bank of Commerce in Detroit. The Smiths sprang into action.

Among the first considerations of the legal scramble which was required on the Smith side of the agreement was to somehow insulate themselves from the sizable federal taxes which would be due for the windfall profits the deal would deliver. Taylor Sieber of the accounting firm of Ernst & Ernst of Detroit had established that should the Smiths simply sell their portion of the stock to the bankers, they would pay an estimated $120,000 in Federal Income Taxes.[6] Accordingly, a strategy known as the *Sieber Tax Avoidance Plan* was developed.

An ingenious ploy, actually, which required Chris, Jay, and Bernard each make a gift of 20% of their holdings to their wives, while Owen gives 20% of his to his mother, Anna. Next, *the wives*, Anna, Maybelle, and Dora form *Smith Investment Company*, trading their boat company stock for the investment company stock. Chris, Jay, Bernard and Owen then form a holding company, *Algonac Investment Company*, trading *their* boat company stock for the holding company stock. Then, Smith Investment Company (owned by the wives) buys the Algonac Investment Company (owned by the men) in exchange for holding company stock, and the holding company dissolves. *Chris-Craft Corporation* is formed, and buys Chris Smith & Sons Boat Co. in exchange for new Chris-Craft Corporation stock. Finally, Chris Smith & Sons Boat Co. dissolves, distributing its shares of Chris-Craft Corporation to its stockholders, the Smith Investment Corporation. The Smiths own only one-twentieth of one percent of the new corporation outright, while 99.96 percent is owned by their Smith Investment Corporation. Ownership of the new corporation is thereby diluted to percentages which are not taxed, or not as heavily taxed, and stock is now owned in the following percentages:

Chris Smith	18.75%
Jay Smith	18.75%
Bernard Smith	18.75%
Owen Smith	18.75%
Anna Smith	12.50%
Maybelle Smith	6.25%
Dora Smith	6.25%

In January of 1930 the Smiths introduced their most ambitious offerings to date, twenty-four models of boats ranging from a 20-foot, 8-passenger runabout at $1,895, to the 30-passenger 48-foot yacht selling for $35,000, their largest production craft yet. It was a clear signal to both consumers and the marine industry that Chris-Craft was not affected by widespread rumors of impending disaster as a result of the crumbling American economy. "Here they come," an article begins, "a long line of 24 new Chris-Craft — the largest and most complete motor boat spectacle ever presented."[8] Indeed, no other manufacturer in the world could offer such diversity and value. The review of the 1930 Chris-Craft fleet in *Motor Boating* reveals the increased emphasis on the higher end of their fleet market.

Eleven runabouts lead the procession ranging in speed from 28 miles an hour to a dashing forty-five miles. Following closely are the sedans — nine of them, deluxe sedans, convertible sedans, and all-mahogany sedans; a model to

Courtesy Mariners' Museum, Newport News, Virginia

This unique cut-away drawing of a 1930 Chris-Craft 22-foot runabout shows the major components and general layout of a typical triple-cockpit runabout. Powered with the optional 125-horsepower Chris-Craft engine, this model 102 could carry nine passengers to speeds of 36 mph.

suit every man's requirements. Then comes the 34-foot commuter, one of the fine new boats this year; a boat of which Chris Smith & Sons are justly proud; a dashing craft with twin motor installation designed for fast commuting service. Next the 38-foot commuting cruiser, with an alternate floor plan and cabin arrangement, bringing new comforts to water travel. And finally, the Flagship of the Chris-Craft fleet, the new 48-foot express yacht passes before us. Entirely new in its conception, it brings with it luxuries never before found in the water.

...Horsepower ranges from seventy-five up to 450; speed from 28 miles an hour to 45, and seating capacity from eight to thirty persons, in comfort.

In this great array there is truly a boat within the reach of everyone. The startling new 20-foot runabout is indeed a marvel in its field. Never before has such a high quality moderately priced small motor boat been built. This boat, built to the high standards of workmanship which mark all Chris-Craft is truly a brother of the big 26 and 28-footers known the world over for their luxury. No expense has been spared to

make this the outstanding small boat of the season. For over two years this boat has been on the designers' boards, but never until now have standardization methods allowed Chris Smith & Sons to build her and make her the way they wanted to. ... It is only regrettable that this company can build but 500 of these wonder boats in 1930.

Among the closed boats there is presented an entirely new type of convertible sedan. Sedan owners everywhere will welcome this new type of covering which allows the whole rear part of the sedan top to fold forward for easy access and egress. For those that prefer them, there will also be a handsome new all-mahogany sedan.

The 34-foot custom commuter is a boat which, while new in production this year, has long been under discussion as a popular type of boat. First of all, it is fast, forty miles is her speed, and she is equipped with double cabins for protection in any weather. As a commuter for the man who lives a short distance from the city nothing is more suitable. A 38-foot commuter will be available to those who require a larger craft.[9]

Also fueling the confidence in the seemingly depression-proof nature of the boating industry were Chris-Craft's almost unbelievable record-breaking sales at the 1930 New York Motor Boat Show. Setting an all-time record for sales at the show, Chris-Craft accepted orders for four hundred ninety-seven boats for a total value of $2,204,216.50, which represented *over a third of all orders* placed at the mammoth event, which was represented by nearly every major manufacturer in the country.[10] Unfortunately, their joy was dampened as many orders began to cancel, even forfeiting deposits, and the first warning sirens began to blow at Chris-Craft.

Yet, a major marketing effort was underway to increase the already sizable dealer and franchise network. Under the direction of Jack Clifford and the new advertising manager, Gordon Manning, an ambitious campaign was mounted which included production of a twenty-page franchise brochure, a forty-eight page pamphlet on the establishment of a water taxi business, the new forty-eight page *Chris-Craft Care and Operation Book*, fourteen different direct mail pieces, and the dramatic *Ye Mappe of Chris-Craft Activities throughout the World* which appears on the end leaves of this book. Also displayed for the first time in 1930 was the Chris-Craft Heraldic Shield which is still in prominent use today. Potential franchisees were assuaged with statistics like "A million prospects and a three billion dollar market invite you to participate and will pay you well," and "All those who own motor cars are logical prospects for Chris-Craft," or "Any retail sales organization with suitable personnel and sufficient working capital to maintain a showroom with boats on the floor, and a demonstrator in the water during season, can expect success with the Chris-Craft Franchise."[11]

The sale of Chris-Craft at franchises was modeled after the automobile industry, an area where Jack Clifford excelled. The first line of attack for attracting new franchises was the established automobile dealer. "An established automobile dealer," Clifford argued, "should… be able to add anywhere from ten to fifty thousand dollars to his annual net income."[12] And finally, the *lifestyle* marketing which had become the Chris-Craft trademark, was extended to franchise marketing. "A Chris-Craft merchant's time is spent on the clean, open waterways, where every moment is full of the joy of living. He is demonstrating a craft of which anyone could be proud, and meeting a class of people

Courtesy Mariners' Museum, Newport News, Virginia

The 1932 29-foot *level riding* Custom Runabout offered an exhilarating 45 mph speed equipped with a 250-horsepower V-8 Chris-Craft engine. For 1932 it was the fastest boat in the Chris-Craft fleet.

that anyone would be glad to know. Each day is different, contributing some new experience to the constant pleasure of being in this remarkable business."[13]

The Smiths had mastered the advertising media, and by 1930 could boast of nearly 60,000,000 consumer impressions a year. Their advertising placements had spread out from traditional targets like *Yachting* and *Motor Boating*, to include such prestigious family publications as *The Saturday Evening Post, The National Geographic Magazine, Harper's Bazaar, Town & Country, House & Garden, Vogue, Vanity Fair* and *The Literary Digest*. Chris-Craft correctly boasted that, "No other in the field has such an advertising coverage of the market, and no other has the model coverage, or the public acceptance."[14] They would sum up their optimism, accomplishments and forecasts by saying "Chris-Craft has the name, the prestige, the public acceptance. It has consistently advanced from the beginning and maintained the continued success of its merchants. Chris-Craft has been the leader, is the leader, and will continue to lead."[15]

Chris Smith enjoyed the occasional practical joke, and one Sunday was able to convince a group of buyers that he was only an old-time employee or the watchman.

One of the most interesting stories [Chris] tells is of the party of millionaires that came out from Detroit one day to buy a boat. It so happened that they arrived at the plant on a Sunday when there was no one around but old Chris. He was, as usual in an old pair of trousers and

osite left: This 1930 Chris-Craft 48-foot Cruiser
sing Palm Beach carried all the amenities of home,
ıding a full galley and stately *saloon* which converted
double bed. With a pair of 250-horsepower Chris-
t engines, 30 passengers could travel 30 mph.

slouch hat, sitting by the office door with his faithful dog, Jack, at his side. The gay party from the city marched boldly past Chris and on into the office in search of someone from whom they might buy, or at least see a boat. No one was around except Chris. Out they came and asked, in their eagerness, if there was anyone around who could show them through the plant. "I will," says the laconic Chris, as he picks up a stick and motions for them to follow. Then followed a minute exacting description of all the processes incidental to the building of their boats, and finally a trip out on the river, in one of the boats. When it was all over, and they were back at the office again, one of them could contain himself no longer and broke out to Chris: "You must have been with the company a long while to know so much about the way they build boats here."

"Oh, I have," remarked Chris in an offhand way.

"Well, we certainly are sorry not to see Chris here today, as we really wanted to order a boat. But will you tell him that the Van Ripers came out to look at a boat today, and really think he builds a wonderful boat."

Surely Chris would tell himself that as soon as he had a chance to talk with himself. And so the people got into their car and went away, never knowing they had been with that same person, of whom they talked so glibly, for over an hour. But that's Chris Smith, the practical joker. There is always something happening in daily life around the plant which he will comment on in such a humorous way that his employees have come to love him and revere him like a father. Incidentally, the Van Ripers sent their order in by mail the next day, and the joke of old Chris, did not cost the company an order, after all.[16]

By mid-1930, the economy was starting to weaken. The first indications of the coming depression were seen in the increasing unemployment of the lower middle classes, a class into which the Wall Street banking firm of Childs, Jeffries & Co. had heavily invested. One of their strongest holdings was known as the *Chain Store Fund*, and according to the Smiths' main contact, Robert Heller, it "was a bank which we organized for the purpose of aiding small chains of stores not sufficiently large to warrant public financing. This corporation has approximately $3,000,000 at the present time, a

Courtesy Mariners' Museum, Newport News, Virginia

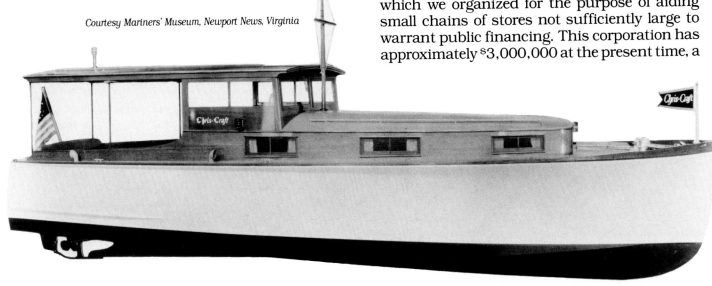

A 1932 36-foot Chris-Craft cruiser, a true cabin cruiser, showing the conversion of the saloon to a dinette. In the evenings, the two saloon seat backs would swing up to create double bunks port and starboard to accommodate a total of six overnight guests.

In June of 1935 the Hudson Motor Car Company demonstrated the strength of its steel roof by loading a Chris-Craft and two passengers on their stock Terraplane. The weight of the new 16-foot *level riding* runabout and passengers was 2,665 pounds.

large portion of which is in cash and is a very successful company."[17] Within their glowing literature, of chain stores they said, "In general, their history has been that their volume of business shrinks but little in hard times, and recovers rapidly in good times," and, "Chain stores...on account of their rapid turnover of merchandise, resist depressions admirably, which makes for stability of earnings on the common stock," and finally, "In hard times, the chain stores thrive especially well, because then the demand for low-priced articles always increases. In consequence, chain stores prosper when others fail."[18]

On June 3rd, Chris Smith & Sons Boat Co. announced their expansion programs, including the formation of a new corporation. Within their announcement, they suggested that theirs was, "another industry added to [the] depression-proof group," and that, "In noticeable contrast to the general hesitancy in current business activity, Chris-Craft plants are and have been running at capacity to meet the demand from record sales."[19] Within ninety days, the reality of the growing economic vortex would finally hit home.

The autumn of 1930 ushered in a chain of events which were to shock both the Smiths and the bankers. First, the third quarter audit of the boat company showed that sales had reached *less than two million dollars,* which surprised even themselves as they had announced eight months ago that New York Boat Show sales alone had been well over two million dollars. Next, Childs, Jeffries & Co. announced to the Smiths that they wouldn't be able to meet their commitments and purchase the stock. The Smiths had kept their part of the bargain, meeting every obligation in the transaction. The contract stipulated that if Childs, Jeffries & Co. defaulted on their part of the agreement, the Smiths could keep the $250,000 deposit. The banking firm quickly re-negotiated an extension for exercising their option to buy a third of the stock by November 1st, *1931,* nearly a year away. Meanwhile, the Smiths deposited the quarter million dollar bonanza into their Smith Investment Corporation, the family oraganization which controlled the Chris-Craft Corporation stock. The money, which as events over the next few years would prove, was to rescue the corporation from insolvency as the depression would plunge

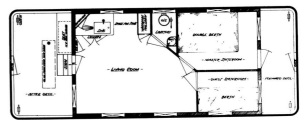

Courtesy Mariners' Museum, Newport News, Virginia

In 1936 Chris-Craft introduced a 30-foot *Houseboat* built of pine and white oak for only $1,590 without an engine. Buyers were encouraged to buy a $695 16-foot Utility Runabout as a combined tug and tender.

nearly the entire marine industry into a corporate and trademark graveyard.

On December 31st, 1930, two chilling statistics were disclosed which seemed ominously related. The American Federation of Labor estimated the nation's jobless population at 4.8 million, an increase of over 360,000 in the last month alone.[20] Chris-Craft Corporation discovered that during their final quarter, from September to end of December, they had *lost over $100,000*. Even the strong showing in the early part of the year worked out to evince a profit for the year of only $51,204. The year before, in 1929, they had netted over $308,000.[21]

At the 1931 New York Motor Boat Show, the new Chris-Craft Corporation unveiled an exciting new concept in family boating which was destined to change the shape of water recreation. The *cabin cruiser*. As one marine writer admitted, "The rich man's sport... transformed into the average man's recreation."[22]

During the past five years Chris-Craft has been planning, experimenting, building, testing, discarding. The goal they sought in addition to their runabout line was a capable, husky sort of boat, built for any kind of water or weather — a boat which would be a floating home for the family.

The problems were many — mechanical reliability and speed, roominess, completeness of equipment, safety, ability to provide comfortable travel under all weather conditions.

Against these problems the Smith family pitted the lessons learned from three generations of boat building. They built experimental cruisers — then took them out and lived on them for awhile, subjected motors and hulls to every conceivable test, found out just how seaworthy and staunch and comfortable they were.

Then they brought them back — modified designs here and there, changed mechanical specifications, added and altered equipment — until this new type of cruiser satisfied them all, from Chris Smith down to the youngest boy on the payroll.

These new cruisers, as they finally emerge from the Chris-Craft shops, fully justify the years of patient study and planning that have gone into them. They really usher in a new era in water transportation. They are big, rugged boats, but beautiful; they satisfy every requirement of speed and mechanical reliability; every square foot of space is packed with the little niceties of home convenience and luxury that would make Cleopatra (or any other woman) clap her hands with delight.

The Smiths of Algonac foresee a time when thousands of families who have vainly sought real recreation on crowded dusty pavements, will find it in a home afloat.[23]

With the very first scars of red ink slashed across the Chris-Craft ledgers, a long and precise series of financial studies began. Trend analysis, percentage estimates, inventory dis-

Among the rules along the assembly line in Algonac, Michigan was *No Spitting In The Boats*. Workers who chewed snuff created a safety hazard for others who would slip in the bilges.

Courtesy Mariners' Museum, Newport News, Virginia

section, departmental breakouts, budget evaluations and forecasts. Though this *get tough* introspection was exhaustive, the great unpredictable was the scale of the plummeting economy itself.

In a burst of bravado and their own unyielding marketing inertia, Chris-Craft introduced thirty-seven models for 1931, twenty-three of which would be enclosed models. Again, the New York Motor Boat Show was a bellwether of forgivable optimism. "Chris-Craft Corporation again out-sold every motor boat exhibitor during the eight days of the National Motor Boat Show.... Orders were received for 316 runabouts and cruisers — a total sales volume of $1,012,854. A large percentage of these were for immediate delivery — and all of them will be shipped by June....Significant...is the fact that an impressive share of Chris-Craft's total production is marketed by men who are also...selling automobiles...."[24] Always the innovator, Chris-Craft mounted a special peripheral exhibit during the show. The *Chris-Craft Salon* was established at the New York factory office to display eleven models that wouldn't fit into the Grand Central Palace. "This is believed to be the first time that a motor boat concern has ever held a private salon of its own simultaneously with the motor boat show itself."[25]

A distinction was first made in 1931 between runabouts and *custom runabouts,* and between Cruisers, *DeLuxe Models,* and *Custom Models.* Chris-Craft offered eleven runabouts, consisting of a 17-foot, 20-foot, two models of 22-foot, three models of 24-foot, and four versions of the 26-foot model, one of which was a convertible sedan. The aft section of the convertible folded *forward,* admitting sunshine in the second cockpit. The runabouts ranged in price from $1,295 for the 17-foot to $5,100 for the 26-foot convertible sedan, with speeds from 25 to 42 miles per hour.

Ten models of Custom Models included four 26-foot versions (two open, two sedans), five 28-foot models (two convertible sedans, two runabouts, one *All-Wood Sedan*), and a 30-foot runabout. The custom models were more luxurious, included real leather seats, additional bright work, other appointments and slightly faster speeds. Prices ranged from $4,450 for the 26-foot runabout to $6,500 for the 28-foot All-Wood Sedan, and speeds varied from 38-45 miles per hour.

Four models of the 31-foot Cruiser were offered, two single cabin models, and two double cabin models. While 70 horsepower was installed in all four, two models had reduction gears which added about four miles an hour to unprecedented *slow speeds* ranging from 12 to 18 miles per hour. Prices ranged from $3,975 for the Single Cabin Direct Drive to $5,170 for the Double Cabin Reduction Drive.

Nine DeLuxe Cruisers were on the menu, but only two lengths, 31-foot and 36-foot. Variations were single and double cabin layouts, and power. Speeds varied from 15 miles per hour for the 70-horsepower models to 33 miles per hour for the Chris-Craft 250-horsepower 36-foot Single Cabin model. Enclosed or open bridge variations could be ordered for any model.

The three Custom Models were the 34 and 38-foot Custom Commuter, and the all new 48-foot Custom Yacht. Quickest was the 34-foot Commuter with a pair of 225-horsepower Chris-Crafts at 40 miles per hour, while the Yacht could make 30 miles per hour with a pair of 250 Chris-Crafts thrumming beneath the cockpit sole.

The unusual design of this 1935 30-foot Cruiser suggests a hybrid between open cockpit runabout and cabin cruiser. Featuring a convertible saloon within the single cabin it offered the best of both worlds.

Courtesy Mariners' Museum, Newport News, Virginia

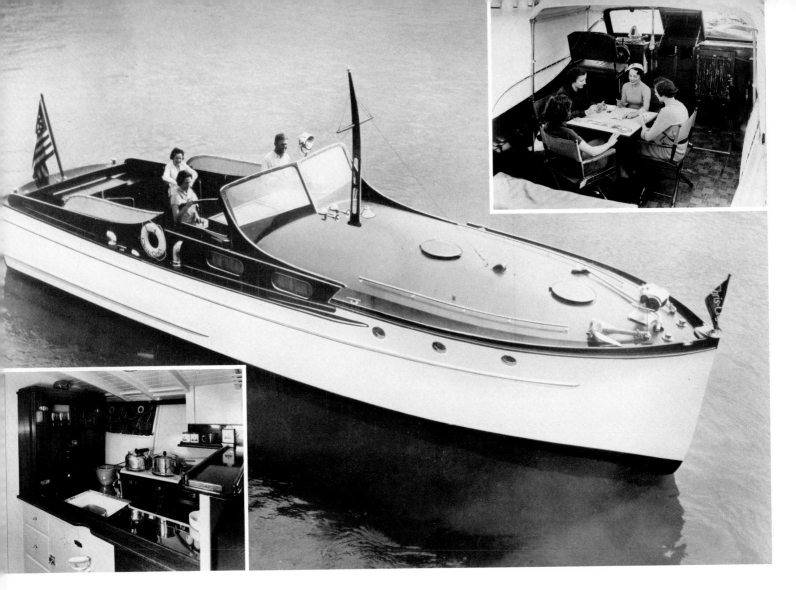

As sales began to fall behind quotas, Chris-Craft introduced what would prove to be their most popular model for the year, a tiny 15½-foot runabout which sold for just $795. The peppy little boat was powered by 43 horsepower, and could propel six adults to 30 miles per hour. Sales of the newcomer would in some months lead all other boats by ten to one. "We are extremely proud of this new runabout," Jay Smith said when it was announced; "It is the first time in the history of the motor boat industry that a manufacturer of quality motor boats has ever offered an over-sized, full-powered, genuine Philippine hardwood runabout for less than $950."[26]

Philippine *hardwood?* A controversy of great proportion had spread throughout the boat-building industry, and the worst fears at Chris-Craft were confirmed by scientists. *There is no such thing as Philippine Mahogany.* Chris-Craft's largest supplier, Indiana Quartered Oak Company of Long Island, importing from the highland plantations of the Philippine Islands, had to admit themselves, in a series of ads, that their product, actually Philippine *Indoako* wood, was "not botanically of the same species as Central and South American Mahoganies."[27]

Because of the suddenness of the disclosure, Indiana Quartered Oak Co. simply made up a name for their wood out of their own name, and this only focused more attention on the perceived deception. No deception was meant, for the Philippine product was demonstrably superior to the African, Central or South American competition in a number of ways. As the Insular Lumber Company, another importer, retorted, "...in addition to its resemblance to the botanical mahogany, it has the added virtues of greater strength and durability, greater freedom from splitting, lighter weight, minimum absorption of water, comparative immunity from the attacks of the teredo worm, freedom from stain at fastenings, and moderate cost."[28]

However, since it was nearly impossible to persuade the public against the popular term *Philippine Mahogany,* within two years of the beginning of the controversy in 1930, everyone was back to using the term again. It is somewhat disturbing, and often near life-threatening, to tell people that Chris-Craft never made a boat out of Philippine mahogany. If that doesn't start a fight, try telling people that the wood can actually scientifically be referred to as *bastard mahogany.*[29]

Previous page: *Climax,* a 1930 28-foot triple cockpit runabout owned by Pete and Jean Henkel of Harsens Island, Michigan. Shot from the same lighthouse near Algonac used by Chris-Craft for their early catalog photos.

Photo by Karine N. Rodengen

Right opposite: Elegant yachts were back in fashion by late thirties, and this 48-foot Chris-Craft Yacht was chtened by the Sydeman family in 1939. If equipped with a of G.M. 165-horsepower diesels, it retailed for $26,

Courtesy Mariners' Museum, Newport News, Virg

Sales began to grind to a near halt by the fall of 1931, and the ledgers ran red with the evidence of a disastrous year. Nearly two hundred thousand dollars would be lost, and a wide axe swung through the 74-acre facilities in Algonac. Among the casualties of this dark year would be sales manager Jack Clifford and production superintendent W. A. "Bill" MacKerer. Within four years, MacKerer would return, and Clifford would be drafted by Chris' old nemesis, Gar Wood.

In 1932, Chris-Craft finally had to admit that a special approach to the marketplace would have to be made in order to survive. In introducing their *Level Riding* fleet of runabouts, they said "…important to the individual is the fact that in this new fleet Chris-Craft gives you the full benefits of today's price possibilities."[30] Without modifying their hull designs, Chris-Craft cleverly deployed a strictly marketing modification to a *new* line of runabouts.

A level ride is a dry ride…it is a *safe* ride. The sensation is that of effortless flight *over* water instead of riding *through* it. …the new LEVEL RIDING principle has cut to a minimum water resistance and "stern drag" at high speeds. The new Chris-Craft develop more speed per horsepower and more speed per foot. Drivers and passengers have a clear, horizontal range of vision that is not possible when bows point up at an awkward angle. Yet at low speeds the bows of these boats ride well out of the water…an added factor in comfort and safety in heavy weather.[31]

The runabout fleet was cut from twenty-one models to twelve. The cruisers fared even worse. Chris-Craft quietly dropped the Custom Commuters and the 48-foot Yacht, and concentrated their efforts solely on the inexpensive 31 and 36-foot family cruisers. They addressed the men and the women differently in their approach to the cruiser market, again a Chris-Craft first. The ladies received the most attention in this article of the day.

The interiors have been designed to delight any woman. They are well planned, beautiful homes. Comfort is combined with charm. There are broad seats at each side of the cabins, deeply upholstered over box springs, which make them into divans by day. At night the backs of these seats swing up and are strapped securely to form comfortable upper berths. The stationary seats are quickly made up into comfortable beds.

As no woman likes crowded quarters, tables which seat six comfortably can be placed between the cabin seats.

There is no lack of household conveniences. The galleys with their dependable stoves, refrigerators, disappearing sinks, handy lockers for storing food and utensils, are most prac-

tical. A specially constructed shelf keeps china and glassware safe in all weathers. Preparation for a bridge luncheon or even a course dinner is a pleasure.

Each of these cruisers has a complete lavatory with toilet, wash bowl, medicine chest and mirror. Running water is provided to the lavatory and galley. The complete electric lighting system has been carefully planned and provides light wherever it is desired.

There is no lack of closet space. Room has been provided to hang clothing and store linen and bedding as neatly and as conveniently as at home.[32]

As early as March, further storm warnings appeared on Jay Smith's desk, this time in a letter from his own accounting staff. "It is almost unnecessary to remark that no matter what savings may be made in manufacturing costs or commercial expenses, we cannot hope to carry our present plant and its minimum required overheads with such a low sales volume."[33]

While sales continued to reflect the deepening reality of over eleven million jobless American workers, an ingenious new approach was quietly rolled out by Chris-Craft. The *Utility* boat. In September of 1932, the 24-foot Utility model was introduced, actually a very stripped-down version of the 24-foot runabout. "Except for forward and aft decks, the cockpit is open, and is finished in all mahogany planking and trim," the announcement said. "Only one built-in seat is provided — for the driver. The motor — 85 h.p. with a speed of 30 miles, or 125 h.p. with a speed of 35 miles — is under a permanent housing which provides added seating accommodations. This new model is particularly well adapted for fishing, cargo carrying and harbor work..."[34]

opposite and above: The 1930 28-foot triple-cockpit runabout ax, piloted by Pete Henkel, shows her championship form e St. Clair Flats near Algonac, Michigan

s by Karine N. Rodengen

Photo by Karine N. Rodengen

Attention to details has always been a Chris-Craft obsession. Here, a unique gas filler cap masquerades as a deck cleat.

Actually the Utility boat was merely a very clever way of drastically reducing the cost of the runabout so that it would be within the means of an increasingly bankrupt world. By naming it the Utility, they carefully avoided any pretense of trying to push the price of a *runabout* down. In the years to come, this practical utility boat concept would be extended to cruisers as well.

Losses for 1932 would mount to $263,730. Their reserves were down to only $350,000, $250,000 of which had been received as a result of the Childs, Jeffries & Co. stock deposit forfeiture. Chris-Craft cut their advertising budget to *zero*, along with their catalog, direct mail, show expense, photo and art budgets. Even the Christmas campaign was scrapped.[35] At this point you could buy a brand new Chevrolet, complete, for $475.[36]

In 1933 the shrinking fleet was reduced even further to five sizes of runabouts and the two cruisers, for a total of just *fourteen models.* Sales continued to drop. With an energetic new president, Franklin D. Roosevelt, promising America a *New Deal,* Chris-Craft was making some remarkable deals of their own. Any form of inventory went up for sale; even the old stock of Curtiss OX-5 engines went for sale at ten dollars apiece.[37] It was all to no avail, as by the end of the fiscal year they had lost another $252,281, losing an incredible $73,594 in July alone. Though Roosevelt would appeal for dignity, "the only thing we have to fear is fear itself," it was Chris-Craft's darkest hour. The Smith Investment Corporation, owners of the Chris-Craft stock, was forced to merge with Chris-Craft Corporation to make available the $250,000 forfeited stock deposit funds.[38] Were it not for the Childs, Jeffries & Co. deposit, Chris-Craft more than likely would have closed its doors by Christmas of 1934, denying millions of boating enthusiasts for generations to come, the pleasure and adventure of the countless boating and recreation innovations yet to be discovered.

In 1934, Chris-Craft would extend the utility concept to 18 and 21-foot runabout models, and add their first cruisers to the fleet in two years, one of which was a 24-foot utility cruiser. Using the hull of a newly-designed 24-foot cruiser, the utility version offered no above-deck enclosure, while still providing sleeping accommodations forward for two in what in later years might be referred to as a cuddy cabin. The barest of accoutrements shaved the price of this 21-mile-per-hour cruiser to only $1,390 complete.

The 24-foot cruiser, with living and sleeping accommodations for four, was available at only $1,590, while the new 30-foot, double stateroom forward cruiser could be your *Summer Home Afloat* for only $2,290, F.O.B. Algonac.

The strategy worked, for while the year still showed a deficit, it was much smaller, and some months even showed a modest profit. Chris-Craft was on the mend.

This tentative optimism continued into 1935, as Chris-Craft introduced new, *moderately-priced* cruisers and more utility products. Three versions of a new 25-foot Utility Cruiser, two versions of a new 25-foot Family Cruiser, and four versions of the new Double Stateroom Cruiser were announced, ranging in price from $1,345 to $3,240. Cruiser power was offered from Chris-Craft's own new 55-horsepower engine to the Chrysler 92-horsepower units. Twenty-two models of runabouts filled out the fleet, from 16-foot to 27-foot in seven size ranges. Prices were advertised from $595 for a 16-foot utility with a Chris-Craft engine to $4,950 for the 27-foot powered with a 250-horsepower Chris-Craft V-8. Jay Smith and his team of engineers were now manufacturing three models of Chris-Craft engines, including economical four-cylinder 45 and 55-horsepower versions.

In addition to the *Streamline Cruisers*, in 25 and 30-foot lengths, in February Chris-Craft announced their new 38-foot *Individualized Cruisers*. This unique concept allowed a wide margin of owner decisions in configuration and layout. Compared, even by Chris-Craft, to a battleship, the sturdy, often twin-engined boats, featured double planked bottoms, double planked decks, transverse framing said to be 30% stronger, forced ventilation and soundproofing.[39]

The mood of the country was changing, and Chris-Craft was one of America's corporations that consistently presented a positive attitude. During 1935 Chris-Craft introduced a new 16-foot, double cockpit forward of the engine model. It was a bit of a tight fit for six adults, but Chris-Craft turned it into an advantage. They staged a national contest for "submitting the best name or phrase descriptive of the double cockpit feature...." The winner would receive a brand new 16-footer for himself. Out of 11,732 enthusiastic entries, the winner was, "Ride gaily through the spray; the chummy Chris-Craft way."[40]

Sales began to increase substantially during 1935, so that by fall Jay Smith announced that "Sales of Chris-Craft motor boats in September were the largest in the corporation's entire history."[41] The statistics, along with the return to the executive staff of W.A. "Bill" MacKerer, were a great boost to morale.

In October, Jay would announce that, "Chris-Craft October sales showed a gain of 360 percent over October, 1934, and 47 percent over the corresponding month of 1929, the corporation's peak year." Jay was able to sum up the struggle of Chris-Craft during the depression in an interview with *Motor Boating*.

> Our business has been on the up grade consistently since September, 1934. This is due, we believe, to the improvement in general business conditions and the increased effort which we have been putting into every phase of our business for more than 18 months.
>
> We are firm believers in hard work and are always open to new ideas. We've taken the opportunity offered by the depression to do additional research work, experimenting, testing...to improve our products wherever possible. The

Courtesy Mariners' Museum, Newport News, Virginia

The highly practical Utility runabouts were born of necessity, reducing the cost of boats in a depressed economy. Left: A 1938 17-foot Deluxe Utility. Above: A 1934 21-foot Standard Utility.

public is quick to recognize quality. They have taken readily to our new models and have made it possible for us to receive a substantial return on our depression investment. Naturally we are gratified at the results.

I don't remember a year in all my experience in the motor boat industry when we have had so many popular models in our line. From the amount of business coming in, the inquiries and interest displayed, it seems more like Spring than Fall in our plant. Last Summer when we enlarged our Cruiser facilities and built a new Engineering Building, we felt that our rush would be only temporary. As it is, we need every foot of available space and by the looks of things, we'll be planning on further additions before the Winter is over."[42]

Chris-Craft had weathered the storm. In 1936 a quiet celebration must have ensued in Algonac, as the Chris-Craft Corporation was to make a $213,131.71 *profit* by the close of their fiscal year. Chris-Craft leapt back into the fold with a passion. No less than 66 models of boats were offered during the year, including names which would remain with the Chris-Craft fleet for decades, like *Clipper, Conqueror, Sportsman* and *Sea Skiff.*

Among the more interesting innovations for 1936 was the introduction of a 30-foot Chris-Craft *Houseboat.* Built without an engine, the purchaser was encouraged to buy a $695 16-foot utility runabout to tow his new home, and then use the inexpensive tug for, "commuting, shopping, fishing, swimming, and other sport pursuits."[43] The boat was built with 2-inch yellow pine bottom and side planking, 2 by 8-inch yellow pine keelsons and white oak chines of the same dimensions. Side frames were 2 by 4-inch white oak and deck frames 2 by 8-inch yellow pine, all covered with a canvas roof. The *very* inexpensive construction explains the $1,590 price tag, and also why none of these houseboats are known to have survived. The living room of the floating home was eleven by thirteen feet, making a combination living, dining room and galley. Master and guest bedrooms rounded out the arrangement, in which six adults could live comfortably all summer long.[44]

Though in later years Sea Skiff would come to mean Chris-Craft's lapstrake line of cruisers, in 1936 it was introduced as the new 23½-foot cruiser, in a big, round, powerful-looking boat with greater than usual freeboard. The Clipper was a 24-foot by 8-foot beam cruiser with spartan accommodations yet unique styling which sold for a mere $1,270. The Conqueror made its debut as a 31-foot by 10-foot beam, husky cruiser

Courtesy Mariners' Museum, Newport News, Virginia
Introduced in late 1939, the 16-foot Racing Runabout, Model 22, powered with a 121-horsepower engine would deliver up to 44 mph for $1,540.

with two staterooms, accommodations for six, and propelled by the new 55-h.p. Chris-Craft four-cylinder engine, among other power options. The Sportsman, at 24 feet, was a clever cross between custom runabout and utility runabout which offered a large, open area behind the engine, and a route from front seat through the second cockpit to the stern so that runabout passengers for the first time wouldn't have to master the high hurdles moving forward to aft. Available with an optional cabin, it was also the first Chris-Craft runabout that would accept a *pair* of 55 or 85-horsepower Chris-Craft engines, though most were equipped with single engines from 85 to 212 horsepower. Also new was a sporty 16-foot, single cockpit, red, white and blue raceboat powered by a Chris-Craft 6-cylinder 85-horsepower engine to speeds of 40 miles per hour.

Among the heralded innovations introduced in 1936 was the *dinette.* Many of the new cruiser models offered this unique concept, which, "... is always available to dine, play bridge or just to sit at and talk with or without refreshments...

This dinette furniture is situated in such a position as to height, that one sitting in it can get good vision out the cabin windows. Still another advantage is that the table can be used for a meal without the necessity of having to clean up immediately and stow the table away before the cabin or aft cockpit can be used."[45]

Business improved to such an extent that Chris-Craft raised the wages of all Chris-Craft employees by five percent in June. In the same announcement, it was learned that "More than 800 employees, the largest total in the corporation's history, are affected by the new wage rates. Sales of Chris-Craft motor boats and marine engines for the current year have surpassed all

previous records excluding 1929. The company is working six days a week and reports a large bank of unfilled orders."[46]

In November, Chris-Craft once again began year 'round production. Jay Smith described the benefits of the accomplishment.

> Continuous production has been the aim of the industry for many years. It is a sound, economic principle with a three-fold purpose. It helps the worker, the builder, and the buyer.
>
> We have been working for many years towards this goal. We believe we have laid a very solid foundation and that the growth of our business warrants taking this important step. During the last eight months, our sales of boats exceeded that of the entire year of 1935. Dollar volume for the eight month period was 60 percent greater than that of the corresponding period last year. Fall business on hand constitutes the largest bank of orders in the history of our company.
>
> Cost records show that by continuous operation, we can make a further saving. This we are passing along in the form of a 10 percent reduction from all list prices, to those who purchase their boats in the Fall. With this extra incentive for Fall delivery and an entire new line of boats embodying many innovations in design, styling, construction and equiment, we feel confident the results will justify our action.[47]

His actions were indeed justified, for when the 10 percent reduction for fall orders incentive program began, orders for the new 1937 models flooded Chris-Craft headquarters. An unprecedented ninety-seven models were offered. More hybrids of existing models were introduced, including what was seemingly a contradiction in terms, a *DeLuxe Utility*. When a boat like the 17-foot Utility becomes a DeLuxe Utility, it then includes a folding windshield, chromium plated cutwater, upholstered lazy backs, paneled cockpits, among a number of other refinements. The 21-foot DeLuxe Utility even offered a streamline cabin enclosure and was available for only $1395, just $200 more than the open model.

For the first time, Chris-Craft offered a *Fishing Cruiser* in 1937, the forerunner of modern sport fishing boats. The 25-foot semi-enclosed cruiser was designed with a large aft cockpit, "the floor of which is mounted in rubber, insulated against motor noises and covered with linoleum. There is ample room for casting and three life preserver cushions form a seat for trolling."[48]

Chris-Craft ventured back into larger boats in '37, with the announcement of a series of 40-foot

This beautiful 1939 24′9″ Deluxe Utility, *Molly-O*, one of only seven made, was originally built for owner Arthur N. Armstrong, Jr.'s grandfather. It features a rear steering bar and live bait well. Taken in the shallows of the St. Clair River Flats.

Photo by Karine N. Rodengen

Courtesy Mariners' Museum, Newport News, Virginia

The 1939 19-foot Sportsman was perfect for the new sport of aquaplaning. Note the unusual rear-facing aft cockpit seat, along with jump seats on either side of the engine box.

yachts. *Streamlining* was in vogue, and the double cabin enclosed bridge models, and double stateroom models would carry a sleek but hefty design to 23 miles per hour, depending on power selection.

The overall fleet showed a greater balance and distribution among models, as America slowly recovered from the depression. Prices, however, still remained low, with utility boats starting at $895 and up, runabouts from $1,150, race boats from $1,450, and cruisers starting at $1,495. For the first time, cruiser ads would entice readers to *Command A Chris-Craft*.

Something else occurred for the first time in Chris-Craft's history during the early months of 1937. Labor unrest, followed by a strike, began on March 13th curtailing production 25% due to "labor agitation and unrest." One week later, on March 20th, the situation had deteriorated to such an extent that it became necessary to close the plants completely, putting six hundred Chris-Craft workers out of work. However, the agitation was begun by a small minority of workers and organizers of the United Auto Workers Union who wished the Chris-Craft workers to become affiliated. Four hundred fifty of the six hundred workers petitioned management, indicating satisfaction with Chris-Craft, and requesting that they be allowed back to work.[49]

This issue, not surprisingly, was wages. Chris-Craft told the strikers they could have a five percent increase in wages on April 1st if they went back to work, followed by an additional five percent a month later on May 1st. By today's standards, an immediate guarantee of a ten percent increase in wages would be enthusiastically accepted. It must be remembered that in 1937, with American production wages running between thirty-five cents and forty cents an hour, ten percent worked out to less than four cents an hour for many employees; less than eight dollars a month.

Harsen Smith, 29, now a very active and capable vice-president, and Bill MacKerer representing management, encouraged the four hundred fifty workers to form their own *shop union*, as they clearly represented a plurality of the work force. But the agitators began to go to extremes. "The [outside union] brought down a bunch of colored guys...they closed the plant and we didn't want to be closed."[50] One day, as tension built to the breaking point, the organizers had "goon squads from Port Huron" above and below the plant at the entrances. They would forbid entrance to a group of workers, sending them to the other entrance where they would be sent back to the first, until the workers would give up. Adding to the confusion was a sound truck, used by the agitators with abandon, stirring up emotions, until the workers got together and decided to take the organizers, "them and the sound truck and throw the whole works in the river."[51] They started to march toward the truck when Bill MacKerer came out and stopped them, saying "Don't worry about it."

An ominous silence permeated the seventy-four acre production facilities, as the strike continued. When Chris-Craft's lines would normally be buzzing with activity, a dream-like, tranquilized quiet replaced the stock chasers, bottom plankers, trim carpenters, mill workers, and an orchestra of electric drills and screwdrivers. When the response to management's offer came back almost three weeks later, it was the United Auto Workers who responded with an offer of their own. Thirty-five demands were listed, including recognition of U.A.W. worker representation, a reduction of weekly work hours from forty-eight to forty-four hours, an across the board minimum wage of fifty cents, and a five cent an hour raise for all employees. Chris-Craft, with a steadily increasing backlog of orders, acquiesced to the union demands, and W.A. "Bill" MacKerer signed the agreement for management, countersigned by five members of the United Auto Workers, local 276. Relations between the front office and the rank and file workers would never be the same again.

A small press release appeared in the April, 1937 *Motor Boating*, whereas the industry never seemed to be aware of the problem. "The Chris-Craft Corporation, Algonac, Michigan, has announced a general wage increase of 5% for all employees working on hourly rates, with an additional 5% to take effect April 1. The new rates will apply to more than 700 workers. Increases in hourly rates for the 12-month period ending April 1, 1937, total 30 percent, according to Jay W. Smith, president."[52]

The Smiths felt slighted by this seeming affront to a long-standing relationship with the work force, predominantly from Algonac and Marine City. Through good times and bad, they would privately argue, Chris-Craft had kept its doors open to workers willing to work, providing wages and security for hundreds and hundreds of families. "They cussed it," a worker who was running the center trim shop during the strike remembered, "I was in the Ford garage one time and Owen [Smith] was in there. He said 'Do you realize how much money we're dumping into this damn little burg here?'"[53]

The strike and negotiations held a very personal character for the family, causing the already quiet group to withdraw even more, a subtle, but further alienation from their own community.

Once the concept of a successful strike was experienced by the work force, in future years it would become a useful tool for less than idealistic principles. "They would always strike in the spring so the farmers in Marine City could get their crops out," a worker observed; "They wanted the time off to go to the farm."[54]

The Chris-Craft family of engines blossomed throughout the decade of the thirties to such an extent that engines were advertised and sold independent of the boats. The engines were very dependable and were held in high regard by owners. By 1937 the line contained twelve engines divided into three basic categories of four-cylinder, six-cylinder and eight-cylinder engines. The four-cylinder engines ranged from 45 to 55-horsepower, direct and gear reduction models, while the six-cylinder engines contained models of 85, 95, 110, 125 and 130 horsepower. The V-8's were available in two basic models, the 275 and 350-horsepower versions, although a number of intermediate sizes were built throughout the decade.

Chris-Craft exploded into the marketplace in 1938 with no fewer than 105 models of boats, far more than any other manufacturer in marine history. Quite possibly the first active proponent of *niche marketing,* their rifle approach to specific markets, and their shotgun approach to value, paid good dividends both to consumers and to the Smith family. Over the preceding nine

months, the Smiths quietly paid themselves over fourteen dollars per share in dividends.[55]

In the new Cruisers, particular stress has been placed on heavier hull construction, beam and freeboard have been generously added, beauty has been enhanced with smooth flowing lines, and marked improvements have been made in the way of added comfort and more convenience for those who live afloat....

New to the fleet is the 1938, 19-foot Chris-Craft Sportsman, an innovation in small craft design. Seating accommodations are provided for eight persons in three separate cockpits — an unusual feature. The aft cockpit, facing the stern, is an innovation that will be especially popular with fishing, aquaplaning, or camera fans....

Characterized by low racy lines, the 1938 Chris-Craft Runabout fleet is faster and smoother than ever before. Planking is narrower and thicker, transoms are more rounded, and all main side and bottom frames are joined by an overlapping knee, and bolted through the chine. Banjo type steering wheels have been made standard equipment on all models of 19-feet and over....

To meet the demand for fast fishing boats with a high degree of practicability and seaworthiness, Chris-Craft announces for 1938 a 24-foot Utility Cruiser and a 25-foot Semi-Enclosed Cruiser. The Utility Cruiser is a completely new boat particularly equipped for salt water. It has canvas decks and a minimum amount of mahogany bright work....

Sleek lines and pleasing cabin contours are features of the 1938 Chris-Craft cruisers. Cruisers are available in sizes from 25 to 40-feet with wide options of cabin arrangements and power plants. New color schemes, streamlined masts, vee type windshields and general streamlining lend a new ultra-modern appearance....

For 1938, Chris-Craft is building the most luxurious and desirable 40-foot Cruiser Yachts ever offered. They are offered in Double Stateroom, Double Stateroom Enclosed Bridge, or Double Cabin Enclosed Bridge types, and feature the latest in streamline designs.... The Double Stateroom Cruiser is particularly adaptable for fishing and may be equipped with harpoon pulpit, crow's nest, fishing chairs, bait boxes, etc.[56]

Late in the year, Chris-Craft surprised the marine industry by announcing a new series of yachts which would include models up to *fifty-five feet.* "Immediate plans call for the production of motor yachts in both 48 and 55-foot lengths, on a line production basis," Jay Smith announced. "Present plans call for the produc-

CHRISTOPHER COLUMBUS SMITH
1861-1939

tion of from 25 to 35 motor yachts in various hull lengths, up to 55 feet overall during the next 12 months."[57]

The great confidence of the Smiths was shown by the introduction of 115 models for 1939. The books for the close of 1938 showed the earned surplus for the Corporation had topped a million dollars for the first time, adding over $127,000 in

profits during the year, even though a full month was lost to the strike.

A sixth division was added to the line-up: *Motor Yachts* now joined the Utility, Runabout, Sport Runabout, Utility Cruiser and Cruiser divisions.

New for '39 were three sport runabouts of 19, 24 and 29-feet, along with a 29-foot Sportsman model. Additions to the cruiser line included three 29-footers, in enclosed, single-cabin or sport flying bridge versions, and three 41-foot models in double stateroom, double cabin and express types. The express cruiser; "...is designed for commuting where speed is an essential factor," and depending on power selected would go as fast as 33 miles per hour.[58]

It was no secret that Chris-Craft was looking in other cities to build additional manufacturing facilities, because of the near saturation of production and work forces in the Algonac and Marine City area. In September, "Rumors concerning a new Chris-Craft factory to be erected at Holland, Michigan, were confirmed by the purchase of 22 acres of land." Jay Smith would say, "The proposed new building will substantially increase present production facilities as well as absorb extra peak manufacturing loads."[59] Actually, a $300,000, 600-foot by 110-foot building was already under construction, and was, "believed to be the world's largest line production factory under one roof."[60] Jay and Harsen would see that the new facility was on-line by the end of November, which is quite remarkable by itself. To provide for the volume construction of boats from 15½-feet to 42-feet in a new structure within four months of ground breaking is testimony to the powerful administrative abilities of the Smith family.

The decade, though, would end on a sad note, with the death of Christopher Columbus Smith. To the end, Chris maintained jovial and good-natured spirits, even managing a joke as he went through the gates of the Chris-Craft plant for what was to be the final time. A man who spent a great deal of time with Chris in the boiler room during these years describes the founder's last day at work.

I went to work one morning and 'ol Chris was sitting on a nail keg out in front of the boilers. I said something, and when I got down...Jesus Christ he was all rugged. Blood all over his shirt from a nose bleed. I said "Did you call anybody?" He said "No, don't, it will stop." I told him I was going into the mill to punch in. I went inside and called Jay and Bernard, who came right away.

They loaded him in the car, and they were on their way out to the highway, when they came

backing up all the way to the boiler room and blew the horn. I went out and Chris said "Luke, keep a damn good head of steam," he said, "Where I'm going I don't want to freeze." And they all started to laugh.[61]

The bleeding didn't stop. Jay, Bernard, Owen and possibly Harsen, among others, gave blood for transfusions. Three generations of Smith blood, mixed together in the vessel from whence it had all begun, was to no avail. After nearly two weeks at St. Joseph's Hospital in Mt. Clemens, at 8:30 p.m. on Saturday, the ninth of September, 1939, he succumbed to the illness which had begun to afflict him seven years before. Perhaps over half a century of heavy cigar smoking led to the ulcers which came to line his nasal passages; perhaps no one will ever know. But of his contributions to the motorboat industry, no one shall ever forget.

Years and years ago, when every Sunday afternoon there was a boat excursion on the St. Clair River to Algonac and back for thirty cents, I would occasionally drop down there and talk to my friend Chris Smith, who conducted a little boathouse on the north channel. Chris was even then trying out motor boats and one day, while a number of us were standing around looking over a new and neat little craft built by him, he remarked: "Some day you'll see a motor boat go over fifty miles an hour!" We hid our smiles and chuckled to ourselves about "poor old Chris." In our opinion, he was just a bit cracked about boats. How could a boat go that fast in the water? Why, it couldn't even be done on land, except by the Empire State express train. Well, the other day Chris Smith died, the Henry Ford of the speedboat world. He had made his wildest dreams come true and lived long enough to laugh at all of us time and time again. In the boating world his name became the guarantee for the best and fastest there is the world over. He built a great boat manufacturing plant, giving employment to hundreds of his fellow townsmen, and made the name of the little village of Algonac known in every corner of the globe. He was one of those rugged, honest, industrious and kindly individuals, who didn't work by the clock and who have helped to make America the greatest of all nations and the best place in the world to live.

Anonymous[20]

Top: Grand Central Station for Chris-Craft's railroad was the shipping and receiving docks
of the Algonac, Michigan factory. Below: Chris-Craft's hard-working thirty-five ton
Plymouth locomotive was dubbed the Toonerville Trolly by local residents.

CHAPTER XI
The Chris-Craft Railroad

Railway termini...are our gates to the glorious and the unknown. Through them we pass out into adventure and sunshine, to them, alas! we return.

Edward Morgan Forster
Howards End, 1910

FEW PEOPLE ARE AWARE that Chris-Craft operated their own railroad for nearly thirty years.[1]

Near the turn of the century, the Detroit United Railway, an electric marvel of the time, was installed from Detroit, through Algonac to Port Huron, bringing a welcome flood of commerce and visitors to the region. "The noisy, clanging electric railroad cars zipped from [Algonac] to Detroit in a little over two hours time."[2]

The vast majority of Chris Smith & Sons boats were placed in box cars or on flat cars from their railroad siding at the Algonac facility, and shipped around the country. The Smiths also received their mahogany, teak, glass, chain, anchors, coal for the boilers, and all other construction and raw materials by rail. But then the Detroit United Railway, DUR, fell victim to the nation's plunging economy in late 1929, and the Smiths were faced with a terrible dilemma. In the absence of a rail system, shipments and deliveries would have to be made by truck, as the St. Lawrence Seaway wouldn't be in existence for another quarter century. Roads in these days were in deplorable condition, limiting truck travel to slow speeds and often violent pitching, pounding and bouncing stretches of dirt roads.

Jay Smith acted quickly to negotiate for the purchase of the approximately seven and a half miles of tracks which ran from the Chris Smith & Sons Algonac plant to Marine City, where the Port Huron and Detroit Railroad, PH&DR, could provide the needed link to the outside world. Jay secured the right of way and rails, including poles and fixtures (less the valuable copper transmission wire) for $20,144, and an additional $7,744 for the spur which connected the Algonac plant to the main line.[3] In May of 1930 Jay purchased a 25-ton Plymouth locomotive, model ML6, Type 3 with air brakes, for $9,950. The Smiths already owned a small, 15-ton gasoline switching engine for use within the plant spur.

In June of 1930, the first month that books were kept, the balance sheet showed the *Jay Smith Railroad* had made a net profit of $274, with shipping revenues of $1,000. It was a trend which would continue almost without exception for the next twenty-seven years. Not only did the Smiths secure the only possible rail link between

A 1937 35-foot Double Stateroom Cruiser with special front cockpit is being prepared for shipment. Once secured to its cradle, the tarpaulin, seen rolled in front, would be lashed tightly over the boat for all-weather transport.

Algonac and the rest of the country, but they would do so *profitably.*

On November 12, 1930, the *Algonac Transit Company* was incorporated, issuing 250 shares of stock at a par value of $100, for a total of $25,000. The stock was divided between Jay W. Smith (84 shares), Bernard T. Smith (83 shares) and Owen N. Smith (83 shares). The Algonac Transit Company, which appeared on the general ledger of the Chris-Craft Corporation beginning in 1930, was established as a *private carrier,* and as such was restricted to the conveyance of products and materials solely for the Chris-Craft Corporation. It was impossible, however, for the Smiths to refuse the many requests for service from other stranded organizations, and so they hauled freight for a handful of companies ranging from privileged family members to Morton Salt. Business became noticeably brisk, and in March of 1941, the Interstate Commerce Commission had to issue a stern warning.

Investigation conducted recently by this bureau has disclosed that the Algonac Transit Company, although chartered as a private carrier, actually is engaging in the transportation of property in interstate commerce, for hire, for shippers other than its parent company, the Chris-Craft Corporation, and holds itself out as ready and willing to transport, for hire, for anyone who may tender goods to it.[4]

Chris-Craft suspended shipments for their other customers, but found that by charging themselves the same, $10 per car, one-way fee, they were still showing a profit for the railroad. Later, during World War II in 1943, the Interstate Commerce Commission rescinded their order, allowing the Smiths to increase their shipping revenues again. By this time the Algonac Transit Company was so busy shipping products for defense, that they often shipped twenty-four hours a day, and weren't particularly concerned with outside freight contracting.

From Chris-Craft, the Algonac Transit Company rails passed right down the mid Michigan Avenue in Algonac, Michigan, scattering city traffic en route to Marine seven and one-half miles down the tracks. Smith ingenuity provided Chris-Craf nearly one-half million rail-miles of shippin

The Algonac Transit Company tracks went right through the center of town, down the middle lane of Michigan Street, which gave the Smith operation the affectionate moniker of *Toonerville Trolley, Doodlebug Trolley* and *Chris-Craft Railroad.*[5]

At least twice a day, automobiles and pedestrians dodged the northbound cars laden with boats under canvas covers which read, *"Another Chris-Craft Boat."* The engineers and brakemen for the line became adept maintenance artists, and on many occasions mastered the art of getting the cars and engine back on the tracks after becoming derailed from ice build-up in the winter months. The train passed through a heavily-wooded section on the north end of town which is now a magnificent State Park, and afforded at least one brakeman a unique challenge.

> [He] was quite a hunter. He'd shoot squirrels and rabbits off the front of the engine on the way to Marine City, out through the back of the State Park with a sling shot. It was not uncommon for him to come back with rabbits or pheasants or stuff on the engine.[6]

On a hot summer day, it wasn't unusual to see the train stop at a bar just outside of town, and see an ice cold pitcher of beer get handed up to the men in the locomotive.

A 35-ton locomotive, which was acquired to increase capacity, could pull eight cars, but often they had to move a dozen or more cars, so the 25-ton engine would be attached to the rear to push. When boat production was busiest, Chris-Craft needed a 44-foot boxcar of mahogany *per day*, stacked floor to ceiling, and at least another car full of accessories of all descriptions.

Several times, boats were nearly destroyed by rail shipments. Four runabouts could be stacked on cradles inside special boxcars which had *ends* which would open. These shipments were quite safe, though on occasion a boat could get loose. Boats shipped on open flatcars were much more exposed, and at least once, a boat too large for a particular route met an embarrassing fate. It was a boat specially prepared for display at the New York Boat Show, something like a 40-foot cruiser. It was magnificent, had special paint, special varnish, a real *show boat*. The boat was expertly cradled and secured on the flatcar, and the canvas cover was carefully lashed over the gleaming Chris-Craft. Somewhere between Detroit and New York, a switchman put the Chris-Craft car on a route which took it under a low bridge, and the *entire cabin* of the boat was sheared off in one mahogany-crunching moment.[7] Normally, all models of Chris-Craft could be shipped safely, up to model lengths of nearly fifty feet.

In September of 1957, the Algonac Transit Company was sold, retaining an earned surplus for Chris-Craft Corporation of nearly a quarter million dollars in profits. Chris-Craft, with a shrewdness worthy of Christopher Columbus Smith, had shipped its boats for nearly thirty years from Algonac to Marine City, accumulating nearly a half million miles of rail shipments in both directions, *for free.*

CHAPTER XII

The Girls of Chris-Craft

A girl never really looks as well as she does on board a steamship, or even a yacht.

Anita Loos
Gentlemen Prefer Blondes

THERE'S A WHOLESOME and refreshing air about her. Hundreds of Chris-Craft girls have adorned the decks and bridges of the world's largest fleet of boats. Since the 1920's, they have helped to stir the imaginations of millions of sailors, both real and imaginary, through the pages of the brochures, catalogs and magazines where Chris-Craft products have been displayed. Though she may range in age from 3 to 93, she is urgently alive, blushing with health, and has been a role model for five generations of youthful America.

She has spent untold thousands of hours smiling from the portholes of displays, cheerfully escorting visitors aboard earthbound models at trade shows and fairs, and has effervesced with buoyant courage, swimsuit-clad in the Algonac winter, to help announce the new model year.

She has also been the tireless hostess to millions of guests aboard her husband's vessels, across the unending miles of Chris-Craft waterways, from slips to seas. She has brightened the twilight salon, and warmed the cool evenings. She is a Chris-Craft girl.

Men scramble aboard Chris-Craft landing craft prior to a battle in the war for control of the Pacific.
The landing craft pictured are Chris-Craft LCPR, Landing Craft Personnel Ramp. Chris Craft would
manufacture more than 12,000 craft for the Armed Services between 1942 and 1945.

CHAPTER XIII

The Forties

In this extreme crisis which we all face today, that danger is not to the other party alone, it is ours individually and collectively. Unless we meet this crisis successfully, we may look for no more favorable treatment than is now being accorded the unfortunate people of the conquered countries of Europe.

Opinion of the Court
Chris-Craft labor dispute, November 4, 1941[1]

ONCE AGAIN, Chris-Craft would enter a new decade ablaze with enthusiasm and confidence, their victory over the anguish and near-fatal depression decisive and complete. Again, too, would events unfold to alter the character of their purpose, and the shape of their product. Newspaper headlines stalked the advances of Hitler's armies across a terrified and wounded Europe. German seizures of Czechoslovakia and Poland had outraged the sensibilities of the free world, climaxing in declarations of war by England and France.

America had other, fresh distractions like nylon, cellophane and television to explore. The economy had recovered, and America was spending money again, freely and unabashedly. The rapidly widening morass in Europe was on everyone's mind, but as a nation, we were reassured by President Roosevelt of our resolute neutrality.

Chris-Craft introduced 98 models of boats in 1940, including sixteen Utility Runabouts, four- teen Runabouts, sixteen Express Cruisers, forty-seven Cruisers, and five models of Motor Yachts. Utility Runabouts ranged from the 15½-foot, 60-h.p. model at $845 to a 29-foot Custom Sportsman with twin 130-h.p. engines at $5,590. Runabouts could be had for as little as $895 for the 15½-foot 60-h.p. model, to $6,290 for the 27-foot, 350-h.p. racing runabout, guaranteed to deliver over fifty miles per hour. Express Cruisers included models from the 95-h.p. 25-foot at $2,690 to a 34-foot, twin Chris-Craft 160-h.p. Express with deluxe navy top for $7,790.

By far the largest group of graduates in the class of 1940 were the cruisers. Though only six basic lengths (25, 30, 33, 37, 42 and 48-feet), variations and options swelled their numbers to forty-seven models ranging from the 25-foot, 60-h.p. model at $1,495 to the 48-foot, twin 165-h.p. G.M. *diesel* model at $26,800. Motor Yachts, which were only available in the 55-foot length, ranged from the twin Chris-Craft 130-h.p. version at $28,300 to the twin 165-h.p. G.M. diesel model at $37,500. The 55-foot Motor Yachts were the first boats that Chris-Craft couldn't ship by rail, due to bridge clearances, and so had to be either shipped aboard steamship or owners could *driveaway*, as Chris-Craft termed their cash and carry, f.o.b. Algonac option, which was exercised by a great many buyers of all cruiser models.

Business had never been better. 1940 sales surpassed, for the first time, the brilliant performances of 1929 as Chris-Craft tallied over $3,665,000 for the year. It has taken an entire decade of sweat and innovation to move sales to a new frontier, and plans were made for sustained and continued growth. An absolutely new market was opening up, one in which Chris-Craft had very limited experience. War materiel.

A blitzkrieg of German invasion forces rolled over Denmark, Holland and Belgium, as Roosevelt signaled American industry to prepare for the worst, the possibility of American involvement in the increasingly global conflict. In early June of 1940, over 340,000 predominantly British and French allied troops were evacuated from the beaches of Dunkirk, where they had been driven relentlessly by a ruthless and obsessed German army. Among the miracle flotilla were Chris-Craft, and one commander wrote to Algonac to describe the struggles of the 32-foot *Bonny Heather*.

> I want to tell you about the "Bonny Heather", a Chris-Craft Cruiser which participated in the evacuation of Dunkirk. I can't even begin to describe the hell under which the operations were carried out — bombed, machine gunned, shelled, caught in parachute flares and bombed — the little ship was certainly built in a lucky zone, and dodging and twisting never once let us down, loaded as she was. The "Bonny Heather" stood up to it like a Trojan, made seven complete round trips, Ramsgate to Dunkirk,

after filling up transports (lying off) from the beaches. About 60 men were carried on each trip, except the last, and on that one the number was close to 80. I selected the "Bonny Heather" as a leader of a convoy of motor boats. Believe me, the choice was justified.[2]

Contrary to popular belief, Chris-Craft began serious efforts to acquire government contracts well before America was drawn into the conflict directly. Following the fall of Paris, and during the battle of Britain in September, 1940, Harsen Smith, Bill MacKerer and Charles "Chuck" Smith reported to the Navy Department at Virginia Beach, Virginia, with a new 30-foot *Landing Boat* they had designed for contract competition.[3] The principal rival for securing landing craft awards was the Higgins *Eureka* Landing Boat, manufactured by Higgins Industries in New Orleans, Louisiana.

Early in the morning of the 17th of September, the Chris-Craft prototype was loaded with 4,050 pounds of sandbags, to simulate a full load of men and equipment under combat conditions. While in this handicapped condition, they had "a brush with a Eureka 30-foot Landing Boat powered with a Hall Scott 250-h.p. motor and having three men aboard and no extra weight." The Chris-Craft was able to "keep broadside of this boat without any gain by either boat."[4] The Chris-Craft was equipped with a pair of 110-h.p. Chris-Craft engines. Two other boats were engaged in the testing for comparisons, a *Bureau Type* 30-foot metal launch, and an older model 30-foot Eureka Boat with a 250-h.p. Hall Scott motor.

The following morning, when the convoy of three test boats were towed to the test beach, only the Chris-Craft was actually ready to begin tests, as the Higgins boat wouldn't start, the Bureau boat had clutch trouble, and the older Eureka had a line fouled in its propeller. The Chris-Craft was asked to make the first run. With Chuck Smith driving the boat for the first time, the Chris-Craft made a perfect 90-degree beaching, picked up an additional eighteen officers and men, including the son of Andrew Higgins, and retracted from the beach without difficulty. "As soon as he was free from the beach he [Chuck Smith] was able to back through the first heavy breaker and had sufficient maneuverability and control to immediately turn the boat and head it out to sea before the second breaker broke."[5]

When the Higgins Eureka made a successful landing on the beach, some observers got off,

Courtesy Mariners' Museum, Newport News, Virginia.

Harsen Smith, seated, then Chris-Craft Vice-President, accepts the largest number of orders ever received at one time by a single dealer. Orders for thirty boats totaling $70,000 were delivered from Chicago franchise president John Rodi (center) and Clyde Erzinger in February, 1941.

and nine bags of sand were dumped before the Eureka retracted and headed out to sea.

The next boat, the 30-foot Bureau-type launch, was caught broadside maneuvering through the surf, and was hurled against the beach with twenty observers aboard. It was unable to retract due to motor failure and the boat filled with water. After about an hour, the Coast Guard and the sailors together managed to pull it off the beach and tow it away. Meanwhile, the older Eureka Boat had motor failure and could not take part in the tests.

Then, the Higgins and the Chris-Craft were asked to beach at the same time, to see which could land further up the beach. The Chris-Craft beached a full twenty feet further inland than the Higgins, and both boats retracted without difficulty. The Chris-Craft had in every respect defeated the Higgins boat, and the crew was preparing to disband when word arrived that *one more test*, not listed, was required. The Chris-Craft crew was told to come into the beach with their motors dead in a *broaching* maneuver. Chris-Craft, thinking the tests were over, had not made minor repairs to their boat, which now would handicap it in this unscheduled test. "Charles Smith told [the Commander] that the boat was partially filled with water due to a broken exhaust line and from surf rolling in the boat and that our bilge pumps were not of sufficient capacity to pump the boat dry in time to make the maneuver. However, after consideration, our operator, Charles Smith, decided to make the maneuver in spite of the fact that he was going to operate under these handicaps."[6] As Bill MacKerer reported, it turned out to be a very costly decision.

> While our boat was lying on the beach broadside the Higgins boat came in and broached sideways in the surf and successfully rode the breakers, but the boat was maneuvered so that it did not land broadside on the beach but on an angle of almost 90 degrees of the beach which made it very easy for the Eureka boat to retract from the beach on this maneuver. The Chris-Craft boat had completed the maneuver *as we had interpreted it* and was then required under the above mentioned handicaps to retract off the beach with full load. Due to the amount of water in the bilge of the Chris-Craft, water splashed on the ignition system and put the starboard motor out of commission leaving the boat to retract under one motor. During the entire time the full crew and observers remained aboard and Charles Smith, our operator, was able to maneuver the boat in such

Courtesy Mariners' Museum, Newport News, Virginia.

The 1940 25-foot Sportsman featured a walk-thru from the center cockpit to the stern cockpit which was wide-open for fishing or water sports. Capable of 40 mph, it retailed for $4,690 with a 223-horsepower engine.

a way with one motor as to bring the boat around to a point at right angle to the beach line and on two specific occasions practically had the boat off the beach but due to the unfortunate circumstances of extra large breakers was thrown up further on the beach. After attempting for approximately fifteen or twenty minutes to retract off the beach and getting the boat to a point where probably in another few minutes the boat would have been free, instructions were given by the Navy officials to the Eureka boat standing by to throw a line to the Chris-Craft and tow it off the beach.[7]

It was humiliating for the Chris-Craft to be pulled off the beach by the competition. MacKerer was convinced that the Chris-Craft had "completed all the maneuvers expected of this type of boat in spite of the fact that we were carrying the additional weight of observers over and above the specified dead load weight [over two tons]." He was also "at a loss to understand why at the last moment this broaching test was required as at no time was this point ever discussed or thought of."[8] A further conclusion was reached that "we had received a bum-steer originally from the Navy Department on the method of handling sea water washed aboard...."

Higgins received the order to build 400 landing crafts, and Chris-Craft would get any overflow, even though Navy engineers admitted that the Chris-Craft "was equally as good if not superior to the Higgins Eureka,"[9] and that the Chris-Craft boat was less expensive even though it was powered by two engines rather than one. At one point, MacKerer was shocked to hear that

These three 1941 runabouts show the new trend of *streamlining* with their stylish *torpedo* sterns. Left to right: 17-foot De Luxe Runabout, 23-foot Custom Runabout and 19-foot Custom Runabout.

Courtesy Mariners' Museum, Newport News, Virginia.

among the considerations in denying Chris-Craft the award was "incidentally, Higgins had received a $113,000 loan from the government which must be protected some way."[10] MacKerer told the Navy that he "questioned Higgins ability to produce these boats immediately, feeling that not only his manufacturing set up was insufficient to take care of any greater volume but also the fact that Hall Scott Motor Company capacity for motors is limited to one a day."[11] His arguments, though valid, were to no avail. The award went to Higgins.

In 1941 Chris-Craft proudly announced 110 models of boats, with an emphasis on minor model variations and increased luxury in existing models. "More beam, more freeboard, heavier construction, twin rudders with twin engines, salt water equipment, easier handling qualities, and higher speeds are among the structural improvements."[12] Among the new offerings were a 16-foot double-cockpit forward runabout powered with a 60-h.p. aft engine, and a new line of *rocket* style runabouts in 19, 23 and 27-foot ranges with wide power options. "Turtle back decks, slip stream folding windshields, and shark nosed bows are a few of the advancements on these craft."[13]

In Express Cruisers, a new 23-foot model was offered "believed to be the world's lowest priced model of its type and size."[14]

Two 40 footers are new, an Express and a Challenger. Both provide self-bailing forward cockpits with ingenious cabin entrances, a forward stateroom, complete galley, toilet compartment, and a large saloon. The Express cruiser has a three piece windshield, practical weather cloths, and features a large open cockpit with fish well and bait box. A demountable navy top is standard equipment and offers shelter for the helmsman. The Challenger has a permanent streamlined top and cozy owner's cabin aft of the bridge. This cabin is a revelation in design and provides comfortable, extra wide berths port and starboard, a lavatory, dresser and toilet.[15]

1941 Cruisers demonstrated further Chris-Craft thinking in making an even greater range of models available to an ever-widening target market. "Just a suggestion of ostentation is apparent on the new 26-foot enclosed cruiser .... The 26-footer has been acclaimed by many yachtsmen to be Mr. Average Man's ideal when it comes to a small boat with real accommodations for short or extended cruising."[16]

On January 15, 1941, Chris-Craft finalized an agreement with the City of Cadillac, Michigan, to acquire an additional 125,000 square feet of production facilities. The clever arrangement stated that Chris-Craft would obtain *free use* of the land for a period of eight years, or until such time as Chris-Craft's payroll in Cadillac exceeded $250,000, at which time the City would turn over title to the land. The enormous structures were sold to Chris-Craft for a mere $35,644.48. By February 24, only five weeks after taking over the facilities, the Smiths were already producing 18 and 22-foot Utility boats, with a new production line being set up for cruisers up to 30-feet.

Chris-Craft made a variety of accessories available to buyers. Pictured here are a pair of 1941 22-foot De Luxe Utility models, identical except for the optional De Luxe Navy Top. Equipped with a 130-horsepower engine these boats would reach 35 mph ad retailed for $1990. For an additional $295 a solid mahogany *Streamline* ventilating cabin could be installed.

Courtesy Mariners' Museum, Newport News, Virginia.

Though the Smiths could have justified the expansion in facilities from increased pleasure boat orders alone, they had good reason to believe that they would be the recipient of sizable government contracts within the year, and that increased capacity would allow them to capture larger awards while still continuing with an ever-increasing civilian program.

By February, Chris-Craft had received its first taste of contracting with the Federal Government. The Wheeler Shipyard in Brooklyn, New York had been awarded contracts for building 26-foot motor mine yawls, employed as auxiliaries in mine planting operations. Chris-Craft was to supply the engines for these boats, and for boats built by the Palmer-Scott Co. of New Bedford and the Southwest Harbor Boat Corp. of Maine. Then, Chris-Craft delivered twenty-seven of their 22-foot utility boats for the Army to use as a rescue or *crash* boat for downed pilots. Chris-Craft would also supply engines to Wheeler for 35-foot patrol boats.[17] Though modest compared to the scope of the new national emphasis on defense preparation, these orders allowed Chris-Craft to sort out and understand the complexities and procedures crucial to government contracting.

By May of 1941, Chris-Craft had penetrated both the Army and the Navy procurement bureaucracies, and had sold four virtually stock cruisers to three government agencies.

Two 30-foot sedan cruisers have been purchased by the Ordnance Department of the Army for use on Lake Erie at a proving ground. They are powered with twin 95-horsepower engines giving a speed of 24 m.p.h. A 26-foot semi-enclosed cruiser has been sold to the Navy for use as a tender on the U.S.S. Barnett and is equipped with a special skeg, lifting rings and dual controls. A 130-horsepower engine gives a top speed of 28-m.p.h. The fourth boat, a 29-footer, was sold to the Public Roads Administration for use on Gatun Lake, Panama Canal Zone. It has berths for two and a speed of 27 m.p.h.[18]

While the nation labored furiously to build up its antiquated defenses, the motorboat industry struggled to convince consumers that there was no need for alarm, no need to curtail recreational boating, no need to put off purchasing decisions. As one leading magazine stated, "Any belief that the purchase of a new boat or the commissioning of an old one might reflect discredit or evoke unfavorable comment against the owner at the present time, is wholly without foundation."[19]

Another public relations problem appeared as more boat builders accepted defense contracts.

The public, fearing their order of boats from contract award winners might delay the construction of critical defense material, turned to other builders or remained within the used boat marketplace. To counter these feelings of boating guilt, a campaign of education and persuasion was mounted.

In the first place, even while the plants and factories of the boat building, marine engine, and equipment and accessory firms throughout America are turning out the products called for by the Government for defense, their great potential productive capacity has hardly been tapped. Every one of these builders is fulfilling every Governmental demand as a first consideration — and may be counted on to continue to do so. If the time ever comes when every such builder in the industry must occupy himself with government work, no one need doubt that that work will take precedence.

Some firms today have established new plants devoted exclusively to Government work, while the pleasure boat division continues to function unhindered in any way by the expansion. Many have not yet been called upon to fill Government contracts.

Never before has there been better justification for building up and improving our pleasure boat fleet. This is a time for national sanity.[20]

Early in the morning of October 2nd, 1941, the labor union staged an unannounced strike, in violation of the two-year contract which they had negotiated and accepted only ten months before, on the first day of the year. Chris-Craft was surprised and becoming increasingly disappointed with the conduct of the union. Picket lines were quickly set up, and "threatened with physical violence non-striking employees and officers...anxious and willing to work..." Also, incredible as it seems, officers of the corporation, the Smiths, vendors and virtually anyone else, were "prevented by means of threats and intimidation...from entering any part of the...Algonac Plant..."[21] The union, in poor judgment, wouldn't even allow Chris-Craft to maintain their sprinkler fire system, and were prepared to allow all the water lines within the plant to freeze and burst. Further, they allowed a large number of recently completed boats to remain exposed to the elements, and allowed water to freeze in the holds and bilges.[22] By November 12th, well over a month since the strike began, a restraining order was issued by the court, prohibiting the union from continuing "violence, threats of violence, or intimidation, [or] interfering with the orderly conduct of...business."[23]

Three weeks after reopening the plant, on December 7, 1941, America was viciously and savagely attacked by Japanese warships and aircraft at Pearl Harbor, Hawaii. Over 360 Japanese warplanes participated in the disastrous attack, sinking or very seriously damaging five U.S. battleships and 14 smaller ships. Over 2,000

Navy personnel perished, along with 400 civilians. Roosevelt called the attack "a brilliant feat of deception, perfectly timed and executed with great skill."[24] Within four days of the attack, the United States would declare war on Japan and her Axis partners, Italy and Germany. America was plunged into the horrible fury of world war.

Chris-Craft, months before, had announced its 1942 line. The fleet contained 79 models of boats, including fifteen models of runabouts from a 16-foot model at $995 to a 23-foot Custom at $3,290; six models of Utility Runabouts from the 16-foot De Luxe Utility at $995, to a 22-foot De Luxe for $2,090; nineteen Express Cruisers from a 23-foot for $1,795 to the stylish new 40-foot Challenger with a pair of 160-horsepower Chris-Craft engines at $12,500; thirty-four Cruisers from the 24-foot Clipper at $1,795 to a 45-foot Double Cabin Enclosed Cruiser with Flying Bridge, powered with a pair of Chris-Craft 160-horsepower engines for $15,400; and four models of the 55-foot Chris-Craft Motor Yacht from $30,900 powered with two 130-horsepower Chris-Craft engines to $39,900, powered by a pair of 165-horsepower General Motors diesel engines.[25]

Even though the nation was swept into war, companies were encouraged to continue normal production, and consumers were encouraged to continue recreational activities. "The morale of a nation at war," one prominent boating publication suggested, "is as vital a factor for victory as the production lines."

Agencies of the government directly concerned in the successful prosecution of the war have stressed repeatedly the need for continuing as far as possible all normal sports activities. The Office of Civilian Defense has established a Division of Physical Fitness and selected a representative group of prominent yachtsmen to foster and encourage motor boat competition and cruising.

While he is enjoying his boat, the yachtsman is fortifying himself by exposure to the pure air and sunshine, which are an important part of boating. He strengthens himself, the better to carry on his activities in the production of defense materials and thus further the war effort.[26]

Chris-Craft was awarded their first major government contract within weeks of Pearl Harbor,

elegant 1941 40-foot *Challenger* featured a self-bailing
ward cockpit with an ingenious forward stateroom
ance. Powered with a pair of 275-horsepower engines it
ld make 32 mph and retailed for $13,990.

Courtesy Mariners' Museum, Newport News, Virginia.

The Navy tests a new Chris-Craft LCVR (Landing Craft Vehicle Ramp) along the banks of the St. Clair River at Algonac, Michigan. Powered by a 225-horsepower Gray diesel engine, this model could even transport the Army's smallest combat tanks.

Courtesy Mariners' Museum, Newport News, Virginia.

for 1,025 36-foot Eureka-style Landing Boats, the same model they felt they had defeated in tests against their own design a year and a half earlier at Virginia Beach. This first contract called for production to be divided among the three plants, with 260 for Algonac, 295 for Holland and 170 for the Cadillac plant. The program was classified as *urgent,* and the schedule of deliveries, starting in June, was so crucial that the Government assigned an AA Rating to the program, and stated that the schedule *"MUST BE MET OR EXCEEDED".*[27] The boats required the use of plywood for the relatively flat sides of the boxy boats, a material basically foreign to Chris-Craft, but which presented no real transition problems. Chris-Craft would also be introduced to a new and valuable adhesive and sealant known as *thiokol,* which would prove crucial to Chris-Craft construction in later years. Armor plate for ramps and for certain strategic bulkheads was supplied by the Government under terms of the contracts. Each landing craft was to cost the government approximately $8,000.

Chris-Craft was then able to respond with breathtaking speed to meet the challenge. With three facilities fully operational, and with a talented and seasoned work force, production lines were quickly converted to accommodate the new Landing Boats. Within weeks of commencing production of the initial order, more contracts flowed in, so that within 90 days, Chris-Craft had received additional orders for 725 Personnel Ramp Landing Boats (LCPR), 400 Vehicle Ramp Landing Boats (LCV), and 200 additional Regular and Personnel Ramp Boats (LCVP).

The Landing Boats were each 36-feet long, with beams between 10-foot 7¾ and 10-foot 9¾ inches, drawing between 2-feet 3 inches and 3-feet 2 inches, and could transport 36 men with full combat equipment (LCVP), or jeeps and men (LCVR), or even small tanks (LCV). The Landing Boats, landing craft or landing barges as the terms were often interchanged, all used engines supplied by the government, and weren't powered by Chris-Craft engines as sometimes thought. The primary power plant for the Landing Boats was the Gray diesel, which developed 225-horsepower at 2100 r.p.m. with a 1.5-to-1 reduction gear, while the Chrysler Royal gasoline engine was designated for use with the Personnel Ramp Landing Boats, LCPR.

Almost simultaneously, Chris-Craft received orders for 105 Navy Harbor Picket Boats, a 36-foot twin screw cruiser type boat powered by a pair of Chris-Craft Marine 150-horsepower engines, set up with two-to-one reduction and counter-rotation, which would push the Picket Boats at around 25 miles per hour. These larger boats were set up within the cruiser and yacht division lines, and were shipped to ten different

Harsen Smith, at the front, and Bill MacKerer, arms folded, go along for speed trials of a new *spoonbill* LCPL (Landing Craft Personnel Light) model in the St. Clair River at Algonac, Michigan in the summer of 1942. Notice the navigation light and horn, accessories which would eventually be eliminated.

Courtesy Mariners' Museum, Newport News, Virginia.

locations around the country, ranging from Seattle to Key West, and from Hoboken to San Diego.

The sheer volume of work to be produced was staggering, and required Chris-Craft to locate, screen, hire and train another one thousand employees distributed throughout the three plants. Birth certificates were now required for workers, and general plant security was provided by the Government. A guard tower was erected, and fully armed and vigilant sentries continuously monitored new anti-personnel fences and approaches to the plant. Saboteurs were said to have infiltrated American society, and had as their targets our military industrial capacity. It wasn't an unjustified Nazi paranoia, for in May, an Axis submarine sank an American cargo ship at the mouth of the Mississippi River in New Orleans, killing twenty-seven people.[28] Employees were required to wear photo identification badges at all times.

Chris-Craft was able to meet and even exceed the fantastic production demands placed by the Government, due to their twenty-year history of precision in-line manufacturing ability. They had very little new ground to break in meeting the challenge; they were instead able to expand on basic and time-proven production principles to increase the flow of production. With a legal pad and shop pencil, Bill MacKerer recorded the reasons he thought Chris-Craft was so efficient and successful in meeting the seemingly impossible schedules.

Before entering the war effort, Chris-Craft was the world's largest builder of motor boats and the leader in a highly competitive field. In order to obtain and maintain this position, it was necessary that Chris-Craft establish leadership in boat production with the lowest labor costs in the industry. This was done by our advanced production methods and trained personnel developed over a period of more than 20 years of production boat building, manufacturing all types of pleasure and commercial crafts.

On January 1st, 1942, Chris-Craft Corporation was in a position to offer the Navy Department the services of a complete engineering staff and production organization thoroughly trained and experienced in all phases of production boat building. The original bids submitted to the Navy by Chris-Craft as compared with competitors bids reflected our confidence in our ability to build boats in quantity, more efficiently and at a lower price...

Chris-Craft was conscious, from the beginning of our Navy Landing Boat program, that manpower would be the bottleneck in quantity production. This factor made it all the more imperative that everything be done to secure the greatest volume of work with the limited amount of trained labor available. To this end, considerable time and expense was [rendered] in order to reduce job man hours, results of which were apparent as production increased and labor costs dropped…

Daily cost records on each hull and operation were reviewed *each day* by [the] plant manager, and in cases where excess time showed up, these cases were investigated and corrected…. When a new manufacturing method was used, an estimate of the time saved was made and deducted from the standard costs…. All our employees are cost conscious, and rivalry exists between various crews…

Each hull is assembled on a moving production line and allotted a certain amount of time for each operation. These boats move on a regular schedule and work must be completed on time by the man power allocated…. Our testing and shipping facilities are excellent and conducive to low cost operation in places where confusion and excessive costs usually exists in other plants.[29]

Chris-Craft efficiency and resolve was rewarded on June 15th of 1942 with the presentation of the prestigious Navy 'E' award, the highest honor an American plant or civilian can receive from the Navy. As Frank Knox, Secretary of the Navy expressed in a letter to Jay Smith, "For nearly four decades this symbol has been eloquent of highest achievement to the officers and men of our naval service. You have now earned the privilege of flying the Navy 'E' Pennant over your plants. Each of your workers has earned the right to wear the Navy 'E' lapel insignia identifying him with the honor of this significant award…. Your Navy and your country are depending on you — all of you."[30]

Each of the plants, Algonac, Holland and Cadillac, Michigan, were presented the award on the same day. The award has a noble and stirring

history, which was conveyed to the assembled employees at each location.

This coveted award for superior service, loyalty and devotion to duty was instituted in 1906. Throughout the Navy, the 'E' is a recognized symbol of excellence. For example, the 'E' is painted on the turret of a ship which excels in gunnery, or on the funnel of a ship which has won it for engineering. The 'E' is one of the Navy's most sought after awards.

By special permission of the President of the United States, the 'E' award has been extended to certain industrial plants demonstrating their patriotism and determination to win by outstanding performance on Navy contracts.[31]

The employees of Chris-Craft wore the lapel pin with pride, and the flags which flew over the plants represented for the men a genuine honor, for they truly had earned it. In return for the award, each worker at Chris-Craft gave their pledge to continue the performance which had made them among the most efficient defense contractors in the country.

We of Chris-Craft accept the insignia of the Navy "E" proudly.

We shall wear this prized token of excellence in production until Victory is won. We will keep on building, with all of the skill and strength at our command, more and more of these essential craft, until their sting be felt by all the serpents that seek to stifle the freedom of the seas.

We will continue to produce to the same high standard of excellence that has won for us, in the three plants of Chris-Craft, the privilege of working under the Navy "E" Burgee. With One Cause, One Single Aim, we are working as One, even as the United States Armed Forces are fighting as One, for Victory.[32]

Chris-Craft sales for 1942 were, understandably, over three times 1941, and would top *twelve million dollars.* Due to operational efficiencies and production streamlining, Chris-Craft was able to return $1.5 million to the Government from January to September alone, a trend that would continue as Chris-Craft defense contracts continued to grow at a dramatic pace through the duration of the war. Chris-Craft and its stockholders would profit handsomely from the mammoth Government contracts, but the record shows that Chris-Craft ingenuity, production excellence and managerial expertise also saved the Government millions upon millions of defense dollars, and the quality and speed of production of Chris-Craft defense products were responsible for saving many thousands of American lives overseas.

Employees of all three Chris-Craft plants received the prestigious "E" Award, which included a lapel pin, on June 15, 1942. The highest civilian award for an American factory enabled the Algonac, Cadillac and Holland plants to fly the "E" flag until victory was won.

Courtesy Mariners' Museum, Newport News, Virginia.

Liberators Courageous..

Brave men . . . massed in landing boats, eager for action, attacking to liberate the oppressed peoples of the world.

Now America strikes with all its might and fury . . . fine fighting forces under capable, courageous officers, with superb equipment.

To make the task easier, to get it done more quickly, American industry must produce more and more . . . all Americans must buy more of the War Bonds that back our fighting forces.

Building the boats shown above in greater quantities than ever before is but a part of the war-time, full-time job of Chris-Craft . . . it's one of our contributions to the cause of Liberty.

ARMY E NAVY

For production "Well Done" we proudly fly the Army-Navy "E" at all three Chris-Craft Factories.

★ ★ ★ **CHRIS-CRAFT** ★ ★ ★

CHRIS-CRAFT CORPORATION • 4611 DETROIT ROAD, ALGONAC, MICHIGAN
WORLD'S LARGEST BUILDERS OF MOTOR BOATS

Courtesy Mariners' Museum, Newport News, Virginia.

Chris-Craft promoted the critical American War Bond drive during the war by placing full-page ads
such as this in national publications.

Opposite Above: American troops run a *spoonbill* Chris
Craft LCPL (Landing Craft Personnel Light) up on a
European beach head. This model was without the forward
ramp common to other models

Courtesy Mariners' Museum, Newport News, Virginia.

Chris-Craft helped the war effort in other ways, by using their advertising commitments to urge Americans to buy war bonds, which they did by the billions of dollars.

Towards the end of 1942, the union representing Chris-Craft employees was reorganized into four separate unions under the American Federation of Labor, one each for Carpenters, Machinists, Painters and Electrical Workers. Though there is some evidence of continued agitation during this period, Federal laws had been set in place which would preclude the temptation of strikes at plants engaged in critical defense production.[33]

All of the Landing Boats had to be sling hoist and water tested. As a consequence, production from the Holland and Cadillac plants were shipped to Algonac, where all completed boats were tested. Once testing was completed, boats were shipped to their final destinations on either the East or West coast. George Smith, son of Bernard, was assigned to the Holland plant, and remembers one day "We had a hundred and seventy of those boats out in the yard, couldn't complete them because we didn't have a piece of armor plate for them, or we didn't have an engine for them, but we were pushing them out every day. We were shipping about ten boats a day,

actually." George also remembers that Chris-Craft had to bail out Higgins, who were building the same model, as they, too, would run short of parts. "I remember one time he couldn't ship any more boats, he was tied down and he didn't have the brass casting to hold the strut to the skeg and the rudder to the skeg. We packaged up a whole bunch of them and sent them down to him so he could ship boats."[34] George also recalled that all along highway 16 in Holland, where the big boxy Landing Boats would be shipped, "for years you could just see the square tunnel where the trees were chewed out, just the size of the boat going through."[35] Another remembered the shipping record established at one point during the war, of six hundred and two boats in *one month.*[36]

To facilitate water testing of Landing Boats and other government contracts in winter, Chris-Craft devised a way of piping steam from their plant heating boilers to underneath the water of the testing basins and slips in Algonac. The project was first completed in December of 1942, when the ice had already formed on the Chris-Craft canal. "I lit both boilers in about five minutes," the boiler operator remembered; "…they were high pressure boilers and took about eighty-five pounds. I turned [the steam]

In 1943 and 1944, Chris-Craft war production was at peak performance. Above: The testing basins at Algonac are crowded with landing craft undergoing static tests. Left: Hundreds of covered landing craft await shipping orders from Washington.

Courtesy Mariners' Museum, Newport News, Virginia.

over to the cut. Chuck, Bernard's son, he took off on a run when I fired one, because I looked outside and that water was, I'd say, ten feet up in the air, brush flying around and everything where it blows over. In an hour I had two boilers going and there wasn't a piece of ice in that cut. But you ought to have seen the fish that lay out there. It got too hot for them. There was carp and bass, sheephead, just about every kind of fish in one little look out there."[37]

Sales for 1943 were almost $21 million dollars, which showed a $2 million profit on the books. Chris-Craft, however, in anticipation of restrictions contained within the War Profits Control Act, voluntarily renegotiated contracts and made a refund to the government of $5.6 million dollars at the end of fiscal 1943.

In an ad describing the virtues of the Army Amphibian Command Boat built during the year, Chris-Craft emphasized their ability to build *fast.*

> The U.S. Army required a new type command boat for its amphibian command. U.S. Army engineers working against time (and around the clock) dispatched complete plans and specifications to Chris-Craft with orders to RUSH! In one tenth of the time that it previously took us to build a pleasure boat of the same length, the new command boat was built, tested and delivered to Army engineers.... Another example of Chris-Craft's ability and willingness

Courtesy Mariners' Museum, Newport News, Virginia.

A Chris-Craft, like the LCVR shown with ramp down above, was the first landing craft to hit the beach at Normandy during the Allied invasion of Europe June 6, 1944.

to co-operate with the United States Armed Forces.... Another real reason why the United States will *win this war!*[38]

Among other defense craft delivered to the Armed Forces during the war was an Army *Target Boat,* essentially a stripped-down 27-foot runabout designed to tow targets. Chris-Craft also produced a number of 60-foot Quartermaster Boats for the U.S. Army, which were basically stretched 55-foot Chris-Craft designs with minor modifications. Chris-Craft, in an ad appearing in *Yachting,* described the role of these "husky" craft.

Photo by Karine N. Rodengen

In Iceland, in the African theatre, in the Solomons, wherever U.S. Army operations require boats, you'll invariably find 60-ft. standard Chris-Craft transporting Army personnel.

In the acid test of war, these sturdy Chris-Craft, with no changes in hull design or construction, with added equipment and carrying capacity, have come through with colors flying. In service months before Pearl Harbor, the U.S. Army has ordered and reordered these husky craft to meet constantly expanding Army needs.

Today building 60-footers for the Army is one of our important war assignments. We're proud of the performance record of all Chris-Craft in Service....[39]

During 1943, with uncertainties concerning the duration of the war, Chris-Craft quietly bought land for additional plants and facilities in Grand Rapids, Michigan, and in Jamestown, New York. Though the purchases were modest, at $7,328 in Grand Rapids and a $600 deposit in Jamestown, it marked the first indication of Chris-Craft's anticipation for postwar expansion. It is also the first indication that Chris-Craft would venture into unknown waters, eventually outboard engines, at the Grand Rapids facility.[40]

1944 sales were almost identical to 1943, as the three plants were working at virtual capacity. Production continued at a feverish pace, while Chris-Craft products were engaged in landings throughout the global theatres of war. From Sicily, Palermo and Anzio in Italy to beach heads in New Guinea and throughout the Pacific, Chris-Craft Landing Boats carried tens of millions of pounds of soldiers and war materiel to hostile shores.

On sunrise of June 6, 1944, a Chris-Craft was the first boat to hit the beach at Normandy, France, as the long awaited Anglo-American invasion of Europe began. Delivered to within striking distance by five thousand battleships and transports, the Chris-Craft Landing Boats were lifted over the sides, and performed brilliantly in wave after wave of landings on beach heads established from St. Vaast to Ouistrham, at strategic locations known as Utah, Omaha, Gold, Juno and Sword beaches. The Allies secured a stronghold on the European continent, and in concert with Russian advances from the East, they together began to close on the increasingly encircled and beleaguered German armies.

Photo by Karine N. Rodengen

A 1942 17-foot (17'5") De Luxe Runabout, *Loan-Sum.* If powered with the 95-horsepower Chris-Craft engine, the double cockpit runabout would do 35 mph and retailed for $1,595.

In February of 1945, a cable was sent by U. S. Navy Rear Admiral E. L. Cochrane, to the men and women of both Chris-Craft Corporation's Algonac, Holland and Cadillac plants.

> On the completion of your 10,000th Landing Craft for the Navy, it is appropriate for the Bureau of Ships to congratulate you for your outstanding accomplishment, and to express its appreciation for your splendid contribution to the war effort. Not only have you built this vast fleet, but you are supplying maintenance and replacement parts in sufficient quantities to keep these boats in action. LCVP's, LCP(R)'s, and LCP(L)'s of your construction have participated in amphibious assaults in worldwide theatres of operation and are now carrying our forces ever closer to the shores of Japan. The Bureau commends your entire organization for the cooperation and unusual ability and craftsmanship which have made possible this notable achievement.[41]

Photo by Karine N. Rodengen

Opposite left and above: *Olde Made,* a 1940 23-foot triple cockpit Custom Runabout races towards the sunset over the St. Clair River at Marine City, Michigan piloted by owner/restorer Ron Danneels.

By October, 1945, as Chris-Craft Landing Boats carried General Douglas MacArthur's forces ashore in the Philippines, the firm's government sales would total over $23.5 million for the year, realizing a profit of $688,458.[42]Production began to taper off during the year, as Roosevelt died in office, Truman becomes president, Mussolini and Hitler are dead, and ultimately, on May 7th, Germany surrenders to the Allies. Deliveries shrank from 300 in June to nearly half by August, as news of the devastation of Hiroshima and Nagasaki by American atomic bombs reached Algonac and the world.

In March of 1943 Chris-Craft built this 42-foot Aircraft Rescue boat equipped with powerful water pumps to quickly extinguish the flames from downed aircraft.

With the surrender of Japan on August 15th, 1945, all military contracts were suspended. Chris-Craft closed a proud chapter in their history, and production was almost immediately launched for civilian production once more. As early as January, 1945, six months before the end of the war, Chris-Craft had already made plans for pleasure production. They knew the demand would be large for postwar boats, as they had received a steady stream of letters during the waning months of the war from G.I.'s and civilians alike, looking forward to taking to the peaceful waters once again.

> "They tell us that we really build good boats," Edward Pickell, public relations director of the company said in an interview. "Since that is our aim here at Chris-Craft, we're very proud of the letters we have received from overseas. Lots of the men tell us that they intend to own Chris-Craft pleasure boats after the war is over."

> While the Algonac plant and two others at Cadillac and Holland are now engaged in 100 percent war production at top speed, plans have already been made for postwar reconversion to pleasure boat manufacture.
> "Within 30 to 90 days after we get the go-ahead signal from Washington at the end of the war, we'll have pleasure boats ready for delivery," a company spokesman said.[43]

True to their word, shipments began to leave Chris-Craft factories by late July, destined for peaceful purposes for the first time in over three and a half years. The 1946 fleet was almost a duplicate of the 1942 line, with only variations in features and model designations. The 90 different Chris-Crafts contained runabouts in three unique categories, Special Runabout, De Luxe Runabout and Custom Runabout. They ranged in price from the 16-foot Special Runabout powered with a 60-horsepower, 4-cylinder Chris-Craft engine at $1,340, to the 23-foot Custom Runabout powered with a 160-horsepower Chris-Craft engine for $4,290. Utility Boats as a category disappeared with the war, and now the redefined Sportsman class contained seven models of De Luxe Utility boats and four models of Sportsmen ranging from an 18-foot De Luxe Utility powered with the 60-horsepower Chris-Craft engine at $1,740, to the 25-foot Sportsman powered with a pair of Chris-Craft 95-horsepower engines listing for $4,490.

Twenty-seven models of Express Cruisers were announced, ranging from a 23-foot, 60-horsepower version at $2,340, to the familiar prewar 40-foot Challenger which could be equipped with a pair of 160-horsepower Chris-Craft engines delivering 26 miles an hour for $15,900.

Thirty-eight models of Cruisers began to flow from Chris-Craft assembly lines, ranging from a 26-foot Semi-Enclosed Cruiser powered by the 60-horsepower Chris-Craft for $2,590, to the largest boat of the year, a 46-foot Double Cabin Enclosed Cruiser with Flying Bridge with a pair of 160-horsepower Chris-Crafts for $20,500.

An interesting thing about the advertising copy for the 1946 line is the curious lack of any mention of construction materials. The word mahogany doesn't appear anywhere, nor is any other type of wood suggested or specified. The truth is, many of the post-war boats were built of cedar, or any other wood they could find. Lumber of all descriptions would remain difficult to acquire in quantities for nearly two full years. As Bill MacKerer characterized the problem during January, 1947, there were occasions when labor negotiations in the plants nearly had to shut down.

> The other thing I must tell you is that our lumber situation is definitely bad. We may have some shut downs. I can't tell you how they will be, or when they are coming, but they are coming. We are rapidly becoming more and more affected by the critical shortage of lumber. We have been in this trouble for over a year, and have done everything humanly possible to keep

this operation going…it's getting worse, and will probably remain that way for another six months or a year. We have had to make numerous substitutions, and in some models have had to cut out mahogany altogether. Consequently, cancellations are coming in from our dealers. I'm not crying "wolf" — he already has one paw inside the door and will be on our chest in another month…

The Smith family put the responsibility in my hands. There should have been a shut down last Spring. You men who have been here know that we are not putting into our boats today the kind of lumber that we formerly used — it just isn't available, and we have been forced to use substitutions in order to keep going… . We don't have a corner on all lumber. The other companies are having the same trouble as we are, but where they use possibly a carload of lumber, we probably use ten carloads, and naturally our problem is more acute.[44]

When the lumber shortages were most critical, Chris-Craft would paint hulls rather than stain them, because the stain on the substituted woods wouldn't look proper to consumers.

Americans were anxious to return to water recreation, and sought out the most respected name in boating as soon as they could. 1946 sales were nearly $6 million, testimony to the resiliency and prewar product loyalty of the American consumer, and heralded the re-estab-

lishment of a continued dominance of the pleasure craft industry by Chris-Craft.

Towards the end of the war, Jay W. Smith was "moving aside to give Harsen plenty of elbow-room."[45] Though Vice-President, Harsen would become clearly the leading administrator in the years to come, and would gain a solid reputation as a level-thinking, honest, and solid leader within both the Smith family and the marine industry.

Outside of cost of living increases, most industries throughout the United States deferred wage bargaining until victory was won. But in 1946, millions of American workers set up picket lines that seemed to stretch across the continent. 800,000 steel workers, 200,000 longshoremen, strikes at General Motors, meat packers, cab drivers, even coffin makers walked off their jobs hoping to adjust wage scales that had been put on hold for so long. Chris-Craft was no exception.

In 1946, negotiations continued between Chris-Craft and her several unions, leading to a series of meetings stretching from the end of the year on into the early 1947. The dollar had declined in purchasing power; some say it was worth about 37 cents. But besides wages that ranged from 85 cents an hour to $1.25, there was a question of an employee's ability to get a raise or move up in job classification if his foremen

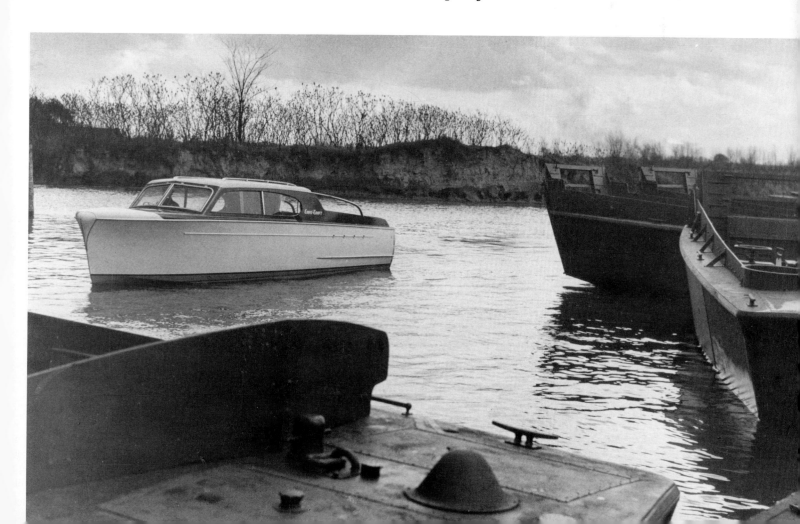

Photo by Karine N. Rodengen

This beautifully detailed horn, one of a pair mounted on each 1940 23-foot Custom Runabout, is pictured aboard *Bye Gone*.

tion must have struck a nerve, for MacKerer left little doubt about his feelings on the matter.

What have we been doing here all these years? I think this discussion is silly and asinine — we damned near had a strike because we didn't have a classification plan in our contract. Are you going to upset a whole amiable relationship that we had in the last year because you suddenly question our classification plan?[46]

Tensions subsided when the international union representative replied to MacKerer's outburst. "I was going to recommend that we have showers installed here for the foreman," he said laconically with a poker face, "because if we have to kiss a foreman's 'hind end' in order to get a raise, we want to make damned sure it's clean."[47] The joke was enough to move the meeting on to more meaningful discussions, and eventually a strike was averted. During the protracted negotiations, however, MacKerer was to describe the rapidly changing nature of the marine industry.

During the war a lot of people went into new industries. Before the war we could count our competitors on the fingers of one or two hands — today the position has changed a lot — there are at least three or four times that many. A lot of these companies started up pretty well organized in production facilities and finances. I am not in a position to say what the future will bring for Higgins and Truscott [MacKerer had previously disclosed a $2 million loss by Higgins in 1946].... We are hoping for the day when things will be more stabilized and will return to normalcy....

didn't like him. During an animated exchange between Bill MacKerer, representing Chris-Craft, and one of the international union representatives, the employee classification plan was in question, specifically, "is there a chance for a man to go over his foreman's head?" The ques-

A reflection on Chris-Craft artistry is the barrel-back stern of this 1941 16-foot Hydroplane, *the Fifth*, which in the catalog carried the stern warning: *For Racing Only*. Photographed in the boat house of E.J. Mertaugh Boat Works, the very first Chris-Craft franchise, in Hessel, Michigan.

Photo by Karine N. Rodengen

Another one of our contemporaries is going out of business. Gar Wood Industries closed their Newport News plant some time ago and are now closing up their Marysville [Michigan] plant.[48]

Before the end of 1946, Chris-Craft would purchase additional land and manufacturing facilities at Chattanooga, Tennessee, and establish runabout production lines. When boats were ordered from dealers, they really had no idea whether they would be produced and shipped from Algonac, Holland, Cadillac, Jamestown or Chattanooga. With a high degree of quality control and factory-mandated consistency, it really wouldn't matter much anyway.[49]

1947 was a strange year for Chris-Craft. The lumber shortages, as Bill MacKerer described, plagued the industry and forced Chris-Craft to shrink its fleet of introductions quite drastically. Only 21 models of Chris-Craft were offered, four Runabouts, three Sportsmen, six Express Cruisers and but ten Cruisers. It was their smallest fleet in twenty years, and naturally, only the most successful models remained in the abbreviated line-up. The surviving runabouts were the 16, 17 and 20-foot models, ranging from $1,840 to $2,240. The 16-foot model was called the *Rocket*, and powered with the 92-horsepower Chrysler engine would make 36 miles-per-hour in the year that Chuck Yeager would travel faster than the speed of sound, over 600 miles per hour in the Bell X-1 *Rocket* plane.

The Sportsmen weathering the cuts were the 18-foot De Luxe Utility Boat at $2,290, and the 22-foot Chris-Craft Sportsman at $2,790. The 22-foot Sportsman would, in later years, gain fame as the boat destroyed in *On Golden Pond*, the motion picture starring Katharine Hepburn and Henry Fonda. The popular, though mahogany-laden 25-foot Sportsman was "temporarily discontinued". Of the Express Cruisers, only two sizes, the 23-foot and 25-foot remained. You could choose from the 23-foot powered by a 92-horsepower Chrysler for $2,970, up to the 25-foot with a pair of 95-horsepower Chris-Craft engines for $5,440.

Hardest hit was the Cruiser division, with only five lengths remaining; the 26, 27, 36, 40 and 46-foot models. They ranged from the 26-foot Semi-Enclosed Cruiser powered by a 115-horsepower Chrysler for $3,690, to the 46-foot Double Cabin Enclosed — Flying Bridge model powered by a pair of 160-horsepower Chris-Craft engines for $24,200. The majority of boats in the 1947

Above and below: A beautiful and rare 1947 17-foot De Luxe Runabout, *Chris' Craft*, piloted by Art Armstrong. The Zenith down draft carburetors atop the Chris-Craft 121-horsepower KBL engine are slightly taller than the engine box, requiring the stylish aluminum enclosure.

Photos by Karine N. Rodengen

fleet sported white-painted hulls, a reflection of the severe amount of mahogany substitutions required. Even before the war, some models of Express Cruisers began to be called the Chris-Craft *Red & Whites,* the predominant colors of the class of fast, open-bridge cruisers.

Even with such a short menu, Chris-Craft sales managed an impressive showing of almost $13.5 million, and registered a profit of over $533,000 for the precarious year of lumber shortages.

Also during 1947, Chris-Craft bought land and manufacturing facilities in Caruthersville, Missouri, and established runabout production lines.[50] The hardest thing about establishing a branch factory is training local labor in company methods, standards and procedures. As with Jamestown, New York and all future satellite plant ventures, pilot programs were developed in Algonac, and then simply duplicated in Caruthersville with skilled operators working alongside the new workers until they could be turned loose on independent production.

By 1948, *postwar* design was the watchword of the industry, and as Chris-Craft asked consumers to *Make a date for '48,* 59 models were detailed for the fleet. Though over twice as many models would be introduced for '48, most of the additions were variations on power, configuration or appointments. Runabouts included models in 16, 17, 19 and 20-foot lengths, with single-engine power ranging from 60 to 145-horsepower, and at prices from $1,790 to $4,060. Sportsmen were offered in 16, 18, 22 and 25-foot versions, with power from 60-horsepower to a pair of 95-horsepower Chris-Crafts, though a 225-horsepower Scripps was offered with the 25-foot model, which for $6,970 would produce the fastest speed in the fleet at 40 miles per hour.

Nineteen Express Cruisers were available in 23, 25, 34 and 40-foot lengths, with a 23-foot, 60-horsepower model going for $3,220 and a 40-foot version powered with a pair of 316-horsepower Scripps going for a cool $25,000. Five models of the 40-foot Challenger returned, with power ranging from a pair of 95-horsepower Chris-Crafts at $18,700, to a pair of 316-horsepower Scripps at $26,300.

Cruisers were available in 26, 27, 30, 33, 36, 40 and 46-foot lengths, making a total of twenty-three variations. Flagship of the fleet, once again, was the 46-foot Double Cabin Enclosed with Flying Bridge model, powered with a pair of 160-horsepower Chris-Craft engines.

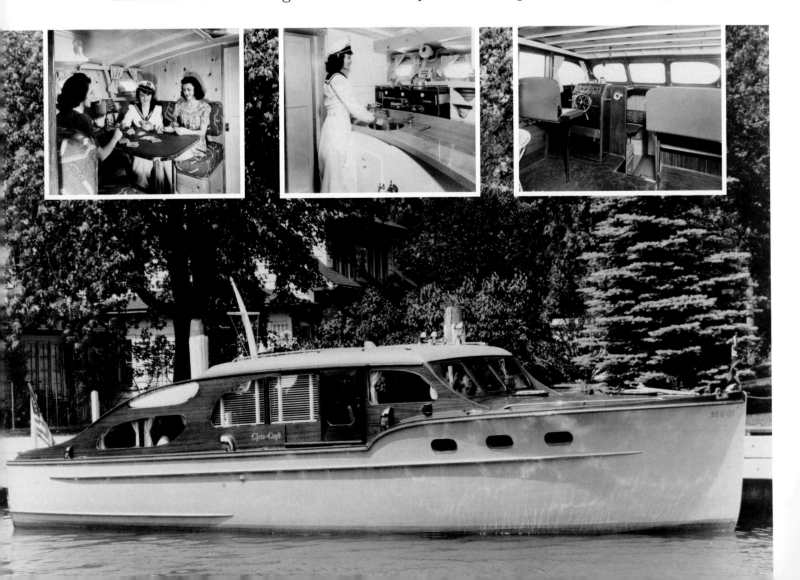

A 1949 48-foot *Catalina* continued Chris-Craft's evolution to the open flying-bridge configuration of mid-size cruisers. The

Courtesy Mariners' Museum, Newport News, Virginia.

greatest benefit to the layout was to move the owner's stateroom aft, where it is more comfortable in heavy seas.

The market for boats was increasing steadily each year, and by August 31, the end of Chris-Craft's 1948 fiscal year, the ledgers reveal sales of over $15 million, with a net profit before taxes of $1.6 million. The brochure for the year could accurately state "TODAY Chris-Craft holds a unique position...more Chris-Craft are sold in every country (with navigable waters) than any other make of motor boat. THE VAST majority of all the power boats at yacht clubs, resorts, and on the waterways of America are Chris-Craft...."[51]

A combination of logistical problems, growth less rapid than anticipated, along with a generous offer, led to the sale of the Jamestown, New York plant and facilities, which was originally considered an emergency war production facility during 1945. Chris-Craft would secure a net profit on the land and buildings of slightly over $90,000 when the sale was closed on September 7, 1948.[52]

Although sales would slip by over $2 million in the last year of the decade, Chris-Craft was rapidly preparing for expansion into new and promising markets. The fleet underwent a dramatic expansion in 1949, increasing to a record 161 models, including a renewed foray into premium sized *Motor Yachts* with the 52-foot *Conqueror*. On the first day of the year, Chris-Craft disclosed more than one new direction that would shape the decade of the fifties.

The new 52-foot Conqueror, latest model to be added to the Chris-Craft Corporation's 1949 fleet, brings a feeling of pride to the 650 employees at the Algonac plant.

The first model of this new motor yacht, which has accommodations to sleep eight people, has just been completed. It is expected to be shown at the New York boat show, Jan. 7 to 14.

The Conqueror, largest of the Chris-Craft fleet, has a 12½-foot beam. Prices [of all Chris-Craft models] range from $1,690 to $54,800.

The company's five plants, in Algonac, Cadillac, Holland, Mich., Chattanooga, Tenn., and Caruthersville, Mo. produce more motor boats than all other makers in the country combined, officials say. They are the largest builder of motor boats in the world....

42 40-foot Double Cabin Enclosed Bridge Cruiser was
ant, if slow yacht. Even equipped with a pair of 130-
ower Chris-Craft engines, it would only make 23 mph,
ailed for $11,900 f.o.b. Algonac.

Courtesy Mariners' Museum, Newport News, Virginia.

The Algonac plant has six main assembly lines. The boat starts with nothing but the keel on one end of the line, moves through the plant and comes out at the other end ready for the water....

Upholstery, berths and curtains are custom tailored in Chris-Craft's own shops. All the marine hardware is designed by Chris-Craft experts....

A new Chris-Craft outboard motor, the Challenger, will soon be put on the market. The new motor is to be built in an outboard plant at Grand Rapids.[53]

Three names were added to an enduring Chris-Craft vocabulary in 1949, *Riviera, Conqueror,* and among the most famous names in Chris-Craft history, *Commander.*

Six lengths of Runabouts were produced in 1949, including 16, 17 (Special and DeLuxe Runabouts), 18, 19 (Racing Runabouts) and 20-foot models (Custom Runabouts). 16-foot, 18-foot and 20-foot *Riviera* runabouts were offered, and while the $2,190 16-foot model was only available with the 60-horsepower Chris-Craft engine, the 18 and 20-footers were powered from 60 to 131-horsepower, producing speeds from 28 to 38 miles per hour respectively, and retailing from $2,430 to $2,820. Sportsmen were manufactured in 16, 18, 22 and 25-foot models, and ranged in performance from the $1,690, 60-horsepower, 30 mile an hour, to the fastest boat in the 1949 fleet, the 25-foot, 40 mile per hour model equipped with a pair of 145-horsepower Chris-Craft engines available for $6,840.

Express Cruisers were produced in 21-foot (Express and DeLuxe Express), 24-foot, 26-foot (Super Express), 30, 34, 40-foot, and the 40-foot *Challenger* models. Prices ranged from the 21-foot model powered with a 60-horsepower Chris-Craft at $2,530 to the 40-foot Challenger, powered with a pair of 316-horsepower Scripps engines at $27,600.

Eleven lengths of Cruisers were available, as 24-foot Enclosed Cruisers with Dinette; 26-foot Super DeLuxe Semi-Enclosed and Enclosed; 28-foot Super DeLuxe Semi-Enclosed and Enclosed; 30-foot Sedan, 33-foot DeLuxe Enclosed; 34-foot *Commander;* 36-foot Salon, Double Stateroom Enclosed, or Quarter-Deck Cruisers; 40-foot Double Cabin Enclosed Bridge; 46-foot Double Cabin Enclosed Bridge or Flying Bridge, and 52-foot *Conqueror* Motor Yacht models.

The new outboard motor production plant at Grand Rapids was in full production by the mid-

A 1947 25-foot (25'6") Express Cruiser, also known as a red and white, showing good speed in light chop off Harsens Island, Michigan. Aboard are driver Art Armstrong and owner Pat Pulk.

Photo by Karine N. Rodengen

dle of 1949, and Chris-Craft began an ambitious program to introduce their new venture to prospective dealers and consumers. The *Challenger*, a 5 ½-horsepower outboard, began to roll off the impressive outboard assembly lines, and like the well-established series of engines in the Chris-Craft Marine Engine Division, it was a superb product. It was superb because of the near obsession for detail and improvement which was heaped upon the outboard program by Jay W. Smith, Harsen Smith and Harry H. Coll, who was to manage the new division.

Winn Morrow, a longtime employee of the Marine Engine Division, remembers the fervent, enthusiasm which Jay W. had with the new project.

> I've gone to work a little early at six o'clock, and he was there long before me, running tests. We were running fifty hour tests or something like that and he was absolutely interested in what was going on with it. He helped to make the breakthrough, he had an awful lot to do with getting a two-cycle engine that would idle, and continue to idle without loading up.[54]

George Smith, son of Bernard, remembered the details of the decisions to mount the program, and the attention to detail which characterized the outboard program as a whole.

> There is quite a story just behind building that engine. They started out deciding what size engine to build. They decided the five horsepower motor was the most popular. They had [done] a survey all over the country. They set up a little room in the back, and tested [competitive engines], and learned all there was to know, and then started to develop their [engine]. When they got into the preignition problem, they called up the Champion Spark Plug people, and said we're having trouble. They came up and they looked at it and then showed them what the trouble was and everything. They [Jay and his engineers] took the spark plug and filed it off so it was half way across. That was all it took. So [Champion] came out with the JA plug.
>
> They had the same problem with the magnetos, the same problem with the carburetor, but when they put their mind to do something, they do it; they go all the way on it. Like I'll always say in the Smith family, there was no such expression as *that's good enough*.
>
> A lot of engines, you know, the flywheel would [come apart and] hit the pilot in the back of the head, you know, racing jocks and so on. They took one of the flywheels down to Packard Motor Company, and let her spin until it would break, and they learned from that so they knew that

they were safe. They also took them engines, and left the propeller off of it to see how fast it would turn. When it gets up around, eight, nine thousand rpm, the little reed valves flutter and it just can't go any faster.

> I can honestly say, as many times as I ran my engine, I never pulled the starter twice to start it. If I had to pull a second time I would take it apart and have to do something first. That's the way they were built to run. We had the magneto people right there, and we said we want a spark that long [George shows about two inches between his fingers] with 200 revolutions. Magneto people tried to tell us it was impossible. Next day they called on us we said, here, I'll show you one. We took a magneto, rewired it long, and did it. That was it. They wanted that engine to run at 200 rpm's for trolling, very slow. Other engines, you rocked the boat a little bit, she'd stall.[55]

By July of 1949, Chris-Craft had distributed 100,000 new brochures on the Chris-Craft *Challenger* outboard engine, and were on their way to penetrating a difficult and highly competitive market. The alternately-firing twin two-cycle engine was renowned for its quick starting, full reverse, simplified controls, 2-port reed valves, automatic rewinding starter, 1 ¼-gallon fuel tank and underwater exhaust. It was a great complement to the Smiths' overall marine industry accomplishments, and seemed to be a logical next step in their marine engine business.

Harry H. Coll, who was named manager of the Grand Rapids outboard motor plant in 1949, remembers the exceptional nature of the project.

> It's the most interesting story that you'd ever imagine. Here was Jay W. Smith, who was the master mechanic, a terrific engineer on engines, along with his brother Bernard.
>
> They took a tool-maker in the Algonac plant, and bought some expensive machines that could do very high tolerance work, and this man they had could operate it. They took outboards apart and found out what was wrong with them and incorporated the changes into the Chris-Craft outboard. Magnetos in those days wouldn't fire below 800 r.p.m., and you can pull only a thousand r.p.m. when you pull by hand, so they made a magneto to start with that would fire at a hundred and fifty r.p.m. There were three or four things that contributed to the idle. The plugs would get too hot running idle because there wasn't as much water circulation and then also you had too much fuel, so we drained the fuel and reused it, which was the first time that had ever been done. The Chris-Craft outboard engine would idle better than any other engine at that time.

Chris-Craft was dominating the elegant look by 1949. Among the 161 models offered were the 33-foot De Luxe Enclosed Cruiser and the rare 19-foot Racing Runabout which could deliver 44 mph with a single 158-horsepower Chris-Craft engine.

You had to buy magnetos from [the same sources], so it didn't take long for other companies to get the same equipment.

Actually, the basic reason for its success was Jay W. Smith and the rest of them over there that actually got to the bottom of what was wrong with outboards at that time and fixed it.[56]

The decade of the forties had been exceptional for the Smiths and for Chris-Craft, for even though the war would prohibit pleasure models for '43, '44, and '45, the war contracts provided the company with equipment and revenues which were to pay tremendous dividends in the postwar civilian marketplace. Though the world war was over, Chris-Craft, by the end of the decade, was rattling sabers in new areas of the marine marketplace, and had openly declared war on some of the toughest competitors in the industry, including Johnson, Evinrude and Mercury.

Courtesy Mariners' Museum, Newport News, Virginia.

On this, and the next few pages, are examples of design serendipity that never saw the
production line. As the war dragged on, Chris-Craft teased an anxious America
with the designs they imagined they would make when the war ended.

CHAPTER XIV

Boats You Never Saw

The mind of man is capable of anything — because everything is in it, all the
past as well as all the future.

Joseph Conrad
Heart of Darkness, 1902

THE FRUSTRATION of a long and agonizing World War was a challenge to the patience of Chris-Craft designers. Accustomed to the gentle curves of recreation, the hard lines of war were stifling and rigid. Anticipation of victory and a return to leisure pursuits swelled the imaginations of both artist and beholder. Together they dreamed of what it would be like when the agony was over. "Tomorrow," was the promise, "command your own Chris-Craft."

While the men and women at all three Chris-Craft factories are 100% engaged in war work, remember, after victory as always, you can count on Chris-Craft for advanced styling, greater values and all that's new and proved and practical in motor boating.[1]

The designs which teased a melancholy audience were a blend of the *streamline* school of the mid-thirties, and the fluid, sweeping exaggerations of *art deco*. They were bold and imaginative concepts, employing new materials and new techniques which were assumed to be available following the technological explosions of war. That the boats were never produced revealed more innocence and naivete than deceit or failure.

When the end of the war neared, the alluring and futuristic designs disappeared, quickly replaced by the realities of peacetime production. The transition from pleasure craft to landing craft had been so sudden, that the designs which were available as early as August of 1945, looked, not so surprisingly, like the tried and true models of 1942. America was anxious to move, and to move on.

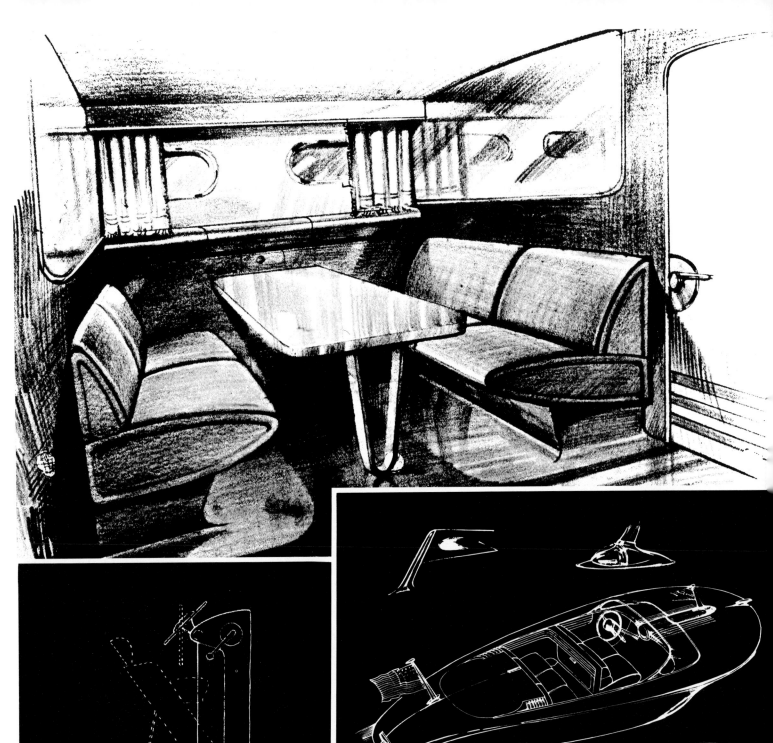

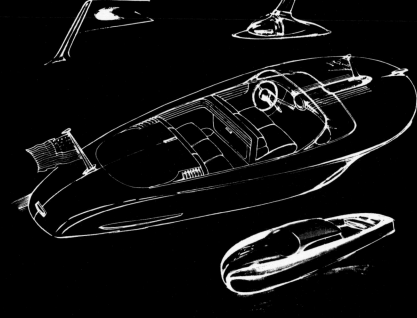

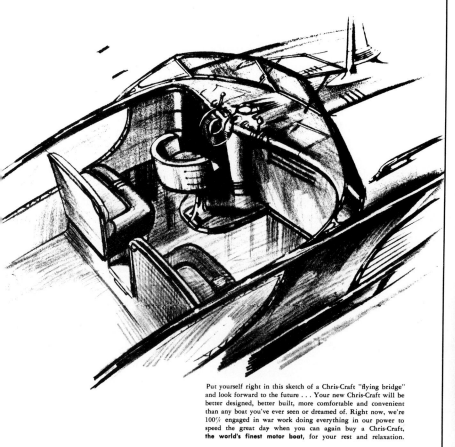

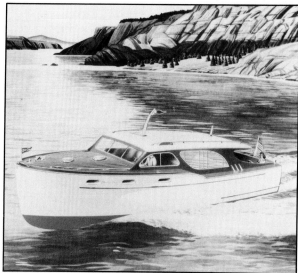

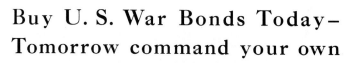

Chris-Craft manufactured solid mahogany skis in the fifties, like these aboard *Jenny,* a 1956
17-foot Custom Sportsman owned by Joe and Jenny Morrison of Algonac, Michigan

CHAPTER XV

The Fifties

We acknowledge your letter...dealing with plastic boat construction and in reply wish to advise that our present intention is not to enter the commercial plastic boat business. However, as has always been our policy, we will continue to entertain an interest in this development...

A. W. MacKerer
April, 1952[1]

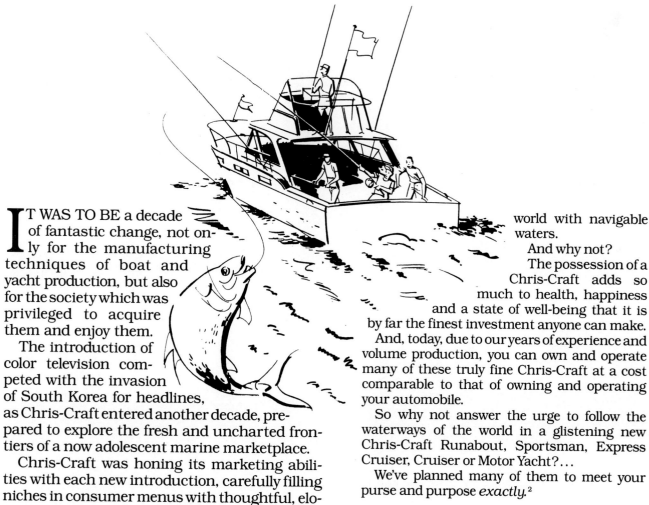

IT WAS TO BE a decade of fantastic change, not only for the manufacturing techniques of boat and yacht production, but also for the society which was privileged to acquire them and enjoy them.

The introduction of color television competed with the invasion of South Korea for headlines, as Chris-Craft entered another decade, prepared to explore the fresh and uncharted frontiers of a now adolescent marine marketplace.

Chris-Craft was honing its marketing abilities with each new introduction, carefully filling niches in consumer menus with thoughtful, eloquent products. "Command a New 1950 Chris-Craft," the brochure suggested, or who could resist a challenge to be "Nifty for Fifty"?

"Command a Chris-Craft" has become a buyword with boat lovers in every country in the world with navigable waters.

And why not?

The possession of a Chris-Craft adds so much to health, happiness and a state of well-being that it is by far the finest investment anyone can make.

And, today, due to our years of experience and volume production, you can own and operate many of these truly fine Chris-Craft at a cost comparable to that of owning and operating your automobile.

So why not answer the urge to follow the waterways of the world in a glistening new Chris-Craft Runabout, Sportsman, Express Cruiser, Cruiser or Motor Yacht?...

We've planned many of them to meet your purse and purpose *exactly*.[2]

In 1950, 139 models of Chris-Craft were fashioned from factories in Algonac, Holland and Cadillac, Michigan, along with Caruthersville, Missouri and Chattanooga, Tennessee. Runabouts were offered in 38 models, but only eight lengths, 16, 17, 18, 19, 20, 22, 23 and 25-foot. The 18, 22 and 25-foot models were the only surviving Sportsmen, while the 16, 18 and 20-foot versions were the Rivieras. The 1950 22-foot Sportsman was made famous in later years as the boat in *On Golden Pond*, starring Katharine Hepburn and Henry Fonda. The Rivieras featured a two-tone, natural mahogany finish, double cockpit forward, red Naugahyde seats and a smooth, compact looking structure which established a good following. A 16-foot Riviera was equipped with a 60-horsepower Chris-Craft engine for $2,290, while the 20-foot could top 40 miles per hour with a 158-horsepower engine for $3,440. Production was stopped on the little 16-footer on June 3, 1951. The boat was underpowered and quite sluggish, and passengers crammed into the little rear seat would get wet in any kind of chop. Fastest in the fleet was the 19-foot Racing Runabout powered with a 158-horsepower at 44 miles per hour and $2,960.

Express Cruisers ranged from the diminutive 21-foot with 145-horsepower at $5,880 to a 40-foot Express with a pair of 160-horsepower Chris-Craft engines at $19,400. In between were twenty models in 23, 26, 30, and 34-foot lengths.

Cruisers dominated the 1950 fleet with eighty models from the 24-foot Enclosed Cruiser and 60-horsepower Chris-Craft engine at $4,430, to the 52-foot Motor Yacht powered with a pair of General Motors diesels at $49,400. The Motor Yachts could be configured with triple engines for an additional $1,240. Among the cruisers were 26-foot Super Semi-Enclosed and Super Enclosed, 28-foot Super Semi-Enclosed and Super Enclosed, 30-foot Sedan Cruisers, 32-foot Super Enclosed, 33-foot DeLuxe Enclosed, 34-foot Commander, 36-foot Salon Cruisers, 36-foot Double Stateroom and Quarterdeck, 40-foot Challenger, 41-foot Double Cabin Enclosed Bridge and Double Cabin Flying Bridge, along with 46 and 48-foot Double Cabin Flying Bridge models.

Chris-Craft added another outboard engine to their popular 5½-horsepower *Challenger*, with the introduction of the 10-horsepower *Commander*. The *preparatory costs* for the new 10-horse were only $152,093.57 according to the balance sheet, which, in contrast with the immediate consumer acceptance of the engine would prove to be an astounding return on investment.[3] As one letter of praise claimed, "We ship water, dousing the engines; run full-throttle in shallow mooring, churning gravel that chews our propeller; and gun the engines through 15-ft. swells. Yes, Chris-Craft Marine engines are the world's best buys."[4]

Among the new ventures which Chris-Craft would undertake in 1950, and which would endure for the entire decade, were boats avail-

The last custom-designed military vessel produced by Chris-Craft was this 52-foot *Aircraft Rescue Boat* completed in 1952. Powered with twin Packard 1500-horsepower engines, it had a unique transom ramp for bringing injured airmen aboard quickly.

Courtesy Mariners' Museum, Newport News, Virginia.

able in *kit* form for consumers to assemble themselves. Since this episode in Chris-Craft history is so unique and intriguing, a chapter is devoted exclusively to this topic. See *The Kit Boats*, Chapter XVI.

Sales crested for all Chris-Craft products in 1950 at nearly $14.5 million, which yielded a profit of over ten percent, or $1.5 million, an indication of good financial and production management in any organization.[5]

America's involvement in the Korean conflict was further cemented as China entered the foray in late 1950. Within months, Chris-Craft would be called upon again to build specialty craft for the Navy, though in a very limited capacity. This time, the design of a 52-foot *Aircraft Rescue Boat* would be Chris-Craft's, and two prototypes were requested within one-hundred days of receiving a letter of agreement from the government.[6]

These fast Naval vessels were "designed for speedy rescue of downed airmen," and were capable of speeds over 52 miles per hour. "Thermostatically controlled heating and cooling systems will maintain constant engine temperatures," the press release disclosed, "so that these new rescue craft can be pressed into emergency service at top speeds, without encountering delays for engine warm-ups."[7] Both boats were to be powered with twin Packard engines that each develop 1500 horsepower at 2500 r.p.m.

One of the prototypes would have a direct drive arrangement, while the other would have an advanced form of "Vee" drive system, and the performances of each would be compared. Each could carry twelve hundred gallons of fuel for a range of 250 miles at full throttle.

Among the interesting design characteristics of the vessels were special transom ramps which were hinged below the waterline, to "enable rescuers to bring injured airmen into a self-bailing cockpit and down into sick-bay without lifting them over the side." As part of this tricky mechanism, "racks that swing down from the transom and from the hull sides, near the stern, will form an underwater cage around the propulsion unit to fend off floating debris and to protect men in the water from the wheels [propellers]."[8] The sick bay took up the after third of the ships, to "accommodate four and if additional litter cases are picked up, four can be treated in the crew quarters, forward."[9] Another unique feature was that if fire would break out in the wreckage of the fallen aircraft "fire-fighters on the new rescue craft, can quickly extinguish the flames to hasten rescue and to enable crewmen to save valuable equipment. A pump pulls water from the surrounding sea to supply six 1½" streams of water."[10] The 46,000 pound hulls were convex, modified-vee, and designed especially for high speed operation. Built of Philippine mahogany outer planking, they used

Photo by Karine N. Rodengen

Queen of the Flats is a very rare 1955 18-foot *Fiesta Cruiser Kit Boat*, piloted by owner Jim Chominski of Harsens Island, Michigan.

a mahogany marine-plywood inner planking run on a bias across mahogany frames.

The project was hampered by frustrating delays and red tape by the government almost from the very beginning.[11] By August of 1951, Bill MacKerer had to give Washington a stern warn-

The Choice of Experts

Chris-Craft halted outboard engine production in 1953 due to potential patent infringement concerning the 10 hp *Commander*, above right. The 5½ hp *Challenger* was produced in England by others until the mid-sixties.

ing about their handling of the project, and to remind them of the onset of the Algonac winter.

Chris-Craft is making every effort to complete the two (2) Prototype rescue boats so that they can be tested and driven away before freezing and making the project ice-bound.

The actual production of the boats is proceeding unusually well, considering the late date of the contract and subsequent events, and will normally be completed for testing in late October or early November. However, from a realistic angle, other factors than fabrication are entering the picture and may possibly delay the completion of these boats until December and January (which is too late for testing and drive-away).

These outside influences are beyond the control of the Chris-Craft Corp., and fall more in the realm of control of the Navy and Governmental agencies. Some of the items holding up work are as follows: Inability of some vendors to secure specified material in time, delivery of Government furnished Packard Engines and equipment, fabrication of "Vee" drive gears, inability of some suppliers to meet schedule, etc.[12]

In fact, due to continued delays of the same variety as MacKerer chastised the government, the Rescue Boats wouldn't be ready for testing until June of the following year. Chris-Craft wasn't used to moving slow at anything. The government contract became a sore point in an organization that was bulging with expansion opportunities in the fast-paced pleasure craft marketplace, and was less and less interested in having their hands tied by a Washington bureaucracy. Among the major irritants in the program was the inability of Chris-Craft to get the Government to finalize their agreements, even up to a week before the first boat was launched.[13]

When continual government changes finally pushed the cost of the hulls to over $20,000 more than the Government agreed to pay Chris-Craft on a fixed price contract, MacKerer wrote a detailed letter to the Bureau of Ships which revealed his frustration.

We feel that by establishing a fixed price contract for developing and fabrication of *Prototype* hulls of a complex nature, without firmed-up specifications and "Outline of Work" plus requiring Final Plans completed before hull completion — delays in delivery of material — substitutions, etc., is an unsatisfactory way of being compensated for our work and effort.[14]

Things had changed a great deal since the war, both at Chris-Craft and in Washington. The Korean conflict didn't have the priority that

World War II commanded, and lines of communication were strained and impersonal. Once Chris-Craft delivered the two prototype Rescue Boats, they declined future government contracts, except for the occasional order for stock boats. Concerning a future government development contract MacKerer would scribble in his notebook "In view of past experience with development contracts...too much of a headache."[15] A few years later, in response to an offer to have Chris-Craft take over an assignment to develop a new version of the LCVP Landing Boat produced so successfully during the war, MacKerer spoke for the corporation when he said "After discussing this matter quite thoroughly, it is felt that because of circumstances both past and present-day, we will be unable to take on this additional workload."[16] Chris-Craft still did everything it could to assist

when the Government needed a favor. When a request was made to use the Holland, Michigan plant for three days of seminars to educate Bureau of Ships personnel in modern small boat building techniques, Chris-Craft cordially agreed, and concerning the fee for the use of the plant, sent them a telegram saying "The Bureau can set any amount they choose from $1 – $2,500...for the services."[17]

To introduce their new 1951 line, Chris-Craft waxed poetic and reminded consumers that "There's a new Chris-Craft for every purse and purpose."[18]

You, who have always dreamed of owning a fine boat —
Of flashing across blue inland waters at breath-taking speeds
Or cruising the limitless waterways of the world in luxurious splendor

Photo by Karine N. Rodengen

Even though it hadn't appeared in the catalog since 1948, this 25-foot (24'11") Express Cruiser, also known as a *Red and White,* was built in 1950. Driven by owner Dana Wagenhals of Mt. Clemens, Michigan.

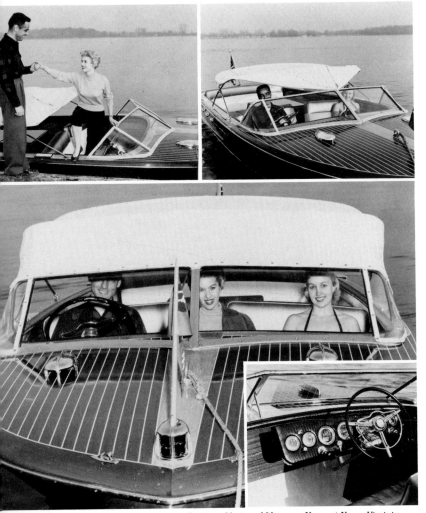

Courtesy Mariners' Museum, Newport News, Virginia.

Chris-Craft was always experimenting with tops for their run-about fleets. This 1954 20-foot *Continental* featured a three-way folding top to fit any occasion.

The warm sunshine on your back and
A fresh breeze against your cheek —
Take the wheel…enjoy life…command a new
Chris-Craft now.[19]

The Chris-Craft fleet for 1951 shrank in size by thirty-two models, for a total of 107 offerings. New for '51 were the 19 and 23-foot *Holiday* runabouts. The Holiday was a premium run-about that seemed to be a cross between the Sportsman configuration and the obsolete DeLuxe Utility boats, sporting wide open spaces, vinyl plastic upholstered bench seating and smooth lines enhanced by two-tone mahogany deck details. The 19-foot model could cost up to $3,786 with a 120-horsepower engine, while the 23-foot could top $5,683 with a 158-horsepower engine. Options would include amidship seat, metal-lined live fish box, folding top with side curtains and ice chest/seat. The

25-foot Sportsman was dropped from the run-about line-up.

A drastic overhaul was made in Express Cruisers, Cruisers and Motor Yachts. Almost all models were new. Among the missing in Express Cruisers were the 21, 23, 26 Super Express, 30 and 40-foot models. Only two new models were introduced to replace them, a 22-foot and 24-foot Express.

Cruisers were almost entirely changed; the only survivors were models in lengths of 31, 32, 33 and 34-feet, including the 34-foot Commander. New Cruisers were introduced in 25, 27, 29, 38, 42 (Commander), 42 (including Challenger), a 47-foot Buccaneer, and 50-foot Catalina models.

Newest flagships of the fleet were Motor Yachts in both 54 and 62-foot models. A new 62-foot Motor Yacht, powered with a pair of General Motors 200-horsepower diesel engines would take a party of thirteen live-aboard guests just about anywhere at over 20 miles per hour for $121,750 f.o.b. Algonac. A year earlier, Bill Mac-Kerer had done some computations to determine the cost to produce the 62-foot boat, and he figured on 13,000 hours of labor per boat, $6,726 in lumber, $12,000 in stores, and an initial cost of 1,542 hours of labor just to fabricate patterns, jigs and the stall for the yacht. His penciled-in total came to $57,300.[20]

Sales jumped nearly $3 million for the year, at $17,701,406, while profits dipped to $851,525 owing to the nearly universal model changes and the purchase of the capital stock of Hercules Motor Corporation at over $600,000, the company which supplied the block for many of the Chris-Craft Marine Engines.

All New for '52 the headlines shouted, as Chris-Craft urged buyers to *Do it today! Get away and play!*[21] As a result of the large-scale overhaul of the '51 fleet, few changes were evident in '52. Marketing direction was further honed, however, and in one communication, Sales Manager Wayne Pickell reacts to an objection over the new *Special Sportsman*, in 17-foot and 20-foot models.

Some of the old timers will turn up their noses at the interior because it is painted instead of being paneled. I am thinking of one in particular (and there are others) that is a high hat guy who does business only with the silk stocking trade. He believes he couldn't sell an unpaneled boat to buyers in his locality and he is very sincere about it. Yet, I know if we were to go to his area and put in an additional dealer

The 1953 63-foot Motor Yacht could fulfill a life
dreams, with a galley suitable for a full-time chef. Eq
with *three* 200-horsepower G.M. diesels, it would m
mph for $1

Courtesy Mariners' Museum, Newport News, Vir

(which we don't intend to do) with the understanding that all this new dealer could buy from the factory is the two 17's and the 20 that this new dealer would enjoy an attractive volume and the senior dealer's business wouldn't be affected. He would sell just as many Chris-Craft as he ever did.

So don't be prejudiced, and don't let your personal likes and dislikes influence you too much in regard to your purchases for resale. Look at it like this, if the models we are offering were not selling, they would not be in the line for long. That's right. Isn't it?[22]

1953 was a year of mixed feelings at Chris-Craft, for though the new fleet of boats would do very well in the marketplace, the outboard motor production plant in Grand Rapids was shut down, a victim of both marketing and engineering errors. After investing well over a million dollars in facilities, exotic and exacting manufacturing equipment, personnel training and fierce positioning, the doors were being locked.

Like many disasters, this one had several causes and produced many explanations. Two

basic facts overshadow the controversy which is today still discussed passionately by those who were ensnared by the events of 1953. First, many say that for Chris-Craft to be successful in the outboard motor business, they would have had to develop an *entire line* of outboard motors. Two engines, the 5 ½-horsepower *Challenger*, and the 10-horsepower *Commander*, could not satisfy the breadth of applications required by consumers accustomed to choosing among dozens of sizes and styles of Johnson, Evinrude and Kiekhaefer — Mercury outboard products. The common explanation continues by pointing out that Chris-Craft's increasingly complex boat product lines required 100% of their effort and concentration to satisfy the greater demands placed on them by more and more sophisticated consumers. But there is another, less appealing answer.

Chris-Craft could not have developed their outboard engine program in such short fashion without paying close attention to the engineering techniques and strategies of other manufacturers. This created a fatal problem with the

10-horsepower *Commander.* Chris-Craft had inadvertently infringed on a patent or patents of the Kiekhaefer Corporation, manufacturers of Mercury outboard engines in Fond du Lac, Wisconsin.

Charles D. "Charley" Strang, then Chief Engineer for Kiekhaefer Corporation, and now Chairman of the Board of Outboard Marine Corporation (OMC), manufacturers of Johnson and Evinrude outboard motors, remembers the Chris-Craft outboard engines well. "We put it out of business. They...duplicated some of the stuff that was patented by Mercury. Carl [Kiekhaefer] said sue them. So we sued them and their solution for the whole thing was to go out of business."[23]

Harry Coll, who was then plant manager for the Chris-Craft outboard motor operations at Grand Rapids, recalls the uncomfortable dilemma.

This beautifully restored 1953 35-foot Commander was captured near Cedarville, Michigan. If equipped with a pair of 145-horsepower Chris-Craft engines, it would deliver 30 mph for $17,830.

Photo by Karine N. Rodengen

It was the ten horse lower unit. We didn't know that we had violated anything until he told us. In order to get it thin, you had to use a certain bearing set up, the thinner you got it the faster the boat would go and we didn't know that we used one of their patents until somebody told us. There was no way that we wanted to continue violating a patent, so we stopped the production of the engine. But that didn't affect the five and a half. It was still made by other companies that we sold it to. It was made in England for ten years.[24]

Chris-Craft's dominance of the pleasure boat industry was not affected in the least by the quiet disappearance of the outboard motors. Insiders agree that the return on investment was much greater for funds placed in the boat divisions, rather than attempting to build a complete line of new engines at tremendous cost, and as Chris-Craft had learned, tremendous risk.

The 1953 fleet of 111 models included an unusually small selection of runabouts, with examples in 17-foot (Special Sportsman and Rocket Runabout), 18-foot (Sportsman and Riviera), 19-foot (Racing Runabout and Holiday), 20-foot (Special Sportsman and Riviera), 22-foot (Sportsman) and 24-foot (Holiday). Prices ranged from the 17-foot Sportsman with 60 horsepower at $2,350, to the 24-foot Holiday with 158 horsepower at $5,730.

Express Cruisers were offered in 22, 26, 28 (Super Deluxe Express), 32, 33 (Capitan), and 40-foot lengths, and prices started at $3,650 for the 22-foot, 60-horsepower model, to $21,850 for the 40-foot Express with a pair of 160-horsepower engines.

Cruisers continued to dominate with forty-five models, with greater emphasis on larger models, increasing in both appointments and capabilities. Models were available in 22-foot (Custom Sedan), 25-foot (Enclosed), 28-foot (Super Deluxe Semi-Enclosed and Enclosed), 31-foot (Sedan), 34-foot (Double Cabin Enclosed Bridge and Flying Bridge), 35-foot (Commander), 40-foot (Double Cabin Flying Bridge), 42-foot (Commander and Challenger), 45-foot (Double Cabin Flying Bridge), 50-foot (Catalina Double Cabin Flying Bridge), and the return of the 52-foot Conqueror (Double Cabin Flying Bridge). Prices ranged from $5,360 for the 22-foot Custom Sedan with 130-horsepower engine to $48,700 for the Catalina with three 145-horsepower engines.

Motor Yachts were available in 55-foot and 63-foot versions, and ranged in price from the 55-foot Motor Yacht with a pair of 160-horsepower engines at $57,720 to the Queen of the fleet, the 63-foot Motor Yacht with three General Motors 200-horsepower diesel engines at $127,980.

Chris-Craft offered boat trailers for the first time in 1953, in four weight capacities, 300 lb., 650 lb., 1000 lb., and 2,200 lb. The trailers were also offered as kits. (See *Chapter XVI, The Kit Boats*). A separate division was established in Algonac for these practical, welded square-tubular, steel chassis products.

1954 would mark the introduction of a whole new class of boats for Chris-Craft, and the unveiling of a brand new production facility to accommodate the new line. No sooner than the doors closed on the Grand Rapids outboard facility, construction was underway on newly acquired land in Salisbury, Maryland. During World War II, Chris-Craft was introduced to a new adhesive sealant known as *Thiokol*. The gooey substance was used to seal plywood to other components in the construction of the Landing Craft. It set up firmly, but was resilient enough to remain intact under stress and movement. And as an adhesive, it couldn't be matched. Chris-Craft was now ready to employ the wonder substance in a new application, sealing between strakes of a new line of lapstrake, clinker-built, round bilge boats known as *Sea Skiff*. The Thiokol, renamed *Chris-Craft Sealer* for mention within brochures and ads, worked so well, that Bill MacKerer along with many employees felt that screws or other fastenings weren't even needed on the strake side planking.[25]

The Sea Skiffs were renowned for their dry, comfortable ride, combined with a husky and rugged styling, and response from the market was almost spontaneous. In a letter to dealers announcing the new 35-foot model, Sea Skiff Division Sales Manager W.S. Vance, revealed the fact that new Sea Skiff orders were running far ahead of production.

> That soft, cushion, dry ride for which Chris-Craft Sea Skiffs have become so famous is in full evidence. Moreover, Chris-Craft Sea Skiff Sealer which virtually adds about four times the strength to a round-bilge, lapstrake boat is used between all seams and joints from keel to sheer. The critic who insists upon the maximum in seaworthiness and wants that additional feeling of security need look no further.
>
> The good news about this great value apparently is getting around, since, in spite of the fact that neither data nor sales promotion effort has been put forth in the usual manner, orders have been received at an unprecedented rate. This fact is best confirmed since the next delivery date, subject to prior sale, is [three months away].[26]

One hundred and forty-eight models of boats, excluding Sea Skiffs and Kits were rolled out for 1954, and new names were added to a growing list of Chris-Craft classics. Newest additions were the 35-foot *Sport Fisherman;* 36-foot *Corvette* Cruiser; a 45-foot *Corsair* Cruiser, and a

name which would overshadow the rest in longevity and prestige, *Constellation*, introduced as the new 53-foot flagship of the Cruiser fleet.

The well-balanced fleet started at $2,380 for a 17-foot Sportsman with a 60-horsepower engine, and climbed to $133,540 for the new 63-foot Motor Yacht equipped with three General Motors diesel engines.

Among the busiest years of the decade was 1955, a landmark year as Chris-Craft initiated a variety of bold new ventures. It would be the year that Chris-Craft first used the new technology of plastic resin reinforced with fine glass fibers spun into a yarn, *fiberglas*, in the construction of a new model of racing runabout, the *Cobra*. Though Chris-Craft completely dominated the pleasure craft industry, they were not the first to embrace fiberglas technology, but waited a couple of years for the new substance to prove itself, and began to experiment with it themselves.

Early experiments around the industry in the manufacture of fiberglas boats were less than successful. In the early fifties, the catalyst chemistry involved in the resin hardening process hadn't been fully discovered, and the only way to get a hull to set up was to bathe it in very hot heat lamps for quite some time. Once removed from the mold, the sides would be wavy, and some areas of the hull would be thick, others would be thin, and finishes came out looking dull and spotty.

Two of Chris-Craft's most fascinating classic boats, the 18 and 21-foot Cobras, were the first to use fiberglas components in their construction. At first glance, the boat is absolutely dominated by a large, golden-colored single dorsal-type fin on the after deck. The fin, along with the supporting panel, was made of fiberglas, the rest of the boat built out of traditional Chris-Craft mahogany construction. Only 106 Cobras were built from January until discontinued due to poor sales and somewhat skittish performance in July of 1955, with slightly more 21-foot models being produced, at 55, than the 18-foot model. The 18-foot could be equipped with Chris-Craft engines of 95, 105, 120 and 131-horsepower, while the 21-foot version could accept a Chris-Craft 158-horsepower, Chrysler 200-horsepower or even Cadillac 285-horsepower V-8 power plants.[27]

Another overhaul of the product line-up occurred for '55, with new models grouped into "series" for the first time. Following the 17-foot

Above: The 1955 19-foot *Capri* would deliver 39 mph with a 131-horsepower engine.

Fleet flagship honors were shared between the 53-foot Conqueror and 53-foot Constellation as the larger, considerably more expensive Motor Yachts were quietly scuttled. You could drive-away a new 53-foot Constellation from the Algonac plant with a pair of 223-horsepower General Motors diesels for $55,330, or whisk away aboard a new 17-foot Sportsman for $2,390.

Two bold new divisions were inaugurated in 1955, as far apart in the boat construction spectrum as you can get. Chris-Craft *Plywood Boat*

Middle below:
A four-sleeper
1955 34-foot *Capitan*.

Below: Built with 5-ply Philippine Mahogany plywood, this late 1954 17-foot *Cavalier Utility* delivered up to 38 mph.

Photos Courtesy Mariners' Museum, Newport News, Virginia.

Sportsmans were the Holiday Series of 18, 20 and 22-foot models; the Continental Series of 18, 20, 22 and 25-foot models; the new *Capri* series in 19 and 21-foot versions; the Racing Runabout Series containing the Cobras; a Two-Sleeper, Low and Medium Priced Express Cruisers Class containing Expresses in 23, 25 and 27-foot variations; the 26-foot Series of Semi-Enclosed, Sedan and Flying Bridge Cruisers; the 29-foot Series of Sportsman, Semi-Enclosed, Sedan, Express and Capitan Cruisers; the 33-foot Commander and 34-foot Capitan; the 37-foot Series of Commander and Corvette Cruisers; and the 42-foot Series of Express, Commander and Commodore Cruisers.

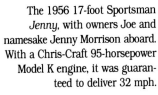

Photo by Karine N. Rodengen

A rare 1950 22-foot *Sportsman* with a factory optional *Streamlined ventilating cabin* hurries across the St. Clair River Flats driven by owner Jeff Mily.

Division, and the purchase of the *Roamer Boat Corporation* in Holland, Michigan, manufacturers of *steel* cruisers, established firm beachheads in both high and low ends of the market.

The Plywood Boat Division was established in response to consumer demands for inexpensive boats, while still maintaining styling appeal. Owens Yacht Company had introduced a line of plywood cruisers, and rumors of record sales filtered back to Algonac. A number of sources indicate that the decision to enter the plywood boat business was a difficult one for the Smiths. Clearly, the quality of the boats was not in the same league as their planked mahogany products, but unmistakable and irresistible signals from consumers indicated a growing need for an economy line of boats.

Only four plywood models were introduced in 1955, the 15-foot *Cavalier* with 60-horsepower inboard at $1,595, the 16-foot outboard Express Cruiser at $699, a 17-foot *Cavalier* capable of 40-miles per hour with a 131-horsepower Chris-Craft engine at $1,795, and the 20-foot outboard Cruiser *Gay Paree*. The *Gay Paree* was virtually the same boat as available in kit form for around $700, while fully assembled came to $1,099. Styling of the boats was slightly boxy, owing to the limitations of large plywood sheets bent for hull bottoms, sides and decks. Solid mahogany lumber was still used on all keels, skegs, frames, stem and forefoot components. Known as "Chris-Craft's New Big-Value Line", the marketing approach was straightforward and to the point.

> Now step up into the runabout or cruiser class in a smart new Chris-Craft Plywood boat! Outboard and inboard models — with prices starting at only $699!
>
> All are exciting performers! Swift and easy handling; light in weight, yet ruggedly strong — thanks to sturdy, full-length panel-plywood construction, which brings manufacturing costs down. And *you* benefit from the savings!
>
> If you'd like a bigger, faster, better-looking boat, you can't do better than buy a sensational new Chris-Craft Plywood Boat![28]

The 1956 17-foot Sportsman *Jenny*, with owners Joe and namesake Jenny Morrison aboard. With a Chris-Craft 95-horsepower Model K engine, it was guaranteed to deliver 32 mph.

Photo by Karine N. Rodengen

Photos by Karine N. Rodengen

Using 5/16" to 3/4" mahogany and fir plywoods, Chris-Craft insisted on using only the very best sheet plywood available in the industry. In fact, so much wood was rejected, and so much pressure placed upon suppliers for the highest quality sheets, that the industry, of its own accord, named a new, ultimate mahogany plywood quality category *Chris-Craft Grade,* a category which had already been established in the industry for solid mahogany sent to Algonac.

Literally down the street from the Holland, Michigan plant, a small welded steel boat company called Roamer Boat Corporation began building steel tugs for the war effort while the

The 1958 22-foot Chris-Craft *Cavalier Express* 2-Sleeper was the affordable dream. Built of Philippine mahogany plywood, a family could own a cabin cruiser equipped with a 60-horsepower Chris-Craft engine for only $3,770.

Courtesy Mariners' Museum, Newport News, Virginia.

Chris-Craft facility turned out Landing Boats. In 1955, an opportunity to purchase the company surfaced, and nearly overnight, Chris-Craft was in the steel boat construction business. The leading product of the Roamer Boat Corporation in 1955 was a stylish 35-foot Express Cruiser built of "lifetime steel".

As you know, there are many advantages to steel hulls — freedom from rot, safety from unknown underwater obstructions, minimum upkeep, to mention a few. Particularly gratifying to the economy-minded owner is the minimum upkeep required on all ROAMER Cruisers, which is made possible by our special, highly adhesive paint which we apply to the hull after sand blasting has produced an absolutely clean surface. Further, the inside of the hull is covered with a bitumastic compound that dampens sound and also makes the inside rust-free in both salt and fresh waters. A non-bleeding paint over this protective coat produces a fresh, clean appearance. All hulls, of course, whether wood or steel, must have normal maintenance and care, however, we feel from a do-it-yourself standpoint that the steel hull is by far the easier to maintain.[29]

The 35-foot Roamer was available with engines ranging from a pair of 95-horsepower Chris-Crafts at $15,520, to a pair of 200-horsepower Chryslers at $19,120, which compared favorably to the 37-foot mahogany Commander, similarly equipped at $21,490.

Chris-Craft built a new 200,000-square-foot plant to supplement the existing facilities, devoted exclusively to the construction of welded-steel and, later, welded-aluminum Cruisers and Motor Yachts.

Courtesy Mariners' Museum, Newport News, Virginia.

Chris-Craft purchased the Roamer Boat Corporation in 1955, and overnight were in the steel boat-building business. Shown above left is the 1957 28-foot *Roamer* Express Cruiser. Top and right; A 42-foot steel *Roamer* prototype is welded together in Holland, Michigan in 1957.

Rigged for action, this 1957 22-foot *Sea Skiff* shows the versatility of the lapstrake design. The durable hulls are very seaworthy, able to take abusive conditions and still give many years of faithful service. Owned by Paul Conroy of Port Huron, Michigan.

Photo by Karine N. Rodengen

Above and right: Bill Buckley's 1954 36-foot Commander Express Cruiser Four-Sleeper, *Tonofun V.* The flying bridge model, including a folding top with side curtains, was an option at no charge which replaced the standard hard top.

Photos by Karine N. Rodengen

Opposite left: *Outpost,* a 1958 32-foot *Commander* from New Baltimore, Michigan, driven by owner Mel Mathias. Powered by a pair of 6-cylinder 130-horsepower Chris-Craft Model M engines, it retailed for $17,780.

Photo by Karine N. Rodengen

Sea Skiffs were available in '55 from 18 to 35-feet, including a new open and roomy 26-foot Sea Skiff with a whopping 8'4" beam for $3,750.

A renewed enthusiasm for the fast-growing sport fishing market segment was shown by the introduction in 1956 of the 38-foot *Sport Fisherman*. The rugged and well-designed mahogany fishing machine accommodated four in upper and lower berths, and included a full galley, dinette and lounge.

Slashing "swords", screaming lines and salty sea-air introduce you to a thrilling new concept of fun and freedom as you "hunt" the seas from the fishing flying bridge of the sleek new CHRIS-CRAFT SPORT FISHERMAN! Exceptional *visibility* is matched by amazing *maneuverability*, with twin engine options up to 500 total horsepower. When a big one socks your bait and the fight begins, the skipper can scramble below to a dual control station in the cockpit. After your fish is brought to gaff you'll haul him over the low unobstructed cockpit rim

and onto the teak deck where the battle will finally be won.[30]

The Chris-Craft "Boat Division" introduced 150 models for 1956, apart from Roamer, Sea Skiff, Plywood, Kit and Trailer Divisions. Notable new additions to the line-up included the 33-foot *Futura* Cruiser; a new small *Constellation* in 35, 38, 42 and 46-foot sizes; along with *Conquerors* and *Constellations* in 54-foot lengths to top the fleet.

Sportsmen were available in 17 and 20-foot versions; Holiday Series included 18, 20 and 23-foot sizes; Continentals came in 18, 20, 23 and 26-foot lengths; while Capris were offered in 19 and 21-foot versions.

Express Cruisers were represnted only in 23 and 25-foot lengths, while an altered Cruiser line-up contained models in 24, 26, 27, 30, 33, 35, 38, 42, 46 and 54-foot versions. Prices fluctuated somewhat in '56, and ranged from $2,530 for the 17-foot Sportsman with 60-

In 1956 you could order a 38-foot *Constellation* many ways. Two possibilities were the Four-Sleeper flying bridge model below, or the Six-Sleeper with hard top (insert).

Courtesy Mariners' Museum, Newport News, Virginia.

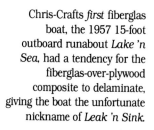

Chris-Crafts *first* fiberglas boat, the 1957 15-foot outboard runabout *Lake 'n Sea*, had a tendency for the fiberglas-over-plywood composite to delaminate, giving the boat the unfortunate nickname of *Leak 'n Sink*.

Courtesy Mariners' Museum, Newport News, Virginia.

horsepower engine, to $60,920 for the 54-foot *Constellation* with a pair of General Motors diesel engines.

Plywood boats surged in sales rapidly following their introduction, and as a result several new models made their debut including a 20-foot Cavalier, 16-foot outboard Express Cruiser, and a 21-foot outboard or inboard Cabin Cruiser, and a 22-foot outboard or inboard Four Sleeper Express Cruiser with Flying Bridge.

The popular Sea Skiff line grew to an incredible sixty-one models, in lengths of 18, 22, 26, 30, 35 and 40-feet. They ranged in price from the 18-foot model with 60-horsepower engine at $2,660 to the 40-foot Salon Deckhouse Cruiser Sea Skiff with a pair of 200-horsepower Chrysler engines for $28,090 f.o.b. the busy Sea Skiff plant at Salisbury, Maryland.

Emotions ran high among Chris-Craft's Algonac employees early in 1957. The Smith family, backbone of Algonac manufacturing since the 19th century, and whose traditional administrative headquarters at Algonac was seemingly intractable, spread shock waves throughout the organization by announcing they would move all corporate offices to Pompano Beach, Florida. They had quietly bought a spectacular stretch of land along the northern coast of Pompano Beach, between Race Track Road and Cypress Creek. With a shrewdness worthy of Christopher Columbus Smith, subdivision and resale of much of the property generated nearly suffi-

cient profit to build the Pompano Beach plant and a new, two-story, 34,000 square feet Administrative Headquarters Building.[31]

Chris-Craft was willing to relocate valued executives to the new Pompano offices, but a sense of gloom and abandonment permeated the Algonac manufacturing facilities. The year-round fair weather of Florida would permit continuous testing and experimentation, the Smiths would say, and Florida was much closer to the center and pulse of the growing marine industry than Algonac. Others mentioned the possibility that Florida represented less tax liabilities for the Corporation.[32] A steadily greater percentage of boats were shipped to Florida markets, and logically a plant located there would also reap dividends in shipping delay and expense.

Harsen Smith, by now Chairman and chief executive of Chris-Craft Corporation, authorized construction almost immediately on a portion of the retained sixty-six acres of property, for a new Manufacturing and Engineering Center. The three-story M & E Center was envisioned to be a focus of research for the corporation, and home of over fifty naval architects, engineers and stylists challenged to "explore new ideas aimed at attracting more potential boat buyers into the cockpits of Chris-Craft boats."[33]

Boats are conceived that will match varying tastes and budgets. Big boats and small boats. Those that sleep two and those that sleep ten.

Below and uppermost right: A 1957 27-foot Sedan with Flying Bridge, *Peg O My Heart* built in Chattanooga, Tennessee. With a pair of 95-horsepower Chris-Craft Model K engines, it retailed for $8,890.

Opposite right, top to bottom: 1957 27-foot Sedan with Flying Bridge, 1950 25-foot *Red and White* Express Cruiser, 1947 25-foot *Red and White* Express Cruiser.

Photo by Karine N. Rodengen

Fast runabouts and commodious cruisers. Big luxury yachts and low-cost craft for family outings.

As soon as innovations or improvements for any one of the models have been proved at the Manufacturing and Engineering Center they are immediately incorporated in to the boat's design. Chris-Craft does not reserve major changes or even new models for yearly announcements. They introduce them when ready. Every detail of each boat is carefully plotted and drawn full-size before engineering drawings are sent to the [7 plants]. The drawing board in the M & E Center is 80-feet long, accommodating full-size drawings of all Chris-Craft boats.

Performance and construction development are the major concern of Chris-Craft's M & E Center staff, but style, comfort and adaptability of new models is also their responsibility. An average day for the head of the M & E Center, A.W. MacKerer, veteran Chris-Craft Vice-President in charge of Manufacturing and Engineering, might start with a research and development committee meeting attended by representatives from sales, service, accounting, purchasing and production departments. Here, new ideas are presented and evaluated from the standpoint of salability, maintenance, cost, availability and installation.

Photo by Karine N. Rodengen

Courtesy Mariners' Museum, Newport News, Virginia.

Chris-Craft began building the line of lapstrake, Thiokol-seamed *Sea Skiff* boats in 1954. Shown above, top to bottom are the 1959 40-foot Semi-Enclosed Cruiser with Fishing Bridge, 30-foot *Open*, 36-foot *Hard top*, and 18-foot *Ranger*.

Next can come a conference with quality control personnel whose inter-plant liaison man may be reporting on a new method or material found to save time or money, or enhance the value of the product. Often, the production staff at one factory discover materials or develop production techniques that can benefit production at other plants. A free flow of such ideas to the M & E Center quickly brings these changes into play throughout the organization.

The continually changing needs of the worldwide market require frequent revisions in production schedules at various factories. Maintaining flexibility and efficiency simultaneously is another M & E assignment. Production must be geared to sales. The closer the ratio, the easier it is to supply market needs on time and avoid inventory build-ups.[34]

Befitting a year of dramatic and, for some, traumatic change, in 1957 Chris-Craft also bought a small boat manufacturing company in Pompano Beach, builders of the 15-foot fiberglas *Lake 'n Sea* outboard runabout. It was Chris-Craft's first all fiberglas boat, and an introduction to both the benefits and hazards of the new technology.

The Lake 'n Sea had compound curvatures which would never be attempted in traditional planked wood construction, particularly the stylish and critically flaring spray deflectors along the hull which really served more cosmetic purposes. The cockpit seated six quite uncomfortably on seat backs and bulkheads molded along with the deck. Another innovation was the capture of Styrofoam within some hull areas, the new wonder material from the Dow Chemical Company.

The hull was molded from what was called *special formula Chris-Craft Polyester Lami-*

Opposite right: The modern look in big game fishing a in 1959 with this 40-foot Chris-Craft *Sport Fisherma* five-sleeper fishing machine could be equipped with of 197-horsepower G.M. diesels for $

nate, or CPL for short. The transom of the boat was a composite construction of 1 ¼" plywood sheathed in fiberglas. The cockpit flooring was also fir plywood. The hull of the lightweight, 425-pound runabout had the advantage of being offered in a variety of colors, Sunrise Pink, Yellow Chartreuse or Seafoam Green.[35] The promotion for the boat emphasized the maintenance-free attributes of the new technology.

The Lake 'n Sea combines the durability and watertightness of tough, molded fiber glass with the safety of built-in Styrofoam flotation. Store outdoors — hull never needs caulking or protective painting; won't shrink, swell, rot, or dry out! This beauty is ready to go all the time in fresh or salt water.[36]

The combination of fiberglas over plywood and styrofoam turned out to be the Achilles heel of the sporty little boat. The fiberglas tended to delaminate from the other materials, allowing water to seep inside, swelling the composite structure, which caused further delamination until the boat was virtually unusable. This characteristic gained for the Lake 'n Sea the unfortunate nickname of *Leak 'n Sink.*[37] Hundreds of the fiberglas boats were built before, as Christopher James Smith, son of Bernard remembered, they "determined that it wasn't the thing to build boats out of and sold the whole business, molds and everything."[38]

The Chris-Craft *Showboats* for 1957 were designed "to put a new lift in your life…open up an exciting new world of fun and adventure!"[39] Among highlights within the *Sport Boat* fleet were the 17-foot runabouts; 17 and 20-foot Sportsmen; 18 and 20-foot Holidays; 18, 21, 23 and 26-foot Continentals; and 19-foot Capri. A sedan hard-top with ventilating windshields was available for most models. Most interesting of the runabouts was the unique styling of the 21-foot Continental runabout. The '57 Chevrolet Bel Air was among the most popular cars of the year, a fact not lost on Chris-Craft stylists. A pair

of beautiful, rounded-edge fins appeared on the Continental, the first time that Chris-Craft had ever so obviously followed a consumer trend in boat styling and building, rather than setting one.

Classic contenders among the cruisers included a 23 Express Cruiser; a two-sleeper, 24-foot Semi-Enclosed Cruiser with a toilet and twin berths; a 24-foot Sedan with Flying Bridge for four; a large cockpit 26-foot Sedan Cruiser with Flying Bridge; a flush deck cockpit model of the 27 and 28-foot Sedan Cruiser with Flying Bridge; along with a 27-foot Semi-Enclosed Cruiser.

Larger cruisers were dominated by the Constellation Series, starting with the 30-foot considered "as new as tomorrow, with clean, sweeping lines, modern yacht styling."[40] The 35-foot "Connie" offered walk-around side decks, while the 38-foot, six sleeper had a fully paneled salon and optional hard-top. The 42-foot version proffered a large owner's stateroom with private bath, and the 55-foot constellation was described as "Classic beauty and luxurious cruising accommodations for ten."[41]

Queen of the fleet for '57 was the 56-foot Salon Motor Yacht, which "can truly be called a *floating palace.*"[42] Among the design considerations for the Motor Yacht was the mandate to have "all the roomy comfort of your own living room — with big picture windows all 'round for complete visibility."[43]

Even a strike in the fall of 1957 at the Salisbury, Maryland Sea Skiff plant couldn't dampen enthusiasm for the growing Sea Skiff line, as no less than 61 models were produced, including the new 40-foot Salon Deckhouse Cruiser. Models were offered in 18, 22, 26, 30, 35 and 40-foot versions, ranging in price from the open 18-foot model with 60-horsepower engine at $2,660 to the 40-foot Cruiser with a pair of 200-horsepower Chrysler engines for $28,090. Hulls could be ordered in blue, yellow, green, gray, white, buff or black at no additional charge, and demand was still ahead of production, with some dealers waiting two and three months for delivery of the most popular models.

The *Cavalier Division*, changed in name and image from the Plywood Division, manufactured twenty-seven models in 1957. Utility Boats were available in 15, 17, and 20-foot Cavalier versions; Runabouts in 17-foot Double Cockpit Forward Cavalier models; Outboard Cruisers in 16-foot Cavalier Semi-Enclosed Sports, 19 and 22-foot Cavalier Express versions; and Inboard Cruiser Models in 19, 21 and 22-foot varieties. The economical plywood boats ranged in price from $1,025 for the 16-foot outboard 2-sleeper to $3,920 for the 22-foot Cavalier Express 4-sleeper with a 95-horsepower Chris-Craft engine.

"Make a Date for '58" announced the new Chris-Craft *Super Fleet* for 1958. The traditional *Chris-Craft Division* which moved to Pompano on November 20, 1957, offered 147 different models in 21 hull sizes from 17 to 65 feet.

Perhaps the boldest entry in the fleet was the 19-foot *Silver Arrow*, a carefully measured return to fiberglas following the disappointment of the Lake 'n Sea program. The hull sides of the flashy five-seat runabout were built of fiberglas-reinforced spruce, while the side decks, forward deck and aft deck were reinforced molded fiberglas. Basically, the Silver Arrow was a planked and battened mahogany runabout with a fiberglas skin. It wasn't a particularly light boat, for at 2,860 pounds it outweighed the 19-foot all mahogany Holiday by over 500 pounds. It also wasn't especially cheap. When equipped with the same 131-horsepower Chris-Craft engine, the Silver Arrow retailed at $5,290 while the popular 19-foot Capri went for $4,100, a difference of nearly $1,200. If you installed the optional 215-horsepower Dearborn Interceptor V-8, the price zoomed to $6,170. For many, though, it's revolutionary styling, canted fins and 42-mile-per-hour speed overshadowed the price tag.

> So new and different, it'll take your breath away! The action-packed Silver Arrow is designed for the man who wants a modern "sports car of the waterways." Power-packed engines to 215 hp, speeds to 42 mph make it a honey for water skiing .... Sleek, canted fins ... deluxe appointments ... one-piece, reinforced fiber-glass deck...and a host of fresh, new styling features. One look and you'll want a new Silver Arrow![44]

Like the Cobra, the Silver Arrow wasn't especially popular, and only 92 were built before production was discontinued.

Also sporting the trendy automotive style fins were the 21-foot Continental and 21-foot Capri.

The Sportsman Series contained 17 and 20-foot models; the Holiday only contained the 18-foot model; Continentals were available in 18, 21, 23 and 26-foot models; the Capri Series contained the 19-foot Capri and Silver Arrow; and the 25-foot Series revived the venerable name *Cadet*, among the most successful names in pre-war Chris-Craft runabout history.

Cruisers for 1958 included the 25-foot Semi-Enclosed; 26-foot Sports Express, *Commuter* and *Clipper;* 28 and 31-foot Constellation; 32-foot Express, Sedan and Commander; 33-foot *Futura;* 35 and 38-foot Constellation; 38 and 42-foot *Corsair;* 40-foot Sport Fisherman; 40, 48 and 55-foot Constellation; 55-foot Conqueror; 56-foot Salon Motor Yacht; and 65-foot Constellation and Motor Yacht. The first 65-foot Constellation didn't roll off the Algonac yacht assembly line until late April, 1958, and retailed

Above, below and opposite top right: Driven by owner John Kovach, the 1957 21-foot Continental, *Smoove*, sported the latest in automobile-style tail fins, and could be powered up to 300-horsepower with speeds to 45 mph.

Photos by Karine N. Rodengen

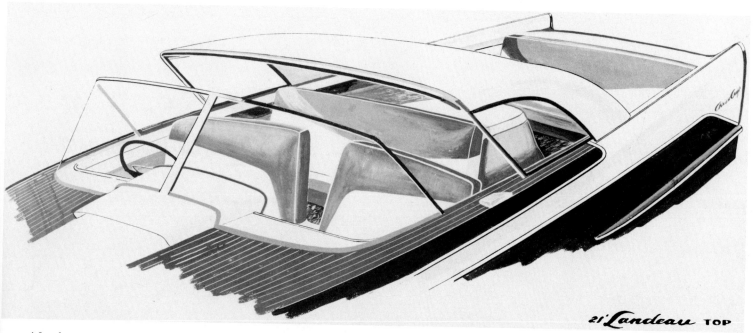

21' *Landeau* TOP

A Landeau top option was available for the 1957 21-foot *Continental*, featuring a unique sliding forward canopy.

Below: Also from the class of 1957, the 21-foot Chris-Craft *Capri*. Driver/owner Jim Mertaugh of Hessel, Michigan, is the son of E.J. Mertaugh who secured the very first Chris-Craft franchise in 1926.

Photo by Karine N. Rodengen

From bottom clockwise: All from 1959, the 19-foot *Silver Arrow*, 33-foot *Sport Fisherman*, 55-foot *Constellation* and 18-foot *Continental*. The 1959 Chris-Craft Division fleet alone numbered seventy-two models.

for $139,000 with a pair of 300-horsepower GM diesel engines.

Sea Skiffs for '58 came in 73 models, including the new 40-foot Convertible Sedan retailing for $29,440 with a pair of 225-horsepower Chrysler engines. Also built in Salisbury, Maryland were hulls in 18, 22, 26, 30 and 35-foot lengths. With talk of economic recession prevailing, Sales Promotion manager Chuck High of the Sea Skiff Division distributed a parable with a point for his dealers.

A man lived by the side of the road and sold hot dogs. He was hard of hearing, so he had no radio. He had trouble with his eyes, so he had no newspaper. But he sold good hot dogs.

He put up a sign on the highway telling how good they were. He stood by the side of the road and cried, "Buy a hot dog, mister." And people bought. He increased his meat and bun order, and he bought a bigger stove to take care of his trade. He got his son home from college to help him. But then something happened.

His son said, "Father, haven't you been listening to the radio? There's a big depression on, the international situation is terrible, and the domestic situation is even worse." Whereupon the father thought, "Well, my son has been to college. He listens to the radio and he reads the papers, so he ought to know.

So the father cut down on the bun order, took down his advertising signs, and no longer bothered to stand on the highway to sell hot dogs.

His hot dog sales fell almost overnight. "You were right, son," said the father to the boy, "We are certainly in the middle of a great depression!"[45]

The new fleet of Cavalier Division boats offered a popular new accessory approved for factory installation, a fiberglas-covered bottom. A great many of the boats shipped from Cavalier production lines at Caruthersville, Missouri and Salisbury, Maryland were equipped with the optional bottom. Models in the line ranged from the 60-horsepower, 15-foot Utility Cavalier to the 95-horsepower 22-foot Cavalier Express 4-sleeper.

Five basic models of the all-steel Chris-Craft Roamer Cruisers were also marketed in '58. The 42-foot class included the *Riviera*, *Regal* and *Royal*, all with options of paired engines from 200-horsepower Chris-Crafts to 300-horsepower Cadillacs, or GM diesels of 197-horsepower. Two Express Cruisers were also welded together in Holland, in 28 and 35-foot versions. Prices ranged from the 28-foot Express Cruiser with a pair of 130-horsepower Chris-Craft engines at $14,685, to a 42-foot Royal equipped with a pair of 197-horsepower diesels for $50,120, f.o.b. Holland, Michigan.

The exciting 1958 19-foot Chris-Craft *Silver Arrow* had bottom and sides of fiberglas reinforced spruce, while the decks were molded fiberglas. With a 215-horsepower Dearborn Interceptor V-8, the heavy boat would give 42 mph.

Courtesy Mariners' Museum, Newport News, Virginia.

In 1958 a tradition which stretched back to the very roots of the company was broken. Most people are unaware that Harsen Smith was never President of Chris-Craft, as he had been elevated to Chairman of the Board from his long-standing position as Vice-President. Jay Smith had remained as President, though admittedly semi-retired. With Jay wishing to enjoy his retirement completely, Harsen Smith appointed his old college friend and rock-solid Chris-Craft administrator Harry H. Coll as President of Chris-Craft Corporation. Coll would be only the third person to be President of the boat building firm, following Christopher Columbus Smith and Jay Wesley Smith. It was quite an honor, but one which Coll deserved, for he had proven his

Opposite right: A days end in Algonac. The sun sets over the
St. Clair River and the 1957 27-foot Sedan with Flying
Bridge *Peg O My Heart* idles downstream towards home.

Photo by Karine N. Rodengen

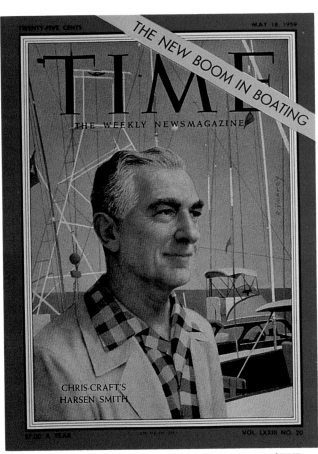

Harsen Smith, Chairman of the Board, graced the cover of *TIME*
on May 18, 1959. Said Harsen, "The Smith family — and not any
single Smith — is responsible for Chris-Craft's success."

administrative skills during World War II as the
Holland plant manager, became manager of the
Grand Rapids outboard motor facility, President
of the Roamer Steel Boat Division, and ultimately Group Vice-President for all three Western Michigan plants.

With the burgeoning models of the Sea Skiff,
Cavalier and Roamer Divisions, the Chris-Craft
Division of traditional mainstream products
slimmed down to a manageable 72 entries for
1959. Survivors of the cuts included Series 17,
20 and 24-foot Sportsmen, along with a new
concept model, the 17-foot *Ski Boat*. The Ski
Boat was available with engines ranging from
100 to 185-horsepower, and could be delivered
with optional chrome ski-tow, folding top with
curtains, mahogany paneled cockpit and
linoleum flooring.

Made-to-order for fast-action skiing and
aqua-planing thrills, this sleek six-passenger
speedster is just as perfect for fishing trips and
all water sports. The secret of her quick
response: a high-performance hull with non-
trip chines for smooth, flat turns, and a V8
engine for wildcat acceleration to 42 mph.
Another big feature: the sturdy ski tow (optional
extra) is mounted amidships with concealed
bracing. A two-tone Philippine Mahogany hull,

Photo by Karine N. Rodengen

custom two-tone upholstery, walk-thru to front seat, and sparkling chrome trim highlight a boatload of beauty.[46]

The Continental Series contained the 18, 21-foot with stylish fins and 26-foot models, while the racy Capri Series carried the 18-foot and fin bedecked 21-foot models, along with a single model of the 19-foot fiberglas Silver Arrow, now offered only with a 185-horsepower Chris-Craft V8.

A 27-foot Constellation was a nice surprise to mid-size cruiser buyers who wanted legendary Constellation quality. It truly was a generous design for a small boat, and could be equipped with a single 185-horsepower V8 or a pair of 100 to 185-horsepower engines for less than $10,000. For the single engine version, you could tell your friends you owned a Constellation for only $8,360. Constellations were also available in 31, 35, 40, 42, 50, 55 and flagship 66-foot versions. The new 66-foot constellation powered with a pair of 336-horsepower GM diesel engines could be driven away from Algonac for $157,860.

Other cruisers included the 32-foot Commander, 33-foot Sports Cruiser, 33-foot Sport Fisherman, 40-foot Conqueror and a 40-foot Sport Fisherman all loaded with practical options.

By Spring of '59, another 18 models sailed into the fleet, including 25-foot Semi-Enclosed Cruisers, 26-foot Commuters, and the return of the 33-foot Futura.

Thirty-seven models of Sea Skiffs were produced in '59, with very little changes except for options and prices. Models were available in 18, 22, 26, 30, 35 and 40 foot versions, with the 18-foot *Open* with 60-horsepower engine retailing for $2,660, while the 40-foot Semi-Enclosed Cruiser with a pair of 197-horsepower GM diesels was available for $37,310.

The plywood Cavaliers were produced in 15 and 17-foot Sports Utility and in 18, 23, 25, and 30-foot Express Cruiser models. Prices ranged from the 15-foot Sports Utility with 60-horsepower engine at $1,995 to the 36-mile-per-hour 30-foot Express Cruiser with a pair of 185-horsepower V8 engines for $9,695.

The Steel Roamers continued to grow in popularity and fleet size in 1959, with a carefully styled selection ranging from 25 to 52-feet. Sportsmen Roamers were built in 25 and 28-foot versions for offshore fishing and cruising, while Express versions were welded together in

In 1957 Chris-Craft moved its corporate offices to Pompano Beach, Florida, seen here in 1959. Harsen Smith's ingenuity in real estate subdivision provided enough profit to build the enormous Pompano manufacturing facility, below.

Photo courtesy Ray LaParl

Photo courtesy Ray LaParl

The Pompano Beach, Florida plant cruiser lines overflowed with the Chris-Craft Division fleet in January of 1959. Notice the small, inverted experimental fiberglas runabouts in between the huge cruisers.

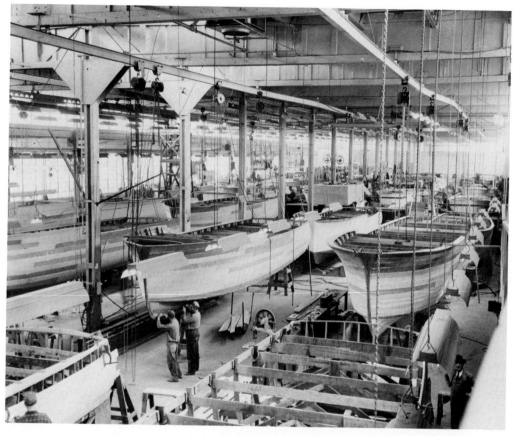

It has been calculated that it actually took *less* time to build cruisers out of double-planked Philippine mahogany than it would in later years out of fiberglas. Here, the Holland, Michigan cruiser facility displays the efficiency and cleanliness of Chris-Craft operations in the fifties.

Courtesy Mariners' Museum, Newport News, Virginia.

25, 28, 31 and 35-foot models. Always slightly ahead of industry styling, the mainstays of the Roamer fleet were the 35 and 42-foot Regals, the 42-foot Royal, and the Queen of the fleet was the all new 52-foot Motor Yacht with a 15-foot beam, three staterooms and two showers.

The decade of the fifties was packed with experimentation, expansion and energy for Chris-Craft. The test programs in fiberglas had been less than they had hoped, but the experience they gained would become valuable in the tumultuous years to come. New Sea Skiff, Cavalier and Roamer divisions appeared, grew and flourished, offering a remarkable variety of products to a seemingly insatiable market. The movement of corporate management and key divisions to Florida had set the stage for further growth. Although the bonds which cemented Chris-Craft with Algonac traditions and memories were broken, the boating public's love affair with Chris-Craft had blossomed.

On May 18th, 1959, Harsen Smith graced the cover of *Time* Magazine, a tribute not only to the Smiths and their dedicated pursuit, but also to generations of boat buyers who had benefited from the products of the most respected name in boating history. The article provides a rare glimpse into the private thoughts of Harsen Smith, and reveals his deepest sentiments.

The biggest thing in Harsen Smith's life is the conviction that the Smith family — and not any single Smith — is responsible for Chris-Craft's success. When the company moved its headquarters from Algonac to Pompano Beach last year, the family followed as a matter of course. Today, most of the Smiths live within miles of the Pompano Beach factory (19 of them recently attended a Smith bridal shower). Harsen calls "family meetings," not board meetings, still listens to the advice of his semiretired father and his uncles, Owen, 61 and Bernard, 70.

Harsen himself has not yet bought a house, lives with his wife in a simply furnished apartment overlooking the harbor in nearby Fort Lauderdale, keeps a weather eye on the passing parade of boats ("When 70% of them are not Chris-Craft's, I'll know something is wrong").[47]

1929 24-foot Runabout.

1936 18-foot De Luxe Utility.

1949 15'9" Sportsman.

A DASH OF CLASS

The Chris-Craft dash has reflected the fluid tastes of five generations of boat buyers. The elegant artistry of instrumentation has transcended the mundane requirement to monitor performance.

Photography by Karine N. Rodengen

1953 18-foot Sportsman.

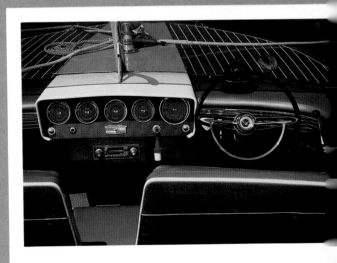

1960 21-foot Continental.

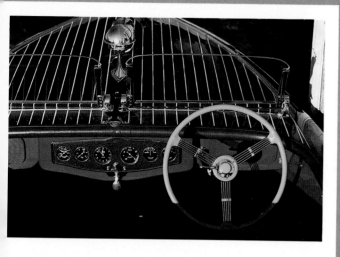

1939 19-foot Custom Runabout.

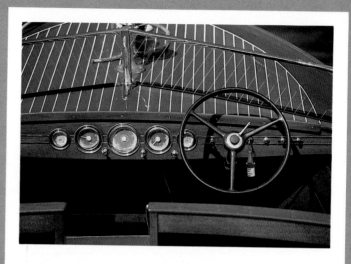

1941 22-foot De Luxe Utility.

1946 22-foot De Luxe Utility.

1949 25-foot Sportsman twin engine.

1957 21-foot Continental.

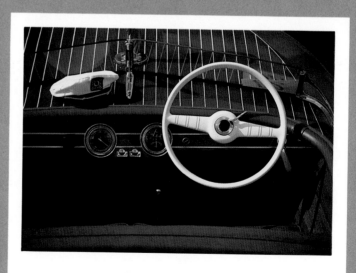

1949 17-foot De Luxe Runabout.

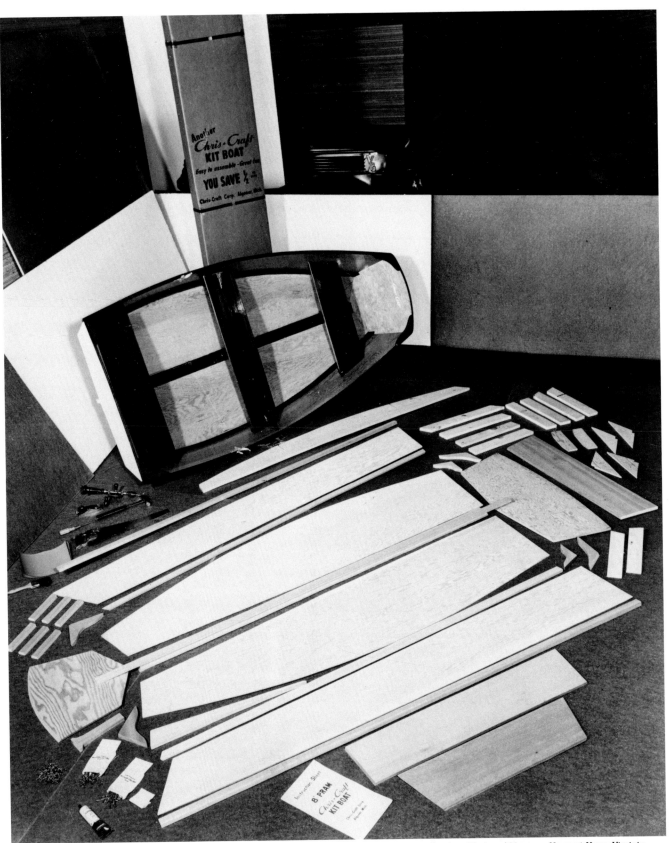

Among the very first Chris-Craft *Kit Boats* was this 8-foot *Pram* which was designed to be built
by inexperienced builders in 8 to 10 hours. Selling for $39, boys tried to order the kit fifteen
years after production stopped in 1958.

CHAPTER XVI

The Kit Boats

The whole difference between construction and creation is exactly this: that a thing constructed can only be loved after it is constructed; but a thing created is loved before it exists.

Preface to Dickens, *Pickwick Papers*

FROM THE MOMENT they were introduced in the summer of 1950, the Chris-Craft *Kit Boats* became the fastest selling new product line in company history. Since the components used in the assembly of the production line boats were so uniform and accurately milled, why couldn't even more simple models be assembled by budget-conscious hobbyists at home? When Chris-Craft introduced the first three models, an 8-foot *Pram* for $39, 14-foot *Rowboat* for $99, and 14-foot *Outboard* Kit Boat for $148, the response was overwhelming.

Think of it! Only $39 plus freight brings you this Chris-Craft Kit for a real 8-ft. Pram! A dandy boat for youngsters and grown-ups — for rowing, fishing, sailing and outboarding. It's lightweight for convenient car-top carrying, ideal for use as a dinghy.

This Pram is a cinch to put together...and fun, too! Genuine Philippine Mahogany parts and top-grade Marine Fir-Plywood panels accurately precut by precision tools. Included in each kit is a jig frame on which to assemble your Pram and a special screw driver for the recessed-head brass screws.

Put one together in 8 to 10 hours of your spare time...have fun doing it...and SAVE ½ or more![1]

The kits arrived at buyers' doorsteps in metal-banded corrugated boxes, and the sight of the oversized packages with "Chris-Craft Kit Boat" emblazoned across them set hearts pounding in the breasts of young boys all across America. The kits were very complete, including pre-cut mahogany seats, fender rails, chines, and keel. Sides, bottom, bow and transom panels were pre-cut from marine fir-plywood, and the shipping box became a ready-made jig for coordinating the assembly. Brass recessed head screws, special screwdriver, seam compound, oarlocks and Chris-Craft decalcomania were all included along with step-by-step-instructions. Buyers were required to supply a drill, saw, hammer, wood plane, paint and varnish brushes.

The larger 14-foot kits came with fully assembled Philippine mahogany frames, machined and assembled stem, and assembled transom. The brochure suggested 48 hours to build, but as the kit boats got bigger, they got harder to put together.

Among the reasons kit boat sales skyrocketed was that Chris-Craft realized the opportunity for entirely new merchandising methods. Not only could traditional Chris-Craft dealers distribute the new kits, but marine stores, hardware stores, lumber yards and mail order distribution would work as well. Advertising targeted new markets during kit boat production, reaching out to hobbyists from the pages of *Popular Science Monthly*, *Popular Mechanics*, *Mechanix Illustrated*, *Boy's Life* and *Life* magazines, along with their traditional mix of marine and recreation publications. Chris-Craft wasn't the first in the kit boat field, but from almost the moment of their announcement, they became the largest and most successful kit boat manufacturer in history.

Within a year, in 1951, Chris-Craft expanded their line of kits to include a Pram *Sail Kit* for $65, a 12-foot Runabout Kit at $118, a 14-foot Fishing Skiff for $111, a 14-foot De Luxe Runabout for $149, an 18-foot Outboard Express Cruiser for outboard or inboard power at $895, a 21-foot inboard Sportsman for $614, a 21-foot Express Cruiser for $747, and the flagship of the Kit Boats, the 31-foot Express Cruiser with double-planked bottom for $1,995. The primarily outboard fleet was a perfect match for the 5½-horsepower Chris-Craft *Challenger*, or the new 10-horsepower Chris-Craft *Commander* outboard engines being produced in Grand Rapids, Michigan.

As sales continued to surge, Chris-Craft added a 10-foot *Utility Racing Pram* for $84, a 16-foot *De Luxe Runabout* for $239, and a 17-foot Speedboat for $449. Chris-Craft also branched out by offering a *Boat Trailer Kit* for $125, which could be assembled in an hour, and would carry a 650-lb. boat. With an optional *Stake Body Conversion Kit*, the boat trailer became a utility trailer for an additional $36. Recognizing the needs of people who wished the very economical designs, but were unable to assemble the boats themselves, Chris-Craft offered several of the models assembled at the factory. These first factory assembled Kit Boats were the real forerunner of the Plywood Boat

Division, which would become the highly successful *Cavalier* Division.

Also available in '52 was a knotty pine gun cabinet kit for $66 which could also be used as a china or linen cabinet. Many children were delighted with their new Chris-Craft *Treasure Chest* Kit which, for $39 featured knotty pine components with a hinged cover for toys, blankets, clothing or could be used as a seat, sea chest or wood box. The kits had become so popular, that Chris-Craft established the *Kit Boat Division* in 1952, with their own sales, production, and shipping departments.

In 1953, the legacy of Christopher Columbus Smith had come full circle with the introduction of a *Duckboat Kit*, over fourscore years since the master had fashioned the first. The 14-foot duckboat could be finished as a double-ender for canoe-style paddling, or with an outboard motor transom. Also new to the Kit Boat fleet were a 12-foot *Penguin* Sailing Dinghy, a 14-foot Sportsman, and a 26-foot *Cruiser*, along with additional trailers in 300, 1000 and 2200-lb. capacities.

The 31-foot *Express Cruiser* Boat Kit was a giant-sized project for even the most adept craftsmen, let alone the casual hobbyist. It offered a host of possibilities for interior finishing, depending on the builder's fancy.

Big-Cruiser design, carefully fabricated parts, proved procedure enable you to assemble

Courtesy Mariners' Museum, Newport News, Virginia.

Above: Few people knew that Chris-Craft manufactured furniture kits in the fifties, including knotty pine gun cabinets and treasure chest.

Left: The Chris-Craft 14-foot *Land Cruiser* kit appeared in 1954, featuring accommodations for four adults.

Courtesy Mariners' Museum, Newport News, Virginia.

Chris-Craft Land Cruiser

Above: A completed 8-foot *Pram* kit was just the ticket for taking your favorite gal on an afternoon adventure.

Right: The completed 12-foot Chris-Craft *Meteor* kit in 1956.

Courtesy Mariners' Museum, Newport News, Virginia.

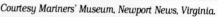

Courtesy Mariners' Museum, Newport News, Virginia.

this 31-ft. Boat Kit into a smart, sturdy Express Cruiser with ¾" double planked bottom; ½" Fir marine-plywood sides; Philippine Mahogany transom; stringers for single and twin engines.

Each hull is set up on a master jig at the factory for predrilling bolt and screw holes into frames, keel, stringers and transom frame to insure easy and proper assembly. Cabin can accommodate dinette, galley, toilet, wardrobe, 2 berths forward.[2]

In 1954 Chris-Craft astonished just about everyone when they introduced their new *Land Cruiser* Kit, a 14-foot mobile home that would sleep four adults. The kit contained everything from a steel chassis, aluminum roof covering, aluminum frame windows with screens, to wheels and a hinged door with lock. Since the product was so unique, Chris-Craft formed the *Land Cruiser Kit Division* just to accommodate the new product.

Think of it! Now you can own your own mobile home. You can go wherever you want, whenever you like, without the fuss and bother of stopping at expensive hotels and restaurants. You can follow your heart to new fun and adventure — and take your home right along with you!

The new Land Cruiser Kit by Chris-Craft makes all this possible. Now — for the first time! — anyone who can afford to drive an average car can afford this big, comfortable mobile home.

Finished in gleaming aluminum, with an all-steel chassis, the Land Cruiser is a full 14-feet overall. Inside, there's plenty of room for a double bed, a dinette that converts into another bed, a heating unit and cook stove, refrigerator, closets and cupboards!

Right: A 12-foot Chris-Craft *Penguin* sailboat kit became available in 1951 for only $65. The little known kit was actually Chris-Craft's *first* sailboat.

Courtesy Mariners' Museum, Newport News, Virginia.

Courtesy Mariners' Museum, Newport News, Virginia.

Above: A 1954 14-foot *Caribbean* kit boat, atop a Chris-Craft *Boat Trailer Kit* which was also available for $125.

Left: The 1954 16-foot Chris-Craft *Express Cruiser* kit offered V-berths for two overnight guests.

Courtesy Mariners' Museum, Newport News, Virginia.

Below: Among the more ambitious kit boats was this 1954 Chris-Craft 21-foot *Monterey Express Cruiser*. Similar to the 18-foot *Fiesta* kit shown on page 162, it was designed to be an affordable overnight outboard cruiser.

Courtesy Mariners' Museum, Newport News, Virginia.

…You don't have to be an expert carpenter or mechanic to put together your Chris-Craft Land Cruiser. Not a bit of it. If you can use a hammer, a saw, a wrench and a screwdriver, you can do a real professional job. Ordinary household tools are all that is required.[3]

Unfortunately, market acceptance for the innovative product didn't live up to expectations, and the mobile homes were discontinued after little more than a year of production.

It was quite possible to get into trouble building a Kit Boat indoors and not having a way to get it out. A retired Chris-Craft sales executive remembers "one guy locally here tried to build one in his basement…big, big mistake. He had to take it completely apart cause he couldn't get it out, put back every piece of wood, put it in his garage and then he got it back together again."[4]

By 1955, the Kit Boat Division exploded with 28 models. Popular designs picked up sporty names, like the 12-foot *Vagabond*; 14-foot *Dolphin, Zephyr, Hornet, Caribbean*, and *Barracuda*; 15-foot *Marlin*; 18-foot *Fiesta*; 20-foot *Gay Paree*; and 21-foot *Monterey Express*. Prices ranged from the 8-foot Pram at $49 to the 21-foot Monterey Express at $814, while the difficult-to-assemble 31-foot *Express* had been dropped from the fleet.

Chris-Craft distributed manufacturing chores for the Kit Division among five plants: Algonac, Cadillac, and Holland, Michigan; Caruthersville, Missouri; and Chattanooga, Tennessee.

In 1957, automobile-style *tail fins* had reached into the kit fleet, as the 12-foot *Meteor*, 14-foot *Comet* and *Barracuda* all succumbed to the new rage in sleek-looking outboard runabouts. Also new to the fleet were the 14-foot *Grayling*, 15-foot *Tarpon*, 19-foot *Sports Convertible*, and 22-foot *Express Cruiser*.

New materials were being incorporated into the increasingly sophisticated Kit Boats, including pre-formed wrap-around plexiglas windshields and one-piece, molded fiberglas cabin roofs on some models.

Mainstream production line boat activity was requiring all of Chris-Craft's attention by 1958, and the Kit Boat Division was slowly disassembled. Close-out sales were the order of the day, and even though kits would continue to be sold through 1959, no new kits were being manufactured. Among key factors in the decision to dissolve the Kit Division, was the growing popularity of the economically priced plywood *Cavalier*

Courtesy Mariners' Museum, Newport News, Virginia.

Among the most interesting Chris-Craft runabout kits was this 1956 19-foot *Sports Convertible* which featured a three-way top and convertible bench seating which became a double bed or sun lounge.

boats which were competing with kits for the low end of the market.

The Chris-Craft Kit Boats provided thousands of young and old Americans with the opportunity to fashion a boat from their own hands, and to become captains of their labors. The program demonstrated for untold youth the safe use of hand tools, and offered the retired, but ambitious hobbyist, a unique and genuine pride of accomplishment. C. Gordon Houser, who was a longtime Vice-President of Advertising and Public Relations at Chris-Craft, recalled how hard it was for boys around the country to believe that it was really over. "Fifteen years after the program was abandoned, we still got coupons clipped out of *Boy's Life*, the publication of the Boy Scouts of America. Some boy would see it in an old issue, clip it out and send it in…and want their kit."[5]

SMITH BROS. BOAT BUILDERS
1874 – 1900

C. C. SMITH BOAT BUILDER
1900 – 1904

C. C. SMITH & CO.
BOAT BUILDERS   ALGONAC, MICH.   BOAT LIVERY
1904 – 1909

Smith-Ryan Boat Co.
1910 – 1912

Smith-Ryan Boat and Engine Company
1912

C. C. SMITH BOAT & ENGINE CO.
1913 – 1916

Gar Wood / C. C. Smith Boat & Engine Co.
1916 – 1921

Chris Smith & Sons Boat Co.
1922 – 1929

Chris-Craft Corporation
1930 – 1960

NAFI
Chris-Craft Corporation
1960 – 1962

Chris-Craft Industries, Inc.
1962 – 1981

Murray Industries, Inc.
1981 –

Chris-Craft
1924

CHRIS CRAFT
1924

CHRIS-CRAFT
1925

Chris-Craft
1926

Chris-Craft
1927

Chris-Craft
1947

Chris Craft
1988

CHAPTER XVII

The Sixties

…We look entirely to the present management to operate the business without interference on our part. We believe you are competent to do the job ahead, otherwise we would have been very foolish to have bought the business.

Paul V. Shields
February 16, 1960[1]

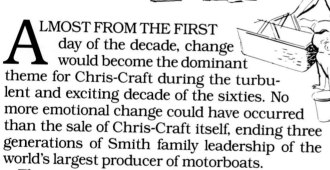

ALMOST FROM THE FIRST day of the decade, change would become the dominant theme for Chris-Craft during the turbulent and exciting decade of the sixties. No more emotional change could have occurred than the sale of Chris-Craft itself, ending three generations of Smith family leadership of the world's largest producer of motorboats.

The story of how Chris-Craft Corporation came to be sold on February 7th, 1960, is an intriguing tale of chance encounters, reluctant negotiations and passionate family emotions. Two written accounts of the events leading to the transaction survive. One is written by Cornelius Shields, partner in the Wall Street investment banking firm of Shields & Company, which negotiated the sale on behalf of the company they controlled, NAFI, and appears in his book *Racing with Cornelius Shields and the Masters*, an anthology of sailing exploits and

techniques. The other version, a detailed and well researched account of the exciting and complex transaction, appeared in the May 7, 1960 issue of *Business Week*. Both accounts are in complete agreement of the facts, but approach events from differing perspectives.[2] The tale begins in early 1960.

Last Jan. 18 at about six o'clock in the evening, Joseph Flannery, 44 year old assistant to the president of NAFI Corp., was struggling into his overcoat and overshoes for the cold and slushy commutation ride home from New York City to Bernardsville, N.J. All afternoon he had been at the Boat Show in the New York City Coliseum, talking business with the officers of a boat manufacturing company. Now he was running late; he had missed his regular train, was bound to be late for dinner.

At just this moment Owen Smith, one of the founders of Chris-Craft Corp. and then major stockholder in this family held company that is the giant of the pleasure boat business, swung around the corner of the exhibition booth where Flannery was standing.

Smith and Flannery had first met two years previously, so they had a few of the usual pleasantries to exchange. Then Flannery asked: "How's Chris-Craft?"

He got anything but a run-of-the-mill reply. Said Owen Smith: "It looks as if we might be getting ready to sell the company."

"Well for pete's sake, I wish we had known about it."

"Oh," said Smith, "there's nothing final about it yet. It's just that we're talking to people who want to buy."

"I hope it isn't too late for us to get into the picture."

"No," said Smith, "It mightn't be."

"Well, look, we can't talk here. Let me buy you a drink tomorrow night and we'll talk about it."

"You can't buy me a drink," said Smith, "but you can buy me something to eat."[3]

Four years previously, in 1956, Shields & Company had bought control of NAFI, then known as National Automotive Fibers, Inc. NAFI was a leading manufacturer of interior trim for automobiles, and one of its specialized products was the fibrous insulating blanket that lines trunk and engine compartments. Even though NAFI's sales in 1956 were $46 million, it had lost more than a million dollars. Shields trimmed some of NAFI's marginal product line, and diversified into oil and gas operations, along with radio and television broadcasting enterprises. This combination of trimming and diversification lowered NAFI's annual revenues to $23 million, but increased profits to $1.2 million. By 1960, when the possibility of a Chris-Craft purchase surfaced, NAFI was quite solid, with over $10 million in cash, securities and other liquid assets. The purchase of Chris-Craft by NAFI would generate rich fees for Shields & Company, while giving NAFI an unbeatable opportunity for expansion into a fast-growing marine industry.

Four of the Smiths were trustees for all other shareholders in the family: Jay, Owen and Bernard, sons of Christopher Columbus Smith, and Harsen Smith, son of Jay and Chairman of the Board of Chris-Craft Corporation. Only 55 stockholders held shares in Chris-Craft, all Smiths.

Five years ago they faced a temporary crisis when Owen Smith, who then held about 30% of Chris-Craft wanted to sell part of his stock. The family settled that one by itself; other members

bought one-third of Owen's holdings. That time, according to outsiders, Owen wanted the cash. Owen himself will not speak for publication, but outsiders who are close to him say, "He lives somewhat differently from the other Smiths." The others live quietly, some of them almost austerely. Though Owen doesn't live lavishly, he does have a different conception of the value of money.

Late last year another crisis began brewing. Owen again wanted to sell stock — this time his remaining 20%, and this time for diversification. Says Harsen Smith: "In January, Owen became quite insistent about selling. It was plain to us that this would involve a public offering of his 20%."

Owen was, of course, no more than one of four trustees. But with his 20% he had the largest single block of stock in the family. It was clear to the other three trustees that they had to satisfy Owen, and this time they did not feel the rest of the family could absorb Owen's holdings.

Early in January, the Smith trustees talked with two or three New York underwriters — Kidder, Peabody among them, but not Shields & Co. — of the chance of selling a public issue. The underwriters, estimating from a few reports on Chris-Craft but not from the company's books, produced a valuation of the company of between $45-million and $50 million.

This was stunning news for the Smiths. Says Harsen: "We'd never realized the company was worth that much. I certainly hadn't. But I guess that was because I was running the business and not paying attention to market values."...

News that they were sitting on a gold-mine far richer than they had thought traveled fast around the family. Harsen took a poll in mid-January and found that more than 50% of them, attracted by the promise of so much money, wanted to sell. But it was up to the four trustees to decide what to do. They split 2-2 on the question of whether to accept Kidder, Peabody's proposal to market up to about 35% of Chris-Craft's stock to the public.

Harsen was against the idea. He felt so strong an emotional attachment to Chris-Craft that he simply didn't want public trading in its stock...

That vote couldn't end the crisis. Owen was just as insistent on selling his stock. So the vote meant, in effect, that the Smiths would now take more seriously the bids for acquisition that had come from several industrial companies.

The first of these was from Brunswick-Balke-Collender Co. (now Brunswick Corp.). Last October, Brunswick's business development manager L.T. ("Casey") Peifer made his first approach to Harsen Smith. Says Peifer: "We went to Chris-Craft simply because we decided that we wanted to buy a boat company. I had detailed reports on 140 of them. We started with Chris-Craft because it was the biggest." Peifer didn't know then of the crisis that was brewing inside the Smith family, and he didn't find out about it at that first meeting. Harsen simply pointed out that Chris-Craft wasn't for sale.

Early in January, Peifer tried again. He met Harsen in his Pompano Beach office on Jan. 6, and they talked for a couple of hours. This time, says Peifer, Harsen was much more interested in Brunswick's ideas. Brunswick made no offer to Harsen, but Peifer explained to him that if Brunswick did acquire Chris-Craft it wanted to do so through an exchange of stock. Harsen says now: "I was against this method of selling." But at the time, he closed no door in Peifer's face, and agreed to meet a group of Brunswick's top men, including Pres. B. Edward Bensinger, later in January. Meantime, Brunswick's estimators went to work and put a tentative valuation of from $36.7 million to $42 million on Chris-Craft.

At the same time, says Harsen, two other companies were eager to talk and, he believes, were ready to offer cash. Who these two were, he won't say. But it is a fact that Singer Mfg. Co. was among those inclined to talk business with the Smiths. Rumor had it that American Motors Corp. was also seeking Chris-Craft, but AMC says it didn't approach Chris-Craft, nor did Chris-Craft approach it.

This was how the stage was set when Flannery of NAFI Corp. had his brief but vital meeting with Owen Smith at the New York Coliseum...

TALKS BEGIN

A business novelist would require that Flannery rush back to his office and start telephoning his superiors, who were at that time spread out over the country — one in Florida, others on the West Coast, and one in New York. But instead he rattled home on the Lackawanna commuter train, ate his late dinner, and at 5:30 next afternoon kept his date with Owen Smith.

They met in Owen's hotel room at the Savoy Hilton and talked a while, strolled around the corner of Fifty-Eighth Street to Trader Vic's, had their meal and talked a lot more, returned to the hotel and kept talking until almost midnight. They talked for six and a half hours of Chris-Craft's past and of its probable future, of the value that had lately been put on the company and of the talks then going on between Chris-Craft and possible buyers, of the Smith family and of the positions that its members held on the question of selling, and of NAFI's chance of buying the company.

Owen, of course, could not talk for Chris-Craft as a corporation; only Harsen could do

that. But he could — and did — help establish some of the foundations for the deal.

"Owen," says Flannery, "did most of the talking. It amounted to a great mass of background detail — the kind of detail that is invaluable in a deal like the one we were entering."...

It was by now obviously time for the top brass to begin talking. Next day Flannery set up lunch for Owen Smith with Paul Shields, chairman of NAFI and senior partner of Shields & Co. and Macrae Sykes, a Shields partner. Paul Shields and Sykes got a precis of Flannery's six-and-a-half-hour talk with Owen Smith. This time, Owen made it plain that if the Shields-NAFI combination were to move in, they would have to move fast.

They took him at his word. That afternoon Cornelius Shields, Paul's brother and also a senior partner of Shields & Co., was routed out of his vacation at Palm Beach, where he had reached the third round of a golf tournament, and appointments were set for the following day with Harsen Smith in Pompano Beach. Flannery took the midnight plane from Newark airport, fell into bed in his Fort Lauderdale hotel room at 6 a.m., and at three o'clock that afternoon he and Cornelius Shields met Harsen Smith.[4]

Cornelius Shields begins his account following the meeting between Flannery and Owen Smith, and before the meeting with Harsen Smith in Pompano Beach.

> ...I was playing in a golf tournament at The Breakers in Palm Beach when the New York office called to say that the Chris-Craft Corporation might be for sale. I was asked to make an appointment with Harsen Smith, chairman of the company...
>
> For several years we had heard rumors that Chris-Craft was planning to sell out, but nothing had ever come of them, so I was neither optimistic about our chances nor enthusiastic about withdrawing from the golf tournament. But I went down to see Harsen Smith...the next day.[5]

* * *

It had been a breathless three days for Flannery since he met Owen Smith at the Coliseum in New York. Harsen Smith, who had been working quietly in Pompano Beach unaware that all these preliminaries were going on, chuckles in recollection and says: "They didn't waste any time getting here, I'll say that."

But, because of Flannery's long talk with Owen Smith, Shields and Flannery came primed for their meeting with Harsen. Says Cornelius Shields: "We had been warned that Harsen was a quiet, reserved man, difficult to approach. I knew he didn't want to sell Chris-Craft. Owen had told us 'You'll be lucky to get what you want from him...you'll have to be very lucky to get any figures at all.'"

For a while they skirted the subject, chatting about yachts and power boats, cruising and yacht-racing. Cornelius Shields, famed for years as a blue-water skipper of sleek racing yachts and more recently as trainer of the crew of the last America's Cup winner, *Columbia*, had the salt water in common with Harsen. Harsen says, "We got along fine. When two nautical families get together they usually hit it off. They talked our language and that helped things."[6]

Shields remembered well the difficulty which he faced given the reluctance of Harsen Smith to sell Chris-Craft.

He was rather quiet and reserved, and as we began talking I thought to myself how difficult it would be to make a living trying to sell securities to men like him. Time was short, because I had been told that several other companies and banking firms were sitting on Smith's doorstep, notably the Brunswick Corporation. It was the plan of Shields & Company to have the NAFI Corporation, a diversified industrial company that we controlled, make the offer to acquire Chris-Craft.

I soon surmised that Harsen Smith himself didn't want to sell Chris-Craft, but that he might be outvoted by the other trustees...After a while, Smith said, "We should be able to do business, because we have a common love — the water." He also mentioned that we were both members of the same "club"; he was referring to our both having been *Time* magazine cover subjects. [Cornelius Shields was on the cover of *Time* magazine July 27, 1953.]

Encouraged by the freeing up of his attitude, I felt at least I was making progress. We talked further about the company and I told him I would very much like to see the company's figures — balance sheet, income statements, etc., to guide us in our bid for the company.

Harsen Smith opened the top drawer of his desk, but made no move to bring out the sheets that I knew must be inside. Instead he spoke of the company his family had built and of its tradition of fine workmanship. If they sold it, it must be to people who would preserve the excellent condition, spirit, and happiness that prevailed in the organization.

I assured Smith that we wanted to keep Chris-Craft intact and that it was our desire to preserve the present management in its entirety; that the company would be run by them, not us, and that it would not become a divison of a giant corporation. This obviously impressed him. Nevertheless he continued to open the drawer partially and close it without producing the figures. I sensed his growing enthusiasm for my presentation and at last he produced the balance sheet and income account. I tore off the top part, which contained the company's letterhead, so if by chance the sheets went astray, no one could relate the figures to Chris-Craft.[7]

* * *

Despite Cornelius Shields' outline of the future for Chris-Craft and despite Harsen's inclination to do business with another nautical family, it was still far from certain that Chris-Craft would deal any more with Shields-NAFI. As Flannery looked through the company's accounts he could see that he needed more figures and that a more expert eye than his should look over them, so he asked that the head of Shields & Co.'s research department, Ted Crockett, go through the accounts. Said Harsen: "Sure, but you'd better get him down here soon. There's another company coming in next Tuesday and they're bringing a big contingent."

Crockett flew down from New York on Sunday afternoon, Feb. 24, spent all day Monday and — persuading Harsen there would be no harm in his taking the figures back to his hotel — also spent a large part of Monday night working over Chris-Craft's accounts.

Together Crockett and Flannery returned the accounts to Harsen early on Tuesday. Almost as they walked out of Harsen's office, the "big contingent" — a group of eight executives from Brunswick — walked in through Chris-Craft's front door. Brunswick's men knew they were in competition, but at this stage they didn't know that the competition was the Shields. While the Brunswick group talked to Harsen, Flannery and Crockett were out the back door, in Chris-Craft's Pompano Beach manufacturing plant, talking with department managers about new designs, new products, new sales opportunities.

In Harsen's office, the Brunswick group, which included Edward Bensinger and three of his vice-presidents, was having some difficulty presenting its plan for acquisition. For one thing, Harsen apparently was upset by the size of the Brunswick group. But there was more than that. Says Peifer: "I'd got on well with Harsen in my earlier meetings with him, even though he is a hard man to talk to. But this time he had Chris-Craft's lawyer, Wayne Van Osdol, there. Van Osdol made it virtually impossible for us to present our plan. Every time we tried to explain the benefits that could come of an exchange of stock, Van Osdol interrupted and told Harsen 'This will mean six months of waiting; you don't want that. You want your money now.'"

Brunswick's top men spent about two hours with Harsen and got practically nowhere, apart from learning that their competition was the Shields.

THE PRICE RISES

For the Shields group, all the predictables that would go into the bargaining were by now collected. There was a basis for mutual trust. It took Crockett one more day to produce, from the figures he had collected and from a series of long-distance telephone talks with his superiors in New York, an offering price for Chris-Craft. It was apparent that Chris-Craft's net worth — its plant, equipment, inventories and other tangible assets — was about $15 million. (Brunswick had also come up with that figure.) What remained was to put a price on the broad category of intangibles, the strength and talent of management, of the sales and distribution systems, of research and development, and the probable future sales — as well as good will, the name and reputation of the company. For this, they decided they would have to go high.

By Thursday, Jan. 28 — 10 days after the chance Coliseum meeting that triggered the talks — it was time for the Shields-NAFI negotiations to reach a new critical point.

Paul Shields and Virgil Sherrill, the Shields senior partner and NAFI director who would handle the final negotiations, flew in from New York that morning. Cornelius Shields, who had returned briefly to his Palm Beach vacation, came back to Pompano Beach. Owen Smith was back from New York and Bernard and Jay were in Pompano Beach to make the full group of Chris-Craft trustees.

They met for three hours on Thursday afternoon, Paul Shields talking for Shields-NAFI and Harsen Smith for Chris-Craft. It was Paul Shields' turn to show Harsen that there would be no sweeping changes at Chris-Craft, that a sale would be in the best interests of the Smith family. He put the offers to Harsen: Shields would underwrite the issue of 60% of Chris-Craft's stock to be offered to the public for $30-million, and would take $2.4-million as underwriter's fee. Alternatively, NAFI would pay $35-million in a private sale for the entire company.

In recollection, Harsen says, "We knew we would get less in private sale. But a sale to the public just didn't appeal to most of us." Still, the Smiths apparently did not expect so much less. That evening the four trustees met, decided to reject the proposed stock offering and voted 3-1 to sell the whole company — but for a minimum of $40-million.

HOLDOUT

The holdout was Harsen Smith. He was still against selling any part of the institution that had fed, clothed, housed and trained him, and had been his life for his 53 years. Behind his lone vote were the 13% of the company that he and his immediate family owned, and 14% more for which he was trustee; the votes of his father and his two uncles far outweighed his. So Harsen, as chairman, now had to negotiate the sale of a company that he didn't want to sell.

He met the Shields group next morning, told them of the trustees rejection of the stock plan.

"We like the idea of the second proposal," said Harsen. And then, in an offhand way, "Of course $35-million isn't enough. Chris-Craft is worth more than that and we have enough interest from others to assume we can get more."

Paul Shields turned his palms upward on the table and said, "Harsen, you know we're in no position to horse trade with you. You tell us how much you want and we'll see if we can meet the price."

"We decided," said Harsen, "that we will sell for no less than $40-million."

Paul Shields glanced at his colleagues and replied, "I'm sure we can meet it."

But the Shields group asked for a few days to arrange financing and they agreed to meet Harsen next on Feb. 3 in Detroit, where lawyer Van Osdol has his offices.

FINANCIAL REEFS

Responsibility for making the deal now fell on Virgil Sherrill, who at 40 is among Shields & Co.'s top men. He had the weekend to devise a plan that would provide $40-million for the Smith family, and two working days to persuade bankers that the plan was not only sound but attractive. His plan was complicated. It called (1) issuing the $15-million worth of new NAFI stock, (2) getting a $15-million bank loan, (3) drawing $6-million in cash out of NAFI, and (4) giving the Smiths a note from NAFI for $4-million.

Sherrill could see his plan had some disadvantages. It would involve much watering down of the interests of NAFI stockholders and would rely heavily on the banks at a time of tight money and high interest charges. But Harsen Smith apparently wanted all — or almost all — the 40-million as soon as possible and this seemed the only way to produce it. On Monday and Tuesday, Feb. 1 and Feb. 2, Sherrill talked with six major New York commercial bankers and failed to get from any of them a solid commitment to lend NAFI $15-million.

But he had not been flatly rejected, so he was able to fly to Detroit on Tuesday night with the plan ready to present to Harsen Smith. As insurance, he had in mind a second plan, one that would require a much smaller loan from banks and a far smaller new issue of NAFI stock — but this plan would not produce $40-million for the Smiths in one neat bundle.

Sherrill met Harsen Smith next morning. He described his plan to Harsen and to Harsen's lawyer. They rejected it.

Says Sherrill, "They didn't like the idea of the deals that would be involved. It would have taken the Securities & Exchange Commission at least 90 days to approve a new issue of NAFI stock. And they didn't like the idea of the whole deal hanging so heavily upon a stock sale."

The rejection didn't upset anyone's appetite. They went to lunch and over the table Sherrill put up his second plan. Harsen liked it much better than Sherrill thought he would, for this plan called for down payment and installments spread over the next five years, with the installments covered by NAFI's note at 6% interest. They bargained most of the afternoon over the size of the down payment, finally agreed on a figure of almost $12-million.

This gave the Smiths a tax advantage. Had they taken as much as one-third of the total price, the Internal Revenue Service would have sliced the entire capital gains tax out of the downpayment. Taking less than 30%, the Smiths have to pay only $3-million in capital gains tax at the start and they can spread the remainder of the tax payments over the next five yearly installments.

WARMER WELCOME

With that much settled, Sherrill dashed back to New York to make the rounds of the bankers again and get their backing for the smaller loan he sought. This time, the down payment would be financed by a short-term $6-million bank loan and $6-million in cash from NAFI's treasury. Earnings and some sales of NAFI property would cover the later installments. The New York banks gave Sherrill a warmer welcome. He saw four of them, wound up with a tentative agreement that Manufacturers Trust Co. would lend the $6-million. This would be paid back within a few months from the proceeds of the sale of 200,000 new shares of NAFI stock.

All day Thursday, Sherrill talked with the bankers. He flew back to Detroit on Thursday night and began bargaining again with Harsen Smith on Friday.

LOOSE ENDS

The acquisition was still not sewed up. Three more solid days of negotiation remained. There was no disagreement about price — that had been settled. But there was plenty of trading to be done over terms.

Harsen, recalling those three days, says, "Here I was negotiating the sale of a company that I didn't want to sell. You can imagine what kind of a bargainer I was."

Sherrill, in recollection, says "Harsen was hard, but he was square with us. All the time we were in Detroit he was called to the telephone several times a day. He told me that several of these times Brunswick was on the line, and that at one stage they were offering him as much as $47-million for Chris-Craft."

Harsen, however, says now, "In Detroit I talked again with the Brunswick man before our negotiations with the Shields group. There was never any offer made. The talk was always of an exchange of stock."

And Brunswick's Peifer says: "I called Harsen about every other day during that week they were in Detroit. We never did make him an offer."...

THE NEWS LEAKS OUT

In the midst of this trading over terms, other things began to happen. Word of the talks between NAFI and Chris-Craft leaked out. Says Sherrill: "It was inevitable. At least half a dozen bankers knew what we planned to do. The bulk of the Smith family, of course, knew what was going on."

The word spread out and the stock market responded. NAFI's stock, which stood at 13 on Jan. 29, the day Harsen Smith asked for $40-million for Chris-Craft, jumped to 19 by Feb. 5, two days before the sale agreement was signed. That day, a Friday, the New York Stock Exchange called Paul Shields at noon, demanded a public announcement so that rumors of NAFI's activities would cease and that trading would be done on the basis of fact. NAFI replied the following day, and said that it was still negotiating.

Not until late on Sunday did Harsen Smith and Sherrill, and their attorneys, finally write the last sentence of the eight page sale agreement. Sherrill's work still wasn't over. He flew back to New York, on February 8 — 21 days after Flannery met Owen Smith in New York — and got his formal commitment for the $6-million loan from Manufacturers Trust Co., organized a NAFI directors' meeting for the following Thursday, at which the directors approved the deal, started work on the complex proxy statement that sought NAFI stockholders' approval and on the much larger registration statement by which NAFI sought SEC's approval of the new issue of 200,000 shares.[8]

An interesting phenomenon occurred in the market as a result of the NAFI-Chris-Craft sale. On Friday, February 12, five days following the acquisition, NAFI stock was so active, actually three times the next most actively traded shares, that the Exchange had to ban the use of stop-loss orders in NAFI trading to "prevent possible future wide fluctuations in the issue." NAFI was called "the market sensation of the last fortnight."[9] Also among the most actively traded issues was Brunswick-Balke, though the irony was that they were one of only a few of the most actively traded issues that was trading *at a loss.*

Cornelius Shields was on a roll. He had watched with intense interest Brunswick's unsuccessful acquisition of Chris-Craft, and put yet another plan into motion.

> Obviously I knew that Brunswick was eager to acquire a boat manufacturer to add to its varied line of leisure-activity products. As a director of Owens Yacht Company, second only to Chris-Craft in the industry, I thought I might persuade the four Owens brothers to sell their company. I told Paul after our second meeting at Pompano that if we were successful in closing the Chris-Craft deal, I was going to try to sell Owens to Brunswick.
>
> Several days later, on a bleak, snowy Sunday after Virgil Sherrill had been successful in his final Chicago negotiations and I had returned to New York, I suddenly decided I could not wait until Monday to contact Brunswick — when someone else might approach them with the same idea. I did not know the name of the Brunswick president, but I finally got in touch with a member of the White Plains office of our organization and asked him to open the office for me so I could obtain Brunswick's financial manuals.
>
> I called all over Chicago that afternoon and finally tracked down Edward Bensinger, the president of Brunswick, at his club. He knew only too well who I was, as he had just learned of our purchase of Chris-Craft the day before.
>
> Before calling him I had telephoned the Owens brothers and obtained their authority to deal with Brunswick. When I told Bensinger of this possibility he was casual, but I knew he was seriously interested. A few days later he came to Baltimore with his associates to meet the Owens brothers, whose father had founded the company in a Chesapeake Bay backwater. The negotiations were completed in less than a

week, and Brunswick acquired Owens for $16,000,000.

> We had made a real double play. My Sunday efforts were most timely; on Monday, a St. Louis firm tried to obtain an option from the Owens brothers, stating that they were confident they could quickly sell the company. I learned later that their prospective buyer was Brunswick. This fortunate Sunday urge once again bore out what I have experienced so many times: If you are blessed with an idea, capitalize on it immediately; otherwise there will be a dozen reasons for delay. Enthusiasm may then evaporate or some enterprising competitor will make your deal.[10]

Once the sale of Chris-Craft was final, Harsen vacated his offices in Pompano Beach very quickly.[11] Though over a half-century had been spent with Chris-Craft, he still had a large job to do and he wanted to get started quickly.

> Harsen Smith has...moved to a still barely furnished room in a new office building in Fort Lauderdale. From there he will direct the investment of most of the $40-million ($30-million after taxes) that will be paid to the Smith family over the next five years. "Even though most of the family wanted to sell," he says, "they would sell only if I handled the investing of the profits. And that's what I intend to do by setting up a trust company."
>
> Harsen will not, however, handle Owen Smith's investment. Owen keeps his 20% share of the proceeds to himself.
>
> It may seem that Harsen, wading almost hip-deep in money now, should be happy. He isn't. "I don't feel any differently now than I did at any other time," he says. "I feel we should have kept ownership and control. From the first I wasn't in favor of selling, and I'm still not..."[12]

Chris-Craft was in its prime in 1960, and at the time of the sale to NAFI, employed three thousand five hundred employees. Sales, at over $40 million, were three times their closest competitor in the industry, Owens Yachts. Chris-Craft built over eight thousand boats in 1960, at a profit of over $2.5 million.[13] It was a sprawling, well balanced company that emerged from the bargaining table, and at the beginning, both sides were in agreement that the less tinkering by the parent organization the better. Harry Coll, President of the boat operations, was given a free hand by the Shields brothers, and as *Time* reported, took the opportunity to roll up his sleeves and literally go back to the drawing boards.

Coll himself took a pencil to Chris-Craft's blueprints. A mechanical engineer with a flair for design, he slimmed the bulging bow line, streamlined the superstructure to give the boats a racier silhouette. To please lady sailors, he installed molded fiber-glass vanities and washbowls in the heads, put pile carpets in the cabins, and picture windows in the galleys. As a result of the new look, Chris-Craft is once again, according to Coll, "at least two years in front of its competitors — and I intend to keep it there."[14]

A renewed aggression was also demonstrated in Chris-Craft marketing, as the company realized that more and more boat builders were competing for the same consumer dollars. *Time* magazine quoted a "top Chris-Craft executive" as saying "We had gotten so we didn't pay attention to the market trends. The philosophy was: let the pioneers get the arrows in their behinds."[15]

to $7,590. A single *Capri* was available with either 100 or 185-horsepower V-8, at $4,200 to $4,290.

The 21-foot Continental incorporated very futuristic design elements to attract an expanding sport boat market. It set new design precedents in an industry scrambling for image and identity.

Elegant new Continental introduces luxury and beauty never seen before in sports boats. Gull-Wing hatches on unique fiberglass hardtop flip up for easy boarding, are removable for open-air cruising. Sleek white fins contrast smartly with rich two-toned hull of matched Philippine mahogany. Cockpit seats eight comfortably and is completely upholstered in shimmering gold, sea-mist green, and charcoal vinyl. V-8 engines to 275 hp, flashing speeds to 42 mph. Every detail shows superior quality, every line speaks eagerness to provide water thrills![16]

The 1960 Chris-Craft 21-foot Continental had an optional fiberglas hardtop with removable gull-wing hatches. V-8 power to 275 hp delivered 42 mph in style.

Courtesy Mariners' Museum, Newport News, Virginia.

The Chris-Craft Division, competing for central focus of the Corporation with the Cavalier and Roamer Divisions, was slimmed down to 44 models in 12 series, of which seven could be modified for status as Express Cruisers by the addition of a folding top and side curtains.

Two hull lengths were offered in the *Sportsman Series*, of 17 and 24-foot versions, with power plants ranging from 100-horsepower to a pair of 185-horsepower V-8's, and were available from $3,335 to $7,990. Two versions of a 17-foot ski boat were also included in the group. The *Continental Series* also provided two basic choices, in 18 and 21-foot versions, with the same power options for between $4,210

From this point the fleet jumped all the way to the *Twenty-Seven Foot Series*, with three models of a 27-foot Semi-Enclosed Cruiser and three models of the 27-foot *Constellation*. Power options were the same, with choices of a single or pair of 185-horsepower V-8's or a pair of 100-horsepower engines. Prices ranged from $6,990 to the Constellation with a pair of V-8's for $10,180. A *Thirty-Two Foot Series* contained only a *Commander* at $16,720, and a Constellation at $17,720, each with a pair of 185-horsepower V-8's with reduction drives. A similarly equipped 33-foot *Sport Fisherman* was available for $20,740, and a 40-foot model drew $56,130. By comparison, three versions of the

40-foot *Conqueror* ranged from $30,990 to $44,790.

In absolute dominance of the fleet were the larger Constellations available in 36, 40, 45, 50, 55 and 60-foot versions, and ranging in price from the 36-footer with a pair of 185-horsepower V-8's at $19,790, to the 66-foot with a pair of V-12, 504-horsepower General Motors diesels, and accommodations for twelve at $139,970.

Gone were the bull nose bows of the fifties, replaced by the sleek new *Clipper* bows of the sixties. This styling change was enthusiastically accepted by buyers, and gave their Constellations the look of much larger custom-built yachts. Actually, Chris-Craft was working hard to attract the custom yacht buyer by running ads which suggested that "Knowledgeable yachtsmen are discovering that Chris-Craft builds custom quality motor yachts...and save up to 40% over boats built the old-fashioned way."[17]

Among the hottest selling boats for 1960 were the 20 models of *Cavalier* from 18 to 30-foot. The plywood boats were available in 18, 23, 25 and 30-foot models and ranged from $2,965 for an 18-foot Cavalier with a 100-horsepower engine to $9,920 for a 30-foot Express Cruiser with a pair of Chris-Craft 185-horsepower V-8's.

While only minor changes occurred in the steel Roamer Division offerings, Sea Skiff Division products were available in 18, 20, 23 and 27-foot Open; 23-foot *Ranger*; 30-foot Open with fiberglas Hard Top; and Cruisers in 30, 32, 36 and 42-foot versions.

With a year of better than average sales and stable production under their belts, the parent organization, NAFI, gave the green light for expansion. On January 27, 1961, not long after 43-year-old John F. Kennedy was sworn in as President of the United States, Chris-Craft Corporation formed Chris-Craft S.A. in Lausanne, Switzerland, to centralize new forays into European sales and production activities. On December 13, 1961, Chris-Craft S.A. established an Italian subsidiary, Chris-Craft of Italy, S.p.A., and in 1962 opened a manufacturing facility in Fiumicino, Italy, to better serve a growing European market.   From the *World Headquarters Building* in Pompano Beach, Chris-Craft supervised operations in twelve plants and one major overseas display and marketing facility. Plants were operating in Algonac, Cadillac, and Holland (2), Michigan; Caruthersville, Missouri; Chattanooga, Tennessee; Hayward, California; Pompano Beach, Florida; Salisbury (2), Mary-

land (Ocean Side Drive and Lee Street plants); Chris-Craft of Italy, S.p.A.; and the new Thompson facility in Cortland, New York.

In the year that both the Soviet Union and the United States would launch the world's first men into space and Chubby Checker had America dancing the *Twist*, the 1961 Chris-Craft fleet underwent a continuing overhaul. The Chris-Craft Division alone lost seven models for a total of 37 offerings. Only two minor changes occurred in the runabout ranks, with the disappearance of the 17-foot Sportsman with 100-horsepower engine, and the 18-foot Continental became a 19-foot model.

A new *Twenty-Five Foot Series* emerged, with a pair of Constellations, one a *Custom Deluxe* with 185-h.p. V-8 for $7,345. The old 27-foot models were discontinued, and a trio of 28-foot Constellations took their place. The 32-foot *Commander*, which was to be the last mahogany Commander built by Chris-Craft, was displaced in the fleet, while the Constellation remained.

The 40-foot Constellations and *Conquerors* became 41-foot, and only one model of 50-foot Constellation would be available, equipped with a pair of 275-h.p. V-8's for $53,990. Both 66-foot Constellations would be G.M. diesel powered, with a choice of a pair of 308 h.p. V-8's for $142,900 or 456 h.p. V-12's at $159,970.

The Cavalier Division stretched the 21-foot models into 23-foot versions, and added four models of 23-foot Express Cruisers for a total plywood fleet of 24 models with only minor price increases.

Virtually no changes were made in the increasingly popular Sea Skiff fleet for '61, with interior appointment and materials simply reflecting the changing tastes of the times.

The Roamer steel boats offered an unprecedented 23 models for 1961, in sizes from 31 to 56-foot. Leading the fleet in popularity and variations were sixteen models of 35-foot Roamers, which varied by power and appointments known as *Express Cruiser, Express Cruiser Deluxe 6S (Six Sleeper), Riviera* (Hardtop 6S and Deluxe 6S), *Regal,* and *Sport Fisherman 4S*. A 56-foot *Motor Yacht* equipped with a pair of 336-h.p. G.M. diesels was priced at around $90,000 with a hardtop, which compared favorably with a 55-foot mahogany Constellation for around $86,000. Years of production at the Holland Roamer plant had succeeded in submerging the price of steel hull construction to less than comparable mahogany yachts.

Overall sales volume for the Corporation for 1961 would yield $42 million, increasing to nearly $44 million for 1962.

1962 was a year of surprises at Chris-Craft. First, the Board of Directors of NAFI agreed to change the name of the corporation to Chris-Craft Industries, Inc., which would more appropriately identify the company with the well-known trademark of the boat division.

Next, plans were announced in September for production of a 35-foot, sloop rigged fiberglas motor sailer, a Chris-Craft sailboat. The sailboat program, which would ultimately number eight models, was such a unique episode in Chris-Craft history, that a separate chapter has been devoted to the subject. See *The Chris-Craft Sailboats,* Chapter XVIII. The all-fiberglas sailboat program helped to accelerate Chris-Craft's lagging fiberglas programs, bringing in needed expertise from a segment of the industry which had much greater and more varied experience.

A new Research and Development Center was completed in Pompano Beach during 1962, and among the priorities was to advance Chris-Craft's fiberglas programs. Chris-Craft was slow to embrace all the design and manufacturing possibilities for the new technologies, and the new research center represented a corporate commitment to stay abreast of changes in polyesters, laminate application, resin curing schedules, and efficient manufacturing techniques.

On January 12 of 1962, Chris-Craft Corporation purchased the assets and designs of Thompson Boat Company of New York, Inc., manufacturers of an abbreviated line of small fiberglas cruisers and outboard runabouts, for $550,000. Since the discontinuation of the Kit Boat Division, the purchase was designed to establish Chris-Craft's presence in the outboard boat field once again, as well as acquire more technical ability in fiberglas fabrication.[18] The Thompson acquisition in Cortland, New York, provided Chris-Craft with another opportunity to develop an advanced fiberglas program. Thompson had firmly established four basic fiberglas models in the marketplace, 16-foot and 17-foot *Traditional* and *Luxury* outboard runabouts, and two principal models of a 20-foot hull, *Traditional Open,* and *Traditional Cruisette.* Prices ranged from $1,095 for a Traditional (outboard) 16 to $2,150 for the Traditional Cruisette.

Along with Thompson came Chris-Craft's first exposure to *transdrive,* or inboard/outboard engine technology. Both 20-foot models could be equipped with either 80 or 100-horsepower Volvo inboard engines attached to the Volvo outdrive unit, basically an outboard lower unit. This new combination of inboard and outboard power offered many advantages over either parent technology, mainly safety tip-up, extra cockpit area, quick prop changes, full height transoms, low center of gravity, and excellent turning performance.

A new identity was quickly established for the Thompson, Cortland, New York plant, with the introduction in October of the *Corsair* line of fiberglas runabouts and express cruisers. A new reinforced fiberglas hull construction technique, far in advance of the old Lake 'N Sea programs, was developed principally by Thompson for the new models.

It features a sandwich-type bottom of fiberglass with longitudinal reinforcing stringers — wood core permanently molded in place, and solidly packed plastic flotation between the inner and outer hull bottom. This makes for outstanding flotation, strength and rigidity. The multi-laminate construction is built by hand — and is quality-control inspected many times. It will withstand impact, weather wear and deterioration with a minimum of upkeep.

Its unique, speed-stability bottom design also makes for positive control at high speed. You bank without skip or slip.[19]

Two 15-foot models, the *XL 150 Sunlounger* and *XL 150 Runabout* were distinguished only by seating configuration. Three 17-foot models were also introduced, an *XL 170 Sunlounger, XL 170 Runabout,* and *XL 170 Express Cruiser* which included a small galley area with sink. Chris-Craft Transdrive (Volvo) power was available on the XL 170 models only. The Corsairs were the prototypes of a whole new look in Chris-Craft runabouts, and a glimpse into the future direction of the marine industry. Featuring anodized aluminum windshields, sun-lounger seats and simple designs, they offered quick, basic transportation with contemporary styling.

Another new innovation hit the water in '62, the 16-foot Chris-Craft *Ski-Jet.* Powered by a 185-horsepower V-8 coupled with a Buehler Water Jet Propulsion unit, the Ski-Jet had no propeller, but three small impellers, which forced water out of the lower unit of the inboard/outboard style unit at tremendous pressure to produce speeds up to 43 miles per hour. Only 46 of the unique boats were produced. In 1962 the price was $4,595 and plummeted to $3,680 in 1963 before being discontinued.

The Chris-Craft Division built eighteen different hulls for '62, which with differences in power made forty-one models. Along with the 16-foot Ski-Jet, a 16-foot *Ski-Boat* was built for $1,200 less for traditional inboard 185-horsepower V-8 power. Three *Holiday* models were produced, including 18-foot, 20-foot and 23-foot versions. The 20-foot was the fastest boat in the fleet at 47 miles per hour. It featured a rakish new bow design, and longitudinal steps on the double-planked mahogany bottom.

The Sport Fisherman was available in 28, 33 and 40-foot models, with a 40-foot equipped with a pair of 181-horsepower G.M. diesels going for $50,095.

Constellations made up the majority of the fleet with models offered in 25, 32, 36, 37 (Tri-Cabin), 45, 50 and 55-foot versions. A 25-foot "Connie" with a single 185-horsepower V-8 went for $7495, while a 55-footer with a pair of 308-horsepower G.M. diesels would fetch $86,965 f.o.b. Algonac. A 41-foot Conqueror was also available.

Queen of the fleet was the 1962 60-foot *Motor Yacht*. A truly spacious boat, it accommodated eight guests in three double staterooms aft, a captain's quarter forward with double berths, and contained three "lavatories" with optional showers. It could be equipped with a pair of 460-horsepower G.M. diesels for $157,270.

Many changes were made in the Cavalier Division for 1962, starting with the addition of a 40-mile-per-hour 16-foot *Custom Ski Boat* for $2,870 with 150-horsepower V-8. An 18-foot *Sport Utility*, 2-sleeper 21-foot *Sportsman* and *Express Cruiser*, were added along with 25-foot Express Cruisers in 2 and 4-sleeper models. Other 4-sleepers included *Custom Cruisers* in

Courtesy Mariners' Museum, Newport News, Virginia.

Only 46 of the 1963 Chris-Craft 16-foot *Ski-Jet* were built, with slow sales blamed on the unusual and often cantankerous jet-driven system. Powered by a 185- horsepower Chris-Craft V-8 and a Buehler Water Jet Propulsion unit, the Ski-Jet delivered 43 mph for only $3,680.

The acquisition of the Thompson Boat Company in Cortland, New York helped Chris-Craft to quickly establish the new fiberglas *Corsair* Division, here seen manufacturing sport boats in the mid-sixties.

Courtesy Mariners' Museum, Newport News, Virginia.

26 and 28-foot models, with some of the 26-foot production available at the Hayward, California plant. Two 6-sleepers topped the plywood fleet, a 30-foot *Custom Cruiser* and a 35-foot *Custom Yacht* for $18,995 equipped with a pair of 285-horsepower V-8 Chris-Craft engines.

Another overhaul took place in the Sea Skiff Division, which offered 11 basic models ranging from 18 to 42 feet. New names and designations were apparent, starting with *Sportsman* in 18, 20, 23 and 27-foot varieties. A 2-sleeper, 23-foot *Ranger* remained. Cruisers came in 27-foot (Express Cruiser), 30-foot (Sports Cruiser), and four models of the new *Custom Corinthian* cruisers in 30 (4-sleeper), 32, 37 and 42-foot (6-sleeper) versions. A 42-foot Custom Corinthian with a pair of 180-horsepower G.M. diesels retailed for $45,645 f.o.b. Salisbury, Maryland.

The welded steel boat Roamer Division added *aluminum* to its hull-making capabilities by the introduction of a new 27-foot cruiser known as the *Silver Comet* and *Custom Comet*. Also new to the fleet was a stylish 32-foot and 36-foot series called *Express Cruiser, Express De Luxe,* and *Riviera De Luxe* models. Top of the line were the 44-foot Riviera and 56-foot *Motor Yacht.* Prices ranged from the 27-foot Silver Comet with a single 185-horsepower V-8 at $10,890, to

the 56-foot Motor Yacht with a pair of 308-horsepower G.M. diesels for $87,290.

Sales increased more than $2 million for 1963, to over $46.3 million as additions were added to the top and bottom of the fleets. Added to the Chris-Craft Division were 17-foot models of *Ski Boat* and *Custom Ski Boat*, and 20-foot *Caravelle*. Gone were the 25, 32, 36, 45 and 55-foot Constellations, replaced by new "Connies" in 27, 30, 42, 46, 52 and 57-foot models. Also missing were the Sport Fisherman models, which made room for a new 34-foot *Sedan*, and a slightly stretched 42-foot *Conqueror*.

Top of the line for 1963 were the 60-foot and 65-foot *Motor Yachts* at $159,605 and $178,030 respectively, equipped with twin 456-horsepower G.M. diesel engines. In 1963, Chris-Craft began to use the term *Command Bridge* to describe the elevated control bridges, also known as *flying bridges*, of the Constellation and Commander series, a term which they would eventually trademark, and is still in active and exclusive use today.

Six standard hulls were available in the 1963 Cavalier line of plywood boats, and the reduced number of models were given catchy new names. Smallest was the 16-foot *Custom Ski Boat*, followed by the 19-foot *Golden Arrow* which was available with the Chris-Craft (Volvo) transdrive which was proving so successful in the Corsair line. A 24-foot *Fiesta*, and *Futura* models in 26, 28 and 31-foot versions could be powered by either single or twin 185-horsepower V-8 Chris-Craft engines. Queen of the Cavalier fleet was still the 35-foot 6-sleeper *Custom Yacht* at $19,495, equipped with twin 185-horsepower V-8 engines.

Nearly every Sea Skiff model for '63 was new, including the 19, 21, 24 and 28-foot *Sportsman*, 24-foot *Ranger*, 27-foot *Corinthian Express Cruiser*, 31-foot *Corinthian Sports Cruiser*, and *Corinthian Custom Cruisers* in 31, 34, and 38-foot models.

Something new was brewing at Chris-Craft that would change the focus of most of the boat divisions over the next few years. Intense research and experimentation was being carried on at the new Fiberglass and Tooling Activity Division at Holland, Michigan, and at the Research and Development Center in Pompano Beach, Florida. It was a dramatic and important new creation, unveiled on a giant castered cradle at the top of the escalators at the National Motor Boat Show in New York in January of 1964. It was a 38-foot *all fiberglas* Commander, Chris-Craft's first fiberglas cruiser, and one of the largest production fiberglas boats which had

ever been built. Chris-Craft had made genuine progress in fiberglas manufacturing technology, and instead of trailing somewhat behind other boat builders in application techniques, they were now moving ahead.

A new fiberglass process has been developed by our Fiberglass Development and Tooling Activity Division at Holland, Michigan. Savings in labor, material costs and weight have been so substantial that we believe a significant breakthrough has been made that will contribute to efficiency and new product development.[20]

This first 38-foot fiberglas Commander sold for $29,900 equipped with a pair of 210-horsepower Chris-Craft V-8's, which compared quite well with a similarly equipped 38-foot *Challenger Salon* at $30,190, or a 38-foot Sea Skiff *Sea Hawk Sport Fisherman* for $26,795. As we shall see, it was to be the first in a very successful series of fiberglas cruisers that would within a very few years begin to dominate the entire fleet.

As the *Beatles* invaded America for the first time, the Chris-Craft Division for 1964 introduced twenty basic models, from 17 to 65-feet. A new class of boats was offered, known as the *Super Sports*, represented by 18, 20, and 21-foot Super Sports. Each took advantage of the addi-

W.A. "Bill" MacKerer was the guiding hand of Chris-Craft manufacturing, production and naval architecture for nearly a half century. In the heat of the day during the twenties, MacKerer would jump into the canal in Algonac fully clothed, then resume work while the evaporating water cooled him off.

Courtesy Mariners' Museum, Newport News, Virginia.

tional speed gained by using streamlined rudders, propellers designed for top speed, and a choice of a 327 or 430-cubic-inch engine. A 20-foot Super Sport with a 275-h.p. V-8 was advertised at 47 miles per hour and $6,495, the fastest in the fleet. The only other runabouts available were the 17-foot *Custom Ski Boat*, 18-foot *Holiday*, and 21-foot *Continental*.

Besides a 34-foot *Sedan* and the 65-foot *Motor Yacht*, it was Constellations all the way

in 24, 27 and 31-foot models, borrowed years of proven bonding experience from the other division.

The smooth-and-dry-riding hulls have sturdy lapstrake sides made of overlapping planks of tough, marine-grade plywood. For lasting strength and watertight bonds, high-quality polysulfide sealant — impervious to gasoline, oil, and fungus — is used between the strakes.[21]

Courtesy Mariners' Museum, Newport News, Virginia.

In 1965 Chris-Craft was building boats out of just about every available material. Top left and clockwise: Roamer 48-foot Riviera (steel or aluminum): Commander Thirty-Eight (fiber-glas); Cavalier 33-foot Futura (marine plywood); Chris-Craft 37-foot Constellation (solid Philippine mahogany); and Sea Skiff 35-foot Sea Hawk (lapstrake).

from 27 to 65-feet, with models in between of 30, 34, 37, 42, 46, 52 and 57-feet.

Challengers were grouped and marketed separately in 1964, with only three versions available, in 36-foot (including Sedan), and 38-foot Salon models.

A new innovation in the plywood Cavalier Division produced three models of a lapstrake design hull, and gave the inexpensive boats the look of the popular Sea Skiffs. The *Seastrakes*,

Also available in plywood were the 16-foot *Ski Boat*, 19-foot *Golden Arrow*, *Futura* in 24, 26, 27 and 31-foot versions, and the venerable 35-foot *Yacht*.

Sea Skiffs for 1964 included *Sportsman* in 19, 21, 24 and 28-foot models, along with *Rangers* in 21 and 24-foot variations. *Corinthians* were offered in 28-foot (Express), 32 (Sports Cruiser) and 35-foot Corinthian 6-sleeper models. The 35-foot Corinthian, and soon 38-foot models, were *smooth-sided* Sea Skiffs, while still retaining the round-bilge architecture. Also available were the new 38-foot *Sea Hawk Sedan* and *Sea Hawk Sport Fisherman* models. Prices ranged from the 19-foot Sportsman with single 185-h.p. Chris-Craft V-8 at $3,650 to the 38-foot Sea Hawk Sport Fisherman with a pair of 181-h.p. G. M. diesels for $39,940.

Chris-Craft expanded again in 1965, with the announcement in February of the formation of a Canadian subsidiary to manufacture boats. A survey had been conducted, which showed the strengthening Canadian economy had produced "increased discretionary income", creating "...a substantial market for Chris-Craft's quality boats."[22] An over 78,000 square foot plant was built in Stratford, Ontario, and was in production by the fall of 1965. The completion of the Canadian plant marked the zenith of Chris-Craft's manufacturing capacity. With eleven manufacturing facilities in three countries, nearly two million square feet was dedicated to the production of Chris-Craft products. Harry H. Coll, president, ordered an analysis of plant floor area in September, and the list clearly showed why Chris-Craft was still the largest manufacturer of motor boats in the world. Missing from the list were the discontinued operations at Hayward, California and Caruthersville, Missouri.

PLANT	SQ. FT.
Algonac, MI	263,808
Cadillac, MI	175,134
Chattanooga, TN	157,706
Holland, MI	339,963
Pompano Beach, FL	198,162
Pompano Administration	42,290
Roamer (Holland, MI)	186,829
Salisbury, MD	315,020
Thompson Boat (Cortland, NY)	183,024
Stratford, Ontario (Canada)	78,803
Fiumicino, Italy	14,385
Total	**1,962,124**[23]

The overwhelming success of the 38-foot all-fiberglas Commander led quickly to the establishment of a *Commander Series Fiberglass Division*, and to the addition of the 38-foot *Commander Sedan*, 38-foot *Sport Fisherman*, and a new 27-foot Commander to the all-fiberglas fleet. Naturally, efficient modifications were made to the wetted surfaces of the new fiberglas versions, as the new medium allowed generous design flexibility.

The decks, superstructure, and hull are low-maintenance, reinforced fiberglass, and they're bonded together into a one piece, extra-strong unit. The bottom is inset at the chine to deflect spray and aid stability. Vertical speed stabilizers run the length of the hull between the keel and the chine. The transom is styled, like the Commander 38, with a slight vee shape.[24]

The 4-sleeper 27-foot Commander with a single Chris-Craft 210-h.p. V-8 was a reasonable $9,995, which compared favorably with a similarly equipped 27-foot mahogany Constellation at $9,345.

Twenty-three basic Chris-Craft Division models were available in '65, representing excitement from 17 to 65-feet. A dwindling runabout fleet contained but five models: the 17-foot Custom Ski, and four models of Super Sport in 17, 18, 20 and 21-foot lengths.

Except for the fiberglas Commanders in 27 and 38-foot (including Sedan and Sport Fisherman versions), and the 65-foot Motor Yacht, every model in the Chris-Craft Division fleet was a Constellation. Twelve hulls were available, in 28, 30, 32 Express or Hardtop, 36 (including Sedan), 37, 38 Salon, 43, 46, 52, 57 and 65-foot models. Prices ranged from a 28-foot Constellation with a single 210-horsepower Chris-Craft engine at $9,995 to the 65-foot Constellation with a pair of 478-horsepower G. M. diesel engines at $181,290. An identically powered 65-foot Motor Yacht brought an additional $3,700, which shows how similar in production value the two flagships were designed.

An even dozen models of Sea Skiff were manufactured in 1965. Only minor changes were made in the fleet, with a 22-foot Sportsman replacing last years 21-foot model, a 28-foot *Express Cruiser* replacing the Corinthian Express, a 32-foot *Sea Hawk Express* and 35-foot *Sea Hawk* replaced the 32 and 35-foot Corinthians, and a new 38-foot Corinthian 6-sleeper was offered.

By contrast, nearly every model in the Cavalier fleet was changed for 1965, increasing the plywood division's selections to 15 models. Economical recreation was manufactured in lengths ranging from the 16-foot *Ski;* 18-foot *Custom;* 22-foot *Dory,* 22-foot *Cutlass; Futura* and *Seastrake* models in 25, 27, 30 and 33-foot versions; 28-foot *Crusader;* along with 36-foot Seastrake and *Yacht* models.

The economic benefits of the Cavaliers were beginning to be less meaningful, as lowered pro-

duction costs in other divisions began to compete with the traditional economy line. For example, a 36-foot double-planked mahogany Constellation could be bought for only $21,990, as compared to an identically powered 36-foot plywood Cavalier Yacht at $20,745, a difference of only $1,245. It was a situation that, in years to come, would cause the eventual deterioration of plywood boat sales at Chris-Craft, and throughout the industry at large. For now, though, thanks to aggressive marketing by Division Sales Manager Bruce Donaldson (who was also Sailboat Division Sales Manager), Cavalier sales were up over 30 percent from 1964.[25]

The all fiberglas Corsair (previously Thompson) Boat line, manufactured at the new 48-acre Industrial Park in Cortland, New York, offered only six models for 1965. Most interesting was the petite 15-foot *Jolly Boat,* a twin sponson outboard runabout with a sunwell forward. It was designed to be very stable, and continued in the Thompson tradition of foam-flotation, fiberglas encapsulated bottom.

> Corsair's multi-laminate hull is handcrafted (more costly "hand-layup" method). The outer and inner hulls have 3 to 8 fiberglass layers impregnated with polyester resin...A balsa wood core is permanently molded-in and reinforces the outer hull.
> A high density urethane filling (5 to 10 inches thick) is foamed under 38,000 lbs. pressure between these two hulls, to fill every cavity. It makes for outstanding strength and rigidity — and curbs vibration and bottom noise.[26]

Corsair also manufactured models in 16-foot (XL 155 Sunlounger), 18-foot (Sunlounger and Express Cruiser) and 20-foot versions. A Corsair transdrive (Volvo) was available on all but the Jolly Boat, and the 20-foot runabout offered an inboard 185-horsepower V-8 option.

Seven Roamers were available in 1965, offering choices between welded steel or aluminum hulls. Fiberglas superstructures and a new Capac electronic electrolysis protection system helped increase sales for the well-found boats. The appeal to consumers was basic: safety and low maintenance.

> The hulls are made of plates of steel or aluminum, welded to sturdy frames. There are no seams to leak, no planks to crack, no rivets, screws, or nails to work loose, no dry rot or borers...and there's no worry about salt-water corrosion.[27]

Sporting the latest fad in tail fins, three beautiful Chris-Craft take an autumn sojourn near Hessel, Michigan. Top to bottom: John Kovach aboard his 1957 21-foot Continental *Smoove,* Frank and Marcia Bronson aboard their 1960 21-foot Continental *Buckwheat,* and Jim Mertaugh aboard his 1957 21-foot Capri.

Photo by Karine N. Rodengen

A 30-foot steel *Dispatcher* would sleep four comfortably from $14,665, while the 37-foot 6-sleeper *Riviera*, available in steel or aluminum, started at $23,475 for the steel version. The 38-foot *Offshore* was offered in steel only, whereas the 48-foot *Riviera* 8-sleeper could be built in steel or aluminum starting from $49,995. A significant premium was paid for aluminum construction. The elegant 57-foot *Motor Yacht* retailed for $95,410 in steel and $107,975 in aluminum, a difference of $12,565.

In 1966, eighty-one total models were available throughout all Chris-Craft fleets. Only minor changes were made to the Chris-Craft Division line-up, such as the elimination of the 32-foot Constellation; replacement of the 38-foot Constellation Salon with a Tri-Cabin version; addition of a 40-foot Constellation Salon; and replacement of the 46-foot "Connie" with a 45-foot version.

The all-fiberglas Commander fleet continued to grow in 1966 with the addition of the new 31-foot *Commander Express*. Seven fiberglas Commanders were now available, including the 27-foot Commander Sports Express and Commander Express, and 38-foot Commander, Commander Sedan and Commander Sport Fisherman. So sure was Chris-Craft that their fiberglas techniques were superior, that they challenged buyers to compare hulls with the competition.

> Sight down the length of the hull for imperfections. Notice that Commanders have none of the ripples, waves, or indentations you'll see on some other hulls. The smoothness is due to Chris-Craft's painstaking preparation of the molds, which are cleaned and polished to mirror-like perfection...
>
> Find out if the hull has been painted. Commander hulls have an outer layer of color impregnated, high quality gelcoat. They're never painted. Inferior gelcoats may necessitate painting at the factory, and will require periodic painting thereafter.
>
> Pound the side of the hull in the amidships sections. If the side flexes under your fist, or if you hear a booming drum sound, the hull side isn't as strong as it could be. Commander hulls are solid. The strength...comes from the use of extra fiberglass reinforcement in the polyester lay-ups. Layer after layer of fiberglass roving or matting is applied until Chris-Craft's requirements for strength are achieved.[28]

Wood construction, far from being neglected in the face of Chris-Craft's fiberglas revolution, was still being refined, still being updated. A comparision of this 1966 wood boat construction description with procedures used in the 1920's shows more similarities than differences. Except for some advanced materials, most techniques have remained the same.

> At Chris-Craft, engineers choose different kinds and types of lumber to fit the need of different parts of the boats. White oak and Philippine mahogany are used extensively. Tough, stringy pieces are chosen for keels, chines, and fender rails. Strong, vertical-grain fir is used for hull stringers. After the keel has been laid, sawn Philippine mahogany main frames are bolted to it, and stout steam-bent white oak ribs are placed alternately between the frames. Beautifully grained and properly dried Philippine mahogany is picked for natural-finish surfaces. It's known for its strength and close grain; it shows little tendency to check, and expansion in water is minimal.
>
> Chris-Craft double-planked bottoms have an inner planking of marine-grade plywood sheets for strength and resiliency without extra weight. The large plywood sheets also contribute great transverse and longitudinal stiffness to prevent "racking" and "working" of the frames. Gaskets saturated with canvas bedding compound are placed over all seams before Philippine mahogany outer planking is applied.
>
> Batten-seam hull side construction produces a strong, lightweight, watertight hull. Solid Philippine mahogany battens back each seam between the planks. Because of precision precutting, planks do not have to be forced into place. They fit at the start. This saves time and eliminates any stress that would cause planks to spring loose. Silicon bronze screws and bolts are used for all hull fastenings...
>
> The transom is solid Philippine mahogany. Screw holes are filled with plugs (bungs), matched for grain and color with the planks in which they're placed. When finished, the bungs are almost invisible.
>
> "No bare wood" is a strict Chris-Craft mandate, and all sections of every model, inside and out, are sealed, painted, or varnished.[29]

Fiberglas spread to the Sea Skiff fleet in 1966, with the introduction of 18 and 20-foot models of fiberglas Sportsman. The entire Sea Skiff fleet was divided into two groups, one containing the Sportsman and Sea Hawk products, and the other, the new Corinthian, carvel skiff. Within the Sportsman and Sea Hawk group were Sportsman models in 22, 25 and 28 feet, along with a 25-foot Ranger and 32-foot Sports

Cruiser. Sea Hawk models included 28 and 32-foot Express and the 35-foot Sea Hawk 6-sleeper.

Five models of the new Corinthian *carvel skiffs* made their debut in 1966. The rugged round bilge design of the traditional Sea Skiffs was enhanced with smooth sides for consumers with more traditional tastes, making a practical hybrid series. The great strength of the boats was due to unique design and construction.

> The Corinthian hull has an inner keel of tough Philippine mahogany, flanked by main stringers of seasoned fir. The outer keels are of stout oak. Frames of steam-bent white oak are bolted into place on the keels. They're strong, yet resilient. The frames are long enough so that each extends not just from the sheer to the keel, but past the keel and to the turn of the bilge on the other side of the boat. This overlapping doubles the strength of the bottom, where strength is needed most.
>
> The 43-foot Corinthian's round bottom has an inner planking of large marine-grade plywood sheets for strength and resiliency without extra weight. Gaskets saturated with polysulfide bonding compound are placed over the seams, and then solid Philippine mahogany outer planking is applied. Double-bottom round-bilge hulls are extremely rare in production boats.[30]

Corinthians were available as the 32-foot Express, 35-foot and 38-foot Corinthian, 38-foot Sport Fisherman, and 43-foot Double Cabin models. Prices ranged from the 32-foot Express with a pair of 185-horsepower Chris-Craft V-8's at $14,290, to a 43-foot Corinthian Double Cabin with a pair of 258-horsepower G.M. diesels for $51,340.

The Cavalier Divison was also split into two distinct product groups in 1966, following the introduction of the all-new mahogany *Crusader* product line. The presence of a line of solid Philippine mahogany boats in the traditional plywood fleet was further indication of a move towards the abandonment of plywood as as primary construction material. In the plywood group, the only changes were the disappearance of the 28-foot Crusader and the addition of a 25-foot Futura transdrive and 26-foot Cutlass models.

This new Crusader line of boats was designed in an apparent effort to fill the mid-range cruiser void left by the disappearance of the wooden Commanders. Only three models were built for 1966, in 28, 30 and 36-foot variations. They ranged in price from the 28-footer with a

single 210-horsepower Chris-Craft V-8 for $8,130, to the 36-footer with a pair of 210-horse V-8's for $18,690, compared with a comparably equipped all-mahogany 36-foot Constellation at $25,190.

For 1967, the only change made in the Chris-Craft Division mahogany fleet was the elimination of the 28-foot Constellation. The lack of changes were more than made up by the explosion of models in the fiberglas Commander program, which had increased to nine models in sizes ranging from 27 to 47 feet. Offered were the 27-foot Commander and Sports Express; 31-foot Commander and Sports Express; 38-foot Commander, Sedan and Sport Fisherman; 42-foot Commander and 47-foot Commander. Prices ranged from $9,790 for a 27-foot Commander Sports Express with a single 185-horsepower V-8, to $80,910 for the 47-footer with a pair of 258-horsepower G.M. diesels.

The fiberglas program was in full bloom by 1967, and spreading throughout the entire Chris-Craft organization. Boughton Cobb, Jr. described the Commander molding process in *Yachting* after visiting one of Chris-Craft's plants. "...She is one of the most beautiful fiberglass moldings we have ever seen. The high-gloss finish, the absolutely fair form of her hull and superstructure are the product of carefully built precision molds."[31] Chris-Craft boasted that the Commander hulls were built to be able to withstand three times the strains and stresses of running through 6-foot seas at full speed.

The Corsair fiberglas fleet of Cortland, New York also expanded in 1967, to nine models, including a new 23-foot *Lancer* designed by offshore racing authority Jim Wynne of Miami. Included in the line-up were the 15-foot *Castaway Outboard* and *Sport-V Outboard;* 17½-foot *Sport-V Outboard* and *Sport-V Transdrive;* 18 and 20-foot *Sea-V Transdrive;* 20-foot *Sea-V Inboard,* and 23-foot *Lancer* in *Transdrive* and *Express Transdrive* models.

Cavalier offered fourteen models in their plywood fleet, in both smooth side models (Futura) and lapstrake designs (Seastrake). 1967 models included the 17-foot Ski Boat; 22 and 26-foot Cutlass; Futuras in 25 (including Transdrive), 27, 30 and 33-foot models; Seastrakes in 25, 27, 30 and 33-foot designs; and the top of the line 36-foot Yacht and Seastrake models.

Though solid mahogany, the Cavalier Division also built Crusaders in three models for 1967, the 28, 30 and 6-sleeper 36-foot Crusader cruisers.

The same Sea Skiff models appeared again in '67, while some interesting changes occurred in the carvel skiff Corinthian line. A new 4-sleeper, 28-foot *Sports Cruiser* was offered, followed by 32, 35 and 38-foot (6-sleeper) Corinthian models. An unusual 40-foot Corinthian *Sedan/Fisherman* was introduced, which was an early hybrid between a sport fisherman and luxury cruiser. It had a lapstrake bottom, two private staterooms, and a low freeboard cockpit for fishing. Top of the Corinthian line was the 43-foot Corinthian with accommodations for eight in spacious comfort.

Holland's Roamer Division welded together five different models for 1967, in steel and aluminum from 33 to 57-feet. The 33-foot Riviera was offered in steel only, while the 37-foot Riviera could be ordered in steel or aluminum, as could the 48-foot Riviera. Queen of the Roamer fleet, the 57-foot *Motor Yacht* was an elegant long-range cruiser with self-contained owner's stateroom aft, guest stateroom with pri-

Opposite left and right: *Fishin' Fever*, a 1961 27-foot Sea Skiff carries a 1952 10-horsepower Chris-Craft Commander outboard motor on her transom for an emergency auxiliary. Piloted by owners Richard and Paullette Louzon of Canada.

Photos by Karine N. Rodengen

Below: *Michelle*, a 1961 23-foot Sea Skiff, owned by Jerome and Barbara Emery of Canada, is a perfect boat for cruising the reed laced shallows of the St. Clair Flats near Algonac.

Photo by Karine N. Rodengen

Courtesy Mariners' Museum, Newport News, Virginia.

Chris-Craft's *Roamer* Division welded together a wide collection of cruisers and motor yachts from 27 to 58 feet during the sixties, in both steel and aluminum.

vate bath, and a full crew's quarter, head and shower forward. Powered with diesels to a total of 700-horsepower, the steel version would reach 22 m.p.h., while the lighter aluminum model would top 25 m.p.h.

It was inevitable. From the moment Chris-Craft Industries, Inc. began trading on the New York Stock Exchange, savvy investors began to take notice. The company with nearly three-quarters of a century of leadership within the ever-expanding pleasure boat building field was a solid investment for individuals and organizations alike. In January of 1968, Chris-Craft Industries, Inc. welcomed a new President and Chairman of the Board, Herbert J. Siegel, who had led an enthusiastic and successful takeover of the corporation starting in the fall of 1967. Siegel, a young and energetic entrepreneur with broad business experiences in industries as diverse as breweries and juke boxes (Siegel, then only 28, was chairman of Seeburg Corporation from 1958-1960),[32] had recognized Chris-Craft's enviable stable history of profitability, cash reserves and industry leadership. Siegel was Chairman of Baldwin-Montrose, a chemical manufacturing company, and had significant experience in corporate acquisitions and takeovers. Siegel and Baldwin-Montrose had acquired up to 70% of General Artists in 1965, and then sold their shares back to General Artists management. Later in 1965 Baldwin-Montrose bought a large block of Paramount Pictures stock, and resold them to Gulf & Western Industries, Inc.[33]

C. Gordon Houser, who was vice-president of Advertising and Public Relations for the Boat Division at the time, remembered the irony which was created with their display at the National Boat Show in New York.

> We had a number of paper sculptured *sea gulls* over the Chris-Craft booth at the top of the escalator at the New York Coliseum...hung on monofilament. One day I was talking to Herb Siegel and he said, "Remember the ad in the *New York Times* that said *Watch Out For The Sea Gulls?*" He said, "You weren't far wrong were you?"[34]

Chris-Craft Industries, Inc. moved from their offices in Oakland, California, clear across the continent to 600 Madison Avenue in New York City. The Corporation was becoming more and more diversified and complex. Among the first orders of business for Siegel was a reorganization of the corporation into major areas of emphasis.

> After the merger, Chris-Craft was organized into three major divisions: the Boat Division with the largest dollar volume of pleasure boat sales in the world; the Television Broadcasting Division with VHF television stations in Los Angeles, Minneapolis-St. Paul and Portland, Oregon; and the Industrial Division, which manufactures and sells a variety of foams, films, organic chemicals, carpet, carpet yarns and other products. The Industrial Division also manages the 50% owned affiliate, Montrose Chemical Corporation of California.[35]

The first annual report to be issued by Chris-Craft Industries, Inc. following the takeover, showed revenues of over $89 million for all operations, showing a profit of $3.48 million. The Industrial Division was the world's producer of DDT, "...the insecticide so important in the control of malaria in many countries around the world."[36]

Among the Chris-Craft Industries, Inc. board of directors was Alvin R. "Pete" Rozelle, the Commissioner of Professional Football. Years later, Rozelle would have the distinction of purchasing the last wooden boat to be manufactured by Chris-Craft, a 1972 57-foot mahogany Constellation.[37]

Early in 1968 the houseboat returned to the Chris-Craft product line. A 33-foot powered fiberglas houseboat was followed in September by the launching of a 46-foot model. Part of the reasoning for the houseboat line was to compete for dollars American consumers were spending for second homes. Another project which never fully matured was the production of a special series of specially designed houseboats which could become *instant hotels* and be located at traditional vacation destinations.[38] The 33-foot model was designed to accommodate six live-aboard guests, and included a full galley and shower. Though the hull was fiberglas, decks, roofs and hatches were vinyl-covered plywood. The houseboat was equipped with a single 185-horsepower Chris-Craft 283-F V-8, or pair of 150-horsepower V-6 engines with *opposite rotation* Volvo outdrive and power-tilt for navigating basically calm, shallow rivers and lakes.

The 1968 Chris-Craft Division of Sport Boats, Constellations and Motor Yachts was slimmed down to 11 mahogany models from 17 to 65 feet, as the product lines continued to be spread out among all Chris-Craft Divisions. Only three sport boats remained, a 17-foot SS 283 Ski Boat, along with 17 and 20-foot *Grand Prix* models. Fastest boat in all the fleets for '68 was the 20-foot Grand Prix with a pair of 300-horsepower V-8's that would push the $7,725 boat to 45 miles per hour. It featured a 3-place lounge seat forward, the port side of which would swing out to become a ski observer's seat.

Constellations were available in 30, 41 Salon, 45, 52, 57 and 65-foot models. A 36-foot *Corvette* was also available.

Top of the line in both dimensions and price tag was the 65-foot Motor Yacht. With a pair of 478-horsepower G.M. diesels, the triple stateroom aft luxury yacht fetched $240,400.

The fiberglas Commander line continued to grow in '68 with models from 23 to 47-feet, for a total of fourteen different variations to choose from. Models included 23, 27 (including Sports Express), 31 (including Sports Express), 35, 38 (including Sedan and Sport Fisherman models), 42 (including sports Convertible), and three 47-foot models (Single Stateroom Aft, Double Stateroom Aft and with Cockpit, Command Bridge & Single Stateroom Aft). Prices ranged from the 23-foot Commander with a Single 210-horsepower Chris-Craft V-8 at $7,290, to the 47-foot Commander with a pair of 258-horsepower G.M. diesels at $98,190.

A trim tab system, known as *Cruise Control,* was available for the first time aboard Commanders in 1968. It allowed the pilot, by pushing two switches at the control station, to adjust twin trim tabs faired into the bottom at the stern. With correct adjustment, proper planing attitude could increase speed and decrease fuel consumption, as well as compensate for list when the boat was unevenly loaded.

The 1968 Sea Skiff line was narrowed down to just eight models, from 25 to 43 feet, which included Corinthian modes. Smallest, a 25-foot *Corinthian Sportsman,* was followed by a 28-foot *Clipper Sportsman,* 31 and 35-foot *Clipper,* 38 and 40-foot *Corinthian Sedan/Fisherman,* and top of the line 43-foot *Corinthian Double Cabin.* Prices ranged from the 25-foot Corinthian Sportsman with a single 185-horsepower Chris-Craft V-8 at $6,850, to $42,900 for the Corinthian Double Cabin with a pair of 258-horsepower G.M. diesel engines.

The plywood Cavalier fleet manufactured ten models in 1968, from 17-foot to 36 feet, in Sport Boat, Futura and Seastrake versions. Models

Chris-Craft returned to the houseboat market in 1969 with the introduction of new 33-foot (pictured) and 46-foot fiberglas floating homes. Powered with either single (33-foot) or twin V-8 power with sterndrives, both models were designed for calm water recreation.

Courtesy Mariners' Museum, Newport News, Virginia.

The 1962 Chris-Craft 37-foot *Tri-Cabin* Constellation was cleverly designed to accommodate six adults in three cabins, with two private heads. Powered with a pair of 185-horsepower Chris-Craft V-8's, it retailed for $27,990.

Courtesy Mariners' Museum, Newport News, Virginia.

included the 17-foot Ski; 22 and 26-foot Cutlass; 26, 30 and 33-foot Futura; 33 and 36-foot Seastrake; and 36-foot Yacht. Transdrive models were conspicuously missing, as a general trend away from plywood sport boats continued. Only two models of the all-mahogany Crusader were built, the 30 and 36-foot cruisers, both powered with a pair of 210-horsepower Chris-Craft V-8's.

Three *Corsair* hull designs were available in '68, as more emphasis was placed on fiberglas diversification: "Sport V, with smooth sides and longitudinal stabilizers on the bottom; Sea-V, with lapstrake sides, bottom stabilizers and a 16-degree deep-vee aft; and Lancer, with a

patented 24-degree deep-vee hull bottom designed by noted ocean racer and naval architect Jim Wynne."[39] Only one *inboard* Corsair was available, the 20-foot Sea V; all others were equipped with the Volvo I/O with either the 150-horsepower Chris-Craft V-6 or 185-horsepower V-8 engine. Models included the 17½-foot Sport V Transdrive, Lancer 19-foot Transdrive, 20-foot Sea V Transdrive, 20-foot Sea V Inboard, Lancer 23 Transdrive and Lancer 23 Express Transdrive.

Only two changes occurred in the Roamer line for '68, that of dropping the 33 48-foot Rivieras, and adding four versions of a 46-foot Riviera in

A 1963 34-foot *Corinthian* Custom Cruiser from the fast growing Sea Skiff Division. With a pair of 185-horsepower Chris-Craft V-8's it would carry a party of six to 30 mph.

Courtesy Mariners' Museum, Newport News, Virginia.

either steel or aluminum. Prices ranged from the 37-foot steel Riviera with a pair of 210-horsepower Chris-Craft V-8's at $31,490, to the 57-foot aluminum Riviera equipped with a pair of 320-horsepower G.M. diesels for $143,640 f.o.b. Holland, Michigan.

Near the end of 1968, Chris-Craft Industries, Inc. Chairman Herb Siegel contacted Lee Iacocca, Vice-President of Ford Motor Corporation, in an attempt to recruit him for president of Chris-Craft Industries, Inc. Henry Ford had passed Iacocca over as president of Ford, and Iacocca was bitter about it. Iacocca recalled his great temptation to accept Siegel's offer in his book, *Iacocca, An Autobiography.*

> For a few weeks I seriously considered resigning. There had been an attractive offer from Herb Siegel, a Lehigh graduate who was head of ChrisCraft [sic]. Herb wanted to expand Chris-Craft into a small conglomerate in the leisure business. He liked me and respected what I had accomplished at Ford.
>
> "Look," said Herb, "if you stay here, you're always going to be at the mercy of Henry Ford, and if he was dumb enough to pass you over for president, he'll probably zap you again."
>
> I was tempted. I even went so far as to look for houses in New York and Connecticut. Mary, too, liked the idea of going back East. "If nothing else, we can get fresh seafood again," she said with a twinkle in her eye.

Courtesy Mariners' Museum, Newport News, Virginia.

The 1964 46-foot Roamer *Riviera* was built of steel, featured a one-level main salon with shore-sized dimensions, large aft owner's stateroom, guest stateroom forward and two private heads. With power to 600-horsepower, the 24,800 pounds of steel would deliver 26 mph.

The 1961 55-foot Constellation would accommodate up to ten guests for extended cruising in two double staterooms aft and a guest stateroom forward. It could be powered with up to 616 total horsepower, and cruise at speeds to 24 mph for a retail price of $85,990.

Courtesy Mariners' Museum, Newport News, Virginia.

In the end, I decided to stay at Ford. I loved the car business and I loved the Ford Motor Company. I really couldn't imagine being anywhere else.[40]

On October 1, 1969, Harry Coll, who had been president of Chris-Craft since 1958, resigned. Only the second president of Chris-Craft since founder Christopher Columbus Smith, Coll contributed greatly to Chris-Craft's progress during the crucial transformation from Smith ownership to NAFI, NAFI to Chris-Craft Industries, Inc., and now entering a new phase as part of an organization striving to become a giant in the leisure and recreational industry. It seemed fitting that Coll, who had been with Chris-Craft since 1939, the year *Gone With The Wind* was produced, would depart only months following man's first landing on the moon. James J. Rochlis, who had been president of the Industrial Division, was appointed president of the Boat Division by Chairman Herb Siegel.

The most impressive addition to the Chris-Craft fleets for 1969 was a luxurious, all-fiberglas, 60-foot Commander *Motor Yacht*. Not only the largest boat in the entire fleet, it was the *world's largest* fiberglas yacht. The over $290,000 Commander was testimony to the concerted efforts of Chris-Craft research, development and manufacturing expertise. Also available in the all-fiberglas Commander group were the 27-foot Sports Express, 31-foot Sedan (six-sleeper with private forward stateroom), 35-foot Sedan, 38-foot (including Sedan), 42-foot (including Sports Cruiser), and 47-foot Commander with 3 different layouts to accommodate between eight and ten guests.

The Constellation fleet continued to shrink in direct proportion to the growth of the fiberglas Commander fleet. In 1969, Constellations were available in 31-foot (six sleeper), 36-foot and 36-foot Corvette, 41-foot (including Salon), 45-foot and 57-foot models. The 57-foot Constellation which accommodated 12 for extended cruising, featured amenities considered top of the line for 1969, like color television, automatic blender and icemaker.

The Sea Skiff Division fleet was pared down to only six models by 1969, in models from 27 to 40 feet. The only survivors were the cruisers in 27, 31, 35 (Sedan and Corinthian), 36-foot Yacht, and 40-foot Corinthian Sedan/Fisherman models.

Most of Chris-Craft's sport boats were being concentrated in the Chris-Craft Division, where the *Lancer* series, designed by Jim Wynne, was quickly growing in response to consumer demand. Among the Lancers were models in 17, 19, 23, 25-foot Lancer, Lancer Sportsman and Sport Fisherman. Rounding out the fleet were the 17-foot inboard Ski Boat and 22-foot Cutlass. Except for the 17-foot Ski Boat, all models were equipped with Volvo transdrive installations, using the Chris-Craft 150-horsepower V-6, 185-horsepower, V-8, or newly introduced 230-horsepower V-8 engines for power.

Roamers for 1969 included the 38-foot Regal and Riviera in either steel or aluminum, 41-foot aluminum Regal, 46-foot Riviera in either aluminum or steel with single or double stateroom aft, and the queen of the fleet, the 58-foot aluminum Riviera.

In 1969 a nationwide search and contest for the "Oldest Living Chris-Craft" was conducted. In ads placed from coast to coast, entrants were encouraged to submit their boats to scrutiny by judges A. W. "Bill" MacKerer, retired senior vice-president of Chris-Craft, and Christopher James Smith, grandson and namesake of Christopher Columbus Smith. Over 400 entries were received, and each was evaluated on criteria ranging from age, condition and amount of remaining original equipment.

The winner was *Miss Belle Isle,* a 1923 Open Double Cockpit ten-passenger runabout. The boat was located in Portage Lake, near Akron, Ohio, owned by W. R. Jerrel. As part of Jerrel's prize, the beautiful runabout was completely refurbished in Algonac, Michigan, under the direction of one of the men who helped originally to build her.

Even the Philippine mahogany was treated in the manner appropriate in 1923: six coats of varnish and hand-rubbing with rottenstone. The fire extinguisher, a type now considered illegal, was replaced with an empty container of the same vintage. Linoleum, upholstery and step pads are all original, as is the power plant, a single eight-cylinder Curtiss OX-5 which develops 90-hp. at 1400 r.p.m., a top speed of 28 m.p.h. with an 18 x 20 Hyde Propeller.[41]

Jerrel also received a brand new 23-foot fiberglas Lancer Offshore sport boat. He was eventually persuaded to sell *Miss Belle Isle* to the Chris-Craft Corporation, where it remained in excellent storage for over seventeen years before being donated by Chris-Craft Industries, Inc. to the Mariners Museum in Newport News, Virginia in the spring of 1987, where it can be viewed on display. The facility, among the lead-

Courtesy Mariners' Museum, Newport News, Virginia.

After a nationwide search in 1969 for the *oldest living Chris-Craft*, the beautiful 1923 26-foot runabout *Miss Belle Isle* was acquired by Chris-Craft. Powered by the original Curtiss OX-5 Jay W. Smith converted aircraft engine, the boat was later donated to the Mariners' Museum in Newport News, Virginia by Chris-Craft Industries, Inc.

ing maritime museums in the world, was also the recipient of the considerable archives of the Chris-Craft Corporation through approximately the 1960 time frame. See Apprendix A, *The Mariners' Museum.*

The sixties represented the decade of most universal change for Chris-Craft, from the release of the Smith family owned enterprise to public corporations, to the dramatic evolution of the product line from primarily mahogany to primarily fiberglas. Rich with tradition, Chris-Craft had expanded its facilities to reach the summit of their manufacturing abilities. Coming from behind in fiberglas manufacturing technology, to leading the industry in advanced materials engineering, Chris-Craft by 1969 was producing the largest fiberglas yachts on earth. Through constant research and manufacturing innovation, Chris-Craft had proven that whether they chose mahogany, plywood, steel, aluminum or fiberglas, they were still the world leaders, and the Chris-Craft signature was still the premier trademark of excellence for boating excitement around the world.

Following pages: The 1961 27-foot Sea Skiff *Fishin' Fever,* piloted by owners Richard and Paullette Louzon of Canada, shows off the dry ride of the famous Chris-Craft lapstrake design. On the stern is a standby 1952 10-horsepower *Commander* outboard engine.

Photo by Karine N. Rodengen

At only $5,395 less sails, the *Capri 26* was an immediate hit in 1964. It could sleep four, had a full galley and an outboard well.

CHAPTER XVIII

The Chris-Craft Sailboats

Referring to power boats, Cornelius Shields once remarked, "They're only good as sail lockers. I never wanted to own a big powerboat; it's just a floating hotel."

Cornelius Shields
Sports Illustrated, 1962

MUCH TO THE SURPRISE of the boating industry and consumers alike, was the announcement in September, 1962 of plans to build a 35-foot sloop rigged fiberglas motor sailer. Chris-Craft *sailboat*. To insiders, the decision was inevitable, for Cornelius Shields, of Shields & Company, majority stockholders of Chris-Craft, was a brilliant competition sailor, and was eager to add sailboats to the fleet. In his book, *Racing with Cornelius Shields and the Masters*, he recalled his excitement for the new venture.

Our relationship with Chris-Craft was an extremely pleasant one. Because boats were involved, it was all the more enjoyable for me. I was delighted that I could persuade the company to enter the sailboat field with a 35-foot fiberglass motor sailer, which seemed a logical first sailboat for a powerboat manufacturer. We engaged Sparkman & Stephens to design her, and she was an immediate success. A keel centerboard 30-foot cutter, also designed by Sparkman & Stephens, followed next in a line that ultimately included five different sailing craft. The most successful of these was the Shields one-design....[1]

The 35-foot *Sail Yacht*, later known as the *Caribbean Motor Sailer*, was a practical, comfortable boat that was easy to handle. Twenty were built in 1963 at the Algonac plant, but demand continued to outstrip production as a result of the fine design and the young and energetic Sailboat Division Sales Manager, Bruce Donaldson, who would ultimately become President of Chris-Craft over two decades later.

The entire hull and deck was built of reinforced fiberglas, which was color impregnated white. The decks had a non-skid surface pattern molded in, and were molded integrally with the cockpit. Cabin sides and cockpit coamings were solid, clear dark mahogany, while the cabin top was marine grade plywood covered with reinforced vinyl with a textured PVC coating.

The well-appointed main cabin included a pair of lounges which converted into double deck berths, accommodating four. The design eliminated bunk boards, as berths were longitudinally hinged which permitted the inboard section to be raised for sleeping security when the yacht was heeled. Central to the main cabin

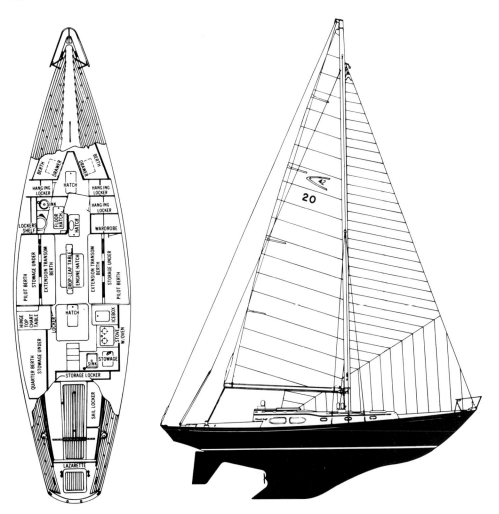

Every sailboat manufacturer has a symbol for their sails to identify the type and class of boat. A single, and sometimes double, elongated "C" distinguished a Chris-Craft from the rest. Inside the "C", a number would designate the length of boat.

Courtesy Mariners' Museum, Newport News, Virginia.

Chris-Craft's largest sailboat, the 1968 *Comanche 42*, was a tank-tested Sparkman & Stephens design that had a skeg modeled after the America's Cup Defender *Intrepid*. It featured a large forward stateroom, a main cabin with two transom berths, full galley and Universal 30-horsepower Atomic 4 auxiliary. Retail price in 1968 was $40,000.

Courtesy Mariners' Museum, Newport News, Virginia.

was a mahogany drop leaf dining table between the berths, seating six. The galley included an alcohol stove in gimbals, CPL ice tray and fresh water system.

The aft cabin included berths port and starboard with 4" foam pads, ample storage and a hand-operated head. Among the nice features of both cabins was over 6'2" of headroom.

The Sail Yacht was equipped with a rubber mounted 60-horsepower Chris-Craft engine with a 2:1 reduction gear, fed by 120 gallons of fuel in two tanks. Gordon Houser, long time vice-president of advertising and public relations at Chris-Craft, remembers the surprising speed of the 35-footer.

> This thing really moved under sail. Some fellows told me once about being in a race on Chesapeake Bay in a fog bank. They said they were heavy to windward. And then just zipping out of this fog bank came this thirty-five foot motor sailer. He said all these people were sitting on the deck sipping their cocktails and he said, "They went by me like I was standing still! And here I am in this big race and I'm trying to win!"[2]

The brisk market acceptance of the Sail Yacht at $25,790 led Chris-Craft to quickly formulate plans to inaugurate a complete line of sailboats.

At the New York Boat Show in January of 1964, Chris-Craft announced production of a new 30-foot *Capri*, a trim keel-centerboarder with five berths which sold for nearly half the cost of the 35-foot Sail Yacht, at a remarkable $15,670 equipped with a 25-horsepower Graymarine gasoline engine. Part of Donaldson's sales strategy for the new Capri was distributing information showing the new model to be superior to major competitors like the Pearson *Vanguard*, and Columbia 33. He even went so far as to demonstrate that the Chris-Craft had the most attractive list price *per pound*. Among the features which beat the competition were structural integrity and living space.

> We have from 8 to 10 laminates giving our hull a thickness of 5/16" to 5/8". The keel, stem and quarters are 1 1/4" thick. The centerboard trunk has a molded in wall thickness of 1/2"...

Note the comparison figures...clearly indicate that the Capri "30" is a far larger boat in waterline, beam [9'8"], headroom and general living area than the competitors that have overall length two and three feet larger. The displacement of 11,740 pounds clearly indicates the amount of hull material and size offered by the Capri "30"...

The Chris-Craft Capri "30" and the "Sail Yacht" are the only sailboats available in the market today with a 2-year warranty.[3]

In January of 1965, Chris-Craft announced the *Capri 26*, followed in April by the $7,490 30-foot *Shields One-Design* racing sailboat. The Capri 26 was a light and fast, all-fiberglas 4-sleeper auxiliary with clean, unobstructed decks and an outboard well for mounting auxiliary power. Two quarter berths were located in the main cabin, two located forward, and the galley featured turquoise counters and a large insulated top-loading fiberglas ice box. At only $5,395 without sails, the Capri 26 was eagerly accepted by a ready market.

The Shields One-Design, brainchild of Cornelius Shields and Olin Stephens of Sparkman & Stephens, was designed almost strictly for the racing environment, and was in production at Cape Cod Shipbuilding before coming to Chris-Craft. The boat was devoid of a cabin or other accoutrements, and many considered the boat to resemble a miniature 12 meter racing yacht, though carrying only 360 square feet of sail area. The concept of a *one-design* sailboat is that identical boats test the skills of skipper and crew without equipment variations. Rules for class competition are strictly worded to insure equipment uniformity, and are stringently enforced by the class organization. Every element of construction had to be identical for each boat built. Templates were used to locate cleats and other rigging elements, and even minor variations in weight of fittings and components were not tolerated. George M. Irvine of Owens-Corning Fiberglas, who would later join Chris-Craft as president, wrote a detailed survey and analysis of the construction techniques used for building the quick and precise race craft.

The hull itself is made of Fiberglas mat and woven roving (heavy fabric) impregnated with polyester resin. Chris-Craft's engineering has come up with an idea, a combination of these products, that gives them a higher reinforcing glass content than found in structures of similar thickness. Higher Fiberglas reinforcement content means higher strength and stiffness for a given thickness of laminate....

The Fiberglas hull and deck weigh 845 pounds ±8 pounds. It is not felt that other ma-

terial could hold such close tolerance from hull to hull on a one-design boat and sell for the same price.

The hull is inverted on the deck and bonded to it while both structures are still in the mold, thus assuring an exact fit, full waterproof bond, virtually making the hull and deck one piece. Five layers of Fiberglas are used to bond the deck to the hull. Besides the obvious safety factor of having essentially a one-piece structure, the owner is assured that the breadth of his boat is identical to the others.... I measured hulls...and did not find 1/16" difference in the length or beam, truly a remarkable feat in "one-design."...

Accuracy on the ballast is considered amazing by many, as Chris-Craft has it cast at ±3 pounds on 2,965 pounds of lead!...

All Fiberglas is pattern cut and weighed to assure that each boat is the same, a true one-design.... The resin is carefully weighed before going into the boat and every fitting, bolt, piece of wood, fasting, etc. is placed on the boat by a template or jig to assure even the most minute

Courtesy Mariners' Museum, Newport News, Virginia.

The 35-foot Chris-Craft *Sail Yacht*, or *Motor Sailer*, was a Sparkman & Stephens design that featured a simple rig, amidships cockpit, and an elegant interior designed to cruise four adults. Retail price in 1964 was $25,790.

distribution of weight or placement of a fitting is identical from boat to boat...

There are many other features in rigging and handling characteristics I have not attempted to cover...but to sum all this in a few words — The Shields 30 is a true thoroughbred of racing and is the closest to perfection in one-design sail yachts as we have seen to date.[4]

Next to follow was the *Capitan 26*, known later as the *Pawnee 26* when Chris-Craft began naming their sailboats after American Indian tribes in 1967. Sharing the same fiberglas hull

as sister ship, Capri 26, the Capitan had a larger cockpit, a pair of vee-berths, and more austere central cabin which contributed to a very low $4,990 price less sails.

A new racing/auxiliary sailboat, the *Apache 37* became available in 1967. Powered by a Universal Atomic 4 auxiliary engine, the Apache was large enough to attract the family cruiser market at $21,990. A pair of vee-berths and a convertible dinette accommodated four guests overnight, while a practical galley with gimbaled two-burner alcohol stove and top-loading foam-

The Chris-Craft *Capri 30* was a five-sleeper auxiliary designed by Sparkman & Stephens. Featuring a keel centerboard, sloop rig and 25-horsepower Graymarine auxiliary, the quick fiberglas sailboat had a beautiful natural mahogany interior, enclosed lavatory, modern galley, convertible dinette and over 6'2" of main cabin headroom. Built in the Algonac, Michigan plant, in 1964 it retailed for $15,670.

Courtesy Mariners' Museum, Newport News, Virginia.

insulated fiberglas-lined ice box made weekend trips comfortable. In quick succession followed the *Cherokee 32*, a six-berth ocean racer with a light displacement, high performance hull, which was also powered by the Universal Atomic 4 auxiliary engine.

Finally, in October of 1967, Chris-Craft built its first 42-foot sloop from plans by Sparkman and Stephens.

> It incorporated many of the features used in their hull design of the 1967 victorious Americas Cup defender, "Intrepid". Called the Comanche 42, this new model compiled an outstanding racing record during the season, climaxing its performance by winning the important Chicago-Mackinac race in a fleet of 185 boats. It was selected as "The Great Lakes Boat of the Year" by the Chicago Tribune.[5]

The Comanche 42 was a Sparkman & Stephens tank-tested design which featured a light-displacement hull with a fin keel and a blade rudder on an integral skeg. Aloft, it featured a large, powerful foretriangle with $15/16$" rig and running backstays. In 1968, Chris-Craft was the only production auxiliary to have running backstays, which "though not needed for mast support, enable you to keep the jibstay standing to maintain your windward ability when beating into a wind of 15 knots or more."[6]

It also offered a private stateroom forward with twin berths and hanging lockers, and a pilot berth and transom berth on each side of an amidships drop-leaf table. A complete galley contained an oven and gimbaled stove. A navigator's station included a hinged-top chart table. Including a 30-horsepower Universal Atomic 4 engine, the Comanche 42 sold for a reasonable $40,000.

In 1968, at the peak of their efforts, Chris-Craft had a fleet of eight sailboats, ranging from the Capri 26 to the Comanche 42. By 1972, only the 35-foot motor sailer, the *Caribbean 35*, would remain in production. Chris-Craft had experimented with having some of their sailboats manufactured in Taiwan, from 1970 to late 1975, which proved to be a major mistake. As C. Gordon Houser, who was in charge of advertising and public relations at the time

remembers, it was among the reasons for the disappearance of the line.

> There was a guy who had been a roommate at the University of Colorado with Chiang Kai-shek's son. We opened a plant [in T'aipei, Taiwan]...the company was called Argonaut Taiwan and they blistered us good. When we went in there the hourly wage was about 25 cents, and when we left it was about forty-three cents. People built their little lean-to's on the walls of the plant, and they had their little hibachis and lived in there. [There was] a wild dysentery.[7]

The fuel crisis of the early seventies gave the Sailboat Division a welcome boost in sales, but it's becoming clear that the marketplace would

not continue to sustain a sailboat program with a trademark so deeply associated with powerboats. The 35-foot Caribbean was continued until 1976, when the last Chris-Craft sailboat was manufactured. Many are still in use today, and Christopher James Smith, grandson and namesake of Christopher Columbus Smith, still enjoys sailing his Shields One-Design on the lakes near his home in Holland, Michigan.

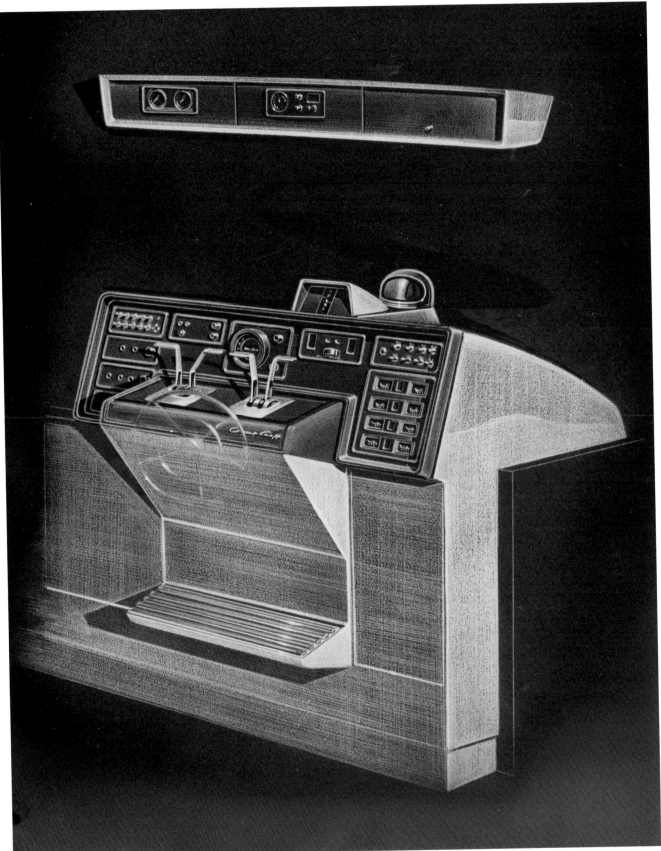

Illustration Courtesy Bob MacNeill

Chris-Craft developed a state-of-the-art *integrated electronics command center* for all models 41-feet and over starting in 1970. The futuristic, modular design was far ahead of its time, including line-of-sight engine performance and heading instruments. Results of Chris-Craft's innovative *human factors* engineering program, are still without equal in the marine industry.

CHAPTER XIX

The Seventies

...Here you'll see the new ideas. That's what we at Chris-Craft are famous for. Innovation. Putting imagination to work to build boats the way people like you dream they ought to be built.[1]

James J. Rochlis, 1970
President, Chris-Craft Corporation

THE DECADE OF the seventies was for Chris-Craft Corporation a bittersweet combination of technological advance and financial decline. Over the next ten years, five presidents would direct worldwide activities from Pompano Beach, each eager to champion their unique causes, each bringing to Chris-Craft their own brand and style of management.

It was also a period of fluctuating markets, fuel shortages and other frustrations, beyond the control of Chris-Craft, which would in combination check the growth of the marine industry in general.

Within just over a year of assuming control of Chris-Craft Industries, Inc., Chairman Herb Siegel had directed the investing of over $46 million in an effort to secure a controlling interest in Piper Aircraft Corporation. It was part of Siegel's strategy to diversify Chris-Craft Industries into a position of leisure and recreational industries dominance. The maneuver was thwarted by Bangor Punta Corporation, which, in aggressive stock purchases secured 52% of Piper Aircraft against only 42% for Chris-Craft. Chris-Craft Industries sued Bangor Punta, among others, seeking substantial money damages for alleged violations of the securities laws. It was a legal brawl that would involve an enormous expenditure of concentration by Chris-Craft Industries, and would not be settled for six years of protracted litigation. In 1975, the United States Court of Appeals, Second Circuit, would award Chris-Craft Industries $25,800,000 in damages and more than $10,000,000 in interest. Finally, in 1978, Chris-Craft Industries, sold their interest in Piper Aircraft to legally vanquished Bangor Punta Corporation for nearly $50,000,000.[2] Within a year, Siegel and Chris-Craft Industries would reinvest the Piper proceeds in a lucrative fourteen percent holding in Twentieth Century Fox Film Corporation, prompting *Forbes* magazine to characterize Siegel as "Crazy like a Fox".[3]

During the period of uncertainty over the Bangor Punta lawsuit, Chris-Craft Industries was not receiving an appropriate return on their $46 million investment in Piper Aircraft stock. Though Industries would end up profiting by nearly $40,000,000 for their adventure with Piper, the struggle meant less emphasis on their Boat Division, and Chris-Craft began to lose the complete dominance they had so long enjoyed in American pleasure boat production.

To add to the distractions of Chris-Craft Industries was the 1970 "...cancellation by the federal government of all but two significant domestic registered agricultural uses of DDT and the increased attacks upon that product."[4] The Montrose Chemical Corporation of California, in which Chris-Craft Industries held a 50% interest, would be prohibited by the Environmental Protection Agency after December 31, 1972, from producing DDT for any U.S. agricultural uses.

To make matters worse, the United States economy began to deliver unsettling signals to the marine industry in 1970. Chairman Herb Siegel noted the ominous instability in a letter to shareholders in the early winter of 1970.

> The national economy is going through a difficult period. While interest rates have receded from their highest point, and business may already be on its way up from its lowest level, the near term outlook is unpredictable. Early in 1970, management retrenched in certain areas while retaining the more important programs to insure the company's expanding future.[5]

Among the casualties of decreased sales and uncertain dealer financing was the closure of the Canadian manufacturing facility in Stratford, Ontario. For a while in 1970, Chris-Craft had leased a manufacturing facility in Mexico, but plans for Mexican production were never brought on-line. Also, a small plant in Edenton, North Carolina was prepared for production and then operations were suspended. Late in 1969, the Engine Division was moved to new facilities in Gallipolis, Ohio. In early 1970, Chris-Craft established a large-scale factory-owned dealership and marina in Marina del Rey, California.

Probably the biggest shock of all, however, was the closure of the Chris-Craft production facilities in Algonac, Michigan in the summer of 1970. Since the late 19th Century, Algonac had been home to powerboat production, and many Algonac residents assumed that the tradition would never end. It had been over ten years since Chris-Craft had been sold by the Smiths, and now the last link with the first family of American powerboating had been severed. The parts division would remain in the old Engine assembly plant, but the sounds and smells of mahogany boat production would issue no longer from the cradle of American powerboating.

1970 began a decade of cautious model offerings, as the general slowdown within the industry also produced lighter production schedules for Chris-Craft facilities worldwide.

A new fiberglas sport cruiser fleet was introduced in 1970, the *Catalina Fleet*. Emphasizing practical weekend-style family recreation, the Catalinas were offered in 26, 28 and 33-foot models, including a 33-foot Sedan. Prices ranged from the 26-foot Catalina with a single 200-horsepower V-8-Q at $8,990 to the 33-foot Sedan with a pair of 145-horsepower Perkins diesels for $33,900. As Chris-Craft suggested, the "...Catalina is perfect for the young family who wants a lot of boat for its money."[6]

The Commander line of fiberglas Cruisers, Sports Cruisers and Motor Yachts grew to sixteen models from 27 to 60 feet. Now the most sought after models in the fleet, the Commanders had for many years proven themselves under a wide range of operating conditions. Models were offered in 27-foot, 31-foot (including Sedan and Sports Express), 35-foot (including Sports Cruiser), 38-foot (including Sedan), 42-foot Sports Cruiser and Salon, 47-foot Single or Double Stateroom Aft, 55-foot and 60-foot Motor Yacht versions. Prices ranged from the 37-foot Commander with a pair of 200-horsepower V-8-Q engines at $17,900, to the opulent 60-foot Commander Motor Yacht with a pair of 478-horsepower G.M. diesels at $350,000.

Radical changes occurred in the nomenclature and distribution of models throughout the rest of the Chris-Craft fleets in 1970. A new *Cruiser Fleet* contained models which traditionally resided in the Cavalier, Sea Skiff and Chris-Craft Divisions. Now, these combined divisions offered only six total models. Included in the Cruiser Fleet were Futuras in 26, 30 and 36-foot Salon models, Sea Skiff in 30 and 33-foot models, along with a mahogany 31-foot Constellation. Prices ranged in this odd assemblage of models from the 26-foot Futura with a pair of 200-horsepower V-8-Q engines at $9,900, to the 36-foot Futura Salon with a pair of 230-horsepower V-8-QR engines for $37,500. Also built were mahogany Constellations in 38,

42 and 57-foot models, and Aqua-Home fiberglas houseboats in 34 and 46-foot versions.

The difficulties of designing the perfect combination of livability and performance was illustrated by noted small boat designer Richard C. Cole, who was instrumental in the development of the cathedral-style runabout hulls for companies like Outboard Marine Corporation and Thunderbird. He described a whimsical boat, the *S.D.E.* in an article on design considerations.

> ...My overall favorite is the little-known S.D.E. It's about the maximum trailerable size — 25-feet long and eight feet wide. She's unusual in that she has fore, and aft cabins and a hardtop covering the cockpit. The forecabin is conventional with a head in the forepeak and vee berths. The cockpit is also pretty conventional, with pilot to starboard and a matching lounge seat to port.
>
> The aft cabin, however, is divided from the cockpit by a sink to starboard and a galley stove to port. Aft of this is a dinette arranged athwartships and this, of course, converts into a double berth. Farthest aft is the engine compartment. She has other unusual features: alongside the pilot, in the center of the console, is a plexiglass chart holder that keeps the chart in full view; the side curtains roll up and clip in place under the hard top.
>
> S.D.E. stands for "She Doesn't Exist." Pity, isn't it?[7]

Sport Boats for 1970 included the 17-foot Ski-Boat; Lancers in 17, 19, and 23-foot Offshore and Premiere models, along with 25-foot Lancer, Lancer Sportsman and Lancer Sport Fisherman models.

A bold initiative in human factors electronics engineering came out of the labs and into the cockpits and command bridges of Chris-Craft cruisers in 1970. Starting in 1968, research had been conducted concerning the frustrating method of equipping Chris-Craft boats with owner selected electronics following purchase of the basic boats from dealerships. Chris-Craft had recognized that owners would spend up to ten percent of the cost of the boat itself on added electronics, representing an impressive amount of equipment and investment. After the boat owner chooses from a large array of available electronics, the local marine electronics distributor ends up nearly disassembling the boat to install all of the owner selections. The headliners are stripped, bulkheads bared, carpets pulled up, holes drilled everywhere, and when the work is finished, more often than not much of the hardware is incompatible. Robert F. Mac-Neill, today president of Carver Boat Corporation, was in charge of the Human Factors Engineering Project at Chris-Craft during the development of a whole new approach to pleasure boat electronics engineering. In 1970, Mac-Neill wrote of the hazards of poor integration in the *Journal of the Industrial Designers Society of America.*

> Mr. Mariner's problems occur when he operates the equipment. Since he chose it from the vast array the distributor had to offer, the equipment that he chose was not designed as a working system. Therefore, he finds he must add electronic noise suppression kits to the engines before the radiotelephone will operate; the depth finder must be turned off before keying the transmitter; and so must the automatic direction finder or it makes an ear-splitting squeal. Besides that, the tachometers feed a false signal into the depth sounder, and the radio speaker magnet has put a deviation into the compass.
>
> Have I exaggerated the situation? No, this is virtually the case with every pleasure boat being sold today — except Chris-Craft.[8]

MacNeill and Chris-Craft designed a state-of-the-art integrated electronics command center targeted for models 41 feet and over. Components were completely modular, mounted in a thoughtful, logical sequence for the operator to quickly reference information, and accurately back-lit for pleasant and safe night operation. Such logical refinements as a single microphone with a selector switch for hailer, VHF or single side band radio, and tilting helm station wheels for standing or sitting operation put Chris-Craft decades ahead of the industry. In fact, nearly twenty years later, no company has yet matched the degree of sophistication which Chris-Craft demonstrated in electronic display and integration back in 1970. Chris-Craft eventually abandoned the program, however, due to unanticipated warranty problems associated with swapping complete modules at the dealer level. MacNeill remembered how local electronics dealers balked at servicing components they hadn't sold or installed.

> ...They didn't get the profits on selling and installing the stuff. They looked at it, and it was all remote kind of stuff, fancy wiring and gold plated connectors, and they threw their hands up and said "We don't know anything about this" and refused to work on it. ...We didn't do the homework that we should have done...[9]

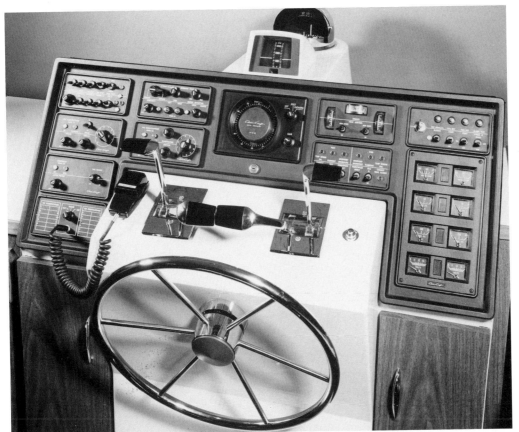

The second generation of the *Integrated Electronics Command Center* had practical features like a single microphone with switching between VHF, single side band and hailer functions. Whenever the owner had a problem, the affected module was swapped in the field by the dealer.

Photo courtesy Bob MacNeill

During 1971 a total of forty-seven models of Chris-Craft were manufactured, and seven new models were introduced. The new models represented nearly both extremes of complexity and price, including the 17-foot Outboard which was designed to look like an inboard, a 60-mile-per-hour 18-foot Jet-Drive (XK-18) high performance ski-boat, a 28-foot deep-V offshore Sport Fisherman, a 31-foot Catalina, a 35-foot Salon Commander with aft master suite, 42-foot mahogany Constellation and a brand new 66-foot aluminum Roamer Motor Yacht. Another factory owned dealership was established in Pompano Beach, Florida during the year, in an effort to guarantee Chris-Craft sales in a traditionally large-order territory, similar to the strategy begun in Marina del Rey, California in early 1970.

A radical design departure was unveiled with the new 31-foot Catalina for 1971. The hull sported a broad, flattened forward section without a traditionally pointed bow. Among the suggested advantages of the strange looking craft were twenty-three percent more interior space and a comfortable ride. A spacious six-sleeper in a 31-foot length, the boat was powered with a pair of 235-horsepower engines to retail

for $21,900. Among other Catalina offerings were the 26, 28 (including Coho Sedan), and 33-foot (including Coho Sedan) models. Prices ranged from the 26-foot Catalina with a single 235-horsepower Chris-Craft engine at $9,500, to the 33-foot Catalina Coho Sedan with a pair of 145-horsepower Perkins diesels at $34,795.

Experimentation in turbine power was revealed in 1971, with the announcement that Chris-Craft had been seriously investigating turbine based sport cruiser development.

Chris-Craft has been experimenting with turbines, looking toward the time when this form of boat power will be available at supportable cost. The XP-36 was created on a Chris-Craft deep-v cruiser hull modified to accommodate twin 300-HP turbines and was clocked at about 50 MPH. Turbines are smaller than reciprocating marine engines of comparable power and have a lower weight to horsepower ratio. Tests showed that heat and noise disadvantages can be overcome and that turbines are practical for boats.[10]

By the 1972 model year, Chris-Craft would be offering five models of Commander and Roamer boats with optional turbine power. "These engines," Chris-Craft stated, "emit cleaner exhaust, require less maintenance, produce less noise and vibration, and are capable of sustained operation at high speeds. The Ford turbines are significantly lighter in weight than equivalent diesel power [and] represent the most attractive power option for certain models."[11]

In January of 1971, Chris-Craft bought the *Gull Wing* Sport Boat line from Outboard Marine Corporation, OMC, manufacturers of Evinrude and Johnson outboard motors, and manufacturers of their own new inboard-outboard propulsion unit. By April, both 16 and 19-foot versions of the cathedral-style fiberglas tri-hulls were being shipped to Chris-Craft dealers. In the bargain, Chris-Craft found itself back in the boat trailer business, as the purchase included matched 16 and 19-foot trailers for the new models.

Among other Sport Boats available in 1971 were the 17 and 19-foot Lancer Custom, XK-18 Jet, XK-19, XK-22, and 23-foot Lancer and Lancer Inboard models.

Aqua-Homes continued to be built in both 34 and 46-foot models. A 34-foot Aqua-Home equipped with a single 200-horsepower Chris-Craft Transdrive retailed for $15,440, while the 46-foot Aqua-Home, often compared to a floating two-bedroom apartment, equipped with a pair of 145-horsepower Perkins diesels sold for $40,400.

The Commander Cruiser fleet for '71 included thirteen models from 28 to 45 feet, with larger models (47, 55 and 60) placed in the *Luxury Yacht* fleet. The cruisers included 28-foot Sports Express, 31-foot (including Sports Cruiser and Sedan), 35-foot (including Sports Cruiser and Salon), 38-foot Sedan, 41-foot, 42-foot Salon and Sports Cruiser, and 45-foot (including Tournament Fisherman) models. Prices ranged from $18,175 for the 28-foot Commander Sports Express with a pair of 200-horsepower Chris-Craft engines, to $146,300 for the 45-foot Commander Tournament Fisherman equipped with

a pair of 390-horsepower G.M. 8V-71T diesels. The Tournament Fisherman could also be equipped with a pair of the new Ford 400-horsepower Turbine engines, but no price was ever quoted.

The Luxury Yacht fleet for 1971 was a grouping of Chris-Craft's elite models, and offered elegance from 42 to 60-feet. Within the group were the 42 and 47-foot Constellations; Commanders in 47-foot Single Cabin, Double Cabin and Cockpit models; and Commander and Roamer in 60-foot models. Prices ranged from the 42-foot mahogany Constellation with a pair of 235-horsepower Chris-Craft V-8's at $51,700, to the 60-foot fiberglas Commander with a pair of 595-horsepower G.M. V-12's at $280,000, compared with a 60-foot aluminum Roamer with a pair of 480-horsepower G.M. V-12's at only $209,450.

At the end of the 1971 fiscal year, Clifford M. Fellows was appointed President of the Boat Division by Chris-Craft Industries, Inc. Chairman Herb Siegel. He had been an executive with the Ford Motor Company before he was recruited by Siegel in 1969. He became Vice-President of Finance at the Boat Division, before being promoted to Executive Vice-President. Fellows was one of approximately ten executives from other major industries which Chairman Siegel had recruited for the Boat Division in 1968 and 1969. Other executives had come from such divergent talent pools as General Electric, General Motors and Fairchild Industries.[12]

Sport Boats for 1972 included the Gull Wing cathedral-hull boats in 16-foot *Explorer* and 19-foot *Dolphin* models, deep-V *Lancer* models in 17-foot (including Ski), along with 19 and 23-foot (including Lancer Inboard). The XK-18 Jet returned to the line-up, as well as the XK-19 and XK-22 sport boats.

Seven Catalina models were produced in 1972, with one (the Coho) being produced in the Taipai, Taiwan facility. The all-fiberglas fleet contained models in 26, 28 (including Coho Sedan

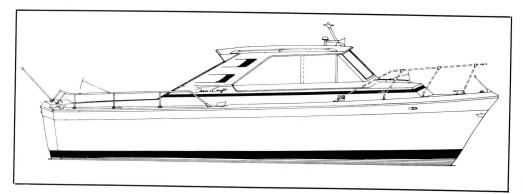

The 1971 31-foot Commander *Sports Cruiser* had accommodations for four in vee-berths and a convertible dinette. If powered with a pair of 300-horsepower Chris-Craft engines, it retailed for $24,550.

Courtesy Mariners' Museum, Newport News, Virginia.

The very last boat to leave the Algonac, Michigan plant was this 46-foot *Aqua-Home*, hull number 2173, on March 25, 1972. In continuous operation for over a half-century, the facility *where it all began* fell victim to wide-scale plant consolidation.

Photo courtesy Ray LaParl

and Sportsman), 31 and 33-foot (including Coho Sedan) versions. Prices ranged from the 26-foot Catalina with a single 235-horsepower Chris-Craft V-8 at $9,500, to the 33-foot Catalina Coho Sedan with a pair of 145-horsepower Perkins diesels for $34,795. Aqua-Home houseboats continued in production for '72 in both 34 and 46-foot models.

Commanders were available in the cruiser fleet in thirteen models for '72, from 28-45 feet. Important new additions were two *Flush-Deck* Commanders, in 41 and 45 feet. The flush-deck cruisers were designed so that the deck level remains constant from bow to stern, thus eliminating an aft cockpit along with any fishing possibilities. The design provides a generous master stateroom aft, along with a sun deck level with the bridge. Other Commanders included the 28-foot Sports Express, 31-foot (including Sedan and Sports Cruiser), 35-foot (including Sedan and Sports Cruiser), 38-foot Sedan, 42-foot (including Sports Cruiser), and 45-foot models, including the popular 45-foot Commander Tournament Fisherman. Prices ranged from the 28-foot Commander with a pair of 200-horsepower Chris-Craft V-8's at $18,175, to the 45-foot Commander Tournament Fisherman with a pair of Ford 373 Continuous Horsepower Turbine engines for $169,500.

The *Luxury Yachts* for 1972 included the 47-foot Flush Deck Commander, 55-foot Flush Deck Commander, 55-foot aluminum Roamer Flush Deck, 57-foot mahogany Constellation, 60-foot aluminum Roamer Flush Deck, 60-foot Commander Flush Deck, 68-foot aluminum Roamer Motor yacht, and the new queen of all Chris-Craft fleets, the 73-foot aluminum Roamer Motor Yacht. For design and technical

assistance, Chris-Craft enlisted the help of Robert E. Derecktor of Mamaroneck, New York, one of America's most significant naval architects and a leading proponent of large aluminum yacht construction. Even with Chris-Craft's abbreviated fleets during the early 70's, it was still the largest group of *production* yachts available from any single source in the world.

The last mahogany Chris-Craft, a 57-foot Constellation, was built during 1972, and was delivered to Chris-Craft Industries, Inc. board member Alvin R. "Pete" Rozelle, Commissioner of the National Football League. Changing over from wood construction to total fiberglas production was a difficult transition for Chris-Craft. Harry H. Coll, Chris-Craft Corporation president from 1958 to 1969, remembered the dangers of the transformation which occurred largely within his period of leadership.

> ...When you have ten plants and four or five thousand people working on wooden boats and you decide to change over to fiberglas, you better know what you're doing. Pacemaker [a contemporary competitor] went ahead and made a mold from their wooden boat and the thing wouldn't run. And that happened to a lot of companies. So, we had to go carefully, and people since then have criticized us that we didn't move fast enough, you know. But we made money. We only moved as fast as we were sure we were right, and that's the important thing. We designed new hulls and tested them in fiberglas, not just the same bottoms as the wooden hulls.[13]

In April of 1973, the first 73-foot aluminum Roamer was delivered to owner Fred Kirk. Kirk had owned ten Chris-Craft previously, starting with a 30-foot Sea Skiff in 1956. This type of

Chris-Craft loyalty, along with steadily moving up in class and size of boat has always been common for Chris-Craft buyers. On the maiden voyage of the 73-foot Roamer, Kirk ran 1,080 miles from Ft. Lauderdale, Florida to his home port of Mystic, Connecticut in a little over fifty hours, stopping for engine checks each six hours and one fuel stop. The Roamer was able to deliver around 22 knots for the distance, which was a record for a boat of this size and class from Florida to Long Island Sound.

A new technological achievement was converted into widespread sales during 1973, with the production of a new *modular* 25-foot Express Cruiser.

> It's the first Chris-Craft of its kind. The result of an engineering breakthrough that calls for a completely new type of fiberglass construction. Instead of the usual steps (molding the hull, reinforcing it, building various sections inside it, then adding decks and superstructure), this cruiser is built in three parts: hull, inner liner and cabin-deck. Each of the three parts performs a variety of functions, and they work together...[14]

It was the first in a long line of affordable modular cruisers which were designed to bring more first-time customers into Chris-Craft showrooms. George M. Irvine, Jr., who became president of the Chris-Craft Boat Division in late 1972, is credited with one of only three profitable years during the decade, as the Boat Division recorded sales of nearly $47 million and profits of nearly $2 million for the 1973 fiscal year.[15]

A total of thirty-six models (down from forty-seven) were manufactured in the remaining seven boat manufacturing facilities during 1973. Sport Boats were unchanged except for the addition of a new XK series 27-foot Sport Boat.

In late 1973, an all-new 25-foot Tournament Fisherman was introduced, and was enthusiastically accepted by both dealers and consumers alike. With only a small cuddy-style cabin accommodating two in vee-berths, the small boat was dominated by a large, wide open configuration which made the addition of a small tower, fighting chair and outriggers popular accessories. Built with the new modular three-piece construction formula, it was powered with a pair of 130-horsepower Chris-Craft V-8 engines.

Few changes were evident in family cruisers which still ranged from 25 to 38-feet, Luxury Yachts in fiberglas from 41 to 60 feet, and aluminum Roamers from 55 to 73 feet.

Chris-Craft did, however, introduce two new engines from the Gallipolis, Ohio plant during 1973, a 181-cubic-inch, four-cylinder compact unit for runabouts and small cruisers, and a 307-cubic-inch power plant with a four barrel carburetor.

During 1974, America became enmeshed in a confusing and constricting energy crisis which not only affected industries competing for discretionary income, but hit hardest those industries that used gasoline for recreational purposes. The shortages reached their peak during early 1974, and combined with the resignation of embattled United States President Richard M. Nixon, created confusion and indecision in economic circles. As Chris-Craft Industries, Inc. Chairman Herb Siegel reflected, it affected almost every profit area in his diversified portfolio of companies.

> Starting with the energy crisis in mid-November, national economic conditions deteriorated rapidly. The sudden rise in petroleum product costs accelerated the inflation spiral which caught businesses with price-controlled products and services, such as boats, airplanes and television advertising time, in an unshakable squeeze.[16]

Sales for 1974 lagged sometimes as much as 50% behind comparable quarters in 1973. Adding to Chris-Craft's challenges were material shortages and increased costs associated with economic inflation.

As a result, only a few new models of boats were introduced during the year, making a total of thirty-seven total offerings. In the runabouts, a new 8-Meter (also called 27-foot) luxury model was announced, which followed the styling lines of the XK series very closely, but with a walk-through double-cockpit design piloted from the aft starboard seat. Again using the modular fiberglas construction approach, hull, deck, inner liner and cockpit were built using hand lay-up application schedules. Standard power for the 8-Meter was a pair of Chris-Craft 300-horsepower engines with Volvo 1:16:1 outdrives.

Among the more popular additions to the fleet in recent years was the introduction of the 22-foot Tournament Fisherman. The wide-open, center-console fisherman sported a dory-like design which *Yachting* Associate Editor Jack Smith said looked familiar.

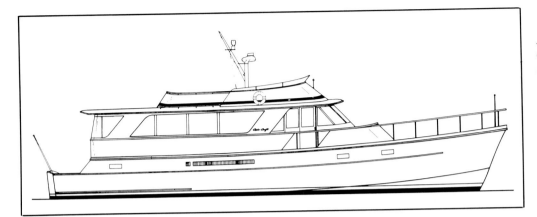

Among the largest and most opulent ways to go fishing was aboard the 1975 Chris-Craft 73-foot aluminum *Yacht Fisherman.* With 1,900 gallons of fuel aboard, the majestic yacht could travel to fishing grounds anywhere on the seven seas.

Courtesy Mariners' Museum, Newport News, Virginia.

Chris-Craft's 22' Tournament Fisherman is an up-to-the-minute fiberglass beauty, but your senses aren't deceiving you if her profile looks familiar — it belonged to the Cavalier Dory introduced by Chris-Craft in 1965. Or you might associate it with the Cutlass — a cuddy-cabin model built to the same hull design, in which lapstrake plywood sides adjoined a sheet plywood V bottom...

Basically the hull is the same... It is the fiberglass construction and the reworked interior that make the Tournament Fisherman a considerably different boat.

Construction in fiberglass allows the boat to be built in two basic parts: the hull, in which the lapstrake side planking is simulated, and the inner liner, which incorporates the decking, cockpit sole and a pair of bonded-in... engine stringers.[17]

A great distinction was afforded Chris-Craft's 45-foot Tournament Fisherman during 1974, as it was selected by the America's Cup defender *Courageous* as official assist boat. The *Escort,* as the Tournament Fisherman was named, would tow the 65,000 pound 12-Meter yacht to the starting line for practice and trials, as well as during *Courageous'* successful defense of the America's Cup. A super-strong stainless steel bit was mounted in place of the fighting chair for towing in the often rough chop off of Newport, Rhode Island where the races were staged.[18]

The Roamer Division introduced new 60-foot and 73-foot aluminum Motor Yachts during the year, continuing Chris-Craft's emphasis on the high-end, or supposedly recession-proof, end of their line.

In 1975, Chris-Craft added important new models to its growing Tournament Fisherman fleet with new 30 and 42-foot models. With six Tournament Fisherman now available from 22 to 45 feet, Chris-Craft had one of the largest pro-duction sport fishing lines available in the industry. Late in the year, Chris-Craft introduced perhaps the largest and most opulent fishing craft yet, a 73-foot aluminum Yacht Fisherman. Designed very much along the lines of the 73-foot aluminum Motor Yacht, it featured a generous cockpit below what would be considered the normal flush deck limit aft. With accommodations for nine in traditional Roamer splendor, the 85,000 lb. displacement Yacht Fisherman was equipped with a pair of G.M. diesel 12V-71TI engines and long range cruising tanks of 1,900 gallons. To round out a remarkable fishing fleet, Chris-Craft followed with a new 68-foot Yacht Fisherman, featuring a rakishly futuristic command bridge which would take up to eleven pampered cruising fishermen to hunting grounds virtually anywhere in the world.

On the other end of the spectrum, Chris-Craft introduced a new 10-foot *Yacht Tender,* a sprightly and wide-beamed spoon-bill fiberglas outboard boat designed for use on Chris-Craft yachts and for relatively calm harbor use. The only power offered by Chris-Craft were an optional pair of oars for $25. A fun variation of the tri-hull tender was the 10-foot *Streaker,* looking somewhat like an overgrown jet-ski ahead of its time; it carried two passengers straddling a transverse center bench seat with storage below, and featured a control console along with enclosed forward deck.

With red ink flowing throughout the Boat Division ledgers during the mid-seventies, it's understandable that the fleets began to shrink and that few new models were introduced. Consolidation and administrative economy were the corporate watchwords, rather than speculative new models. 1975 was the hardest year in Chris-Craft history, as over $5.5 million dollars was lost on sales of less than $40 million. It cannot have been pleasant for Chris-Craft Industries, Inc. Chairman and President Herb Siegel to inform his stockholders.

The severely weakened economy took its toll of the boating industry worldwide during the 1975 season. A group of strong deterrents combined to reduce Chris-Craft's Boat Division sales by 12 percent and caused the Division to suffer a loss. These factors included general buyer reluctance, difficult dealer financing conditions, low dealer inventories at peak sales periods and the usual long lead time to manufacture specific boats when demand did improve.

These conditions required strong production retrenchment measures to bring inventories in harmony with dealer orders. Chris-Craft, operating four boat plants and one engine plant in the U.S. and one boat plant each in Italy and Taiwan, was faced with difficult decisions as to which to close and how to rearrange production of 48 models of boats from 10 to 73-feet long, frequently on short notice...

Lower manufacturing levels at each plant increased unit costs and this was additionally complicated by industry-wide price cutting. Thus, even the higher materials cost could not be passed on. As a result, profit margins were severely depressed in some cases and wiped out on certain models.[19]

Only thirty-four models were produced during 1975, from 10 to 74 feet. The Sport Boat line included the 10-foot Yacht Tender; 16-foot Sportsman; 19-foot Dolphin; Lancers in 17, 19, and 23-foot models (including the 23-foot

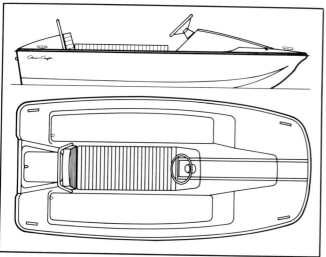

Courtesy Mariners' Museum, Newport News, Virginia.

The smallest fiberglas boat ever manufactured by Chris-Craft was this 10-foot outboard powered *Streaker*, which used the same tri-hull of the 10-foot *Yacht Tender*.

Lancer Inboard); 19 and 22-foot XK; and 8 Meter designs.

Among the surviving cruisers were Express Cruisers in 25 and 30-foot models; 33-foot Sports Sedan; Coho in 33 and 38-foot models; and a 35-foot Double Cabin model. Six models of Tournament Fisherman were produced in 22, 25, 30 (new for 1975), 36, 42 and 45-foot varieties.

In the luxury cruiser and yacht fleet for 1975 were only four fiberglas offerings, the Flush Deck models in 41 (Commander), 45, 47 and 55-foot Enclosed Flush Deck. Amazingly, all other models for 1975 were built of aluminum in Pompano Beach, FL. The seven aluminum yachts were the 60-foot Enclosed Flush Deck and Motor Yacht models, 68-foot Enclosed Flush Deck and Yacht Fisherman models, and the 74-foot Enclosed Flush Deck, Motor Yacht and Yacht Fisherman models.

A great deal of renewed design emphasis was placed in the Sport Boat lines for 1976, resulting in fifteen models out of a total Chris-Craft fleet of forty-three boats for the year. Among the more ingenious of these new designs was the Chris-Craft 23-foot *Overnighter*. Basically a convertible cruiser, the do-it-all boat had a transom seat that folded out into a double bed, a small dinette for two that converted into a single bed, V-berths forward and a galley with sink and refrigerator. Built into the aft deck was a fish/cold drink keeper. If you stripped the cabin off of a cabin cruiser, this is basically what would be left behind. Topping it all off was a nearly tent-sized optional camper top with vinyl rear windows. Powered with a Chris-Craft Transdrive package, it was designed to accommodate a family of five, just as the name implied, on an overnighter.

Also new for '76 was the flashy Chris-Craft XK 6.9 Meter sport boat. The nearly 23-foot boat came equipped with a stylish landau sun roof which raked *forward*, looking very much like a radar arch, forming the back of a smart wraparound windshield. With a pair of fully adjustable 360-degree swivel bucket seats and a spacious sunning cushion on the aft deck over the engine hatches, the 6.9 Meter was a breath of fresh air to a sport boat line that had in recent years been ignored in favor of Chris-Craft's large aluminum yacht programs.

Another innovation for '76 was an outboard version of the 22-foot Tournament Fisherman, known as the *Sportsman*. It had an outboard engine well built into a cut-down transom, making the molded lapstrake, dory-like design a safe but lively offshore performer. A new 22-foot Lancer, nicknamed *The Spoiler*, also evoked a modish design with a low wrap-around windshield which flowed into the hull design aft. A pair of 16-foot cathedral-hulled Sportsman were also introduced, one inboard, one outboard, each featuring a pair of lounge seats forward of a walk-through windshield. The inboard came equipped with a 105-horsepower Transdrive system with underwater exhaust. In a design frenzy absent for many years, Chris-Craft quickly followed with an XK 5.4 Meter, a 17-foot Lancer and a new 20-foot hull available as the 20-foot *Fisherman* or Sportsman.

The only significant introduction outside of the sport boats for 1976 was the new 55-foot aluminum Tournament Fisherman, bringing to seven the popular fishing fleet starting at 22-feet.

Among the reasons for the nearly $5 million loss sustained by the Boat Division during 1976 was the major distraction of consolidating the four remaining domestic manufacturing facilities to only two. As stockholders learned from the *Annual Report,* it's not an easy thing to do.

Sport boat manufacturing at Chattanooga was moved to the Holland, Michigan fiberglass facility and the aluminum yacht production was transferred from the Roamer plant in Holland to Pompano Beach, Florida. The Holland fiberglass facility, with 324,000 square feet, is the largest boat building structure in the world. The effort to employ it fully and maximize its potential profit brought problems which were not completely solved during the 1976 fiscal year.

The transfer of aluminum yacht production had been contemplated for some time, because the yachts built in Michigan were most often required to be delivered to Florida under their own power for fitting out, and delivery to customers was prevented by the winter freeze.[20]

The European facility in Fiumicino, Italy sustained a difficult sixty-day strike during 1976, which was the beginning of escalating difficulties due to absenteeism, stifling Italian taxes, and a worker pension system known as *casa de grazione*, whereby workers who are relieved continue to benefit according to an ever diminishing rate of standard pay.[21] Even though the factory was finally shut down in late 1978, some workers still continue to receive pay for punching the time clocks of a nonexistent factory over ten years later.

The one and only Chris-Craft work boat was built in 1977 and known as the 18-foot *Crooked Island Catboat.* With a broad beam nearly half its length, the Catboat was powered by a small diesel engine and was steered with a wooden sail boat style *tiller* by a standing operator. No seats, no wood, no windshield, no railings, no fooling. Designed for working fishermen, small cargo transport (over a ton) or yacht club launch, the anticipated third world demand for the rugged little boat never materialized, and it disappeared after only one year in the fleet.

A new 17-foot *Super Sport* was introduced for '77, in a true inboard version. The configuration made the all banana-yellow runabout popular

The only commercial work boat ever manufactured by Chris-Craft was this 1977 18-foot *Crooked Island Catboat.* Powered by a small diesel engine, and steered with a stern tiller-bar, it could carry over a ton of cargo.

Courtesy Mariners' Museum, Newport News, Virginia.

with skiers because of quick acceleration without the stern squatting down hard with the application of power.

Among the highlights of the cruiser fleets for 1977 were a pair of 25-foot Catalinas. The 25-foot Catalina Sportsman, though designed primarily for fishing, was popular for all-around use. It had a wide-open layout in the tradition of Sportsman from days of old, but with modern accoutrements like a pair of bow seats that convert into a 6'6" double bed, and a pair of V-berths forward, below a shortened cuddy-style cabin. It was powered by a pair of Marine Power Corporation (Chris-Craft) inboards.

The other 25-foot Catalina, the *Catalina Express,* was targeted to be the average consumer's first family cruiser. With a design that made it look larger, the four-sleeper provided a galley, dinette, V-berths and yacht-like teak accents.

A 28-foot Express Cruiser was designed with an exceptionally large cockpit area, though Chris-Craft naval architect Tracy Van Buren, Jr. explained that designers had more than fishing in mind.

This boat wasn't designed as an all out sportfishing machine, although her generous cockpit will lend itself to the installation of fighting chairs for those owners who want them. Our main purpose was to design a *family* cruiser, and almost everything in the boat was considered in that light.[22]

Courtesy Mariners' Museum, Newport News, Virginia.
The 1972 *Gull-Wing 16 Explorer* was among three cathedral-hull designs purchased from Outboard Motor Corporation (OMC) in early 1971, and powered with the original OMC sterndrive.

Among the nice features of the compact design was a 6'2" long by 2'3" wide settee, the back of which would swing up to create a great pair of bunk beds. With a modest price of less than $19,000 equipped with a single 225-horsepower Marine Power Corporation (Chris-Craft) V-8 engine, the 28 Express Cruiser became a first boat for many families.

In the 30-foot class, a pair of Commmanders offered a clear-cut choice. The 30-foot Com-

The 1972 Catalina *Sportsman* was a practical and inexpensive family sport fisherman. There were no gauges on the Command Bridge, but rather a *view glass* through which could be observed the lower control station instruments.

Courtesy Mariners' Museum, Newport News, Virginia.

mander offered all of the traditional cruiser amenities, including full-height head, optional hot water shower, complete galley with home-style refrigerator, and accommodations for four or five depending on configuration. Among the most popular features of the 30-footer, though, were the spacious (over 11' wide) cockpit which properly equipped made a wonderful sportfishing machine, and a command bridge large enough to seat a whole family on the move. Actually, the boat used to be the 30-foot Tournament Fisherman, modified for a family cruiser. Using the same hull, a 30-foot Commander Sportsman was reminiscent of the open Sea Skiff models. Again, it seemed as if the cabin were simply sawn off the 30-foot Commander, with the only remaining shelter being a pair of V-berths forward in the cuddy-style cabin. A snap-on convertible top was optional.

A new 38-foot Corinthian set some design precedents that were great news for the combination family cruiser/sport fisherman set. Touted as a two-bedroom home with a view on the water, the 38 offered a large aft owner's stateroom, forward stateroom with V-berths, and enough windows in the salon to qualify for a greenhouse. Powered with either a pair of gas-fired 330-horsepower V-8's or diesel engines, Chris-Craft characterized the practical new design as "...the one you've been waiting for."[23]

Chris-Craft continued to down play the Tournament Fishing fleet during 1977 due to sagging sales, and to promote the boats within the series as family cruisers renamed Commanders, that could also be great fishing machines.

Boats falling into this target consumer limbo were the six-sleeper 42-foot Commander (used to be the 42-foot Tournament Fisherman), and the 45-foot Commander (used to be the 45-foot Tournament Fisherman), and *Commander Yacht*. The Yacht was a flush-deck version of the 45-foot hull, which created an unusually large stateroom aft for owner live-aboard or extended cruising comfort. Buyers could order the Yacht with either a single or double stateroom forward floor plan, an unusual benefit for a 45-foot design.

Chris-Craft waxed poetic for the introduction of their 1978 Sport Boat line, fourteen familiar models with only minor adjustments in styling and performance.

> Screaming across the water with the wind in your face and the wheel in your hand. Dropping a line in the glassy stillness of a quiet lake at dawn. Blasting along the shoreline with a couple of skiers out behind and a couple of wet bikinis shining in the sun.
> That's Chris-Craft.[24]

Sport Boats for '78 included the 17-foot Super Sport, 17-foot Lancer and Lancer *Stinger*, 19-foot Lancer, 21-foot Lancer Inboard and Lancer Cuddy, 23-foot Lancer (including inboard) and Overnighter, 24-foot Lancer Express, and a series of *Cutlass* in 20-foot *Frontrunner* and 22-foot Cutlass, Cutlass Cuddy and Cutlass Outboard.

Chris-Craft offered MerCruiser inboard/outboards on a modest and exploratory basis for three models of Sport Boats, namely the 17-foot

A 1978 31 Catalina *Express* featured an oversized cabin, convertible dinette, galley, enclosed head, accommodations for four and 90 sq. ft. of deck space.

Courtesy Mariners' Museum, Newport News, Virginia.

Lancer, 19-foot Lancer and 20-foot Cutlass Frontrunner. All other models were equipped with Chris-Craft inboard or Transdrive systems powered by engines with 225 and 250-horsepower (Transdrive) and inboard power in 130, 225 and 250-horsepower ranges.

In 1978 the Catalina line was increased to five models, with the introduction of the six-sleeper 31-foot Express, another multi-mission, family cruiser/sport fishing type arrangement that featured a very large central main salon. Among the other Catalina-built were the 25 (including Sportsman), 28, 33 and 35-foot (including Double-Cabin) models.

The metamorphosis of the Tournament Fishing fleet was complete by 1978, with a firm marketing emphasis on the all-around family cruisers now referred to as the Commander 36, 42 and 45-foot models, along with the 30-foot Commander, 30-foot Commander Sportsman and 41-foot (flush-deck style) Commander Yacht.

Understandably in a year which registered a $1.6 million dollar loss for the Boat Division, no other new models were introduced, though a broad new menu of interior fabrics, colors and designs were promoted throughout cruisers from 25 to 45 feet.

The continuing losses by the Boat Division led Chris-Craft Industries, Inc. Chairman Herb Siegel to seek out one of the boating industry's outstanding executives and turnaround artists, Richard E. "Dick" Genth. James McQueen, who was president of the Boat Division, stepped aside in August of 1978, eventually to head Trojan Yacht, as Genth took charge of the ailing company.

Genth had a phenomenal record within the pleasure boat industry, starting with his quick rise to the presidency of Thunderbird, and turning around the company from one of marginal profitability to a successful acquisition by Fuqua Industries for $7.5 million. As the President of Wellcraft for six years, Genth was responsible for engineering a transformation from $2 million to over $44 million in annual revenues. He has been described as a "hell bent for leather" ocean racer and former test pilot, and a savvy marine executive who has a sixth sense about consumer priorities and taste. *Business Week* recorded Chris-Craft Industries, Inc. Executive Vice-President Lawrence R. "Larry" Barnett's praise for Genth. "We couldn't have gotten a better man," Barnett said. "His expertise is in the field where we need the biggest help — boats 17 ft. to 38 ft."[25]

Genth's help didn't come cheaply. As *Business Week* reported, his contract seemed like it came from another kind of leisure industry.

Genth says he finally accepted the job [following a two year courtship] partly because of "a very lucrative contract." When Chris-Craft approached him this year, he says, "I told them, 'I'll write up the terms, and I don't think you can afford me.'" Sources close to the company say the three-year contract is much like that of a professional football player. Barnett says only, "He can do extremely well if Chris-Craft makes money in the Boat Div."[26]

The acquisition of Genth marked the beginning of a new era at Chris-Craft. Genth, long accustomed to fast and furious manufacturing decisions, recognized the magnitude of the job ahead.

I was the first person who was brought into the company that came from sport boats, so to speak. I knew dang well the industry would be concerned about the small boat guy. "What the hell does he know about big boats?" It's certainly easier to be sport boat oriented and go to large boats than it is [the other way around].

Small boats are very price sensitive. Hourly sensitive. Everything about a seventeen foot boat is a hell of a lot more difficult to make money out of than a sixty footer. A sixty-five footer takes approximately twelve thousand hours to build. A seventeen footer takes fifty-five hours to build, so everything on that small boat is very sensitive, and you've got to stay on it every second. You know, when you squander a hundred, four hundred hours on a big boat you never see it. That beautiful Roamer? The sixty-eight footer? They said it took twenty-four, twenty-five thousand hours. I said "What?!!" All of a sudden it made a hell of a lot of sense to me...[27]

Genth identified a number of key areas where cost efficiency, plant utilization and product line overhaul would make a difference on the division's bottom line, and wasted little time in instituting the oftentimes unpopular decisions. He needed the support of the Chris-Craft Industries, Inc. Board of Directors to implement his strategy, and Genth says he wasn't sure how they would react to his ideas. The formidable board included Alvin "Pete" Rozelle (Commissioner of the National Football League), John Z. DeLorean (Chairman of DeLorean Motor Company), David Mahoney (Chairman of Norton Simon), among others, along with Herb Siegel, Chairman.

For a country boy like me to walk up there the first time and look at that board — talk about being intimidated. So, I got acquainted with them and they liked me. I was the first person to turn the...company around.[28]

Within the first six months of Genth's tenure at Chris-Craft, he had managed a small profit, reversing the large deficits which had plagued the division for most of the decade. Among the measures which he undertook were the conversion of the Holland, Michigan plant to exclusive cruiser production, quickly marketed nearly three hundred unsold sport boats in inventory, and immediately began to spearhead the design of a complete new line of sport boats for the company. The problem was where to build them.

With the Holland plant dedicated to cruisers, and the Pompano facility largely dedicated to aluminum yacht and cruiser programs, Genth began a state-wide search for a new facility. He had carefully avoided the greater Sarasota, Florida area. Having been president of Wellcraft in the same area, he was sensitive of being accused of recruiting and raiding boat building and executive talent from his previous employer. He ultimately located a facility at Panama City in Florida's northern panhandle, and negotiations had already reached a stage of discussion with the city fathers, when Genth received a call from a well regarded banker in Bradenton, Florida. The banker told Genth he would find him a facility, arrange an industrial revenue bond — in short, make it so attractive that Genth couldn't ignore the offer.

It was dumb for me not to do it. I mean, it was too good to be true. It wasn't because of any other reason than we had the best deal in the country right here [in Bradenton]. They got us an industrial bond right away at a low percentage; we found they had a building for us right away. Everything was put in our hands.[29]

Within five months of tooling start-up on the first new sport boat, the fruits of Genth's labors began to roll down the new Chris-Craft assembly lines in Bradenton.

Genth then had to make one of the most difficult decisions in his career. Wrestling with escalating labor and construction costs at the Pompano Beach plant, he had come to the conclusion that the enormous facility, including the prestigious aluminum yacht program, should be shut down. Genth had walked along the production line of the magnificent 68 and 74-foot aluminum yachts, checking to see who had ordered and placed deposits on the expensive boats. He was shocked to find that none of the boats were sold, and that they were all being prepared for inventory. "I walked out of the building with my head spinning", Genth remembers; "I don't treat a seventeen-foot boat that way, and you're talking a million dollar boat here — unsold!"[30]

Genth flew to New York to discuss the Pompano plant closure with the board of directors. ."I sat down and told Mr. Siegel my recommendation is to close...," Genth remembered. "Well, believe me, that table was silent. They thought I had lost my mind." After he had presented his findings, he gained the support of John Z. De

A 1977 45-foot *Commander Yacht* was powered by twin 320-horsepower diesel engines, came with either one or two guest staterooms forward, a large owner's stateroom aft, abundant teak accents and optional Command Bridge.

Courtesy Mariners' Museum, Newport News, Virginia.

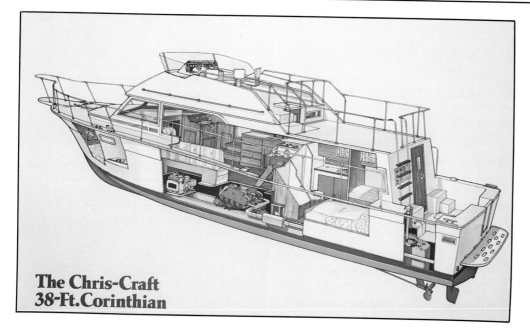

The Chris-Craft 38-Ft. Corinthian

This cutaway view of the 1978 Chris-Craft 38-foot *Corinthian* shows how five adults can be comfortable in two staterooms aboard a mid-size cruiser. Powered by a pair of 330-horsepower Marine Power V-8's it could deliver 27 knots, retailing for $69,990.

Courtesy Mariners' Museum, Newport News, Virginia.

Lorean, among others, and was told by members of the board that "Christ, you're the only guy that had the nerve to sit there and tell Herb Siegel to close the damn Pompano plant." Among Genth's arguments that finally won the day was his admission, "I have nothing against the sixty-eight footer or seventy-four, I love big boats. But until we get a better foundation here, we don't deserve to be building these things. We don't have the money to build them."[31] The announcement was made in July, 1979, that the Pompano Beach, Florida factory, including the prestigious Chris-Craft World Headquarters building, was to be closed. The administrative staff was relocated in modest quarters at the Bradenton facility. Over ten years later, Genth still receives anonymous and threatening notes, usually around Christmas time, concerning shutting down the Pompano facilities.

In 1979, Chris-Craft produced no boats larger than 45 feet, a phenomenon which hadn't occurred for over half a century. With barely any changes, cruisers marketed were limited to seventeen models of cruisers, express cruisers and yachts, ranging from 25 to 45 feet. The Catalina line included the 25, 28 and 31-foot Express, 33-foot Sedan, 35-foot Double Cabin, along with the 33 and 38-foot Corinthian models. Commanders included the 36, 42 and 45-foot models, along with 41 and 45-foot flush-deck style Commander Yachts.

The industry reacted quickly and favorably to the fresh and lively new line of sport boats known as *Scorpion*. The Scorpion fleet included the 170SS, a 17-foot inboard runabout powered

with a 250-horsepower Chris-Craft V-8; the 210SL, a 21-foot design that included a sliding forward hatch accessible via a walk-through windshield and powered with a 228-horsepower Mercury I/O; the 210S; the 211VF which was a toned down family-style runabout available with either the 228-horsepower Mercury package or as an outboard version with transom well; the 23-foot 230S cuddy-cabin design powered with Mercury 260 or 330-horsepower I/O; the 26-foot 260SL which was the first Chris-Craft boat to

Courtesy Mariners' Museum, Newport News, Virginia.

Even in the moonlight it's easy to see that the 1972 55-foot fiberglas *Commander* was designed for entertaining.

have the muscle-style, offshore racing design lines of a Cigarette or Wellcraft *Scarab*, and was powered with either a single 330-horsepower Mercury I/O, or a pair of 260-horsepower I/O engines. Last but not least was the crowning jewel of the new sport boat line, the 39-foot 390 Scorpion which clearly placed Chris-Craft into high-performance offshore racer and competition craft. It was powered by a pair of 370-horsepower Mercury I/O engines with surfacing propellers, fast becoming the standard propulsion system of offshore racing and heart-pounding weekend excitement. Though the other sport boats in the fleet were moderately priced from less than $12,000 to under $20,000, the 390 Scorpion, at nearly $78,000, sent notice to an elite sport boat buying public that Chris-Craft would once again be a major force to be reckoned with.

Following the quick response to the new sport boat line, Herb Siegel was able to report to Chris-Craft Industries, Inc. stockholders that the Boat Division was once again profitable.

The Boat Division returned to profitability in 1979, as it posted an operating profit of $444,000 against a $1,564,000 operating loss last year. The improvement was primarily the result of a 45% increase in boat sales.

The substantial increase in boat sales was directly attributable to the establishment of an aggressive marketing program and the development and successful introduction of an entirely new line of sportboats. Higher unit volume resulted in improvement in manufacturing margins.

The launching of the new sportboat line exemplified the vigorous management action. Within five months of the initial approval date, the Division obtained financing for the project, acquired and renovated a 52,000-square-foot plant located on ten acres in Bradenton, Florida, built a 30,000-square-foot addition and delivered the first boats... The success was even more impressive because the new facility broke even in its second month and recorded a small profit for the year.[32]

Dick Genth still had other seemingly sacred corporate possessions to eliminate in his program of financial and design streamlining. The first was the Chris-Craft engine division, which since 1929 had produced hundreds of thousands of solid performing engines for thousands of models of Chris-Craft, as well as for other manufacturers such as Riva of Italy. Among the reasons for shedding the engine division were sales which, when Genth arrived, required less than five engines per day. The Gallipolis, Ohio facility was distant and awkward to manage from Florida. Further, through Genth's leadership of Thunderbird and Wellcraft, he had successfully used the MerCruiser Sterndrives from Mercury Marine, and had developed an excellent working relationship with then Mercury President Jack Reichert.

Genth had his hands full with new production and new facilities, and asked the Chris-Craft Industries, Inc. Board of Directors to remove all corporate distractions except for boat production itself. The board granted his requests, and the engine, parts division, and

The interior of the 1979 33 Catalina *Sedan* was divided into three sections for three-couple privacy. Usually powered with a pair of 225-horsepower V-8 engines, most owners requested the optional Command Bridge.

Courtesy Mariners' Museum, Newport News, Virginia.

A revitalization of the sportboat program was well under-way by 1979, resulting in a whole new look for Chris-Craft, like the new Scorpion 210SL. Powered with a 260-horsepower MerCruiser sterndrive, the $14,795 boat would do 52 mph. It was among the sportboats that helped a return to profitability.

growing accessories, gift and merchandise catalog sales (now mailing five times a year) functions were all withdrawn from Boat Division supervision and responsibility. Following this, the boat manufacturing functions were divided into separate corporations, Chris-Craft Sportboats, Inc., for the Bradenton operations, and Chris-Craft Corporation for the Holland operations.

Chris-Craft had become a lean manufacturing machine, dedicated to the production of a scaled-down line of premium products, each one with a specific purpose and a carefully targeted market. The decade of the seventies was for Chris-Craft the severest test of corporate judgment and skill. Had it not been for the loyalty of Chris-Craft consumers, who continued to support the company they had known and admired for over ninety years of thoughful boat building, the company, hovering so often near the deepest financial precipice, might have been forced to close. Down to two manufacturing facilities, and with the first black ink in the ledgers in many years, Chris-Craft was poised for a dramatic comeback.

In the midst of this growing optimism, Dick Genth again grimly faced the Board of Directors in New York, and recommended that now was the time to sell the company. Chris-Craft, after twenty years of conglomerate and public corporation dominion, was about to emerge, a sleeping giant, into private ownership once again.

The *Crest* of the Coat of Arms shows the silhouette of the first *Miss America*, emblematic of World Championship and for the Chris Smith built boat that returned the Harmsworth Trophy to American shores.

The *Rising Sun*, representing a new power and majesty upon a blue sea, and signifying "A new day upon the water."

The *Bendy Gules* (red bands) is a mark of high honor, signifying safety and superiority among rivals. The red color represents strength, sincerity, peace and magnanimity.

The *Lymphiad* is an ancient galley, awarded to those who had performed outstanding feats upon the sea. It is colored black to indicate constancy and blue for truth.

The *Two Sable Martlets*, or flying geese, represent strength, speed and resourcefulness. The goose is among the most tireless fliers, and a bird that can do anything, since it walks, runs, swims and flies.

The *Cri de Guerre*, or rallying cry of the house, in this case *Chris-Craft* – universally known name in motorboating.

Chris-Craft

The Heraldic Crest, or *Coat of Arms*, of Chris-Craft has been in continuous use since its first appearance in 1930. Now one of the world's most recognized symbols, each element has a precise meaning rooted in heraldic antiquity.

Taken together, the translation of the Chris-Craft Coat of Arms would be:

I am the boat that brought a new day upon the water, and a new ideal of boating to millions of people. I am safe always for you and your family to use and enjoy, for I have proven myself superior to all rivals and all conditions times without number. My name has been blazoned upon motor boats which have won more competitive events than all others combined – I have speed, strength, and the ability to out-perform others, and to out-live them. I am designed in sincerity, built with honesty, endowed with constancy of performance at all times, sold to you with truth, and am worthy of your loyal regard throughout the many long years you will use me. I am a Chris-Craft.

From a description prepared for the 1930 Chris-Craft catalog.

CHAPTER XX

The Eighties

...Chris-Craft is a real wild card, a genuine legend. We have to protect and preserve that legend. Believe me, I feel that responsibility...The word is out. The drums are beating...I feel we're positioned very, very well to take advantage of the stretch. And that stretch is our *next* hundred years.[1]

G. Dale Murray
Chairman, Murray Industries, Inc.[1]

NEARLY FROM THE moment the decade began, excitement and change filled the air at Chris-Craft. The hard-fought gains of new management were being eroded by tightening credit, rising gasoline costs and the unthinkable discussion by government committees that boating should be banned on the weekends. Shortly following the critical annual meeting of Chris-Craft dealers to view and book orders for the new line of boats, Chris-Craft Industries, Inc. announced that it was writing off, as a onetime charge, the good will of the Boat Division on its books. A *Miami Herald* business writer put the drastic financial measure into perspective.

The good will of an operation represents what management estimates will be the earning power of that operation's products. The move by Chris-Craft, say accountants familiar with the technique, means that Chris-Craft officials are admitting the product name may no longer be worth $19.5 million on the books.[2]

Quickly following the accounting maneuver, was the disclosure by the *Wall Street Journal* that, "Chris-Craft Industries, Inc. said its board has decided to divest the company of the division from which it derives its name and that has been synonymous with power boating in America for generations...The company said the boat division will continue to operate routinely, but it will be accounted for as a discontinued operation in the company's fiscal 1980 financial statement, pending the divestiture."[3]

As soon as word spread that Chris-Craft was for sale, legions of speculators, deal makers, brokers and corporations began to parade through Chris-Craft's new facilities in Bradenton, attracted by the considerable mystique of the name. The majority of them, then president Richard Genth says, were just "nosy". Meanwhile, during this period of uncertainty, a smaller fleet of twenty-nine 1980 models were introduced, including twelve sportboats and seventeen cruisers.

An interesting statistic for the sportboat fleet is that, except for the 17'6" 170SS with a beam of 82", *every boat* in the fleet had the same beam of 8-feet, in models ranging from 20'7" to 39 feet.

The designs were conformed to maximum trailerable dimensions, making the Chris-Craft fleet available to the thousands of navigable inland lakes. Other Scorpions included the 210SL, 211VF, 212VF O/B (outboard version), 213VF O/B, 230S, 230SL, 260SL and top of the line 390SL. Two exciting new Excalibur models were presented in 1980, the 310 Excalibur and 311 Excalibur O/B. The Excaliburs were thoroughbred offshore racing designs, but offered V-berths and other limited overnight amenities below the long sleek deck. Except for the 250-horsepower inboard Chris-Craft powered 170SS and outboard models, every boat in the sportboat fleet was MerCruiser Sterndrive powered. Prices ranged from the 170SS at $11,995 to the 39-foot 390SL Scorpion powered by a pair of 370-horsepower MerCruiser Sterndrives equipped with TRS surfacing propeller units for $77,995. To give you an idea of the bonus paid for the MerCruiser systems, the 310 Excalibur with the same engines retailed for $60,395, while the 311 Excalibur O/B model was available for $16,995 with the customer supplying their own engines.

The 1980 Cruiser fleet reflected the continuing emphasis on mid-range, family-style designs. Models which survived the designers' erasers were the 25, 28 and 31-foot Catalina Express; Corinthian models in 26, 33 and 38-foot versions; 33-foot Express; 33-foot Catalina Sedan; 35 and 38-foot Catalina Sedan; 35 and 38-foot Catalina Double Cabin; 42 and 45-foot Commander; and top of the line 41 and 45-foot Commander Yachts. Prices ranged from the 25-foot Catalina Express with a single 225-horsepower Chris-Craft inboard at $19,695 to the 45-foot Commander Yacht equipped with a pair of 325-horsepower diesels at $254,995, F.O.B. Holland, Michigan.

As prospective buyers continued to browse through Chris-Craft's heavily thumbed books and increasingly distracted manufacturing lines, management was growing weary of playing host to what seemed like an endless procession of long-winded hot-shots.

Genth was preparing to shove off for a few days of relaxation aboard his personal 45-foot Commander Sportfisherman *Sorcerer* in the early summer of 1981, when he received the inquiry that would ultimately lead to the successful sale of Chris-Craft.

> I was cutting my lines to leave Fort Lauderdale on vacation, when a guy who was hanging on the fence says, "Who bought Chris-Craft?" I said, "Nobody." He said his name was Walt Schumacher, and "I've got a friend that might be interested..." I turned to the captain and said "Get me the hell out of here." If I hear one more person that wants to buy Chris-Craft... And as I'm departing he says his friend is F. Lee Bailey and also a man by the name of Dale Murray, and "if you haven't sold it..." And I disappeared.[4]

Though Schumacher remembered the incident somewhat differently, the fact remains that the brief meeting began a chain of events which would ultimately decide the fate of Chris-Craft.

The 1980 311 *Excalibur* outboard version was a fast and classy way to get to the fishing grounds. Without engines, the Jean Claude Simon design deep-vee hull retailed for $16,995.

Photo courtesy Murray Industries, Inc.

Thinking he had made good his escape, Genth set his course for Treasure Cay in the Abacos chain of the Bahama Islands. Once berthed at the tropical resort, his relaxation was interrupted when Schumacher's jet buzzed the docks and then landed. With Schumacher was G. Dale Murray.

Born George Dale Murray on May 29, 1942, he never knew his parents. He was raised in a foster home in Wilson, North Carolina, and from his earliest days learned the merits of hard work and determination. Opportunities were few and far between in the rural tobacco farming community forty miles east of Raleigh. He learned the mechanics of business from delivering both the morning and evening newspaper door-to-door, and from collecting hard-won revenues from his subscribers. In the evenings he worked in the local movie theatre, and dreamed of the far-off places and adventures that flickered across the huge beaded screen. They were more than dreams, though, they were *plans*, for Dale Murray always had the instinctive feeling that he was destined for great achievement. His best teachers were always his own experiences, and he wasn't attracted to scholarly pursuits. He was, rather, the prodigal street-smart kid, confident and cocky with a mind ablaze with life's possibilities. About school he once jokingly remarked, "I slept there. I only think they passed me because I promised to go into the Army right away.[5] Ever faithful to his commitments, three days later Murray joined the Army, and there completed three years of active duty. For a short while following his military duty, he worked as a general construction laborer in Minneapolis, Minnesota. Still nagging Murray, though, was the almost urgent feeling that there were much greater challenges ahead.

Murray developed a personal creed, a private work ethic. He was determined to work his way out of his meager circumstances, but he also knew he needed professional experience. One day, amidst the dust and residue of a full day of building other peoples dreams, he decided to make his move. Searching through the Minneapolis *Star and Tribune*, he circled an ad placed by a bank: "Wanted: College graduate..." Without the prerequisite credentials, most job hunters wouldn't have given the position another glance. But Murray knew banking was the center of the business world, and for him it could be the beachhead of a whole new destiny. So, screwing up his courage, Murray scheduled an interview with the bank manager. As John

Photo courtesy Murray Industries, Inc.

Chairman G. Dale Murray of Murray Industries, Inc., has increased Chris-Craft revenues by nearly a factor of eight since 1981.

Taylor wrote in *Florida Trend,* it was a short interview.

> As Murray remembers it, the job interview went something like this:
> "You have no college degree," the bank officer said.
> "I think I'm qualified," Murray replied.
> "Well, my advice is that you get some experience and come back later."
> Murray returned in 10 days. The officer asked him what he had learned in that short period. Murray said, "All there is to know about banks." A quick question-and-answer session revealed that Murray's knowledge was far from complete. But his chutzpah impressed the bank enough to give him a chance. Over the next several years, Murray did everything from repossess cars to make automobile and business loans.[6]

Most importantly, Murray was on the *inside*. The basic training that he received in the mechanics of finance, and the years of evaluating other peoples balance sheets, gave him the foundation he needed to determine a good deal from a bad one. In 1975, along with a partner, he established his own financial consulting service. Based in Minneapolis, his small company sought out favorable investment opportunities

In 1981 Algonac, Michigan was proclaimed the *Water Speed Capital* by the State of Michigan in recognition of the great achievements of Christopher Columbus Smith and Gar Wood.

for a small retinue of well-heeled clients. It was here, in 1977, that one of Murray's associates brought a young, 25-year-old Certified Public Accountant named Joel A. Schleicher into the company. He was to be a crucial asset to deciphering the complex financial packages to be analyzed.

One of these clients retained Murray and company to investigate coal mine investments in Kentucky, and even paid them well to undertake the extensive background research into the industry so they could ferret out attractive opportunities. After a diligent analysis of existing opportunities, Murray presented his client with several strong opportunities. Believing profoundly in the ability of the properties he had selected to make his client a handsome return on investment, Murray was surprised when the client declined to move on any of his suggestions. With an instinctive bravado that has characterized his professional career, Murray told his client that if they wouldn't buy one of the suggested coal properties, *he would*. With the blessing of the client who had funded the research, Murray's small company bought the Clintwood Energy Corporation in Pikeville, Kentucky for somewhere in the neighborhood of $5 million. It was a critical acquisition for Murray,

and one which drew upon all of his skills as a negotiator and financial analyst.

Murray moved to Pikeville, just twenty miles from West Virginia in the extreme eastern tip of Kentucky, to assume personal management of the operations. The deep coal mine contained what is referred to as high-grade steam coal, or low-grade metallurgical coal, suitable for use in steel-making operations. At the time of Murray's acquisition, the coal mining industry was wrestling for economic survival, and there were some who considered his investment as too risky. As Joel Schleicher explains, Murray's timing couldn't have been better.

Although we didn't have expertise in coal mining, Dale had enough foresight to anticipate what was coming in the industry. Number one, the purchase was done right, which always makes a good deal even better. And number two, there were certain things that were changing in the coal industry. The Reclamation Act of 1978 made it much more expensive to get into new mine sites. We had plowed our earnings back into fixing up additional mine sites, which were grandfathered in [not subject to the new regulations] before the law took effect, which made the property far more attractive to existing operators.[7]

It was demanding work, and required plenty of stamina and ingenuity to learn the ropes. During his first year of operations, Murray faced the worst possible one-two punch for a coal mine operator: a miner's strike *and* a railroad strike. A miner's strike in the coal fields of eastern Kentucky isn't usually settled over tea poured by waiters in pure white tuxedos. Murray was learning the realities of big business the same way he had fine-tuned most of his other skills, by firsthand experience, and by rolling up his sleeves to get the job done. As John Taylor described in *Florida Trend*, long hours made up for any lack of knowledge.

Although Murray and Schleicher knew little about coal mining in the beginning, they proved fast learners. They would show up at the mines every day at 4 a.m., then work till 10 p.m. "One of the things Dale and I believe is that you don't have to have a lot of knowledge about a particular product to be successful. You can learn the business," Schleicher says. "We're not the smartest people around, but nobody outworks us."[8]

After three years of successful operations and expansion, in 1980 Murray sold his interest in

Photo courtesy Murray Industries, Inc.

On Sept. 24, 1981 at the Chicago Trade Show, (L to R) F. Lee Bailey, Richard E. "Dick" Genth, Walter K. Schumacher and G. Dale Murray announced that agreement had been reached to purchase the boat division from Chris-Craft Industries, Inc.

the coal mining company to United Coal Co. headquartered in Bristol, Virginia for a significant profit. At 38, in an enviable emulation of a Horatio Alger success story, Murray retired to fashionable Hilton Head Island off the southern tip of South Carolina. Having become conditioned to the arduous crisis-intensive coal mining operations, it wasn't long before Murray became restless for further entrepreneurial challenge. As John Taylor wrote, Murray would "shift around uncomfortably on the couch [when] he talks about those mornings when he would wake up in Hilton Head... with nothing to do."

The sale of the coal company had made him a rich man, yet he could not stop working. "Each day, I would get up at dawn and ride around Hilton Head looking at all the real estate projects in town," he recalls. "I'd look at every one and still I'd be home at 7 a.m. staring at the shore. I was used to working 16 hours a day, seven days a week. Now there was nothing. It was the dullest and most demoralizing period of my life."[9]

980 45 *Commander* was Chris-Craft's luxury fishing ne, combining spacious accommodations for six with a f 425-horsepower G.M. 6V92TA diesels, for slightly over rter-million dollars a copy.

Photo courtesy Murray Industries, Inc.

Around eighteen months into his "retirement", G. Dale Murray was in the market for a new jet aircraft, and was considering a Gulfstream, following a chance meeting with Allen Paulson, Chairman of Gulfstream at a Hilton Head cocktail party. Paulson had given the lead to Walter K. Schumacher, then 42, who had represented Gulfstream Aerospace for over twenty years. Schumacher, whose holdings included fixed-base operations (executive aircraft support including fuel, hangars, maintenance, etc.) like Skytel Aviation at Fort Lauderdale International Airport, and at Savanna, Georgia, arranged a demonstration flight for Murray from Ft. Lauderdale to Hilton Head. As it happened, Schumacher and Murray took the flight together, and were both in the cockpit when Schumacher recanted the conversation he had exchanged with Dick Genth at the docks earlier in the day. Schumacher dropped Murray off at Hilton Head and returned home. Later that evening, Murray phoned and said, "I was really fascinated by our conversation, and I think we could possibly raise that kind of money. Why don't we continue to pursue this? Why don't you get a hold of Chris-Craft's president and let's have a meeting."[10]

Among Schumacher's many talents was an ability to put his jet-set customers together in interesting deals. Another of Schumacher's clients, noted trial attorney F. Lee Bailey, also flew in and out of the Savanna airport. Bailey, perhaps the most recognized name in the legal profession, gained notoriety from his defense of clients as diverse as kidnaped heiress Patricia Hearst and the Boston Strangler, and as author of three best selling non-fiction books. Schumacher made a note to put the famous attorney together with Murray to discuss the possibilities for the acquisition of Chris-Craft. Following these successful exploratory discussions, Schumacher told Murray that Dick Genth was en route to Treasure Cay, and would be there for several days. It is aboard Genth's yacht that Murray and Genth would first meet.

> Dale and I sat aboard my forty-five footer and we started talking. My pitch towards the end was, "Please...if you're going to buy this company, and you're going to look at the books you're not going to buy it. You're not going to be able to bookkeep this. You're not going to be able to make any sense out of this. You're going to have to look at the picture today, and say for X many dollars I'm going to own this and I'm going to start today." And then I said, "If you try to go

back into this and figure out what happened, how it happened, or what about this, what about that, forget it." I said, "None of this is going to make any sense.

> "You have to take my word for it. Whoever buys it for this price has got a beautiful deal because I've cleaned the company up. There's no large inventories, no obsolete inventories, we've written everything off with the permission of the parent company. I have the company tweaked clean."[11]

Genth's arguments were persuasive, but Murray acknowledged the fact that whoever bought Chris-Craft would be wise to persuade Genth to remain as President. Murray then asked what Genth would like to do in the event of a successful purchase. Genth said he would like to have an equity interest in the new company, and that he was "looking for a partner who wants to give this company the love that this company has to have." Then Genth delivered what was to be his closing argument. Drawing upon John F. Kennedy's 1960 inaugural address he said, "Dale, it's the old Kennedy thing, 'Ask not what this company can do for you, but ask what you can do for your company.'" Murray and Genth liked each other almost immediately, and Murray replied "I'm that person."

Murray credits his successful acquisition of Chris-Craft to fast work and quick decisions, because other buyers were interested.

> There were a number of companies looking at Chris-Craft. Two dozen of them. We made the buy. The people I was competing with were second, third and fourth tier managers in big companies. By the time they made up their minds what they wanted to do, we were able to go to a closing. That's the flexibility and the swiftness that an entrepreneur can work under. A lot of people can *out spend* us, but no one that I've met can *out work* us.

> I can't tell you how many people have told me, "I was looking at that company," or, "I had a chance to buy." I don't think they should be proud of those statements, really. The company had been for sale for ten months before I even looked at it, and for over a year before I closed it. I think my merger and acquisition background allowed me to assess the situation very quickly. From the first day that I got the phone call, five months later we owned the company.[12]

On December 4, 1981, G. Dale Murray, in association with Dick Genth, F. Lee Bailey and Walt Schumacher, purchased the Boat Division from Chris-Craft Industries, Inc. for an estimated $5 million. Murray had borrowed an estimated $3.7 million from two banks in five-year notes, while Genth had put up $1.1 million in Chris-Craft Industries, Inc. stock options.[13] Chris-Craft, after twenty-one years of public ownership, was a private, independent company once again. The actual percentages of ownership are a closely guarded secret, but were originally estimated to be 70% Murray, 20% Genth, 5% Bailey, and 5% between Schumacher and *Tonight Show* co-host Ed McMahon. Since Chris-Craft was the trading symbol for Chris-Craft Industries, Inc. on the New York and other stock exchanges, the name Chris-Craft was actually licensed to Murray Industries, Inc., generally referred to as Murray Chris-Craft, and then representing Murray Chris-Craft Cruisers, Inc. (Holland, Michigan operations) and Murray Chris-Craft Sportboats, Inc. (Bradenton, Florida operations). Retained by Chris-Craft Industries, Inc. were the engine division, the parts division of which was subsequently sold to U.S. Marine Corporation (manufacturers of Force outboard engines), a subsidiary of Bayliner, and the Chris-Craft gift catalog operations, which were also sold.

Months prior to the actual sale, the 1981 Chris-Craft fleet was further reduced to only twenty principal models, with a total of 34 variations. Perhaps most noticeable by their absence were the 42-foot Commanders, and the 45-foot Commander and Commander Yacht. The largest boat in the fleet, the 41-foot Commander Yacht, was only two feet longer than the largest sportboat, the 390SL Scorpion. Also among the missing were the Excalibur sportboats, replaced by the *Stinger* name which was also available in three additional, previously Scorpion, models. Chris-Craft had slimmed down its total models, designing for volume sales, and not one boat was built on speculation.

Twenty Sportboats were manufactured for '81, including the 170SS, 182BR (as in Bow Rider walk-thru windshield style) Scorpion, 183SL (as in Sun Lounger) Scorpion, 184VF Scorpion, 210S (as in Standard) and 210SL Scorpion, 211VF and 212VF O/B Scorpion, 213VF Scorpion O/B, 214VF Scorpion, 230S and 230SL Scorpion, 255CC Scorpion, 260 SL Stinger, 264AC Scorpion, 270VF Scorpion, 275X Stinger, 311SL Scorpion O/B, 312SL Stinger, 390SL Scorpion and 390X Stinger models. Prices ranged from the 170SS equipped with a 250-horsepower Chris-Craft inboard at $13,995, to the 390X Stinger equipped with a pair of 370-horsepower MerCruiser Sterndrives and surfacing drive

units for $79,995. The majority of the '81 sportboats could also be equipped with Volvo I/O power, with engine sizes of 175, 225 and 260-horsepower available depending on the boat.

Cruisers for '81 included the 251 Catalina, 262 Corinthian, 280/281 Catalina, 310 Catalina, 332 Express, 333 Sedan, 334 Trawler, 350 Catalina Double Cabin, 360 Commander, 380 Corinthian, 381 Catalina Double Cabin, 382 Trawler, and largest in the fleet, the 410 Commander Yacht. The new Trawler, in both 33 and 38-foot models, were hybrid models which were designed to combine the spacious living space of the Catalina models, with cockpits for fishing, and a hull with good seakeeping characteristics. The 334 Trawler had a large cockpit reminiscent of the Commander Sport Fisherman cockpits, while the 382 Trawler provided a shortened cockpit to make room for a full aft stateroom. Cruiser prices ranged from the 251 Catalina Express equipped with a single 225-horsepower Chris-Craft inboard at $19,995, to the 410 Commander Yacht with a pair of 286-horsepower diesel engines for $195,995.

G. Dale Murray received an emotional welcome to the boat-building industry, and remembered how both press and competitors alike extended thanks for pledging to carry on the great traditions of Chris-Craft's boating heritage.

> Right after I closed Chris-Craft, I heard from virtually every major manufacturer of boats and engines, as well as the press. I'd hear things like, "Thank you for not allowing Chris-Craft to go by the wayside." Or, "You're going to be tough competition, but it would have been devastating, it would have been a tragedy..." It was so fulfilling to hear from the competition, people I didn't know because I was new to it.
>
> In fact, we had one press conference, and there were probably 60 members of the press there, and one of the guys stood up and said, "I have a question; but first, on behalf of the industry, on behalf of the press, on behalf of everybody that ever had anything to do with boating, thank you for the preservation of Chris-Craft."[14]

It was the 1982 fleet that Murray and Genth would first be able to contour according to their new goals and corporate initiatives. As an introduction to the 1982 Chris-Craft full-line brochure a month following the sale, President Richard E. Genth made the first announcement to the general boat buying public that a new age had begun at Chris-Craft.

Photo by Elizabeth A. Reed, courtesy Murray Industries, Inc.

G. Dale Murray's down-home panche has helped attract great celebrities to his board of advisors. (L to R) F. Lee Bailey, Gen. Alexander Haig, Murray, Pat Haig, and Ed McMahon.

By now, most of the boating world knows that in December 1981 the Chris-Craft Boat Division was sold to a group of private investors.

Along with the sale came a new name, Murray Chris-Craft...and the beginning of a great, new era in which the world's most famous boating heritage returned to private ownership. It is well to remember that during the years of its greatest growth and most innovative product development, Chris-Craft had been a privately-owned corporation.

Speaking on behalf of the Murray Chris-Craft organization, let me assure you — customers and dealers alike — that we recognize the honored traditions which once surrounded the name Chris-Craft. More importantly, we hereby accept the challenge to return the company to its former greatness. That alone is our intent.

There will always be a Chris-Craft.[15]

Twenty-eight models were available in the first Murray Chris-Craft fleet of 1982, ranging in size from 18 to 41 feet. Again, the fleet was carefully contoured to meet dealer and consumer requirements and a renaissance of quality control was in evidence.

The Sportboat line remained largely intact, with the exception of the elimination of the 170SS, 270VF Scorpion, 275X Stinger and 311SL Scorpion O/B models.

Cruisers also stabilized at ten models during the crucial year of management transition. Four models were discontinued, the 310 Catalina, 334 and 382 Trawlers, along with the 360 Commander.

It didn't take long for Murray and Genth to put their plan for the re-establishment of Chris-

292 CATALINA
SUNBRIDGE SEDAN

Photo by Elizabeth A. Reed, courtesy Murray Industries, Inc.

Below: Chris-Craft's largest luxury cruiser in 1987 was the 500 *Constellation* Motor Yacht, featuring wide deck walkways, and a king-size owner's aft stateroom complete with bathtub.

Top: The Catalina remained the *American Dream* for many families during the 1980's. Typical of versatility and value was the 1987 Catalina *Sunbridge Sedan* six-sleeper with flybridge.

Photo by Elizabeth A. Reed, courtesy Murray Industries, Inc.

1982 *Scorpion 264 AC*, even though a fast, express-style er, was a sportboat that could sleep three, including full and dinette. Power options included either the 260-power MerCruiser or Volvo sterndrive packages.

Craft to its prior preeminence in the industry into action. They divided up responsibilities sensibly, with Murray tackling the job of financing and searching for more facilities to build a wider range of boats. To Genth fell the responsibility of developing the dealer organization and planning future models. They both had their work cut out for them, for the purchase had been made with sales and dealer ranks at the lowest levels in nearly fifty years.

Chris-Craft began to grow, and to grow rapidly. In May of 1982, Murray bought the Viking Boat Company in Goshen, Indiana from Coachman Industries. It was precisely the type of acquisition which Murray was after. Viking was doing poorly in the marketplace, down to producing less than a boat a day, but they had good tooling, a great work force and solid manufacturing facilities. The new company, Murray Chris-Craft Sportdecks, was added to the masthead. Almost overnight, Chris-Craft introduced seven new models of Viking's line of wide open, semi-rectangular, *tri-vee*-hulled all-around recreational Sportdecks to the planned 1983 fleet. The practical and stable sportdecks included the 160SI, a 16-foot center console outboard model; the 170SC, a 17-foot I/O model; the 170 *Sprint*, a 17-foot center console I/O model; the 190SI, a 19-foot center console I/O model; the 190SC Sterndrive model which featured an aft sundeck; 190EL Sterndrive model; and top of the line 21'6" 220EL which could be equipped with either 260-horsepower MerCruiser or OMC Sterndrive power packages.

The fast moving Murray organization introduced twenty-two other sportboats for 1983, making for a total of twenty-nine sport models alone. A trio of new, smaller Scorpions were built, including the 168BR, 169S and 169SL models. The nearly 17-foot 168BR featured a walk-through windshield and vee-seating in the bow. The 184VF Scorpion was a center console outboard model popular for fishing, while the 210VR Scorpion I/O model featured a walk-through windshield and vee-seating in the bow. The 210S and 210SL both offered a small storage cuddy cabin, as did both the 211VF Scorpion I/O model and the 212VF Scorpion O/B models. The 213VF Scorpion O/B and 214VF I/O models both featured open bow (bow-rider) configurations. Returning to the line-up were the 230S and 230SL, but new for '83 were the 264AC Scorpion and 265WAC Scorpions. Using the same 26'4" hull, the 264AC was mated with a small cabin and bridge arrangement, while the

265WAC was arranged with a cuddy cabin and wide-open aft deck for fishing. Five strong offshore performers topped off the sportboat fleet, starting with the center console 311VF Scorpion O/B. The 39-foot 390SL Scorpion remained, while three new *Stinger* models augmented the muscle boats of the line, the 260SL Stinger, 312SL Stinger and 1983 offshore flagship 390X Stinger, which could be powered with either a pair of 370-horsepower MerCruiser or 400-horsepower MerCruiser Sterndrives with TRS surfacing drive systems for blazing competition-style performance.

Eighteen cruisers made the 1983 Chris-Craft fleet, with either new models or new options in almost every size range. A new 251 Catalina Express was the smallest cruiser, followed by a new 263 Corinthian Express, all-new 263 and 266 Corinthian Bridge models, two new Catalina Express models in 280 and 281 versions, a brand new 291 Catalina Bridge, an all-new 315 Commander Sport Fisherman/Convertible, 332 Commander Express, 333 Commander Bridge, new 336 Commander Mid Cabin, 350 Catalina Double Cabin, new 360 Commander/Convertible, new 361 and 362 West Indian Trawler, new 380 Corinthian Double Cabin, 381 Catalina Double Cabin, 410 Commander Yacht, and the new flagship of the Chris-Craft fleet, the 421 Commander Convertible. The new West Indian Trawlers were designed by renowned Naval Architect Charles Morgan, and featured a deep forefoot, full-length keel and heavy chines for stability and seagoing ability. Prices for the cruiser fleet ranged from $23,995 for the 251 Catalina Express equipped with a single 225-horsepower Chris-Craft or optional 230-horsepower Mercury Marine inboard engine, to $246,000 for the 421 Commander Convertible equipped with a pair of 500-horsepower 6V92TI diesel engines.

Business soared. The marketplace responded to the new initiatives at Chris-Craft almost immediately. Chris-Craft was on the move and on the mend. As Genth remembers, he and Murray developed an unusually close working relationship, and almost supernatural coincidences in thinking would occur in strategy sessions.

It was twenty-four hours a day. We lived, breathed, ate and slept that thing. Dale was doing what he needed to do. He was guarding my back side, taking care of certain things that I don't care to do and I was running the operations.

It was beautiful. I mean, we had no problems. Dale and I never sat down one single time and had a disagreement. In fact, he will tell you, it was so spooky that it really was scary. I would get ready to say something and he would know what I was thinking or vice versa. I mean talk about being in tune, it was unreal. I've never been around a person like that. We honestly were almost a single person.[16]

The combination was working in brilliant fashion. In the first nine months of operations following the acquisition, sales had doubled from $26 million to $55 million. In fiscal 1983, revenues skyrocketed to $94.5 million as dealers clamored to get on board, totaling 150 by year's end. In March of 1983, Chris-Craft experienced a $10 million month, the greatest sales of any month in the entire history of the boat-building firm. Chris-Craft's share of the highly competitive boat-building market, which had fallen to three percent in 1981, had risen to ten percent by the end of 1983.

By 1984 Murray Chris-Craft was in need of additional manufacturing facilities, and Dale Murray completed the purchase of Uniflite, Inc. in Bellingham, Washington, with another plant located in Swansboro, North Carolina. The acquisition of Uniflite would add eight models to the Chris-Craft line, "... including a 45-foot sea-going Yacht Home that sleeps six and cruises comfortably with twin 340-hp MerCruisers, and a 50-foot Constellation motor yacht that sleeps eight and is powered by twin 500-hp diesels."[17] During the 31 days of May, 1984, Murray Chris-Craft registered sales of over $20 million, and sold nearly as many boats in one month as had been sold in all of 1981. Sales for 1984 would top $125 million.

With record sales tied directly to the popularity of the 1983 Sportboat fleet, many new models were introduced for 1984 to fill in any gaps in the growing line. "Not for the weak of spirit," cautioned the introduction to the 1984 Sportboat line, "They give you the pleasure of owning a Chris-Craft that will run like the wind."[18] Thirty-five models of Sportboats were built at Chris-Craft plants in 1984, including unchanged Sportdeck models. Over one-third of the complete Sportboat line was new for '84. Included in the fleet was the new 167BR to compliment the 168BR Scorpion; new 169S and 169SL Scorpion; new 186BR Scorpion; new 210BR Scorpion to accompany the 210S and 210SL; all-new 210S and 210BR *Ski-Jack;* 211VF and 212VF Scorpion; added to the 213VF and 214VF was the name *Fish-Jack;* new 215WA I/O and 216WA O/B Scorpions; new 217BR Scorpion; new 230SL LTD added to the 230S and 230SL Scorpions; all-new 230XL Stinger with radar arch; new 260SL LTD Stinger joined the 260SL Stinger; 264AC Scorpion; 265WAC Scorpion; all new 300 Chris Cat; 311VF Scorpion; 312SL Stinger and top of the line 390X Stinger.

Among the most exciting developments in the Sportboats was the new 300 Chris-Cat catamaran designed by noted offshore catamaran designer George Linder. As Richard Thiel reported in *Boating,* the Chris-Cat represented one of the finest marriages of racing technology and pleasure craft.

> The hull is a paragon of stability, one of the best examples of racing-cat technology applied to a production boat I've seen. Tabs are virtually unnecessary; the Chris planes quickly with a bit of drive trim, then runs well at any speed above plane with one degree of drive trim. The hull runs flat and is absolutely outstanding in turns. Also the best laid out instrument panel I've seen in *any* performance boat.[19]

The 300 Chris-Cat could be powered with either a pair of 400-horsepower MerCruiser engines with TRS surfacing drives or a pair of KAAMA 420-horsepower performance packages. The decision for adding a high performance catamaran hull to the Chris-Craft Sportboat fleet had roots that went back to the beginnings of the company.

In 1982, Chris-Craft made a commitment to return to powerboat racing as a proving ground for high performance pleasure craft. As Chris, Jay W. and Bernard Smith demonstrated in the early decades of the company's development, racing demands the highest possible skills and abilities to win, and to win consistently. After a hiatus of a half-century, Chris-Craft orchestrated their comeback as if they had only been away for the winter. Murray Chris-Craft called upon boat racing veteran Don Pruett to spearhead a serious commitment to high performance, and move Chris-Craft into the forefront of racing once again. The fact that they called on the two-time world champion offshore throttleman signaled the industry and the racing community that Chris-Craft was serious. In 1968, Pruett competed in eleven offshore events, winning 9, taking second place in one, sank his boat in one, and his team was the overwhelming winner of the world championship. Pruett went on to win the world championship again in

1970. With his 'good 'ol boy' drawl and vast racing experience, Pruett was held in high esteem both on and off the race course. Murray Chris-Craft President Bruce Donaldson called Pruett, "The best there is, we weren't about to settle for anything less."[20]

Pruett commissioned one of the world's foremost racing catamaran designers, George Linder of Long Island, New York, to assist in the development of the company's first *Chris-Cat* high performance catamaran hull. Linder, whose Shadow Cat hulls opened the eyes of many offshore competitors, drew upon his successful experience to design a new 30-foot hull that was to shake up the traditional balance of offshore racing competition. The first boat hit the water in March of 1984. Only a year later, Chris-Craft hulls would win more first and second-place finishes in offshore racing *than any other manufacturer.*

In 1984 a Chris-Craft 312 Stinger won the 115-mile Golden Gate (San Francisco) to Spruce Goose (Long Beach, California) race, sponsored by *Powerboat* magazine to raise more than $500,000 for the Olympics. During the same year, Tim Ciasulli driving *Maxon,* a 30-foot Chris-Cat, set a new American Power Boat Association (APBA) Class II national speed record of 96.48. Another 30-foot Chris-Cat, *Thriller,* would win the APBA Class III National Point Championship. *Spirit of Miss Liberty,* a 30-foot Chris-Cat, established a new one-way and round-trip Hudson River speed record to raise funds for the restoration of the Statue of Liberty.

In 1985, the 30-foot Chris-Cat *Jesse James* was national circuit high point winner, world speed record holder *and* World Champion in the highly competitive APBA modified class. In 1986, twenty-two racecraft were on the water carrying the Chris-Craft colors, including 30-foot Chris-Cats along with 37 and 39-foot Stingers. On the 4th of July, the 30-foot Chris-Cat *Smilin Jacks,* piloted by Jack Bishop of Jupiter, Florida, shattered the World Speed Record in the Modified Class of offshore powerboat racing. Bishop's new American Power Boat Association record of 116.358 demolished the previous record of 101.257 that was set two years previously by the *Jesse James,* another 30-foot

Photo by Karine N. Rodengen

Right: Honors for the most awesome outboard powered sportboat on the market starting in 1985 would have to go to the 30-foot 305 *Chris-Cat*, designed by George Linder.

Photo courtesy Murray Industries, Inc.

305 CHRIS-CAT

Photo by Karine N. Rodengen

Opposite left: *Smilin Jacks*, a 30-foot *Chris-Cat* driven by Jack Bishop established a new world speed record in 1986 at 96.358 mph. Consumers bought standard 300 Chris-Cats with pairs of 440-horsepower MerCruiser engines for $133,395.

Above: *Special Edition*, a 30-foot *Chris-Cat*, driven by John D'Elia, was the APBA National High Point Champion in 1986.

Chris-Cat. The *Smilin Jacks* was powered with a pair of heavily modified 350-cubic-inch MerCruiser engines, with MerCruiser IV surfacing drives. Chris-Craft entered into a limited production agreement with Conquest Marine to produce a 35-foot Chris-Cat which competed successfully in the offshore power boat racing Open Class.

The racing program proved to be valuable to Chris-Craft, as lessons learned in the severe competition environments would assist in the design of performance craft for consumers. Don Pruett explained the reasoning.

> We take what we learn from our race boats, and turn this knowledge right back into our production boats. Our question to our racing boat teams is: "What can you tell us, what can you show us, what can you point out to us that we can apply to our traditional boats that will make our boats the best and safest boats on the water today?"
>
> The objective is to provide the first time boat buyer who buys a 17-foot Cavalier with the same kind of performance and safety considerations that go into our race boats that are winning world championships.[21]

Twenty cruisers were marketed for 1984, nearly half of which were brand new for 1984, in sizes from 25 to 46 feet. The Aqua-Home reemerged in 1984, in a 46-foot version with all the comforts of a modern two-bedroom apartment. With accommodations for eight, the Aqua-Home could be powered with either I/O or inboard gas or diesel power. Other '84 cruisers included the 251 Catalina Express, new 253 Catalina Mid-Cabin, new 268 Commander Sport Sedan, 280 and 281 Catalina Express, 291 Catalina Bridge, new 315 and 316 Commander Sport Sedan, 332 Commander Express, new 333 Commander Sport Sedan, 336 Commander Mid-Cabin, new 337 Commander, 350 Catalina Double Cabin, new 360 Commander Sport Sedan, new 365 Commander Sport Fisherman, 380 Corinthian Double Cabin, 381 Catalina Double Cabin, 410 Commander Yacht, and the stately 421 Commander Convertible.

Somehow, the near Cinderella relationship between Murray and Genth went astray. It was Monday morning, the 22nd of August, 1984, and Genth was preparing to leave for Swansboro, North Carolina when Murray asked to see him before he left. Murray offered Genth the position of Vice-Chairman, to take a greater role in the corporate acquisitions and mergers program, and less of a direct role in the day-to-

day operations of Chris-Craft. Genth, who is most comfortable in direct, hands-on management, balked at the suggestion and told Murray that the position wouldn't work for him. Knowing he would be leaving Chris-Craft after six years, Genth walked back to his office. There, gazing out the window, wondering how to tell his family, how to tie up all the loose ends that a change in administration brings, he quietly reflected on his future. Murray walked back in, and observing Genth looking out the window many stories above the pavement, said, "Are you O.K.?" Genth realized what Murray meant and replied, "If you think I'm going to jump out this window, you're crazy!" Genth's successor was Ernest Schmidt, previously Chris-Craft Executive Vice-President.

The disaffection which ensued following the meeting lasted several years, but now Murray and Genth have patched up their differences, and have been seen lunching amicably and talking over old times. Genth, who profited handsomely from his association with Murray Chris-Craft, purchased Donzi Marine in nearby Tallevast, Florida, with long-time Chris-Craft Vice President of Advertising and Public Relations C. Gordon Houser. Genth, with characteristic pluck, told Murray recently, "You know what we would tell the industry if we ever got together again? We would just tell them we were *too young* when we got married."[22]

Chris-Craft had gained a new reputation for aggressive new model introductions, and the 1985 fleet proved to be no exception. Sixty-six models were manufactured in 1985, as Chris-Craft popularity continued to spread from one end of the diversified line to the other.

Forty-two Sportboats were available for '85, and really represented every corner of the sportboat market from docile to dazzling. Fifteen new models complimented last year's fleet, with only a few changes in basic configurations. New for '85 in the Scorpion flotilla were the 168BR S and 168BR SL, 186BR SL, 187S and 187SL, 210BR S and 210BR SL, 218BR, 232AC, 254WA, 265WA, 266AC and 313VF Scorpions. New to the Stinger high-performance group were the 312 *Competition* Stinger and 314S Stinger. The Sportdeck fleet from the Goshen, Indiana plant was reduced to the three most popular models, the 170, 190 and 220 LTD.

The most dramatic changes in years occurred in the premium end of the '85 cruiser fleet, in a bold offering of 24 models. Nine new models made waves during the year, including the new

Mark and Chris Lavin, driving *Jesse James*, a 30-foot Chris-Cat were the 1985 National High Points Champions, world speed record holders *and* World Champions. Mark Lavin tragically lost his life competing for the world crown in 1986.

282 Commander Sport Fisherman, 382 Commander Sport Sedan, 422 Commander Sport Sedan, 425 and 426 Catalina Double Cabin, 482 Commander Convertible, 450 Yacht Home, and to reintroduce to the Chris-Craft fleet once again the Constellation, in 460 and 500 Constellation Motor Yacht models.

The upgrading of the premium sector of the cruiser fleet was a clear indication of renewed interest in large, opulent and comfortable cruisers with traditional Chris-Craft prestige and flair. The return of the Constellation, Chris-Craft's historic premium yacht line, was the beginning of a restoration of world-class construction and quality controls which were once almost exclusively Chris-Craft trademarks.

Among the charismatic abilities of G. Dale Murray is an almost magnetic, down-home knack of surrounding himself and his companies with among the most well known names in America. As either direct Board of Director members or consulting board members are such notable luminaries as America's foremost defense attorney F. Lee Bailey; *The Tonight Show's* co-host and celebrity Ed McMahon (an ardent boating enthusiast who owns a 500 Constellation Motor Yacht); General Alexander M. Haig, President Ronald Reagan's first Secretary of State, and former Supreme Allied Commander of European NATO forces until 1979; Leon Finley, the senior founding member of Finley, Kumble, Wagner, Heine, Underberg, Manley & Casey, one of the three largest law firms in America; among other notable leaders in banking, manufacturing and aviation. Murray is proud of his relationship with his famous Board of Directors, and is quick to point out that Chris-Craft's magic name is universally respected.

I'm very flattered by that association. It's really Chris-Craft. I thought of Chris-Craft the way I would think of a General Motors. I had no idea the company was in the position it was in when I was introduced to it. It just had such a powerful name; one of the best recognized corporate names in U.S. history. And, if you call someone to join your board, or talk to someone about Chris-Craft, you know you have enormous identification and credibility, so it's not like you have to introduce who you are or what the company does. It's very prestigious. I'm proud to say that I've never talked to anyone about being on the board, or being an advisor, that said "no."[23]

On February 10, 1986, G. Dale Murray appointed Bruce J. Donaldson as President and Chief Operating Officer of the Chris-Craft

Top: The 1988 375 *Stinger*, with near 60 mph speeds set standards for style, comfort and offshore excitement. A full year's production sold out less than a week after introduction.

Left: A 1986 222 *Stinger* was a revolutionary design, demonstrating that even after a century of building high-performance boats, Chris-Craft hasn't lost the Midas touch.

Below: Among the features of the 1988 202 *Stinger* were molded-in swim platform, center-cockpit steering, and with up to a 205-horsepower sterndrive by either OMC or MerCruiser.

Photos by Elizabeth A. Reed and Brian King, courtesy Murray Industries, Inc.

Chris-Craft's crowning design achievement for the 1980's could very well be the *Amerosport* line began in mid-1986. Above: New for 1987 was the 320 *Amerosport*, equipped wih a V-drive 320-horsepower inboard engine. Left: The interior of the 1988 370 *Amerosport* demonstrates the practicality of American market driven design. Below: The modern family six-sleeper cruiser is reborn in the shape of the 1987 284 *Amerosport*.

Photos by Elizabeth A. Reed, courtesy Murray Industries, Inc.

boat companies, replacing Ernest Schmidt. Donaldson's association with Chris-Craft spanned over twenty-eight years, and his rise to the presidency represents a nearly 'mail-room to the board-room' tale of continuous achievement. "I joined the company working for then chairman of the board Harsen Smith, who hired me and put me to work on little tasks here and there," Donaldson says. Starting in 1958, Donaldson graduated to sales, eventually becoming Sales Manager of the Sailboat Division, Cavalier Division, Vice-President of Cruisers, and Vice-President of Manufacturing before assuming the Presidency. Even in the early days of association with the company, Donaldson recognized the sense of deep traditions, quality and the family boating spirit that he has endeavored to instill in the organization.

Chris-Craft restored the venerable name of *Cavalier* to the Sportboat fleet for 1986, replacing models from 17 to 19 feet with the new designation. Also introduced for '86 were the *Limited* series from 17 to 31 feet. The new entry-level Sportboat was the 17-foot Cavalier, an outboard model, which retailed for only $4,795. The other new Cavaliers included the 17BR, 17CD, 19BR, 19CD and 19 Cavalier Cuddy models. All of these Cavaliers could be equipped with either the 140 or 200-horsepower MerCruiser Sterndrive or OMC 140-horsepower packages, while the 17-foot models could also accept the 120-horsepower MerCruiser Sterndrive. A 19-foot Cavalier Cuddy equipped with a 200-horsepower MerCruiser retailed for a modest $17,595. It was a return to the *value line* for the Cavalier name, making available quick and agile pleasure craft for a whole new generation of boating enthusiasts of moderate incomes.

Following the Cavaliers, the Limiteds began with the 179SL, followed by the 196BR, 197SL, 210SL, 210BR, 230SL, and power-packed 312SL versions. Of the new 210SL Limited, Chris Davis, Associate Editor of *Motor Boating & Sailing* would say, "Handling? Power steering and power trimming make it as user-friendly as an Iacocca sedan. And no more difficult to drive."[24] A Chris-Craft spokesman at the time said, "The 210 SL's aimed at someone with boating experience, but a first time operator could go out and have it down in less than 30 minutes. It's like a luxury car — you feel good when you drive it."[25]

The Scorpion line for '86 included the 210S and 210BR, 211VF and 212VF, 213VF, 215WA, 216WA, 217BR, 218BR, 230S, 232AC, 254WA, 266AC, 311 and 313VF models. Also returning

Photo by Elizabeth A. Reed, courtesy Murray Industries, Inc.

Bruce J. Donaldson, President of the Murray Chris-Craft boat companies, was hired in 1958 by then Chairman Harsen Smith.

was the 210BR and 210S Ski-Jack, new 210 Cuddy, and updated Sportdeck models in 170 Limited, 190 Limited and 220 Limited versions.

The Stinger line continued to dominate the increasingly high-performance image of Chris-Craft Sportboats, with the all-new 222, 260SL, 312SL, 314 and awesome 390X Stinger models. Joining the 300 Chris-Cat was a new 305 Chris-Cat outboard version of the offshore champion hull. Prices in the eclectic fleet ranged from the 17BR Cavalier equipped with a single 120-horsepower MerCruiser Sterndrive at $10,695 to the 300 Chris-Cat equipped with a pair of 400-horsepower MerCruiser II SSM Sterndrives for a cool $133,395. Heaviest boat of the fleet was not, incidentally, the Chris-Cat, but rather the 390X Stinger which weighed (hull only) 6,810 pounds, and equipped with a pair of 400-horsepower MerCruiser Sterndrives retailed for $107,995. Each engine weighed an additional 1294 pounds, bringing the 390X Stinger to nearly five tons.

Different construction techniques are used by Chris-Craft depending on the type of model being built. For regular production models, the first layer introduced, the skin coat, is applied using a special gun known as a *chopper gun*, which feeds a precise blend of fiberglas resin and small pieces of glass fiber roving into the mold. Next, a core mat is applied, in which large sheets of woven glass fibers are laid into the mold by hand, and then special di-cycle polyester resins are carefully rolled over the fabric to squeeze out any bubbles or blemishes.

Boats remain in the molds for two days, lay-up the first day and pulled on the second. The two-day mold cycle gives Chris-Craft boats better curing times than some competitors who pull their boats after a single day of curing. Hulls are run two days ahead of decks, to facilitate assembly and engine installations. In 1986, the Bradenton Sportboat facility would coordinate up to thirty different paint and color schemes to accommodate all of the models. "We are running a very aggressive quality control program," the then Director of Manufacturing for the Sportboat division commented, "which includes an in-line quality control program in the lay-up rooms, an in-line quality control program in the finishing line, and a comprehensive quality assurance program for every boat that leaves our factory."[26] An average Chris-Craft Sportboat takes about six to seven days from barrels of resin to sea trials, and in 1986, between 120 and 130 Sportboats would leave the Bradenton facility each month. The Bradenton plant includes a complete upholstery shop, carpentry and paint shops, and employed over 250 boat-building specialists.

In 1984, Chris-Craft began to use sandwich style composite construction techniques in the production of the 30-foot Chris-Cat and the 39-foot Stinger models. The process is accomplished with a hand lay-up of resin, such as Ashland Chemical AME 4000, followed by a tri-axial (woven in three directions) fiberglas mat. Sheets of light but durable foam material, like Divinycell, consisting of small two-inch squares, are laid into the fresh resin. This core material is then covered quickly with a bubble-pack plastic blanket, and the air is pulled out by a vacuum system to about minus 25 psi. The vacuum pulls the core material and the resin together firmly, ensuring a strong and uniform bond. Once the resin has cured, the inner shell is applied using more special resin and another layer of tri-axial glass fiber cloth to complete the composite structure. Hulls built in this fashion are lighter, stronger and more durable than traditional construction and can save as much as 900 pounds of weight on a hull like the 30-foot Chris-Cat. The higher speed capability of the light hulls led the United States Drug Enforce-

Right: The construction of a 1986 Chris-Cat, shows the placement of the foam composite core in the mold. Above: A vacuum hose in place to tightly pull the laminate and core together during curing.

Photos by Karine N. Rodengen

Photo by Karine N. Rodengen

Chris Smith, son of Bernard, grandson of Christopher Columbus Smith, with one of his grandfather's decoys at the Holland, Michigan plant where he works as a special engineer.

ment Administration to purchase six of the Chris-Cats and twenty-four of the 39-foot Stingers to use in smuggling interdiction programs. With pairs of MerCruiser 370-horsepower engines aboard, the boats were capable of 80 m.p.h. without modifications directly from Chris-Craft's Bradenton Sportboat factory.[27]

Twenty-six cruisers were offered in 1986, ranging from 25 to 58 feet. New additions continued to reflect an overall strengthening of the mid to high-end range of the line, with seven new models being introduced. New to the cruiser fleet were the 255 Catalina Express, 338 Commander Sunbridge Sedan, 362 Catalina Double-Cabin, 422 Commander Convertible, 426 Catalina Double-Cabin, 482 Commander Convertible and the limited production 580 Tournament Fisherman. The Tournament Fisherman, at 58½-feet with an 18-foot beam at over 68,000 pounds even with a high-tech sandwich construction, came equipped with a pair of 12V-92-MTAB 1000 Shaft Horsepower diesel engines to rush the luxurious mid-cabin design to fertile fishing grounds fast. A sampling of 1986 retail cruiser prices shows the 253 Catalina Mid-Cabin equipped with a single 230-horsepower MerCruiser Sterndrive at $33,395, the 282 Commander Sport Fish with a pair of 260-horsepower gasoline inboards at $53,895, the 450 Yacht Home with a pair of 205-horsepower 8.2 liter diesel engines at $176,595, and a new 482 Commander Convertible with a pair of

Photos by Karine N. Rodengen

Opposite left and above: Great interest in classic Chris-Craft has spawned nearly 100 boat shows nationwide, and led to the establishment of the popular Chris-Craft Antique Boat Club.

600-horsepower 8V92TI diesels at $382,995 f.o.b. Holland, Michigan.

In the Spring of 1986, G. Dale Murray began to consider methods of providing additional capital for expanding the now over $175 million operations into the over 100-foot, aluminum mega-yacht marketplace. A preliminary survey had shown that an active market was available for plush super-yachts in 95, 110 and 136-foot models, and Brazil was being considered for fabrication. He found an eager venture capitalist in the form of Trafalgar Holdings Ltd. Chairman Charles W. Knapp. Knapp had a long track record of both friendly and hostile takeovers and acquisitions, including participation in such noteworthy gambles as Carl Icahn's bid for Phillips Petroleum Co. and T. Boone Pickens, Jr.'s assault on giant Unocal Corporation. Murray had met Knapp over a year previously, and intermittant discussions ensued concerning a significant interest in Murray Chris-Craft operations. By March of 1986, Murray and Knapp issued joint communiques announcing that

agreement had been reached. The exact percentage of Murray Industries slated for acquisition was not disclosed, but Donald Reynolds, Executive Vice-President of Trafalgar Holdings revealed, "I would call it a major interest, but the size and the purchase price will not be made known."

At the time of the agreement, then Chris-Craft Vice-President of advertising and public relations Tim Clarke stated that, "Trafalgar is an investment banker. They aren't interested in running the company. They know we are a profitable company and saw our potential for growth." Clarke added, "I think it is recognized that to be a successful boat-building company, it is essential to be better capitalized and better run than the others. There are certain indications that, in time, the industry will boil down to having fewer and bigger builders." Even as attorneys on both sides were hurrying to complete

Photo by Karine N. Rodengen

George Smith, son of Bernard, built this Chris-Craft peddle-car for his son, and with the birth of his great granddaughter, seven generations of Smith's will get their start in mahogany boats.

the extensive paperwork required for the major transaction, negotiations broke down and the proposal was scuttled. On July 1, 1986, G. Dale Murray announced the termination of discussions by saying, "It would have been very satisfying to work with Mr. Knapp in making other acquisitions to enhance the further growth of Murray Industries. However, in spite of the progress made toward a closing, we have concluded that a sale of the boating operations is not in the shareholder's best interests at this time."[28]

In December of 1986, a chain of events began which was destined to reshape the character and sophistication of the entire marine industry.[29] It was during the final days of the year when the industry first learned of the bold purchases of Bayliner Marine Corporation and Ray Industries, Inc. (Sea Ray) by Brunswick Corporation, parent organization of Mercury Marine, manufacturers of Mercury and Mariner outboard engines and MerCruiser Sterndrives, the world's largest manufacturer of marine engines. Bayliner and Sea Ray, the largest and second largest boat-builders in the country, represented the most direct competition for Chris-Craft in models ranging from entry-level runabouts through mid-size cruisers. The marine industry was stunned and surprised by the quick negotiations supervised by Brunswick's chairman Jack Reichert. Over the course of three weeks, Reichert's acquisitions catapulted Brunswick into the limelight as the world's largest producer of pleasure craft. Actually, the purchase of Bayliner alone, for $425 million, put Brunswick into first place. Reichert's further acquisition of Sea Ray for $350 million sent the industry notice that a major restructuring of the marine industry was underway.

Before the dust had settled from the Brunswick maneuvers, Charles D. "Charlie" Strang, Chairman of Outboard Marine Corporation, manufacturers of Johnson and Evinrude outboard engines and the *Cobra* Sterndrive, quickly followed with a rapid series of counter-defensive acquisitions. Within a few short weeks of the Bayliner-Sea Ray purchases, Strang announced the acquisitions of Four Winns, Carl A. Lowe Industries, Stratos Boat Company, Sunbird Boat Company and Bramco to OMC's side of the ledger. The combination of purchases by Brunswick and OMC represented a full one-third of American pleasure craft production.

Among the consequences of the mergers was the re-establishment of Chris-Craft as the *world's largest independent boat-builder.* Murray Chris-Craft chairman G. Dale Murray is convinced that the new alliances will create opportunities for his companies, and is delighted with the new degree of sophistication emerging in the marine industry.

We're establishing a very favorable position, being the largest independent. We're going to benefit from this. The strengths that this consolidation brings to the industry is only going to help the rest of us *survivors.* Five years ago, when I got into the boat business, Chris-Craft was a $50 or $60 million company; there were very few of those in sales. Now a number of companies have exceeded the $100 million sales mark, and in this consolidation, they're doing a half-a-billion dollars plus in sales...We're around $200 million in sales. We have a development plan that will get us to about $250 million. Not tomorrow, but we have a strategy...There's a sophistication that's *never, ever existed* in the boat business.[30]

Fifty-three models of boats carried the Chris-Craft name in script for 1987: twelve cruisers, thirty-two sport boats and nine dramatic hybrids, *Amerosports,* that combine the best of both worlds.

The Amerosport line is Chris-Craft's crowning design achievement of the eighties. Starting with the wide-beam, rakish styling trends of European designers, Chris-Craft was able to demonstrate superior entertaining and living space aboard these fast cruisers. From every angle the Amerosport lines flow outward in smooth, graceful contours, without the pyramiding build-up of the Mediterranean cruisers. European style has attracted an American market, but European owners are accustomed to using their boats as day cruisers, and often lack the amenities that American consumers expect for week-end, week-long or vacation cruising. The Amerosports were designed with the American life-style in mind, and are considered more fitting for American pragmatism and how Americans like to use their boats.

When the designs first hit Murray Chris-Craft President Bruce Donaldson's desk in 1986, he was beaming with pride. That is, until he saw the name developed to identify the line, *Eurosport.* "Chris-Craft has been one of America's richest resources for recreational design for well over a hundred years," Donaldson asserted, "We're *America's* boat-builder, a standard bearer for *American* technology, *American* craftsmanship and *American* ingenuity. We're an *American* legend. We'll call it *Amerosport.*"[31]

The first two Amerosports appeared late in the 1986 model year, but by the 1987 dealer meetings a full eleven models graced the greatly anticipated line from 23 to 41 feet. The deep-vee, wide-beam monohedron hull form of the Amerosports was designed with highly efficient lift strakes to reduce wetted surfaces that give a smooth and efficient motion. Skylights over the forward cabin are standard on the whole line, as are an aerodynamically low-drag windshield. All the instrument panels are custom designed with special anti-glare treatment to make performance readings easy in the bright afternoon sun. The best way to sum up the new Amerosports is *high-tech, low-profile.*

Amerosports in the inaugural line-up of 1987 were the 23-foot 230 Amerosport; 25-foot 250 Amerosport; 28-foot 283 and 284 (mid-cabin double berth) Amerosports with accommodations for up to six; 32-foot 320 Amerosport mid-size cruiser with full standing head room, shower, V-drive and radar arch; 33-foot 333 Amerosport flybridge inboard powered version for fishing, cruising or entertaining; 33-foot 332 Amerosport with accommodations for six, inboard engines and large aft entertainment deck; 33-foot 336 Amerosport with V-drive engines and double berth aft; and top of the line 41-foot 412 Amerosport with over six feet of headroom, built-in swim platform, wetbar, cockpit dinette, double berth forward and twin-screw V-drive power.

Catalinas for 1987 featured six hull sizes, from 29 to 48 feet, and offering six distinctive floor plans. The Catalinas in the class of '87 included the 29-foot 292 Catalina Sunbridge Sedan, designed to be an all-around family boat with accommodations for six, a large sport fishing style cockpit and fully instrumented flybridge; the 35-foot 350 Catalina Double Cabin cruiser with master stateroom aft and large sun deck; 36-foot 362 Catalina Double Cabin which featured entertainment areas in the amidships salon, command bridge or aft deck; 38-foot Catalina Double Cabin with queen size master aft stateroom and self contained guest stateroom; 42-foot 426 Catalina Double Cabin dubbed "America's favorite all 'round luxury cruiser" by Chris-Craft, with a master stateroom aft which includes a master bath with tub and shower; and queen of the Catalina fleet 48-foot 480 Catalina Double Cabin with enough cockpit area to qualify as a luxury sport fisherman, but with living room-spaced salon, step-down galley and luxury appointments.

Three stately Commanders were available in 1987, each capable of competing with the finest luxury sport fisherman for power, cockpit design and plush accommodations. Included were the 38-foot 382 Commander Sport Sedan, featuring a double bed in the forward stateroom, and 350 gallon fuel tanks for weekend offshore fishing or cruising; 42-foot 422 Commander Convertible with teak accented interior, upper and lower berths in a guest stateroom that converts to a sofa-lounge, along with double size berth in the master stateroom; and flagship of the Commander fleet, the nearly 49-foot 482 Commander Convertible which featured the fine teak accoutrements of a luxury yacht, and the wide-open sporting layout of the finest tournament fisherman.

Three elegant Constellation Motor Yachts were presented for 1987, the 410, 460 and 500 Constellation Motor Yacht. Each presented luxurious aft stateroom configurations with spacious command bridges ample enough for group entertainment, swim platforms and wide-open salon floorplans. The Constellations, among the most recognized names in yachting, continued to reaffirm Chris-Craft's major stake in cruising elegance for a refined marketplace.

Thirty-two sportboats made waves for 1987, beginning with the four models of Cavalier. As Chris-Craft suggested, "Your first boat should be a Chris-Craft Cavalier."[32] Cavaliers included the 17BR and 19BR, both with the open bow-rider design, and cuddy cabin models in 19 Cuddy Cavalier and 21 Cuddy Cavalier versions. The 17 and 19-foot models were fully flotation-foamed for extra safety. The four Sea Hawk fishing boats utilized two basic hulls, in either center console outboard (213 and 216 Sea Hawk) or cuddy cabin sterndrive versions (215 and 254 Sea Hawk). All featured built-in tackle centers, bow pulpits, windshield vents, aerated bait-wells, built-in rod holders and dry, modified deep V hulls.

Scorpions for 1987 were available in five models using three hull designs. Sterndrive models included the 210S, 210BR and 230S Scorpions, while the Jean Claude Simon designed 311 and 313 Scorpions were designed for a pair of V-6 outboards. The 311 included an outboard well, while the 313 was designed for use with an outboard transom bracket system. Eight models of Chris-Craft Limiteds were built in four hull sizes for 1987, and all featured molded-in swim plat-

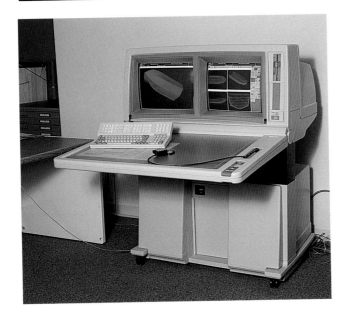

Left: The new million dollar computer aided design and engineering system is part of Chris-Craft's commitment to expanding boating design horizons into the 21st century.

Photo by Elizabeth A. Reed, courtesy Murray Industries, Inc.

Above: The galley of the 1989 501 *Constellation* Motor Yacht is large enough for the most ambitious social occasions. New materials and concepts are being introduced into yacht interior designs that were not possible only a few years ago.

Illustration courtesy Murray Industries, Inc.

Comfort, utility and performance are hallmarks of the Chris-Craft advanced design team. Above: A cross-section of a 1989 287 *Limited* sportboat. Right: The profile and layout of the 1989 334 *Stinger*.

Illustration courtesy Murray Industries, Inc.

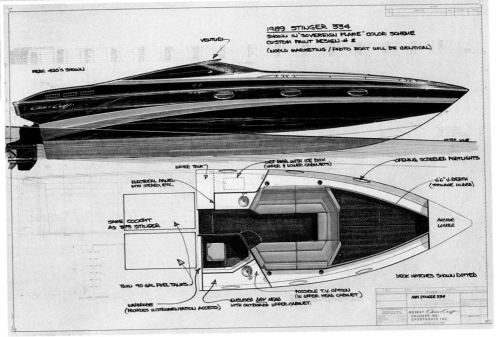

forms, canvas soft tops, lift-out stowage lockers and three-spoke padded steering wheels. Included were the 178BR, 196BR, 197CD S, 210, 210BR, 210BR Ski-Jack, 210CD Ski-Jack and 230 Limited models.

Highest performance for 1987 belonged to the six Stinger models with five different, highly refined hull designs. The newest Stingers, the 202 and 222 share the wide-beam, aircraft style cockpit with center-line helm stations, large sundeck and molded-in swim platform. The 222 has the additional feature of forward or aft facing reversible sunlounge seats that can disappear when mounted flush with the upholstered engine hatch cover. The 260 Stinger, with twin I/O's featured race-inspired instrumentation and a high-tech control center along with molded-in swim platform. In the 31-foot length, a choice was available between I/O power with the 312 Stinger and outboard power with the 314 Stinger. Top of the Stinger line was the all-new 415 Stinger, also designed by Jean Claude Simon, replacing the 390X in the line-up. With a cockpit and performance reminiscent of a tactical jet fighter, the twin 420 MerCruiser powered 415 also offered a plush cabin interior which included a full galley and convertible U-shaped style interior. Returning with only minor style and accessories changes was the 300 Chris-Cat in I/O configuration and the 305 Chris-Cat designed for a pair of the largest V-8 outboards.

In the Spring of 1987, only ten months follownng the collapse of negotiations with Trafalgar's Chairman Charles Knapp, Murray was able to consummate the sale of a significant interest in Murray Industries to Dr. Ghaith R. Pharaon, a billionaire Saudi Arabian financier. Pharaon was best known in the United States for having flirted on the fringes of American politics when he provided much needed capital to a one-time member of the Carter administration. As the *New York Times* reported,

> Mr. Pharaon, whose investments dot the globe, is best known in the United States for an investment made nine years ago. [in 1978] He bailed out the failing National Bank of Georgia, headed by a former aide of President Carter, Bert Lance. Mr. Pharaon, 46 years old, bought most of the stock and supplied the institution some much needed capital.[33]

Following the enormous alignment of boatbuilding and marine engine manufacturers in late 1986 and early 1987, Murray knew that keen success in future competition could well depend on the ability to commit significant capital to expansion, modernization and high-tech strategies.

> We can't compete financially with the Brunswick's or the OMC's, so I sold a piece of my company to someone who shares my growth ideas, so we can take advantage if an opportunity comes to us. If it's an expansion plan that we have, then we can fund it, along with my own financial input. Dr. Ghaith Pharaon, a multi-billionaire...is a very successful businessman. He's an engineer, Graduate School of Mining in Colorado, Ph.D. from Harvard. Of all of his investments, this may be one he enjoys the most. Every moment he has to get away, he goes to his boat. He loves the water. My family and I spent New Years on his 180-foot yacht in the Indian Ocean, for about two weeks. [It was aboard Pharaon's yacht that agreement was reached on the investment.] And he had Chris-Craft tenders, which he had bought before he and I had met, and I, of course, was very pleased to see that. He uses his boats in the toughest conditions. He's a very knowledgeable boat man, having built several of them. We've even exchanged some ideas in accessories, the potential of owning companies in other countries, so he'll bring a lot to the partnership, more than just strong, *very strong* financial ability.
>
> His father was a close advisor to the King of Saudi Arabia, and his grandfather helped finance the wars that brought the kingdom together. He enjoys a close relationship with the kingdom, and he travels with a diplomatic passport. He has...a lot of investments in the U.S., and I'm very proud to have him as a partner. We had many choices.[34]

To introduce the 1988 line, Chris-Craft reminded boating enthusiasts that, "Since... Christopher Columbus Smith launched the world's first power boat, Chris-Crafts have pulled more skiers, caught more fish, won more offshore races and started more families off in boating than any other manufacturer."[35] During 1988, Chris-Craft built fifty models of boats at their five manufacturing facilities located at Bradenton, Florida; Holland, Michigan; Swansboro, North Carolina; Goshen, Indiana and Bellingham, Washington.

The 1988 Sport Fisherman fleet provided a boat for every level of fishing sophistication, ranging from 22 to 58 feet. The fleet starts off with four Sea Hawks, incorporating two hulls, each with the extra-wide bow flare for dry running and fishing. Each have built-in tackle centers, fish boxes, built-in cutting boards, ample rod storage and self-draining cockpits. The 22'9" center-console 213 Sea Hawk outboard was designed as an all-purpose family recreation boat, while the 215 Sea Hawk, in either I/O or outboard transom bracket versions, offered modest overnight abilities and weather-free storage. The 216 Sea Hawk, using the same 22'9" hull, with an outboard well, could be equipped with up to 230-horsepower on the transom. Largest of the group, the 25-foot 254 Sea Hawk sported weekender capabilities, padded cockpit sides, foam flotation, galley and vee-berths. The Commander line of premium Sport Fisherman were designed for every level of performance and mission from 31 to 58 feet. The 315 Commander Sport Sedan, equipped with a pair of T-270 Crusader engines, offered a large command bridge, Venturi windshield and spacious cockpit. The 392 Commander Sport Sedan featured an owner's stateroom forward, full head with shower, elegant salon, large cockpit with big game fish transom door, and a pair of T-350 Crusader engines. The 422 Commander Convertible was a luxury tournament winner with warm teak interiors, three state-rooms for six guests, convertible sofa in the main salon, an 8 KW generator for unlimited operations, and equipped with a pair of G.M. T-6-71TI diesel engines. The 482 Commander Convertible was designed for extended cruising and fishing, and was complete with washer/dryer, queen sized self-contained master stateroom, and additional head with shower for the guest stateroom and convertible salon. Top of the Commander line, and the largest boat in the entire Chris-Craft fleet for 1988 was the 580 Commander. This, the ultimate tournament fishing machine, contained three air-conditioned staterooms, a living room-sized salon, and came equipped with a pair of powerful T-DDA-12V-92 diesel engines to bring even the most remote fishing challenge within range.

With a strong market-driven development organization, each year since 1981 Chris-Craft has been able to introduce more *new* models of Sportboats than nearly any other era in the boat-builder's history. In 1988, Chris-Craft presented a new line of twenty-seven Sportboats, sixteen of which were completely new models. A welcome change in model designations was

Photo by Karine N. Rodengen

Chris-Craft boats have been in continuous production longer than any other pleasure craft manufacturer in the world. Here, sportboats are nearly completed at the Bradenton, Florida sportboat factory, and are being prepared for shipping.

made for '88, with less abbreviations to consider. Returning to the fleet were the ever-popular three models of Sportdecks, the 170, 190 and 220 Sportdecks. New to the Cavalier fleet were the 17-foot Cavalier Bow Rider Outboard and the 17-foot Cavalier Fish Outboard models. A clean sweep was made of Scorpion models for the year, with six completely new models. Available were the 19 and 21-foot Scorpion Cuddy Cabin, 21-foot Scorpion Bow Rider and Closed Deck models, 21-foot Scorpion Bow Rider Ski-Jack and 26-foot Scorpion closed Deck models. Three new Limited were produced in 1988, including the 205 Limited Bow Rider, 225 Limited Closed deck and 245 Limited Closed Deck versions. Returning to the Stinger line-up were the 202 and 260 Stingers, while new models were offered in 311, 312, 313 and 375 Stinger models. Even though the 415 Stinger would remain as the largest and most luxurious offshore missile in the '88 fleet, the 375 Stinger was receiving rave reviews from consumers and from publications like *Powerboat* magazine.

> The 375 is unlike any sport boat we've ever seen. The company has redefined the meaning of European styling and attention to detail. The contour of the 375 is sleek, sassy and comfortable...The boat met with such approval the entire year's production was sold out in less than a week...
>
> Chris-Craft achieved its near 60 m.p.h. goal without sacrificing any controllability. The hull is maneuverable, solid and responsive...
>
> "Chris-Craft should be exceptionally proud of what it has accomplished with the 375 Stinger. The hull performs beautifully with standard power. The design is seaworthy yet nimble, solid yet light on the water." [Bob Nordskog, Publisher]
>
> "What a boat. The 375 will certainly vie for Outstanding Interior Styling honors." [Dick DeBartolo, Eastern Editor]
>
> "If the 375 is a bellwether of what you can expect from Chris-Craft in the years to come, watch out Wellcraft and Thunderbird. Company spokesmen say Chris-Craft is definitely in the high-performance sport boat business up to its gunnels and boats like the 375 ensure it will be around for many years to come." [Randy Scott, Editor][36]

The Amerosports continued to bridge the gap between sportboat and cruisers during 1988, with eight of the stylish, accommodating cruisers. The full line included the 230, 250, new 262, 284, 320 and new 320 Sedan, all-new 370 and returning flagship of the elegant fleet, the 412 Amerosport. Amerosport was honored in January of 1988, as the 320 Amerosport was named to *Boating* magazine's "Ten Best Boats" list from their extensive testing program conducted during the previous year.

> Bright, livable interior spaces with a careful layout make this one a fine choice for a family cruiser. V-drive Crusader power plants provide inboard machinery yet still allow enough hull space to provide a roomy mid-cabin layout.
>
> A well-laid-out bridge provides the helmsman with a good view, with room for company. The engines are monitored with top-notch accessories such as VDO gauges and Morse controls and steering. Deck hardware is of similar high quality and is complemented by minimal teak; easy to own.
>
> A return to basic cabin-cruiser values by those who know them best.[37]

Twelve traditional and luxury cruisers completed the 1988 Chris-Craft fleet, with four completely new models being offered. The Catalina fleet, still the *American dream incarnate*, delivered five versions of family cruising pleasure, including the venerable 292 Catalina Sun Bridge Sedan, the all new 372 Catalina Double Cabin, 381 Catalina Double Cabin, 426 Catalina Double Cabin, and king-size 480 Catalina Cockpit Double Cabin.

The Commander line continued to evolve in 1988, with two new models out of four, offering a broad range of choice between 31 and 49 feet. New Commanders included the 315 Commander Sport Sedan, containing full size V-berths, galley and convertible dinette, along with the new 392 Commander Sport Sedan which featured a well-appointed owner's stateroom forward, large cockpit with transom door, convertible dinette and generous teak accents throughout. Returning to the popular Commander line were the luxuriously appointed 422 Commander Convertible and 482 Commander Convertible models. The highly respected, veteran of Chris-Craft's fishing fleet, the 580 Tournament Fisherman lost its Commander designation for 1988, truly putting the 58'5", 68,000-pound cruising Sport Fisherman in a class by itself.

A trio of timeless and ageless Constellation Motor Yachts presided over the top of the '88 Chris-Craft premium cruiser fleet. Joining the returning 460 and 500 Constellations was the all new 501 Constellation Motor Yacht. The very spaciously designed 501 included a 225-foot main salon, a spiraling staircase leading to the aft master stateroom, self-contained midships guest stateroom, self-contained forward guest stateroom, and huge L-shaped lounge aft of the towering command bridge. The Constellation Motor Yachts are pure elegance combined with a high degree of practical livability that are still the signature of the flagship fleet nearly a half century following its first standard-setting introduction.

In November of 1987, Murray Chris-Craft made a renewed and significant commitment to the future of boat-building, with the dedication of a new Research and Development complex known as Murray Chris-Craft Boat Development, Inc. The group of renovated buildings located in Palmetto, Florida, is home to advanced thinking for the five Murray Chris-Craft boat companies. Within their very private surroundings, the group, led by Vice-President of Engineering Don Thornburg and William J. "Bill" Meyers, Director of Research and Development, perform a broad range of functions with an impressively large staff of high-tech specialists. Among their responsibilities are the testing of new materials to determine the manufacturing suitability, and the examination of existing methodology and consultation with the manufacturing facilities to optimize quality control.

Of equal importance is the Research and Development organization's inquiries into advanced composite structure. Investigations into the suitability of automotive and aerospace composite derivatives continues in an effort, as Bill Meyers says, "To find the safest and most durable products that will keep Chris-Craft as the front-runner in performance and value."[38]

Among the most formidable weapons in Chris-Craft's renewed assault on the technological boundaries of boat-building is a new million dollar Computer Aided Design (CAD) and Computer Aided Engineering (CAE) computer system. Also established in late 1987 as part of the Research and Development organization, the Inter Graph three-dimensional design system is allowing Chris-Craft Naval Architects to investigate the next generation of power boat designs, even into the twenty-first century. Chris-Craft specialists, like Naval Architect Mark Paulhus, Manager of Computer Aided Design Engineering, first feed a complete, hydrodynamically perfect three-dimensional hull image into the system. From the styling department, headed by second generation Chris-Craft executive Craig R. Muir, literally comes the look of the future, a style, design and visual shape that targets a particular boating application and market.[39]

Within the intricate software of the CAD system are routines for the placement of stringers, bulkheads and other structural components which are then tested against hydrostatic formulas and mathematical models for strength and overall structural integrity. Once major structures are modeled within the system, smaller and smaller components are designed, down to the level of nuts and bolts, each of which will fit precisely within the completed program. The goal is to eventually have every common vendor-supplied component, like deck cleats for example, available within a digital library to down-load into the system and place it into a new design within a few moments of operator time.[40]

A small, 18-foot center console fishing boat requires about two months of an operator's time, while a new design of a 60-foot yacht would require twelve to fourteen months of a single operator's time. Among the many benefits of this design and engineering strategy is that information can be shared among several work stations, so that while major components are being finalized, another group of specialists can be working on sub-components to dramatically reduce the time required for the design cycle.

Once the design is finalized, the computer can plot the drawing of full-scale loft drawings which are required for the construction of the plug, used to make the mold, which will ultimately be used to produce the boat in economically attractive quantities. Today, these drawings are converted into plugs, molds, prototypes, test boats, assembly specifications and fixtures which are then delivered to Murray Chris-Craft plants. However, in the not-too-distant future, the system may be able to download its completed program onto digital tape, send it to a special laboratory equipped with six-axis milling equipment, and within a few days receive the entire plug constructed from a derivative of dense foam, ready for finishing. Derivatives of these same digital tapes will be used within the factory environment to instruct computer driven numerical control machine tools to accurately finish components which have already been molded. These techniques are already being used within the highly competitive automobile industry. As marine industry technology continues to mature, it will further adopt the techniques which have at tremendous expense been developed by other industries, including aerospace research, to develop the next generations of boating excitement.

The Eighties were for Chris-Craft a period of prodigious growth, exceeding the growth rate of *any previous era* in Chris-Craft history, even the emergency build-up for America's national defense. When Chris-Craft sales rose from less than $50,000 in 1921 to over $3 million in 1929, there wasn't the competition that there is today. As Bill "The Boss" MacKerer reminded us in 1947, "Before the war we could count our competitors on the fingers of one or two hands..." All are gone. In the early summer of 1988 as this book goes to press, there are over 1,800 boatbuilders in the United States alone. Many are small, nearly garage-sized operations that produce only a few boats a year, but others, like Brunswick's Sea Ray and Bayliner, or Outboard Marine Corporation's Four Winns, Stratos, Sunbird and Bramco boat companies, together represent over a billion dollars in annual competition alone. For Chris-Craft to have tenaciously fought back from being identified as a discontinued operation on the books in 1981 to sales of nearly $200 million dollars by 1988, emerging *once again* as the world's largest independent pleasure craft builder is against all odds. And from Chris-Craft's new position of strength, it is taking advantage of every technological, marketing and styling means available to continue the growth, extend the product line, expand boating horizons and all the while maintaining the deep traditions and stirring legacy that Christopher Columbus Smith established in the nineteenth century.

Chris-Craft is more than a boat-building company; it is a living, breathing force of American culture and tradition, whose history reflects the very rise and fall of national expectation and purpose. Chris-Craft gave Americans the freedom to explore the rivers and lakes, inlets and coves, great bays and distant shores of countless million dreams. Behind her wheel we have broken the glassy skin of a thousand moonlit nights, pulled an unbroken line of skiers across endless summer days, toasted untold memories of youth, and rocked asleep in her arms through the long cool evenings of life. It is still the American dream.

There will always be a Chris-Craft.

APPENDIX A

The Mariners' Museum

LOCATED NEAR THE JAMES RIVER just outside of Newport News, Virginia, the Mariners' Museum is considered among the great nautical and historical marine institutions in the world. As a non-profit, educational institution, the Mariners' Museum has benefited from both the bequeaths of prominent citizens and the enthusiastic support of an ever-growing national interest in maritime history. The extensive museum collections span three thousand years of international watercraft.

The Mariners' Museum is now home to the extensive Chris-Craft Collection, donated by Chris-Craft Industries, Inc. in the spring of 1987. The collection contains the comprehensive archives of the oldes pleasure boat manufacturer, with records, photos, plans and artifacts that made the production of *The Legend of Chris-Craft* possible. The archives contain over 20,000 cataloged photographs, mostly black and white prints, financial records, boat-building plans, and the highly coveted *hull cards* from individual boat production. Though the records were restricted by the donor to information prior to 1960, it is unquestionably the finest individual historical record in the marine industry, and the Mariners' Museum has increased the value of the collection manyfold through painstaking identification, cataloging, fumigating, restoration and research accessibility.

The Museum has a collection of nearly 90,000 Chris-Craft hull cards, detailing the specifications of individual boats in great detail. Each card lists the model number, engine and accessories installed, upholstery type and color, date of manufacture, hull number, BSO (By Special Order) number, dealer destination, and lists the complete inventory of standard items included with the boat at the time it left one of the Chris-Craft factories. To the antique boating enthsiast and marine historian alike, these records are priceless. The Mariners' Museum has patiently re-photographed each card on microfiche, and has made images of them available at a nominal fee to the worldwide community of Chris-Craft boat owners, restorers and enthusiasts. Also included in the Chris-Craft Collection are over 800 plans for Chris-Craft boats, and nearly two thousand catalogs, brochures and other corporate reference materials dating from the early 1920's.

The hull cards and other archives are contained within the Museum's impressive Research Library, which contains over 200,000 marine historical photos of all varieties, and nearly 70,000 volumes on marine history, all available at no charge to researchers who visit the facility. Also available within the research facility is the Rodengen Reference Library, over 25,000 documents representing the several years of cataloged research and the extensive interviews undertaken for the production of *The Legend of Chris-Craft*. By selecting the three-ring binder of the year in question, the researcher is able to survey the articles which were written during the year, copies of the catalogs, brochures, ads, the oral histories and interviews of individuals who experienced the events in question, and comprehensive financial records for the period. Nearly half of the documents originated from the Mariners' own Chris-Craft Collection, so researchers can easily move beyond the scope of the binders with the assistance of the Museum's professional Research Library staff.

On display at the Museum are two of the most coveted antique Chris-Craft, the 1923 26-foot double-cockpit runabout *Miss Belle Isle*, and the 1929 38-foot *Commuting Cruiser*, Chris-Craft's *first cruiser*. Both boats, beautifully restored, can be seen in the Museum's extensive Small Craft Collection. The *Miss Belle Isle*, which contains the original Curtiss OX-5 Jay W. Smith converted aircraft engine, was located by Chris-Craft Industries, Inc., after an intense national search for the *oldest living Chris-Craft* in 1970, and was donated by them to the Mariners' Museum with the balance of the Chris-Craft Collection.

The Mariners' Museum provides a great service to the marine historical community by supporting the continued preservation and accessibility of the Chris-Craft Collection. Whenever the question is raised about the destination of marine antiquities, please remember that with the professional assistance of organizations such as the Mariners' Museum, our treasured marine heritage can be safely preserved and enjoyed by all. Questions concerning the Chris-Craft Collection, artifact or collection bequeaths, should be addressed to:

The Mariners' Museum

Museum Drive
Newport News, Virginia 23606

(804) 595-0368

FOREWORD
ppg VII and VIII

1. The Danish dictionary entry for Chris-Craft means: Pleasure Craft, or Runabout.
2. A 49-million-mile voyage based on 100,000 Chris-Crafts traveling only 490 miles each since delivery to their first owners.
3. *Algonac Courier*, September 9-10, 1939 identified Smith as having worked his way up through the ranks of the White Star Line of Great Lakes steamships to achieve the rank of Captain, and Master of the City of Mackinac.
4. Murray Chris-Craft Sportboats, Inc., Murray Chris-Craft Cruisers, Inc., Murray Chris-Craft Sportdecks, Inc., Murray Chris-Craft Boat Manufacturing Companies and Murray Industries, Inc.
5. Jeffrey L. Rodengen, Ph.D., "Purveyors of the American Dream", *Southern Star* magazine, June, 1986.
6. Bruce Donaldson, President of the Murray Chris-Craft Boat Manufacturing Companies, in a letter to the author of June 15, 1987.

CHAPTER I.
Origins
ppg 1-9

1. J.H. Beers, *History of The Great Lakes: Illustrated*, J.H. Beers and Company, Chicago, Illinois, 1899, Vol. I. Reference for this source was provided by Betty Droulard, Historian, City of Algonac, Michigan.
2. Interview of Marian Dawson, granddaughter of Christopher Columbus Smith, and family historian, in Holland, Michigan, August 18,1986. Mrs. Dawson has one of the original Smith books, and much of the information about the Smith family heritage is available due to the gracious sharing of her many years of genealogical research, and of information contained in the booklet of Chris Smith.
3. Christopher Columbus Smith family book.
4. Ibid.
5. Edmund R. Childs, "Chris Smith — Market Hunter and Decoy Maker," *North American Decoys, Wildfowl Carvers and Collectors News*, Spring Issue, 1970.
6. A special mention of gratitude to Marian Dawson, granddaughter of Christopher Columbus Smith, who graciously shared her many years of painstaking genealogical research with the author.
7. Dawson, op. cit.
8. Childs, op. cit.
9. Childs, op. cit.
10. Childs, op. cit.
11. Interview of Christopher James Smith, grandson and namesake of Christopher Columbus Smith, Holland, Michigan, August 18, 1986.
12. Ibid.
13. Childs, op. cit.
14. Dawson, op. cit.
15. Childs, op. cit.
16. Childs, op. cit.
17. Interview of Luke Stephenson, Algonac, Michigan, October 11, 1987.
18. Ibid.
19. C. J. Smith, op. cit., Dawson, op. cit., and Stephenson, op. cit.
20. C. J. Smith, op. cit.
21. C. J. Smith, op. cit.
22. "Chris Smith, Master Boat Builder," *Motor Boating*, November, 1927.
23. *Port Huron Times Herald*, April 27, 1934, on the occasion of the Smiths' 50th wedding anniversary (actually celebrated on April 13), an article alludes to Anna Rattray's pioneering heritage.
24. Dawson, op. cit.
25. "Where the Thermometer Doesn't Count," re-typed from the original article in the *Algonic Courier*, 1905, probably July, but unknown. Courtesy Betty Droulard, Historian, City of Algonac. Italics not contained in the original.
26. *Motor Boating*, March, 1923, and as reproduced by Michael M. Dixon, *Life at the Flats*, Mervue Publications, 1985, Vol. I.
27. "Concerning Our People, Business and Progress in the Country and Town," *Algonac Courier, Bits of Local Information* Sec., 1903, dealing with social issues and neighborhood gossip. The issue states that "Postmaster C.C. Smith has been appointed for another four years, his nomination being confirmed at Washington on Monday."
28. *Algonac Courier*, May 27, 1904.
29. Article dated 1901 from scrapbook, most likely from the *Algonac Courier*. Courtesy Betty Droulard, Historian, City of Algonac, Michigan.
30. Michael M. Dixon, "An American Venice," *The Flats Golden Era*, Mervue Publications, Vol. II, referring to an undated advertisement for the Hotel Paquette.
31. C. J. Smith, op. cit., Dawson, op. cit., and Jeffrey L. Rodengen, Ph.D., "Purveyors of the American Dream," *Southern Star* magazine, June, 1986.

32. Donald B. Sharp, "The Marine Engine," *Rudder*, month unknown, 1896, as quoted in *Nautical Quarterly*, Nautical Quarterly Company, Essex, Connecticut, Spring, 1983, No. 21.
33. Benjamin F. Bailey, untitled article, *Motor Boating*, June, 1947, p. 120.
34. Robert Hall, "Where the Industry Began," *Motor Boating*, January 1924, p. 46.
35. Bob Solt, article, *Port Huron Times-Herald*, May 5, 1962.
36. Interviews of Pete Henkel, Harsens Island, Michigan, July 4 and 8, 1987.
37. *Motor Boating*, December, 1927.
38. Bailey, loc. cit.
39. *Motor Boating*, December, 1927.
40. Bailey, op. cit.
41. Beverly Rae Kimes, "The Centennial History of Daimler, Mercedes and Benz," *The Star and the Laurel*, an original publication of Mercedes-Benz of North America, Inc., 1986.
42. *TIME*, May 18, 1959. The cover of this issue also carried the picture of Harsen Smith, son of Jay Smith, and then President of Chris-Craft Corporation.
43. During the World's Columbian Exposition held in Chicago, Illinois in the fall of 1893, a young Gottlieb Daimler, destined to join forces with Carl Benz in a future Mercedes-Benz, displayed his gasoline engines in the automotive section of the grand exhibit under the name Daimler Motor Company. Daimler had been building gasoline-powered launches since 1888 in Europe, and brought one of his creations to the Exposition. "On September 3, in a storm, a sailboat capsized on Lake Michigan, tossing its six occupants into the water. The husky lifesaving crew of the USS Illinois rowed furiously to save them and the official launch of the Exposition steamed out as well — but Gottlieb Daimler got to them first with his motorboat. The incident provided the Daimler Motor Company with its best press in Chicago." Quoted from *The Star And The Laurel*, op. cit.
44. Stephenson, op. cit.
45. Stephenson, op. cit.
46. Smith would, in 1938, at 77, a year before his death, suggest in a *New York Times* interview, that his first gasoline boat was powered by a 12-horsepower engine which achieved 16 miles per hour. The preponderance of evidence, however, supports the more modest Sintz application, and a slower initial effort. Source for this reference is unknown, but reported by Joseph Gribbins in "Chris-Craft: That Great American Boat," *Nautical Quarterly*, Nautical Quarterly Company, Essex, Connecticut, 1979, No. 7.
47. *Motor Boating*, December, 1927.

CHAPTER II.
Speed Merchants
ppg 11-15

1. *Algonac Courier*, 1899.
2. Ibid.
3. Ibid.
4. Joseph Gribbons, "Chris-Craft: That Great American Boat," *Nautical Quarterly*, Nautical Quarterly Company, Essex, Connecticut, 1979, No. 7.
5. *Algonac Courier*, undated obituary, probably 1928. It mentions that "Henry M. Smith was the senior partner of the company," and that after retirement, he devoted "the rest of his life to the study of birds, animals and other wildlife."
6. The earliest known advertisement for C.C. Smith, Boat Builder, appears in a 1904 edition of the *Algonac Courier*. The ad states, "If you contemplate buying or having a boat built, call on C.C. Smith, the only practical Boat Builder in Algonac." As evidence that Chris is still quite active in the marketing of wild game, the ad contains an interesting footnote: "The highest market price paid for Fish and Game in Season."
7. An early advertisement for C.C. Smith & Co. was within a passenger brochure for the White Star Line, steamers Tashmoo, Greyhound, City of Toledo, Owana and Wauketa, offering the 1909 summer time table and schedule between Toledo and Detroit, and between Detroit and Port Huron. The ad also states that C.C. Smith & Co. are "builders of Gasoline, Sail and Row Boats, Canoes and Duck Boats," and offering "Launches and Boats of all kinds for Hire," and "Ferry Service to Camp Algonac, Grande Pointe and Tashmoo Park." Discovery of this obscure reference was made by courtesy of Pete and Jean Jenkel of Harsens Island, Michigan.
8. The August 7, 1910 edition of the *News Tribune* referred to Chris Smith's Injun Ferry running between Algonac and Walpole Island. Reference courtesy of Betty Droulard, Historian, City of Algonac, Michigan.
9. Interview of Marian Dawson, granddaughter of Christopher Columbus Smith, and family historian, in Holland, Michigan, August 18, 1986.

10. J. Lee Barrett, *Speed Boat Kings: 25 Years of International Speedboating*, Arnold-Powers, Inc., Detroit, Michigan, 1939. A new printing of this intriguing book was recently undertaken by the Historical Society of Michigan, Ann Arbor. To order the volume, send $17 (includes shipping) to Historical Society of Michigan, 2117 Washtenaw Avenue, Ann Arbor, Michigan 48104.
11. "Where The Thermometer Doesn't Count," re-typed in the *Algonac Courier*, 1905, probably July, but unknown. Courtesy Betty Droulard, Historian, City of Algonac, Michigan.
12. It was more than likely the Van Blerck, as Smith had direct access to Van Blerck through J.W. Gilbert. Also, in *Speed Boat Kings*, J. Lee Barrett contends that following Smith's initial gasoline-powered rowboat, "Smith then bought a few of the early Van Blerck engines, built hulls for them and sold them to fishermen," which further supports the Van Blerck installation.
13. "Chris Smith, Master Boat Builder," *Motor Boating*, December, 1927.
14. Barrett, op. cit., recorded 23 miles-per-hour, while Gribbons, op. cit., supports the faster 26-mile-per-hour figure.
15. Jim Ticknor, "In Old Marine," undated, no doubt part of a Marine City publication. The obscure article is from the private collection of, and courtesy of, Carl Lisee, son of Joseph Napoleon Lisee.
16. William A. Moffett, "Algonac Jumps Into Prominence," chapter of a book of unknown origin.
17. Ibid.

CHAPTER III.
Murder Over Hull Timbers
ppg 17-20

1. The pioneering research for this unusual episode in the life of Chris Smith was undertaken and graciously shared by Betty Droulard, Historian, City of Algonac, Michigan.
2. *Algonac Courier*, Friday, January 20, 1905.
3. Judge Law, as described in the *Port Huron Daily Times*, March 14, 1905.
4. Interview of Luke Stephenson in Algonac, Michigan, October 11, 1987.
5. *Algonac Courier*, loc. cit.
6. Ibid.
7. Interview of Marian Dawson, granddaughter of Christopher Columbus Smith and Smith family historian in Holland, Michigan, August 18, 1986.
8. *Port Huron Daily Times*, January 19, 1905, and *Port Huron Daily Herald*, January 19, 1905.
9. Ibid.
10. *Port Huron Daily Times*, loc. cit.
11. *Algonac Courier*, loc. cit.
12. The Flats, or more correctly, The St. Clair Flats, is a large area of alternately arable and marsh lands, including many navigable channels and islands, bordering the Village of Algonac, and extending as far as 15 miles downstream of the St. Clair River.
13. *Algonac Courier*, loc. cit.
14. Ibid.
15. *Algonac Courier*, January 19, 1905 and *Port Huron Daily Times*, January 19, 1905.
16. *Algonac Courier*, loc. cit.
17. *Port Huron Daily Times* and *Port Huron Daily Herald*, loc. cit.
18. *Algonac Courier*, loc. cit.
19. *Port Huron Daily Times*, loc. cit.
20. *Port Huron Daily Herald*, loc. cit.
21. The Rapid Car was a public electric railway system which went from Detroit through Algonac to Port Huron. It was abandoned in 1930 when purchased by the Algonac Transit Company, actually Chris-Craft, and the section between Algonac and Marine City became a private diesel engine railroad system for Chris-Craft. See The Chris-Craft Railroad elsewhere in this book.
22. *Port Huron Daily Times*, loc. cit.

CHAPTER IV.
The Smith-Ryan Boat Co.
ppg 21-31

1. Joseph Gribbins, "Chris-Craft: That Great American Boat," *Nautical Quarterly*, Nautical Quarterly Company, Pratt Street, Essex, Connecticut, 1979, No. 7.
2. The first was the Baldy Ryan venture capital; the second would be the purchase of the C.C. Smith Boat & Engine Co. by Gar Wood in 1915; the third would be the $350,000 forfeited purchase option from the House of Morgan during the depths of the Depression; and the final time would be the total sale of the Smith collective interests to NAFI Corporation in 1960.
3. Arthur T. Hugg, *Algonac Courier*, August 6, 1910.
4. Ibid.

5. From the only known brochure produced by the Smith-Ryan Boat Co., most likely in late 1911.
6. Ibid.
7. *TIME* magazine, May 18, 1959.
8. It is generally agreed that successful multiple-step hydroplaning hulls had been produced and demonstrated before Fauber patented the hydroplane. His was, however, the first successful and recognized patent on the subject.
9. J. Lee Barrett, *Speed Boat Kings*, Arnold-Powers, Inc., Detroit, Michigan, 1939.
10. Barrett, op. cit.
11. Barrett, op. cit.
12. *Motor Boat*, October, 1911. The article entitled "Buffalo Races" by C.G. Davis was reproduced in its entirety in the Smith-Ryan Boat Co. brochure.
13. Davis, op. cit.
14. Davis, op. cit.
15. Davis, op. cit.
16. Davis, op. cit.
17. Davis, op. cit.
18. *Power Boating*, October 1911. This article, entitled "Honors Divided at Buffalo" was also reproduced in its entirety within the Smith-Ryan Boat Co. brochure.
19. H. Cole Estep, "St. Louis Springs A Surprise," *Power Boating*, November, 1911.
20. Smith-Ryan brochure, op. cit.
21. *Power Boating*, November, 1911.
22. It was also noted in the December, 1927 issue of *Motor Boating* that the *Queen Reliance* was displayed at the Chicago Boat Show and with the same unique pricing system. It gives further evidence that the financial resources of Ryan were considerable, and that he went to great lengths to broadcast the uniqueness of Smith-Ryan talents and products.
23. Undated interview of J. Stuart Blackton by Harry Leduc, *Detroit News*, Detroit, Michigan. Content suggests the possibility of mid-1939 for a date. (Reprinted with permission of *The Detroit News*, a Gannett newspaper, copyright c. 1939.)
24. Barrett, op. cit.
25. Barrett, op. cit.
26. Barrett, op. cit.
27. Barrett, op. cit.
28. Evidence of the change is an invoice, dated January 1, 1912, printed with the new name, which also proclaims the Smith-Ryan Boat & Engine Co. as builders of the world's famous speed marvels, Reliance and Baby Reliance family of speedboats.
29. Ibid.
30. Ibid.
31. Leduc, op. cit.
32. Leduc, op. cit.
33. Barrett, op. cit.
34. Barrett, op. cit.
35. Barrett, op. cit.
36. Barrett, op. cit.
37. A baronet is the holder of a rank of honor below a baron and above a knight.
38. Barrett, op. cit.
39. Barrett, op. cit.
40. "The Man . . . The Boat . . . The Empire," *Florida Journal*, June, 1967.
41. Leduc, op. cit.
42. Leduc, op. cit.

CHAPTER V.
Vision Of Victory
ppg 33-37

1. J. Lee Barrett, *Speed Boat Kings*, Arnold-Powers, Inc., Detroit, Michigan, 1939. A new printing of this intriguing book was recently undertaken by the Historical Society of Michigan, Ann Arbor.
2. Barrett, op. cit.
3. Barrett, op. cit.
4. Barrett, op. cit.
5. Barrett, op. cit.
6. Barrett, op. cit.
7. Interview of Marian Dawson, granddaughter of Christopher Columbus Smith, and family historian, in Holland, Michigan, August 18, 1986.
8. Barrett, op. cit.
9. Barrett, op. cit.

CHAPTER VI.
Racing Dynasty
ppg 39-53

1. Kevin Desmond, "The Grey Fox of Algonac," *Nautical Quarterly*, Nautical Quarterly Company, Essex, Connecticut, Winter, 1982, No. 20.
2. Gar Wood, Jr. as transcribed from a documentary video tape he produced in 1985 about his father, Gar Wood, Sr.
3. Wood, op. cit.
4. J. Lee Barrett, *Speed Boat Kings*, Arnold-Powers, Inc., Detroit, Michigan, 1939.
5. Wood, op. cit.

6. Barrett, op. cit.
7. Barrett, op. cit.
8. Barrett, op. cit.
9. Barrett, op. cit.
10. Barrett, op. cit.
11. Wood, op. cit., and Barrett, op. cit.
12. Wood, op. cit., and Barrett, op. cit.
13. Barrett, op. cit.
14. Barrett, op. cit.
15. Barrett, op. cit.
16. W.F. Bradley, "America Wins Motor Boat Supremacy," *Motor Boating*, September, 1920.
17. During World War I, the British International Trophy, the *Harmsworth*, was kept aboard the *Enchantress*, the official ship of the Royal Motor Yacht Club. A zeppelin raid in 1915 set fire to the ship and an officer of the club rescued the trophy, but not before the original teak foundation was destroyed. The old foundation had recorded all of the winners of the trophy since its creation in 1903. A few years after his victory at Cowes, England in the 1920 *Harmsworth* contest, Gar Wood replaced the missing base from the trophy with mahogany from *Miss America I*. He remarked, "If Europe ever gets this trophy back they'll have to take with them a piece of my *Miss America I*." Quoted from *Speed Boat Kings*, op. cit.
18. Barrett, op. cit.
19. Barrett, op. cit.
20. Barrett, op. cit.
21. Barrett, op. cit.
22. Barrett, op. cit.
23. Wood, op. cit.
24. Wood, op. cit.
25. *Motor Boating*, June, 1921, in an advertisement for Valentine's Valspar (varnish), Valentine & Company, New York.
26. Wood, op. cit.
27. Wood, op. cit.
28. Wood, op. cit.

CHAPTER VII.
Chris Smith & Sons Boat Co.
ppg 55-59

1. J. Lee Barrett, *Speed Boat Kings: 25 Years of International Speedboating*, Arnold-Powers, Inc., Detroit, Michigan, 1939. A new printing of this intriguing book was recently undertaken by the Historical Society of Michigan, Ann Arbor.
2. Barrett, op. cit.
3. Barrett, op. cit.
4. General Ledger, Chris Smith & Sons Boat Company, February 15, 1922.
5. "Chris Smith, Master Boat Builder," *Motor Boating*, December, 1927.
6. General Ledger, op. cit.
7. General Ledger, op. cit.
8. Kevin Desmond, "The Grey Fox of Algonac," *Nautical Quarterly*, Nautical Quarterly Company, Essex, Connecticut, No. 20.
9. Desmond, op. cit.
10. Desmond, op. cit. The Judge was W.D. "Eddie" Edenburn.
11. Desmond, op. cit.
12. Secretary of the Yachtman's Association of America was J. Lee Barrett, who described the incident in *Speed Boat Kings*, op. cit.
13. Pat Paholsky article, *New York Times*, September 5, 1923, as reproduced in the *Courier-Journal/Independent Press*, Wednesday, June 24, 1981.
14. Barrett, op. cit. Italics added for emphasis.
15. Barrett, op. cit.

CHAPTER VIII.
The Twenties
ppg 61-85

1. General Ledger, Chris Smith & Sons Boat Co.; also original stock prospectus of the Chris-Craft Corporation, 1930. These original ledgers, in near-perfect preservation, are part of the Chris-Craft Archives located at the Mariners' Museum, Newport News, Virginia.
2. *Motor Boating*, May 1924, in a full-page ad for Chris Smith & Sons Boat Co.
3. "Eddie and His Gang Run Some Races", *Motor Boating*, October, 1924, referring to W.D. "Eddie" Edenburn, Chairman of the Race Committee of the Detroit Yacht Club, and his assistants, Otto F. Barthel, H.E. Gunnison, Dr. A.A. Hackett and E.V. Rippingille.
4. *Motor Boating*, October, 1924, op. cit.
5. Interview of Tom Cuthbertson, July 8, 1987 in Algonac, Michigan. Tom, now 80 and a master boat builder in his own right, started at Chris Smith & Sons Boat Co. in 1924.
6. Ibid.
7. General Ledger of the Chris Smith & Sons Boat Co., December, 1925 entries. These original ledgers, in near-perfect preservation, are part of the Chris-Craft

Archives at the Mariners' Museum, Newport News, Virginia.
8. *Motor Boating*, March 1925, in a large, double-truck advertisement for Chris-Craft Runabouts, in an ad for Chris Smith & Sons Boat Co.
9. Ibid.
10. Evidence is the original franchise certificate, *number one*, in the possession of the Mertaugh family, who still operate the E.J. Mertaugh Boat Works in Hessel, Michigan. The business, conducted by sons Jim and Jack, provides a great service to owners of antique Chris-Crafts through restorations, hard-to-find parts and repairs.
11. Laura Craska, a story in *The St. Ignace News*, Thursday, July 2, 1987.
12. Ibid.
13. *Motor Boating*, February, 1926, in a multiple-page ad by Chris Smith & Sons Boat Co., "Largest Builders of Fast Runabouts."
14. *Motor Boating*, May, 1926, in an ad by Chris Smith & Sons Boat Co.
15. *Motor Boating*, April, 1926, in an ad by Chris Smith & Sons Boat Co.
16. Ibid.
17. *Motor Boating*, March, 1926, in an ad for the Kermath Chris-Craft, by Chris Smith & Sons Boat Co.
18. "Production Method in Boat Building," an article in *Motor Boating*, May, 1926.
19. In a memo from W. A. MacKerer to J. E. (John) Clifford, Sales Manager, of October 5, 1927, contained in one of the private notebooks of W. A. "Bill" MacKerer, hereinafter referred to as the MacKerer Notebooks.
20. Journal of the Village of Algonac, Michigan, council proceedings of April 4, 1927. These records were made available courtesy of the City of Algonac, Michigan during the summer of 1987.
21. Interview of Emily Stuart, October 10, 1987, in Port Huron, Michigan. Her sister, Ella Stuart, began at Chris Smith & Sons Boat Co. in 1925, and became J.E. Clifford's secretary during Clifford's reign as Sales Manager of Chris-Craft, witnessing the tremendous growth in sales from 1927 to 1931.
22. *Gray Goose News*, undated, a newsletter of fans of the Wills Saint Clair automobile, edited by Bill McKeand, Port Huron, Michigan.
23. Evidence of the opening of the New York office is the mention in the January, 1927 *Motor Boating* ad for Chris Smith & Sons Boat Co.
24. *Motor Boating*, January, 1927, in an ad by Chris Smith & Sons Boat Co.
25. "Modern Merchandising of Motor Boats," an article in *Motor Boating*, March, 1927.
26. "Fast Boats a Florida Hit," an article in *Motor Boating*, April, 1927.
27. "New Engine to be Used in Runabouts," an article in *Motor Boating*, May, 1927.
28. Ibid.
29. "The New Cadet, a Worthy Sister of the 40 Mile Chris-Craft," an article in *Motor Boating*, June, 1927.
30. Interview of Luke Stephenson, September 11, 1987, in Algonac, Michigan.
31. Ibid.
32. Ibid.
33. Ibid.
34. *Motor Boating*, November, 1927, in an ad by Chris Smith & Sons Boat Co.
35. In a brochure section entitled, "A Tour of Inspection Through the Chris-Craft Factory," produced in 1928 by Chris Smith & Sons Boat Co.
36. Stephenson, op. cit.
37. Stephenson, op. cit.
38. MacKerer Notebooks, op. cit., in a memo from W. A. MacKerer to J. E. Clifford of October 17, 1927.
39. Stephenson, op. cit.
40. The beautiful home, located at 2424 St. Clair River Drive in Algonac, is now owned by the Bud Holowicz family, who graciously allowed the first and only known photo session of the interior for the author.
41. *The Jazz Singer* opened October 6, 1927, while the Detroit office of Chris Smith & Sons Boat Co., located at 3107 East Jefferson Avenue, was opened by July, 1927, as evidenced by the announcement in the August, 1927 issue of *Motor Boating*, in an ad for Chris Smith & Sons Boat Co.
42. *Motor Boating*, September, 1927, in an ad by Chris Smith & Sons Boat Co.
43. Ibid.; and in an ad sponsored by Kermath, specifically listing victories achieved by the Kermath-powered 26-foot Chris-Craft in the November, 1927 *Motor Boating*.
44. "New Uses for Runabouts," *New York Times*, undated, most likely in August, 1927, as quoted in *Motor Boating*, *Yard and Shop* section, September, 1927.
45. "Notes of Interest to Both Owner and Manufacturer," *Motor Boating*, *Yard and Shop* section, December, 1927.
46. Ibid.
47. "New Chris-Craft for 1928," *Motor Boating*, February, 1928.
48. Ibid.
49. From the 1928 Brochure and Catalog of the Chris Smith & Sons Boat Co.
50. Ibid.
51. *Motor Boating*, August, 1928, in a double-truck ad by Chris Smith & Sons Boat Co.

52. *TIME*, June 25, 1928, in an ad by Chris Smith & Sons Boat Co.
53. *Motor Boating*, May, 1928, in an ad by Chris Smith & Sons Boat Co.
54. *Motor Boating*, November, 1928, in an announcement entitled, "A New Chris-Craft."
55. *Motor Boating*, December, 1928, in an ad by Chris Smith & Sons Boat Co.
56. Ibid.
57. MacKerer Notebooks, op. cit., concerning an accounting of the exact number of feet of various woods used in the year's construction through December 31, 1927.
58. *Motor Boating*, September, 1928, in an ad by Chris Smith & Sons Boat Co.
59. *1929 Condensed Specifications and List Prices*, Chris-Craft All-Mahogany Motorboats, Chris Smith & Sons Boat Co.
60. 1929 Catalog and Brochure, Chris Smith & Sons Boat Co.
62. 1929 Catalog and Brochure, op. cit.
63. 1929 Catalog and Brochure, op. cit.
64. 1929 Catalog and Brochure, op. cit.
65. 1929 Catalog and Brochure, op. cit.

CHAPTER IX.
Taxis and Tenders
ppg 87-95

1. *Motor Boating*, February, 1927, in an advertisement by Chris Smith & Sons Boat Co., Algonac, Michigan.
2. "Chris-Craft Tested Regardless of Weather," *Motor Boating*, February, 1927, p. 102.
3. *Motor Boating*, March, 1928, in an apparently cooperative ad placed by both the owners of *Savarona* and Chris Smith & Sons Boat Co., displaying both the specifications of *Savarona* and of the Owner's Special Tender.
4. "Round the World in a Dinghy," *Motor Boating*, June, 1939.
5. From the private notebooks of W.A. "Bill" MacKerer, Plant Superintendent and Naval Architect, Chris Smith & Sons Boat Co., handwritten page dated October 13, 1927.
6. Evidence of the total weight, including all extra equipment, is contained in a memorandum from W.A. MacKerer to J.E. Clifford, dated October 13, 1927, and found within the private notebooks of W.A. "Bill" MacKerer, Plant Superintendent and Naval Architect.
7. Condensed from a listing of Chris-Craft tenders and auxiliaries prepared on March 23, 1931, representing the largest and most famous yachts in the world to date. Found within the private notebook of W.A. "Bill" MacKerer, Chris-Craft Plant Superintendent and Naval Architect.
8. *Motor Boating*, July, 1930, in an ad by Chris Smith & Sons Boat Co.

CHAPTER X.
The Thirties
ppg 97-119

1. Each month, Charles F. Chapman, editor of *Motor Boating*, would write a commentary on subjects of timely concern. This scathing indictment of waste and excess was part of his commentary of March, 1931.
2. Evidence of the visit and the negotiated option is contained in a memo to J. E. Clifford from Chris Smith & Sons Boat Co. attorney Wayne Van Osdol of Detroit, on April 13, 1930. The offices in New York had, by this date, moved to Number 1 West 52nd Street.
3. Interview of Judd Gilbert, October 13, 1987, at Algonac, Michigan. The Gilbert family has been in Algonac for three generations and knew the Smith family well. Judd Gilbert's grandfather started in Algonac with a grocery store, and they have been in the funeral business since 1905. Mr. Gilbert was quite helpful to the author in sharing his family scrapbook of newspaper clippings, and has a rather complete collection of Smith family funeral notices.
4. Interview of Ed and Kate Drouillard, October 13, 1987, in Algonac, Michigan. Ed Drouillard started at Chris-Craft in 1935 at the age of seventeen. He lived across the street from the Jay Smith house when he was a young boy. Both he and Harsen Smith were born in 1908.
5. *TIME*, May 18, 1959. The cover of this issue carries the photo of Harsen Smith, then Chairman of the Board of Chris-Craft Corporation.
6. Evidence of the projected tax liability, as well as the specific tax avoidance plan, is contained in a letter from Taylor Sieber to Jay Smith dated April 1, 1930. Another option was contained in the plan, that of using a Canadian Corporation to funnel profits through, a plan which the Smiths rejected.
7. Evidence of the complex legal strategy is contained in a series of documents from early and mid-1930 severally entitled, "Sieber Tax Avoidance Plan," "Structure of Chris Smith & Sons Boat Co.," "Articles of Association" of the Smith Investment Corporation, "Articles of Association of the Algonac Investment Corporation, "Articles of Association" of the Chris-Craft Corporation, and "Capitalization" and "Prospectus" Statements of the Chris-Craft Corporation.
8. "A Parade of 24 Boats," *Motor Boating*, February, 1930.
9. Ibid.
10. *Motor Boating*, March 1930, in an ad by Chris Smith & Sons Boat Co.
11. From the Chris-Craft franchise brochure, 1930.
12. Franchise brochure, op. cit.
13. Franchise brochure, op. cit.
14. Franchise brochure, op. cit.
15. Franchise brochure, op. cit.
16. "Chris Smith, Master Boat Builder," *Motor Boating*, April, 1930.
17. Contained in a letter of April 8, 1930, from Robert Heller of Childs, Jeffries & Co. to Richard Forsyth of the legal firm of Warren, Hill & Hemblen of Detroit, a copy of which was sent to the Smith corporate attorney, Wayne "Van" Van Osdol.
18. Contained within the "Sample Preferred Stock Circular" and "Prospectus," issued by Childs, Jeffries & Co., 48 Wall Street, New York, New York.
19. *Motor Boating*, July, 1930, a general press release of June 3, 1930.
20. *Chronicle of the 20th Century*, Chronicle Publications, Mount Kisco, N.Y., as indicated in the December, 1930 entry entitled, "Jobless reach over four million; aid sought."
21. General Ledger, Chris-Craft Corporation, "Income and Expense - Consolidated for Twelve Months - 1930."
22. "Moderate Price Cruisers for Moderns," *Motor Boating*, December, 1930.
23. Ibid.
24. *Motor Boating*, March, 1931, in an ad for Chris-Craft Corporation.
25. "Chris-Craft Offers 32 [sic] Boats," *Motor Boating*, March, 1931. Actually, Chris-Craft offered thirty-seven models.
26. "New Chris-Craft Announced," quoting Jay W. Smith, President of Chris-Craft Corporation, *Motor Boating*, March, 1931.
27. *Motor Boating*, March, 1930, in an ad devoted to the controversy by Indiana Quartered Oak Company.
28. *Motor Boating*, March, 1930, in an ad for the Insular Lumber Company of Philadelphia, Pennsylvania.
29. *Webster's New Universal Unabridged Dictionary*, Deluxe Second Edition, published by New World Dictionaries/Simon & Schuster Division of Gulf & Western Corporation, New York, 1983.
30. "Level Riding Chris-Craft Fleet" brochure, 1932.
31. Ibid.
32. "Chris-Craft Cruisers Shown," an article in *Motor Boating*, March, 1932.
33. Letter of March 15 (the ides of March) from J.M. Peterson to J.W. Smith.
34. "Chris-Craft Utility Boat," *Motor Boating*, September, 1932.
35. General Ledger, Chris-Craft Corporation, consolidated earnings report of September 31, 1932.
36. Motor Boating, November, 1932, in an ad for *Chevrolet Six*, by Chevrolet, Division of General Motors.
37. Inventory analysis of January 31, 1934, Chris-Craft Corporation.
38. Evidence of the merger contained in notes as to the financial condition of Chris-Craft Corporation from Haskins & Sells, Certified Public Accountants, to Chris-Craft Corporation, October 25, 1935, in which they describe the merger having taken place on July 31, 1933.
39. *Motor Boating*, July, 1935, in which a 38-foot Individualized Cruiser is shown juxtaposed with a battleship in an ad for Chris Craft Corporation.
40. "Ten-Word Suggestion Wins Chris-Craft Runabout," *Motor Boating*, April, 1935.
41. "Chris-Craft Sales Touch New High," *Motor Boating*, October, 1935.
42. "Business Looking Up at Chris-Craft," *Motor Boating*, November, 1935.
43. Chris-Craft Sales Bulletin issued by Wayne S. Pickell, General Sales Manager, September 20, 1935.
44. Ibid.; and "Chris-Craft Offers 30-Foot Houseboat," *Motor Boating*, October, 1935.
45. Chris-Craft Sales Bulletin, August 31, 1935, issued by Wayne S. Pickell, General Sales Manager.
46. "Chris-Craft Raises Wage Scale," *Motor Boating*, July, 1936.
47. "Year 'Round Production at Chris-Craft," *Motor Boating*, November 1936.
48. "Chris-Craft's Fishing Cruiser," *Motor Boating*, September, 1936.
49. In a letter from the Chris Craft Corporation to the 450 employees wishing to return to work, establishing the guidelines under which a return to work could be accomplished, dated March 27, 1937.
50. Interview of Tom Avers, October 9, 1987, in Algonac, Michigan. Avers worked at Chris-Craft from 1935 to 1940, and was an eyewitness to the labor unrest in 1937.
51. Ibid.
52. "Chris-Craft Raises Wages," *Motor Boating*, April, 1937.
53. Ibid.
54. Ibid.
55. In a letter to Harsen A. Smith from Wayne Van Osdol of Van Osdol, McGregor & Dixon, Attorneys at Law, of June 29, 1937.
56. "A Complete New Fleet of Chris-Craft," *Motor Boating*, undated, most likely December, 1937.
57. *Motor Boating*, December, 1938.
58. "Standardized Boats: The Chris-Craft Fleet," *Motor Boating*, February, 1939.
59. "Chris-Craft to Expand," *Motor Boating*, August, 1939.
60. "New Plant for Chris-Craft," *Motor Boating*, October, 1939.
61. Interview of Luke Stephenson, October 11, 1987, in Algonac, Michigan. Stephenson started in the boiler room at Chris-Craft when he was 15 years old, and was 79 when interviewed in 1987.
62. Undated and author unknown, located in the archives of Betty Droulard, Historian, City of Algonac, Michigan. Probably the *Algonac Courier*, mid-September, 1939.

CHAPTER XI.
The Chris-Craft Railroad
ppg 121-123

1. Much of the pioneering research for this unique episode in Chris-Craft history is due to the diligent efforts and courtesy of Don Cuthbertson of Algonac, Michigan. A self-professed "railroad buff", Don interviewed many of the employees of the old rail operation, and slowly collected many of the existing photographs and newspaper articles which have survived. His generosity in assisting the author is greatly appreciated.
2. "End in Sight for Old Rail Line," *Port Huron Times*, Sunday, September 15, 1957.
3. Contained within an account of the operating procedures of the Algonac Transit Company, March 12, 1931, written by J.M. Peterson.
4. Contained in a letter from William H. Bonneville, Director, Interstate Commerce Commission, Bureau of Inquiry, Washington, D.C., to Mr. Wayne Van Osdol, Corporate Attorney for Chris-Craft Corporation, of March 14, 1941.
5. *Port Huron Times*, op. cit.
6. Interview of Don Cuthbertson, October 9, 1987 in Algonac, Michigan.
7. Interview of Tom Avers, October 9, 1987, Algonac, Michigan.

CHAPTER XIII.
The Forties
ppg. 129-153

1. Chris-Craft Corporation vs. Federal Labor Union No. 28783, in the Circuit Court for the County of St. Clair, State of Michigan. The opinion was written as part of an injunction restraining the union from interfering with Chris-Craft's ability to conduct business. Written November 4, 1941, almost exactly one month before Pearl Harbor.
2. In a letter from Lieutenant Charles Waterland Read, an officer in the Royal Navy, convoy leader and Commander of the 32-foot Chris-Craft Cruiser *Bonny Heather*, to Chris-Craft Corportion. The letter was used by Chris-Craft following the war, in the 1947 catalog and brochure, as testimony to the strength and endurance of their cruisers.
3. Evidence of the visit, as well as the conduct and result of testing is contained in a six-page summary of activities entitled, "Report of Chris-Craft Landing Boat Committee, September 19, 1940," and written ostensibly by W.A. "Bill" MacKerer.
4. Report, op. cit.
5. Report, op. cit.
6. Report, op. cit.
7. Report, op. cit. Italics added for emphasis and clarification.
8. Report, op. cit.
9. Report, op. cit.
10. Report, op. cit.
11. Report, op. cit.
12. "Streamlining the Boats," *Motor Boating*, January, 1941.
13. *Motor Boating*, op. cit.
14. *Motor Boating*, op. cit.
15. *Motor Boating*, op. cit.
16. *Motor Boating*, op. cit.
17. "Motor Boats for Defense," *Motor Boating*, March 1941.
18. "Motor Boats for Defense," *Motor Boating*, June 1941.
19. "Boating in 1941," *Motor Boating*, June, 1941.
20. *Motor Boating*, June 1941, op. cit.
21. Bill of Complaint, filed in the Circuit Court for the County of St. Clair In Chancery, Chris-Craft Corporation vs. Federal Labor Union No. 20783, and many individually-named defendants, October 27, 1941.
22. Ibid.

23. Ibid.
24. *Chronicle of the 20th Century.* Chronicle Publications. Mount Kisco. New York. 1987.
25. Chris-Craft Corporation 1942 Price List. printed in September. 1941.
26. "War Time Fitting Out." *Motor Boating.* April. 1942.
27. In a memorandum from the Chief of the Bureau of Ships. Bureau of Ships. Navy Department. Washington. D.C.. to The Supervisor of Shipbuilding. USN. Detroit. Michigan on May 5. 1942.
28. *Chronicle of the 20th Century.* op. cit.
29. These excerpts are contained in several hand-printed sheets of legal size note paper in the Chris-Craft Archives of the Mariners' Museum in Newport News. Virginia. Subsequent to handwriting analysis and content evaluation. the insightful record was attributed to W.A. "Bill" MacKerer. Chris-Craft Plant Superintendent and Naval Architect. Italics added for emphasis.
30. Excerpted from a letter from Frank Knox. Secretary of the Navy. Washington. D.C. to Jay W. Smith. President. Chris-Craft Corporation. of May 20. 1942.
31. Contained within the presentation folio of the presentation of the Navy "E" Award on June 15. 1942 at the Holland. Michigan Plant. accepted by Harry Coll. Plant Manager. Harry Coll. in later years. was to become the first president of Chris-Craft who wasn't a member of the Smith family.
32. Ibid.
33. The National Labor Relations Board. in response to complaints (which turned out to be substantially unfounded). pressured Chris-Craft during 1942 for a detailed examination of employment records. Harsen Smith. on behalf of Chris-Craft. refused. stating that complying with the requests would injure their abilities to fulfill defense contracts.
34. Interview of George Smith. August 18. 1986 in Holland. Michigan. George is one of four sons of Bernard Smith. his brothers being Christopher James. Charles (Chuck) and Elwood.
35. Ibid.
36. Interview of Larry Folker. October 13. 1987 in Algonac. Michigan. Folker started at Chris-Craft in 1930. and worked in the shipping department during his career at the Algonac plant.
37. Interview of Luke Stephenson. October 11. 1987. in Algonac. Michigan.
38. In an advertisement for *The Tatler.* Senior Annual and Year Book. Howe Military Academy. Howe. Indiana. 1943 edition.
39. *Yachting.* June. 1943. in an ad for the Chris-Craft Corporation.
40. Property. Plant and Equipment Analysis. portion of the Profit and Loss Statements for fiscal year's end. August 31. 1945. showing the 1944 purchases. prepared by Ernst & Ernst. Accountants of Detroit. Michigan.
41. In a cable from E.L. Cochrane. Rear Admiral. USN to the Men and Women of Chris-Craft Corporation. February. 1945. The cable was enlarged to two by three feet and the poster was displayed throughout the Chris-Craft plants.
42. Ledgers of the Chris-Craft Corporation for fiscal year ending August 31. 1945.
43. *Port Huron Times Herald.* January 1. 1945.
44. Contained within the minutes of the fourth negotiations meeting held January 21. 1947. between Chris-Craft Corporation and locals of the International Brotherhood of Electrical Workers. United Brotherhood of Carpenters and Joiners of America. International Association of Machinists. and Brotherhood of Painters. Decorators and Paperhangers of America.
45. *TIME.* May 18. 1959. This issue of *TIME* has Harsen Smith on the cover.
46. Fourth negotiations meeting. op. cit.
47. Fourth negotiations meeting. op. cit.
48. Minutes of the third conciliation meeting held March 21. 1947. 1:45 P.M. between Chris-Craft and delegations of the several unions representing Chris-Craft employees.
49. The date establishing the development of the Chattanooga. Tennessee facilities appears in the "Property. Plant and Equipment" section of the profit and loss report of fiscal year 1948. showing the facilities equipped prior to September 1. 1947 therefore during fiscal year 1946.
50. The first mention of the existence of the Caruthersville. Missouri operation was contained in the 1947 Chris-Craft General Catalog and Brochure. which was printed in the autumn of 1946.
51. General Catalog and Brochure. Chris-Craft Corporation. 1948.
52. Evidence of the sale is contained in the 1948 profit and loss statements. prepared for Chris-Craft by Ernst & Ernst. Accountants and Auditors. Detroit. Michigan on November 2. 1948.
53. "World's Largest Builders Plan Latest Model." *Port Huron Herald.* with a dateline of January 1. 1949. but probably appeared in the Sunday edition. December 31. 1948.
54. Interview of Winn and Helen Morrow. October 9. 1987 at Algonac. Michigan. Morrow began at Chris-Craft in 1933.
55. G. Smith. op. cit.

56. Interview of Harry H. Coll. February 24. 1988. by phone at Pompano Beach. Florida. Harry became President of Chris-Craft Corporation in 1958. succeeding Jay W. Smith. when Harsen Smith became Chairman of the Board. He was Plant Manager at the Holland facility. Plant Manager of the Grand Rapids outboard plant. became Vice-President in charge of the group of three western Michigan plants. including the Roamer Division. and became President of the Roamer Division.

CHAPTER XIV.
Boats You Never Saw
ppg 155-157

1. In an ad prepared by Brooke. Smith. French & Dorrance. Inc.. agency. for the *American Power Boat Association Year Book.* March 6. 1944.

CHAPTER XV.
The Fifties
ppg 159-191

1. In a letter from A.W. MacKerer. General Plant Manager and Naval Architect. to Commander J.B. Rawlings. Bureau of Ships. Department of the Navy. Washington. D.C.. April 30. 1952.
2. From the 1950 General Catalog and Brochure of Chris-Craft Corporation.
3. Comparative Balance Sheets. Chris-Craft Corporation. for fiscal year ending August 31. 1950.
4. Letter from Blaine Stubblefield. Weiser. Idaho. describing his trip down the Snake River. according to him. aboard the first passenger vessel to run Hell's Canyon.
5. Statement of Profit and Loss. Chris-Craft Corporation. year ended August 31. 1950.
6. Letter from J.C. Huske. Contracting Officer. Bureau of Ships. Department of the Navy to Chris-Craft Corporation of June 16. 1951 regarding "Design and Construction of Prototype Boats."
7. From a press release entitled "New High-Speed Prototypes." dated 1952. from Chris-Craft Corporation. Algonac. Michigan by Herb Pocklington.
8. Press release. op. cit.
9. Press release. op. cit.
10. Press release. op. cit.
11. Evidence. is contained in a handwritten memorandum by W.A. MacKerer which refers to discussions with J.W. (Smith) about scheduling delays and deadline changes. "J.W. mentioned that approval might be delayed because of clearing through channels...."
12. Letter to Bureau of Ships. Department of the Navy. Washington. D.C. from W.A. MacKerer. General Plant Manager and Naval Architect. August 9. 1951.
13. In a letter to Commander Hazak. USN. Bureau of Ships. Washington. D.C. from A.W. MacKerer. General Plant Manager and Naval Architect. March 20. 1952.
14. Ibid.
15. Excerpted from a 3"x5" card found in the notebook of A.W. MacKerer. General Plant Manager and Naval Architect. and dated November 2. 1954.
16. In a letter to Captain Roe. Code 529. Bureau of Ships. Department of the Navy. Washington. D.C. from A.W. MacKerer. General Plant Manager and Naval Architect. November 17. 1954.
17. Contained in a telegram to Mr. Ladewig. Bureau of Ships. Department of the Navy. Washington. D.C. from A.W. MacKerer. dated October 27. 1954.
18. From the 1951 Chris-Craft Brochure.
19. Ibid.
20. Estimated Cost Summary for 62-foot Motor Yacht with twin G.M. Diesels. dated January 3. 1950. with revisions in pencil on August 8. 1953. prepared by A.W. "Bill" MacKerer.
21. *Life.* November 1951. in a full-color ad by Chris-Craft Corporation.
22. Chris-Craft Sales Bulletin #325. December 17. 1952. to all Chris-Craft boat dealers from Wayne Pickell. Sales Manager.
23. Interview of Charles D. Strang. Chairman of the Board of Outboard Marine Corporation. May 20. 1987. at the OMC testing facility at Stuart. Florida. Strang was Chief of Engineering at Kiekhaefer Corporation in 1953 when he had to confront Chris-Craft with the evidence that they had violated patents held by Kiekhaefer.
24. Interview of Harry H. Coll. February 24. 1988. by phone at Pompano Beach. Florida.
25. Interview of Ed and Kate Drouillard. October 13. 1987 at Algonac. Michigan.
26. Contained in a Sales Bulletin from the Sea Skiff Division dated October 26. 1954 to all Chris-Craft dealers from W.S. Vance. Sea Skiff Division Sales Manager.
27. Interview of C. Gordon Houser. December 2. 1987 at Tallevast. Florida. Houser. whose remarkable career with Chris-Craft actually started at the Thompson Boat Company in 1957. and spanned nearly a quarter century at Chris-Craft. predominantly as Director

and ultimately Vice-President of Advertising and Public Relations. is currently President of Donzi Marine in Tallevast. Florida.
28. From the first Chris-Craft Plywood Boat Advertisement. 1955.
29. Excerpted from the very first Roamer data sheet following the acquisition by Chris-Craft Corporation in 1955. The text. dated May 1. 1955. was written by the previous owners. and only a small reference typed in at the bottom (Subsidiary of Chris-Craft Corporation) indicates the new ownership.
30. From the 1956 data sheet for the Chris-Craft 38-foot Sport Fisherman.
31. Houser. op. cit.
32. Interview of Sam Martin. October 18. 1987. in Algonac. Michigan.
33. "Christopher Columbus and Chris-Craft." *Motor Boating.* February. 1957.
34. *Motor Boating.* op. cit.
35. From the 1957 Lake 'n Sea Boats Brochure. Division of Chris-Craft Corporation. Pompano Beach. Florida.
36. Ibid.
37. Houser. op. cit.
38. Interview of Christopher James Smith. son of Bernard and namesake of grandfather Christopher Columbus Smith. August 18. 1986 in Holland. Michigan.
39. From the Chris-Craft Showboat Brochure and Catalog. February. 1957. Chris-Craft Boat Division. Chris-Craft Corporation.
40. Brochure and Catalog. op. cit.
41. Brochure and Catalog. op. cit.
42. Brochure and Catalog. op. cit.
43. Brochure and Catalog. op. cit.
44. Excerpt from the 1957 Chris-Craft Division Brochure and General Catalog. Chris-Craft Corporation. Pompano Beach. Florida.
45. Contained within a Sea Skiff Divsion Sales Bulletin. 1958. sent out by C.V. High. Sales Promotion Manager.
46. Excerpt from the 1959 General Catalog and Brochure of the Chris-Craft Division. Chris-Craft Corporation. Pompano Beach. Florida.
47. "Boat Fever". a cover story. *TIME.* May 18. 1959. which featured the photo of Harsen Smith on the cover.

CHAPTER XVI.
The Kit Boats
ppg 195-199

1. From the first Chris-Craft Boat Kit flyer. produced in August. 1950. Chris-Craft Corporation. Algonac. Michigan.
2. From the 1953 Chris-Craft Kit Boat Division Catalog and Brochure.
3. From the 1954 Chris-Craft Land Cruiser Kit Brochure.
4. Interview of Sam Martin. October 18. 1987. Algonac. Michigan.
5. Interview of C. Gordon Houser. December 2. 1987 at Tallevast. Florida.

CHAPTER XVII.
The Sixties
ppg 201-229

1. In a letter to Harry H. Coll. President of Chris-Craft Corporation. written by agreement to establish the intentions of Shields & Company as to the relationship between NAFI and Chris-Craft management. by Paul V. Shields. partner in Shields & Company. New York investment bankers. of February 16. 1960.
2. Interview of Ray and Geraldine LaParl. July 9. 1987. in Algonac. Michigan. LaParl had first heard of the contents of the May 7. 1960 *Business Week* article as it was allegedly discovered blowing across the highway in Algonac. Michigan. as old company records were being fed into the boiler long after the sale was completed. The blurry. re-typed. ditto-blue mimeographed copy was held together with a rusty staple. and was at the time thought of as written by an unknown author who had access to key Chris-Craft executives during early 1960. As with other errors which have crept into the history of Chris-Craft. this document. widely circulated. is held in almost mystical regard by Chris-Craft aficionados and memorabilia collectors who are ignorant of its ordinary origins. as an article by a well-circulated and established news magazine. Ray LaParl was a veteran of over thirty years with Chris-Craft. with the majority of his work within the Parts Division. He and his wife. Geraldine. were very helpful to the author during protracted research in the Algonac area.
3. "A Merger is Born — Close-Up View." *Business Week.* May 7. 1960.
4. Ibid.
5. Cornelius Shields. *Racing with Cornelius Shields and the Masters.* Prentice-Hall. Inc.. 1974. This anthology contains guest chapters by some of the world's best racing sailors. including Ted Hood. Olin

Stephens, Robert Allan, Jr., Buddy Melges, Rod Stephens, Bus Mosbacher, Britton Chance, Jr., Robert Bavier, Steve Van Dyck and Ted Turner.

6. *Business Week*, op. cit.
7. Shields, op. cit.
8. *Business Week*, op. cit.
9. *New York Herald Tribune*, Financial Section, February 13, 1960.
10. Shields, op. cit.
11. Interview of Bruce Donaldson, March 15, 1988, by telephone from Bradenton, Florida. Donaldson, current President of the Murray Chris-Craft Boat Companies, was originally hired by Harsen Smith in 1958, and is celebrating his 30th year with Chris-Craft this year.
12. *Business Week*, op. cit.
13. "Corporations: New Skipper for Chris-Craft," *TIME*, February 15, 1960.
14. "CORPORATIONS: New Course for Chris-Craft," *TIME*, July 14, 1961.
15. *TIME*, op. cit.
16. From a 1960 ad sample contained within the Chris-Craft Archives at the Mariners' Museum, Newport News, Virginia. A reprint of the ad was sent to dealers, announcing that "Nearly 6 million readers will see this Chris-Craft ad!". No information as to final placement was available.
17. From an ad prepared for *Fortune*, November, 1960, and for *Popular Boating*, December, 1960.
18. Contained within the footnotes to the "Audited Consolidated Financial Statements and Other Financial Information" of the Chris-Craft Corporation and Subsidiaries, December 31, 1962. These financial records are part of the Chris-Craft Archives of the Mariners' Museum of Newport News, Virginia.
19. From the 1962 *Corsair* Fleet Brochure, Chris-Craft Corporation.
20. From the 1964 Chris-Craft Industries, Inc. *Annual Report*, p.5, signed by John G. Bannister, President, March 12, 1965 in Oakland, California.
21. From the 1964 Cavalier Division Brochure, Chris-Craft Corporation.
22. From the 1964 *Annual Report* of Chris-Craft Industries, Inc. as reported to stockholders by President John G. Bannister in Oakland, California, March 12, 1965.
23. In an Inter-Office Memorandum from Harry H. Coll, President, Chris-Craft Corporation, regarding "Plant Floor Area Summary," dated September 3, 1965. Minor variations in subsequent years would add an additional 50,000 square feet of production space, which would put Chris-Craft at just over two million square feet of manufacturing space.
24. From the 1965 27-foot Commander Brochure, Chris-Craft Corporation.
25. Contained in a Cavalier Division "Sales Bulletin" dated July 23, 1965, by Bruce J. Donaldson, Sales Manager, Cavalier Division.
26. From the 1965 *Corsair* Brochure, Chris-Craft Corporation.
27. From the 1965 abbreviated full-line brochure entitled, "What Can You Get From Chris-Craft in 1965?"
28. From the 1966 Commander Brochure, Chris-Craft Corporation.
29. From the 1966 General Catalog and Brochure of Chris-Craft Division, Chris-Craft Corporation.
30. From the 1966 Corinthian Brochure, Chris-Craft Corporation.
31. As quoted in the 1967 Commander Brochure, Chris-Craft Corporation.
32. "Baldwin-Montrose Makes TV Plans," *Broadcasting*, October 30, 1967.
33. Ibid.
34. Interview of C. Gordon Houser, December 2, 1987, at Tallevast, Florida.
35. Herbert J. Siegel, Chairman and President, "Shareholders Statement", *Annual Report*, Chris-Craft Industries, Inc., November 26, 1968.
36. *Annual Report*, 1968, op. cit.
37. Houser, op. cit.
38. *Annual Report*, 1968, op. cit.
39. From the 1968 *Corsair* Brochure, Chris-Craft Corporation.
40. Lee Iacocca, with William Novak, *Iacocca, An Autobiography*, Bantam Books, Inc., 666 Fifth Avenue, New York, New York, 1984.
41. From the press release announcing the winner of the "Oldest Living Chris-Craft Contest." Undated, but announced in early 1970.

CHAPTER XVIII.
The Chris-Craft Sailboats
ppg 231-235

1. Cornelius Shields, *Racing with Cornelius Shields and the Masters*, Prentice-Hall, Inc., 1974. This anthology contains guest chapters by some of the world's best racing sailors, including Ted Hood, Olin

Stephens, Robert Allan, Jr., Buddy Melges, Rod Stephens, Bus Mosbacher, Britton Chance, Jr., Robert Bavier, Steve Van Dyck and Ted Turner.

2. Interview of C. Gordon Houser, December 2, 1987, in Tallevast, Florida.
3. Bruce J. Donaldson, Sales Manager, Sailboat Division, in a sales bulletin to dealers, January 14, 1964.
4. George M. Irvine of Owens-Corning Fiberglas, in a report entitled, "Survey of Shields One-Design Class Manufacturing & Construction Techniques," reprinted by Chris-Craft in 1965 as a Sailboat Division Sales Bulletin.
5. From the Chris-Craft Industries, Inc. Annual Report for the year ended August 31, 1968.
6. From the Comanche 42 Brochure, Chris-Craft Sailboat Division, 1968.
7. Houser, op. cit.

CHAPTER XIX.
The Seventies
ppg 237-253

1. From the 1970 Chris-Craft Catalina Cruisers Catalog, in a statement by Chris-Craft Corporation President James J. Rochlis.
2. Herbert J. Siegel, Chairman and President, Chris-Craft Industries, Inc., in a letter to shareholders within the 1978 *Annual Report*, October 26, 1978.
3. Thomas Jaffe, "Not Much of a Company But A Helluva Stock," *Forbes*, September 17, 1979.
4. Herbert J. Siegel, Chairman and President, Chris-Craft Industries, Inc., in a letter to shareholders as part of the 1970 *Annual Report*, November 11, 1970.
5. Ibid.
6. From the 1970 Catalina Brochure, Chris-Craft Corporation.
7. Richard C. Cole, "Richard C. Cole On Runabouts and Utility Boats," *Motor Boating*, January, 1970.
8. Robert F. MacNeill, "Human Engineering Pleasure Boats," *Journal of the Industral Designers Society of America*, Pergamon Press, Maxwell House, Fairview Park, Elmsford, New York 10523, June, 1970. MacNeill is today considering a revival of the design concepts and total systems integration which he pioneered during his years at Chris-Craft, and maintains that the entire marine industry would benefit by component and systems standardization practices.
9. Interview of Robert F. MacNeill, March 29, 1987, by phone from Pulaski, Wisconsin.
10. *Annual Report*, 1970, op. cit.
11. From the 1971 Chris-Craft Industries, Inc. *Annual Report*.
12. Interview of Harry H. Coll, April 4, 1988, by phone from Pompano Beach, Florida. Coll was President of Chris-Craft (Boat Divisions) from 1958 to 1969.
13. Ibid.
14. From the 1973 25-foot Express Cruiser Brochure, Chris-Craft Corporation.
15. Patricia Bellew, Business Writer, "Struggling Chris-Craft Bails Out," *Miami Herald*, Monday, September 22, 1980. The article details the financial progression of the decade of the seventies, and discloses the condition of the corporation during its period of greatest economic distress.
16. Herbert J. Siegel, Chairman and President, Chris-Craft Industries, Inc., in a letter to shareholders contained within the 1974 *Annual Report*.
17. Jack Smith, Associate Editor, "Yachting Eyes a Boat: The Chris-Craft 22' Tournament Fisherman," *Yachting*, March, 1974.
18. *Annual Report*, 1974, op. cit.
19. From the 1975 Review of Operations, Boat Division of Chris-Craft Industries, Inc. *Annual Report*.
20. From the 1976 Review of Operations for the Boat Division contained in the *Annual Report* of Chris-Craft Industries, Inc.
21. Interview of Herb Pocklington, April 7, 1988, by phone from High Point, North Carolina. Pocklington was a valuable executive throughout his career at Chris-Craft, spanning the years from 1942 to 1974. He held positions ranging from a sixteen-year-old working summers and week-ends, to public relations, advertising, Director of Product Styling and Planning, to Overseas Operations Manager and President of Chris-Craft SA in Switzerland and of Chris-Craft Italia.
22. Larry Kean and Margaret Sieck, "Boat Test No. 255: Chris-Craft 28 Express Cruiser," *Boating*, May, 1977.
23. From the 1977 38-foot Corinthian Brochure, Chris-Craft Corporation.
24. From the 1978 Sport Boat Brochure, Chris-Craft Corporation.
25. "A Busy Chris-Craft Looks Back to Its Boats," *Business Week*, September 4, 1978.
26. Ibid.
27. Interview of Richard E. "Dick" Genth, March 23, 1988 by phone from Tallevast, Florida. Today Dick Genth is Chairman of the Board of Donzi Marine.
28. Ibid.

29. Ibid.
30. Ibid.
31. Ibid.
32. From the 1979 Chris-Craft Industries, Inc. *Annual Report*.

CHAPTER XX.
The Eighties
ppg 255-283

1. Jeffrey L. Rodengen, Ph.D., "An Old Name with a New Twist," *Boating*, January, 1988.
2. Patricia Bellew, Business Writer, "Struggling Chris-Craft Bails Out," *Miami Herald*, September 22, 1980.
3. "Chris-Craft Decides It Will Divest Itself of Boating Division," *Wall Street Journal*, October 10, 1980.
4. Interview of Richard E. "Dick" Genth, March 23, 1988, by phone from Tallevast, Florida, where Genth is today Chairman of Donzi Marine.
5. John Taylor, "G. Dale Murray: Scrambling To Win His Biggest Gamble," cover story, *Florida Trend*, June, 1987.
6. John Taylor, "G. Dale Murray: Can He Beat the Odds One More Time?", cover story, *Florida Trend*, June, 1987.
7. Interview of Joel Schleicher, April 4, 1988, by phone from Bradenton, Florida. Schleicher, at 36, is Murray Industries Chief Executive Officer.
8. Taylor, op. cit.
9. Taylor, op. cit.
10. Interview of Walter K. Schumacher, April 27, 1988 by phone from Fort Lauderdale, Florida.
11. Genth, op. cit.
12. Interview of G. Dale Murray, June 11, 1987 at Sarasota, Florida and aboard the Murray Industries Sabre 60 corporate jet aircraft.
13. Editor Peter Janssen, "Chris-Craft Comes Back," *Motor Boating & Sailing*, November, 1982.
14. Murray, op. cit.
15. From the introduction to the 1981 Chris-Craft General Catalog, as signed by President Richard E. Genth.
16. Genth, op. cit.
17. Editor Peter A. Janssen, "At the Helm: Looking for George,", *Motor Boating & Sailing*, October, 1984.
18. From the 1984 full-line catalog, Sportboat section, Murray Chris-Craft Sportboats, Inc.
19. Richard Thiel, "Top Cats", *Boating*, July 1984.
20. Interview of Bruce Donaldson, May 18, 1986 in Bradenton, Florida.
21. Interview of Don Pruett, May 17, 1986 at Cape Coral, Florida.
22. Genth, op. cit.
23. Murray, op. cit. This excerpt, among others, also appeared in the January 1988 issue of *Boating* magazine in an article by the author entitled, "An Old Name with a New Twist."
24. Chris Davis, "All American Runabouts," *Motor Boating & Sailing*, July, 1986.
25. The spokesman was then National Sales Manager Steve Pease, as reported in *Motor Boating & Sailing*, July, 1986.
26. Interview of Tony Berky, May 15, 1986 at the Bradenton Sportboat manufacturing facility, Murray Chris-Craft.
27. Ibid.
28. Contained in the official press release of July 1, 1986, announcing the termination of discussions between Trafalgar Holdings and Murray Chris-Craft.
29. Much of the material for this section on the alignment of a significant portion of the marine industry was first published in *Lakeland Boating*, September, 1987, by the author in an article entitled, "Showdown: OMC vs Brunswick. What Their Acquisitions of Major Boat Companies Will Mean."
30. Jeffrey L. Rodengen, Ph.D., "An Old Name with a New Twist," *Boating*, January, 1988.
31. Donaldson, op. cit.
32. From the 1987 Chris-Craft Sportboats Catalog.
33. "Saudi Stake in Boat Maker," *New York Times*, May 23, 1987.
34. Murray, op. cit.
35. From the 1988 Chris-Craft full-line brochure.
36. "Powerboat Performance Report: Chris-Craft 375 Stinger," *Powerboat*, April, 1988.
37. "10 Best Boats," *Boating*, January, 1988.
38. Interview of William J. "Bill" Meyers, May 9, 1988 by phone from Palmetto, Florida. Meyers is Director of Research and Development for Murray Chris-Craft Boat Development, Inc.
39. Interview of Craig R. Muir, September, 1987, in Sarasota, Florida. Muir is Vice-President of Design and Styling for Murray Chris-Craft.
40. Interview of Mark Paulhus, April 25, 1988, by phone from Sarasota, Florida. Paulhus is the Manager of Computer Aided Engineering at Murray Boat Administrative Services, Inc.